Jesus the Inter

Biblical Studies Library

*Jesus the Intercessor: Prayer and Christology in Luke–Acts,* David Crump
*The Descent of Christ: Ephesians 4:7–11 and Traditional Hebrew Imagery,* W. Hall
   Harris III
*Marriage as a Covenant: Biblical Law and Ethics as Developed from Malachi,* Gordon
   P. Hugenberger
*Paul, Scripture, and Ethics: A Study of 1 Corinthians 5–7,* Brian S. Rosner
*The Structure of Hebrews: A Text-Linguistic Analysis,* George H. Guthrie

**David Crump** (Ph.D., University of Aberdeen) is associate professor of religion and theology at Calvin College.

# Jesus the Intercessor

## Prayer and Christology in Luke–Acts

### David Crump

Baker Books

A Division of Baker Book House Co.
Grand Rapids, Michigan 49516

© 1992 by J. C. B. Mohr (Paul Siebeck)

Published by Baker Books
a division of Baker Book House Company
P.O. Box 6287, Grand Rapids, MI 49516-6287

First J. C. B. Mohr (Paul Siebeck) paperback edition published 1992 as volume 49 in
Wissenschaftliche Untersuchungen zum Neuen Testament Series 2

First Baker Books paperback edition published 1999

Printed in the United States of America

Library of Congress Cataloging-in-Publication data is on file at the Library of Congress, Washington,
D.C.

For information about academic books, resources for Christian leaders, and all new releases available
from Baker Book House, visit our web site:

http://www.bakerbooks.com

*This work is dedicated to my parents,*
*who raised me so as to know the Fear of the Lord.*

# Preface

The reader will soon discover that this is not a revised edition of the original work. Consequently, there is no discussion of recent, important works such as Samuel Balentine's *Prayer in the Hebrew Bible* (1993), Oscar Cullmann's *Das Gebet im Neuen Testament* (English translation, *Prayer in the New Testament*, 1994), or Patrick Miller's *They Cried to the Lord* (1994). Hopefully, I will be able to make future contributions to this ongoing investigation into the inter-personal communication lying at the heart of the Christian experience.

I am grateful to Baker Books for the opportunity to include my work in the new Biblical Studies Library. I also appreciate the cooperation of the original publisher, J. C. B. Mohr (Paul Siebeck), in permitting a new printing on this side of the Atlantic.

David M. Crump
Calvin College, Winter 1999

# Acknowledgments

I would like to express my gratitude to those who have taken a particular interest in seeing this work completed. Special mention must be made of the friends who have supported me and my family, sometimes quite sacrificially, during this time of study: thank-you to Ken, Marv, Lynn, Glenn and Marla, Eric and Penny, Heather and Dave, Anthony and Anne, Garth and Fiona, and the people of Immanuel Christian Reformed Church.

Thank you as well to the Hattie M. Strong Foundation, the Tyndale House Fellowship, and the Committee of Vice-Chancellors and Principals of the Universities of the United Kingdom for their financial support.

I am particularly grateful for the discerning criticism and kind guidance of my supervisor, Prof. I. H. Marshall, who has been an example to me of how Christian scholarship can benefit from Christian character.

I am also indebted to the thorough criticisms of Dr. John Nolland, who read the manuscript in its entirety. Dr. Max Turner also offered helpful advice on an early draft of chapter five. The library staff at The Queen Mother Library, Aberdeen also offered many hours of valuable service.

My friends Martin Rodi, Kim Meichle and Chuck Guth have also provided invaluable technical assistance at a critical stage in converting the manuscript from one computer system to another. My thanks must also go to Ilse König of Mohr-Siebeck for her patience during this laborious period of reworking.

Finally, I would like to thank my wife and children for the patience they have shown in enduring the trials of student life throughout the years.

Salt Lake City, Spring, 1992                                      David Michael Crump

# Table of Contents

# List of Journals Consulted

| | |
|---|---|
| ABR | Australian Biblical Review |
| AGB | W. Bauer, W. F. Arndt, and F. W. Gingrich, *Greek-English Lexicon of the New Testament* |
| AJT | American Journal of Theology |
| ALUOS | Annual of Leeds University Oriental Society |
| ANRW | W. Haase (ed.), *Aufstieg und Niedergang der römischen Welt* |
| AshTJ | Ashland Theological Journal |
| ATR | Anglican Theological Review |
| AUSS | Andrews University Seminary Studies |
| BDF | F. Blass, A. Debrunner, and R. W. Funk, *A Greek Grammar of the New Testament* |
| Bib | Biblica |
| Bibl | Biblebhashyam |
| BibT | Bible Today |
| Bij | Bijdragen |
| BJRL | Bulletin of the John Rylands University Library of Manchester |
| BK | Bibel und Kirche |
| BL | Bibel und Leben |
| BLit | Bibel und Liturgie |
| BR | Biblical Research |
| BT | The Bible Translator |
| BTB | Biblical Theology Bulletin |
| BTF | Bangalore Theological Forum |
| BW | Biblical World |
| BZ | Biblische Zeitschrift |
| Cath | Catholica |
| CBQ | Catholic Biblical Quarterly |
| Chr | Christus |
| CJT | Canadian Journal of Theology |
| ClassRev | Classical Review |
| ClRev | Clergy Review |
| CMCSE | Collectanea Mechliniensia Commentarius Scientiarum Ecclesiasticarum |
| CTM | Concordia Theological Monthly |
| CW | Die christliche Welt |
| ETL | Ephemerides theologicae lovanienses |
| EvQ | Evangelical Quarterly |
| EvT | Evangelische Theologie |
| ExpT | Expository Times |
| GL | Geist und Leben |

| | |
|---|---|
| GTJ | Grace Theological Journal |
| HeyJ | Heythrop Journal |
| HibJ | Hibbert Journal |
| HTR | Harvard Theological Review |
| HUCA | Hebrew Union College Annual |
| IBS | Irish Biblical Studies |
| IndTS | Indian Theological Studies |
| Int | Interpretation |
| ITQ | Irish Theological Quarterly |
| JAAR | Journal of the American Academy of Religion |
| JANESCU | Journal of the Ancient Near Eastern Society of Columbia University |
| JBL | Journal of Biblical Literature |
| JBR | Journal of Bible and Religion |
| JEH | Journal of Ecclesiastical History |
| JETS | Journal of the Evangelical Theological Society |
| JJS | Journal of Jewish Studies |
| JR | Journal of Religion |
| JRelS | Journal of Religious Studies |
| JSJ | Journal for the Study of Judaism in the Persian, Hellenistic and Roman Period |
| JSNT | Journal for the Study of the New Testament |
| JSS | Journal of Semitic Studies |
| JTS | Journal of Theological Studies |
| LCL | Loeb Classical Library |
| LTP | Laval Théologique et Philosophique |
| LumV | Lumière et Vie |
| LV | Lumen Vitae |
| MGWJ | Monatsschrift für Geschichte und Wissenschaft des Judentums |
| NJKA | Neue Jahrbücher für das Klassische Altertum |
| NovT | Novum Testamentum |
| NRT | La nouvelle revue théologique |
| NSN | Nuntius Sodalicii Neotestamentici |
| NTS | New Testament Studies |
| Numen | Numen: International Review for the History of Religions |
| OS | Oudtestamentische Studiën |
| Per | Perspective |
| PRS | Perspectives in Religious Studies |
| RB | Revue biblique |
| RechBib | Recherches bibliques |
| RS | Religious Studies |
| RevExp | Review and Expositor |
| RevRel | Review for Religious |
| RevScRel | Revue des sciences religieuses |
| RGG | Religion in Geschichte und Gegenwart |
| RHPR | Revue d'histoire et de philosophie religieuses |
| RQ | Restoration Quarterly |
| RR | Review of Religion |
| RSPT | Revue des sciences philosophiques et théologiques |

| | |
|---|---|
| RSR | Recherches de science religieuse |
| RThPh | Revue de théologie et de philosophie |
| SB | H. Strack and P. Billerbeck, *Kommentar zum Neuen Testament aus Talmud und Midrasch* |
| ScEccl | Sciences Ecclesiastiques |
| Scr | Scripture |
| SD | Studies and Documents |
| SE | Studia Evangelica I, II, III (= TU 73['59], 87['64], 88['65], etc.) |
| Sem | Semeia |
| SJT | Scottish Journal of Theology |
| SO | Symbolae Osloenses |
| SP | Studia Patristica |
| SPAW | Sitzungsberichte der preussischen Akademie der Wissenschaften |
| SR | Studies in Religion/Sciences religieuses |
| ST | Spirituality Today |
| SwJT | Southwestern Journal of Theology |
| TB | Tyndale Bulletin |
| TDNT | G. Kittel and G. Friedrich (eds.), *Theological Dictionary of the New Testament* |
| TG | Theologie und Glaube |
| Th | Theology |
| TijT | Tijdschrift voor Theologie |
| TJ | Trinity Journal |
| TLZ | Theologische Literaturzeitung |
| TP | Theologie und Philosophie |
| TS | Theological Studies |
| TSK | Theologische Studien und Kritiken |
| TToday | Theology Today |
| TU | Texte und Untersuchungen |
| TV | Theologia Viatorum |
| TZ | Theologische Zeitschrift |
| VE | Vox Evangelica |
| VT | Vetus Testamentum |
| WTJ | Westminster Theological Journal |
| ZAW | Zeitschrift für die alttestamentliche Wissenschaft |
| ZNW | Zeitschrift für die neutestamentliche Wissenschaft |
| ZRG | Zeitschrift für Religions und Geistesgeschichte |
| ZTK | Zeitschrift für Theologie und Kirche |
| ZWT | Zeitschrift für wissenschaftliche Theologie |

Chapter 1

# Introduction to the Study of Prayer in Luke-Acts

## Introduction

It is difficult to find a book on prayer which does not at some point lament "the crisis of piety" in the modern church,[1] a crisis often associated with the lack of attention given this subject by biblical scholarship. While such a crisis may well exist, it cannot be attributed to any absence of literature on prayer. The popular bookshelves are filled to overflowing with books on prayer, and the inquisitive buyer never lacks for new titles promising to reveal previously hidden insights into the why, how and wherefore of practical piety. Neither have modern biblical scholars been totally remiss in giving attention to this area. Many important works on prayer have been written this century (to deal with only the last of those nineteen which have followed the writing of the final NT documents), providing valuable insights into any and every aspect of prayer, both historical and theological.[2] The first conclusion to be derived from these observations is rather obvious: if the modern church is peculiarly impious it simply demonstrates that access to literature about prayer does not ensure the practice of prayer. In any event, it is more likely that, except in extraordinary circumstances, what these writers call a crisis in piety is actually the church's normal condition!

However, there is also an important question arising from these observations which is more immediately relevant to the present study: why should anyone feel the need to undertake yet another investigation of prayer in the NT? In response (or defense), it must be said that studying prayer in Luke-Acts is quite a different matter from writing on the theology of prayer in general. In the first place, for as many warnings as one can find about the dangers of modern impiety, there are at least as many observers who have pointed out that Luke has more to say about the place of prayer in the ministry of Jesus and the early church than any other NT

---

[1] For example see G. P. Wiles, *Paul's Intercessory Prayers: The Significance of the Intercessory Prayer Passages in the Letters of St. Paul*, (Cambridge, 1974), p. ix; and W. Bingham Hunter, *The Prayers of Jesus in the Gospel of John*, unpublished Ph.D. dissertation, (Aberdeen, 1979), pp. 1–14, with extensive additional notation.

[2] See the bibliography. H. Schmidt, *Wie betet der heutige Mensch? Dokumente und Analysen*, (Freiburg, 1972), pp. 225–284 lists 1221 works written on prayer between 1960 and 1970 alone.J. Carmignac, *Researches sur le Notre Père"*, (Paris, 1969), provides an 84 page (pp. 469–553) bibliography of works dealing with the Lord's Prayer.

author. This observation has become a commonplace in biblical studies.[3] Yet it is only within the last twenty-five years that any detailed attention has been given to understanding the significance of this theme within Luke's own writings. To elucidate this important point will require a brief look at the history of the study of prayer in Luke-Acts.

## 1.1 A History of the Study of Prayer in Luke-Acts

The study of both Jesus' prayer-life and the gospel of Luke had occupied an important position in the 19th century Liberal "quest" for the historical Jesus. According to A. Deissmann, coming to understand "the inner life of Jesus is the chief task of research in early Christianity."[4] And since Jesus' practice of prayer was the main avenue by which one could come to an understanding of his "unique self-consciousness," prayer was a prime topic for those interested in unravelling Jesus' self-understanding.[5] Furthermore, Luke's gospel in particular had occupied a special place in the Liberal reconstruction of the historical Jesus since it was seen to be "in some measure a rationalised and humanitarian rendering of the Gospel."[6] Therefore Luke's Jesus seemed most amenable to undergirding the doctrine of the universal Fatherhood of God and Brotherhood of Man. However, these two interests in prayer and Luke did not coincide so as to produce a study of prayer *in* Luke specifically. It was not yet time for such literary analysis.

Albert Schweitzer's attack upon the Liberal quest did not eliminate the interest in Jesus' prayer-life; it merely served to redirect scholarly attention on the subject. The main focus was no longer psychological, although this did not wholly disappear,[7] but historical and descriptive; the question now became, how could

---

[3] For example see A. Plummer, *A Critical and Exegetical Commentary on the Gospel According to St. Luke*, (Edinburgh, 1981), p. xlv; J. Fitzmyer, *The Gospel According to Luke*, vol. I, (New York, 1981), pp. 244–247; J. Schmid, *Das Evangelium nach Lukas*, (Regensburg, 1960), pp. 251–253; H. J. Cadbury, *The Making of Luke-Acts*, (London, 1927), p. 269.

[4] A. Deissmann, *The Religion of Jesus and the Faith of Paul*, (London, 1923), p. 43f. Also see his seminal elaboration of this approach in "Der Beter Jesus," *CW*. 13 (1899) 701–707; J. S. Banks, "Professor Deissmann on Jesus at Prayer," *ExpT*. 11 (1899) 270–273 provides an English synopsis of this article. J. D. G. Dunn commends Deissmann as the examplar for the method which he pursues in his own investigation of Jesus' experience of the Spirit; see *Jesus and the Spirit: A Study of the Religious and Charismatic Experience of Jesus and the First Christians as Reflected in the New Testament*, (London, 1975), pp. 11–26, especially p. 15.

[5] Cf. Deissmann, *Religion*, pp. 43–68. "The central question for the history of religion, and for religion in general, is, 'What communion had Jesus with God?' It is to a large extent the same with the question, 'How did Jesus pray?'" (p. 69).

[6] C. H. Dodd, *The Apostolic Preaching and its Developments*, (London, 1972, 2nd ed.), p. 65 (originally published in 1936).

[7] However, it did become more common for such interests not simply to be minimised, but thoroughly expunged; see R. Bultmann, *Jesus and the Word*, (New York, 1958), pp. 8f (originally published in 1934); G. Bornkamm, *Jesus of Nazareth*, (London, 1960), p. 13 (orginally published in 1956).

Jesus' prayer-life be explained in terms of his historical surroundings?[8] For each of these approaches – that of 19th century psychologising and 20th century historicising – the prayer materials of Luke had provided the largest proportion of grist for the mill. Everyone recognised that his gospel offered more examples of Jesus at prayer than any of the other gospels; and, of course, the book of Acts provided the only NT narrative account of the church's early prayer habits. Thus his prayer materials were indispensible for anyone wanting to study Jesus and prayer, whatever their particular agenda might be. But the result, in each case, was the same: while Luke was readily acknowledged to say more about Jesus and prayer than anyone else, Luke's own purpose in having so much to say was never investigated on its own terms. It took yet another development in NT studies before this could happen.

Of course, this new development was the advent of redaction criticism, and the crucial document for Lukan studies was the work of H. Conzelmann, *Die Mitte Der Zeit* (1953). Conzelmann's work opened the door for the proper investigation of Luke's prayer materials in their own right.[9] However, with Conzelmann now acting as chief-guide in this new Lukan wilderness, the first to follow him along his paths of redaction quite predictably imbibed not only of his new methodology but also some of his idiosyncratic understanding of Luke's theology. This was no less true of the earliest studies in Lukan prayer than it was of other post-Conzelmann investigations into the theology of Luke-Acts, as will be seen.

### 1.1.1 Wilhelm Ott: Prayer and Eschatology

The first study of the Lukan prayer theme was published in 1965 by Wilhelm Ott and was entitled *Gebet und Heil: Die Bedeutung der Gebetsparänese in der lukanischen Theologie*. Ott's work focuses primarily upon Luke's didactic material, particularly the parables found in Lk. 11:5–8, 9–13; 18:1–8, to which he devotes lengthy tradition-critical and redactional attention. His primary conclusion is that the centre of Luke's teaching on prayer is neither a concern for true piety, nor the goodness of God in hearing the believer's requests, as is the case in Matthew (p. 137f), but the exhortation *to be persistent in prayer*. The motivation for this restructuring of the tradition is Luke's concern over the parousia delay.[10] Whereas the prayer teaching in both Mark and Matthew was guided by their near expectation of the parousia, Luke has surrendered this hope. The pressing issue for him is not an imminent return of the Lord, but the survival of the church in an indeterminably long period of temptation in this world. The solution to this problem is

---

[8] A good example of this approach would be J. Jeremias' article "Das Gebetsleben Jesu," *ZNW*. 25 ('26) 123–140.

[9] Originally published by J. C. B. Mohr (Paul Siebeck), Tübingen; first English translation by Faber and Faber and Harper & Row in 1961, entitled *The Theology of St. Luke*.

[10] According to E. Bezzel it was originally a Würzburger dissertation entitled *Die Mahnung zu unablässigen Beten bei Lukas*; see his review in *ZRG*. 18 ('66) 377f. This title succinctly expresses Ott's conclusions regarding Luke's teaching on prayer.

persistent prayer; it is the chief means of persevering in Christian discipleship. In fact, Ott is so emphatic on this point that prayer actually becomes a means of salvation; at least it becomes *the* means of ensuring that one will eventually be able to stand before the coming Son of Man (pp. 64f, and pp. 73–75 on Lk. 21:34–36). This is most clearly illustrated in his comparison of Luke with Paul. According to Ott, Paul also emphasises the importance of persistent prayer. But he prays to express his gratitude to God for salvation, whereas in Luke one prays to receive salvation (pp. 139–143).

There are several important results of this Lukan focal point. First of all, Luke presents Jesus as the paradigm of Christian perseverance through prayer. Luke is not interested, like Matthew, in the "How" of prayer (pp. 92–94), but simply in the "That" of prayer, especially as this can be illustrated through the life of Jesus (particularly Lk. 11:1–13 and 22:39–46). Consequently, Luke's special interest in Jesus' prayer-life does not stem from any biographical or even a christological concern; rather it is only the "Vorbildcharacter" of Jesus' prayers which interest Luke (p. 97). Jesus is the prime example of how to survive temptation by means of prayer. This also explains why Ott's brief treatment of prayer in Acts (pp. 124–136) focuses primarily on how the early church followed Jesus' example.

Secondly, because the church's chief danger lies in the possibility of being distracted by worldly cares, Luke eliminates any suggestion that one should pray for material things (pp. 111f, 139). In Lk. 11:11–13 Luke reinterprets the tradition to show that the only good gift is the Holy Spirit, all other requests are for harmful things. Thus, in Luke's view, the delay in the parousia means that God intends prayer to be made only for spiritual requests, and the true answer to such prayer is always the Holy Spirit.

Obviously, Ott begins his study by accepting Conzelmann's convictions concerning Lukan eschatology, ie. Luke's guiding concern is the parousia delay, which causes him to recast salvation-history into a three-fold scheme which sees Jesus' ministry as a Satan-free period (p. 85) and the era of the church as the time of temptation (pp. 65f, 119, 138f). However, this means that the fortunes of Conzelmann's eschatology are also those of Ott's main thesis. There is no need to rehearse here the many legitimate critiques which have been launched against Conzelmann's views over the years;[11] suffice it to say that they are sufficient to call for a major revaluation of the significance which Ott attaches to the paranetic prayer materials in Luke-Acts. Even granted that Ott has shed important light upon Luke's emphatic exhortation "to pray" – and this is an important, beneficial part

---

[11] See W. C. Robinson, *The Way of the Lord: A Study of History and Eschatology in the Gospel of Luke*, Ph.D. dissertation, (University of Basel, 1962); *Der Weg des Herrn: Studien zur Geschichte und Eschatology im Lukasevangelium, ein Gespräch mit Hans Conzelmann*, (Hamburg, 1964); H. H. Oliver, "The Lucan Birth Stories and the Purpose of Luke-Acts," *NTS.* 10 ('63–4) 202–226; F. O. Francis, "Eschatology and History in Luke-Acts," *JAAR.* 37 ('69) 49–63; S. G. Wilson, "Lukan Eschatology," *NTS.* 16 ('70) 330–347; I. H. Marshall, *Luke: Historian and Theologian*, (Grand Rapids, 1970), pp. 144–147; P. Minear, "Luke's Use of the Birth Stories" in *Studies in Luke-Acts*, (Philadelphia, 1980); R. Maddox, *The Purpose of Luke-Acts*, (Edinburgh, 1982), pp. 100–157.

of his study – it is far from clear that in following Conzelmann he has provided the proper explanation for that emphasis. While looking at Luke's paranetic materials will not be a major part of the task undertaken by the present study, it will have a role to play in what follows.

Also, one must question Ott's restriction of Jesus' role to that of a simple paradigm. Jesus certainly is presented as the great model of prayer in Luke. But does this necessarily exhaust the significance of Luke's portrayal? How can Ott exclude *a priori* any christological import from Luke's descriptions of Jesus at prayer when he makes no effort (at least none is revealed) to discover what possible christological interests might be found in Luke's prayer materials if one were to look for them?

It is also difficult to see how Jesus can be an example to the church of how to survive demonic temptation through prayer if the largest part of his ministry was itself a temptation-free era. This leaves only the prayers offered on the Mount of Olives and Golgotha as having any relevance to what Ott describes as the sole significance of Jesus' prayer-life in Luke. What, then, is to be made of all those prayer notices found between Lk. 4:13 and 22:3? Ott seems not to have thought through the compatibility of his thesis and his presuppositions. Clearly one (Jesus prays only as paradigm) or the other (Jesus' life is free of Satanic temptation) or even both of them must go.

It also seems likely that Ott's preoccupation with Conzelmann's eschatology has caused him to misread the significance of Lk. 11:9–13. Is it self-evident that this passage describes all prayer for material things, in other words, prayer for anything other than the Spirit, as being harmful? To anticipate only slightly, it would appear that Luke's beliefs concerning the sovereignty of God – a readily recognised and important theme in Luke-Acts – are more immediately relevant than artificial eschatological constructions.[12]

## 1.1.2 O. G. Harris: Prayer and Heilsgeschichte

In 1967 O. G. Harris produced an unpublished Ph.D. dissertation at Vanderbilt University entitled *Prayer in Luke-Acts: A Study in the Theology of Luke*. Harris distinguished himself by being the first to attempt a comprehensive analysis of the prayer theme in Luke-Acts, as compared to Ott's more restrictive discussion of the parabolic material in the gospel. Harris' main thesis is that "Luke conceives of prayer as an important means by which God guides the course of redemptive history. This is his controlling and distinctive idea of prayer" (p. 3). Secondarily, Jesus is presented as a paradigmatic example of piety which the church is to emulate. But this is a decidely minor point.

Harris thoroughly endorses Conzelmann's view of redemptive-history and Luke's "historicising" tendencies in the face of a delayed parousia (pp. 209 ff, 222 f,

---

[12] The influence of Ott's main thesis has been widely felt; see for example A. Wurzinger, "'Es komme Dein Königreich': zum Gebetsanliegen nach Lukas," *BLit.* 38 ('64–65) 94; J. Schmid, *Das Evangelium nach Lukas*, (Regensburg, 1960), Excursus on "Jesus und das Gebet," pp. 200–202.

239f). Therefore, even though he gives no indication of being familiar with Ott's work (perhaps due to the nearly simultaneous completion of their theses), Harris also views prayer as the chief means by which the church is to "endure" until the parousia. Consequently, Harris relates Luke's prayer theme to both his eschatology and his paradigmatic portrayal of Jesus in much the same way as does Ott.

Harris' primary thesis concerning prayer and decisive turning points in salvation-history has been largely accepted by NT scholarship.[13] There is no doubt that his was a groundbreaking work in the field of Lukan studies and he has demonstrated an important connection between the activity of prayer and the way in which God guides salvation-history. But the present study will also indicate the need for significant readjustment in the details of Harris' thesis. In the first place, it is not obvious that Luke considers every mention of prayer in Luke-Acts as marking a critical turning-point in *Heilsgeschichte*, a fundamental assumption in the course of Harris' argument. For example, what is "pivotal" about the situation in Lk. 5:16? Without the establishment of some prior, evaluative criteria it is too easy to describe virtually anything associated with prayer as comprising a turning point.

Secondly, is it quite correct to say that prayer is *the means* by which God guides salvation-history? Could there be other ways of describing this relationship? For example, in view of Luke's concern with the sovereignty of God and (as this study hopes to show) with the way in which prayer serves to attune the will of the individual to the will of God, would it not be more correct to say that Luke reveals various ways in which God is already guiding salvation-history, and prayer is a means of human perception of, and thus participation in, what God is doing? Harris posits a cause and effect relationship between prayer and the progress of salvation-history; prayer is one of the tools through which God is able to act historically. However, it may be more correct to say that prayer is one of the tools through which an individual becomes properly aligned with God's predetermined action and so is able to obediently participate within God's appointed framework.

Harris also suffers from major methodological flaws which severely limit the value of his work. In keeping with the earliest work in redaction-criticism, he tries to separate tradition from redaction in order to base his exegetical conclusions

---

[13] For example, see S. Smalley, "The Spirit, Kingdom and Prayer in Luke-Acts," *NT.* 15 ('73) 60f; P. T. O'Brien, "Prayer in Luke-Acts," *TB.* 24 ('73) 112, 123–127; A. Trites, "The Prayer Motif in Luke-Acts" in *Perspectives on Luke-Acts*, (Danville, 1978), pp. 181, 185f; Fitzmyer, *The Gospel*, vol. I, p. 772; I. H. Marshall, *The Gospel of Luke: A Commentary on the Greek Text*, (Grand Rapids, 1978), p. 366; L. Feldkämper, *Der betende Jesus alsHeilsmittler nach Lukas*, (Bonn, 1978), pp. 22f. Harris' influence upon Trites seems to have been mediated through Smalley and O'Brien.

Others had observed a connection between prayer and important events in Luke-Acts before Harris; see A. Hastings, *Prophet and Witness in Jerusalem: A Study of the Teaching of St. Luke*, (London, 1958), pp. 89–91; Jeremias, "Gebetsleben," p. 131; J. Margreth, *Gebetsleben Jesu Christi, des Sohnes Gottes*, (Münster, 1902), pp. 42f, 199. But it was left to Harris to nuance the position by defining "important events" as turning points in salvation-history.

only upon those prayer notices which derive from Luke's own hand (pp. 3f, 23 n. 1). Consequently, significant portions of Luke-Acts are excluded from consideration because they are "traditional" and thus irrelevant (Lk. 20:46f; 22:31–34; Acts 6:1–6; 16:25; 20:36; 21:5; 27:35; 28:8, 15; see p. 196). In addition, other material is omitted (Acts 9:40; 14:23) because even though it is redactional it makes little or no contribution to the proposed thesis as this "develops" from the material remaining (pp. 172, 192f). Aside from the obvious prejudice which Harris' thesis has exercised over the assembly and exegesis of Luke's materials, it should be plain that Luke's inclusion of traditional material is itself an editorial decision which merits every bit as much attention as do his alterations.[14]

This methodological fault calls for a renovation of the main thesis itself since one of its prime supports is the apparent "absence" of any Lukan prayer notices after Acts 13:1–3 (p. 198), where the mission to the Gentiles – according to Harris, the last major turning point in salvation-history – is inaugurated (pp. 242f). Harris indicates his own dissatisfaction with his method when he concedes that the prayer notices in the conversion of Cornelius (Acts 10:2–4, 9, 30f; 11:5) are traditional, yet deals with them nonetheless because they are amenable to his argument!

Finally, Harris like Ott sees no need to explore any christological import in Jesus' prayer-life. Jesus is simply the church's paradigm. However, the criticisms of Ott on this point apply to Harris as well. Is this simple conclusion really as self-evident as these scholars seem to believe?

### 1.1.3 Louis Monloubou: Prayer and Jesus' Model

*La Prière selon Saint Luc: Recherche d'une structure* by L. Monloubou appeared in 1976. This is a wide ranging study which investigates the various prayer practices of 1st century society, both Jewish and Gentile (pp. 25–34), as well as the general interest in prayer found in Luke-Acts. The largest sections of this work are taken up with a study of the different sorts of prayer language used by Luke (pp. 101–170), giving significant attention to how this vocabulary reveals Luke's general outlook on prayer, and a detailed analysis of Mary's Magnificat (pp. 219–237). Jesus' own practice of (pp. 57–72) and teaching on (pp. 73–92) prayer receive less attention, although Jesus serves as the key to unravelling the rest of Luke's material. This is so because the whole of Luke's treatment of Jesus is intended to present him to the church as their only model of true discipleship: the One who perseveres through prayer.

According to Monloubou, Luke presents Jesus-as-Paradigm in two ways, through the two types of prayer texts found in the gospel. First, there are seven texts which simply mention that Jesus prayed, without conveying any content (3:21; 5:16; 6:12; 9:18; 9:28f; 11:1; 22:41) (p. 57). He then points to the number

---

[14] For an excellent critique of this assumption which so often accompanies redaction-criticism, together with a detailed defence of the claim that traditional material may be as reflective of an author's theology as his own redaction see I. H. Marshall, "Tradition and Theology in Luke (Luke 8:5–15)," *TB.* 20 ('69) 56–75.

seven saying it is unlikely that it be "merely fortuitous" (p. 58). Monloubou does not elaborate upon this suggestive remark, but he seems to imply that Luke is playing at numerology, using the number of perfection to draw the reader's attention to Jesus as the perfect pray-er.

Secondly, Monloubou notes those texts where the content of Jesus' prayer is recorded (10:21f; 22:41–44; 24:34, 46).Through studying Luke's redaction of Mark, especially of the scene in Gethsemane, he believes that Luke's alterations may consistently be explained by the same motivation: to present Jesus as the model of Christian discipleship (pp. 59–61). In fact, Luke's only real interest in Jesus' prayer-life is how it may instruct the church. "La prière de Jesus, telle que la présente saint Luc, est donc une catéchese sur la prière que pratiquent les chrétiens" (p. 61). This also explains why the whole of Monloubou's discussion of prayer in Acts concentrates upon the parallels between Jesus' prayer habits and those of the early church.

Consequently, Monloubou's treatment of Luke's paranetic material, especially Lk. 11:5–8 and 18:1–8, is not unlike Ott's. There is a slight difference in that Monloubou makes the element of persistance an implication of the primary point which has to do with God's goodness in hearing prayer (pp. 77, 79). But, with Ott, this didactic emphasis upon ceaseless prayer serves to suppliment Jesus' model of faithful prayer. However, it should also be noticed that Monloubou appears to have reached this formulation independently, without a single-minded dependence upon Conzelmann's eschatology.

Monloubou has probably most thoroughly explored the exact manner in which Luke-Acts presents Jesus as the church's model pray-er. And there can be no doubt that this is an important element in Luke's overall presentation. However, it hardly needs to be said that Monloubou's justifications for describing this as the only reason for Luke's interest in Jesus' prayer-life are less than convincing. His allusion to the number seven is hard to believe. Even if one were to assume that Luke could have supposed his readers to pick up on such a subtle idea, why should he have counted only those references which lack content, especially since there are only six of them anyway (22:41 is not contentless!)?

Finally, there remains the perennial question: Why is it automatically assumed that Luke had no christological interests in his prayer motif? Is it really defensible to claim that Luke had nothing but a paradigmatic view of Jesus in mind?

### 1.1.4 Ludger Feldkämper: Prayer and Christology

A major treatment of prayer in Luke-Acts appeared in 1978 from Ludger Feldkämper, originally submitted as a doctoral dissertation at the Pontifical Biblical Institute in Rome, and entitled *Der betende Jesus als Heilsmittler nach Lukas*. The title immediately reveals the primary interest of the work. For as Feldkämper says, the distribution of the Lukan prayer texts throughout the ministry of Jesus, the fact that it is so often Jesus who is at prayer, as well as the content of the prayers themselves, all indicate that Luke's interest is not simply in prayer in general but in Jesus' prayers in particular (pp. 17f). At last, someone had stepped forward to investigate the christological significance of Luke's prayer materials beyond their simple paradigmatic function. In doing this Feldkämper asks two questions (pp. 18f). First, what significance does prayer have for Jesus' person; "was bedeutet die Betonung des Betens für die Darstellung des Gesamtmysteriums Jesu?" (p. 18). Secondly, what is the importance of prayer for Jesus' relationship to God and the church?

Jesus' prayers reveal his unique relationship as the Son. This is discovered in the dialogical nature of prayer which is seen in Luke's overall organisation of prayer texts. In the first half of the gospel Jesus is addressed by God as "Son" while in prayer (3:22; 9:35). In the second half Jesus responds by praying to God as "Father" (10:21f; 11:2; 22:42; 23:34, 46) (pp. 333f). This also reveals the general theological truth that true prayer is always a human response to the personal initiative of God (p. 334).

Secondly, Jesus' prayers always occur in one of two contexts: either that of Jesus' powerful words and deeds, or the discussion of his future suffering (p. 335). These various contextual associations make prayer the meeting ground for Lukan christology and soteriology, for at just these points Jesus is revealed as the Son sent by the Father to bring the Kingdom of God and to suffer in Jerusalem. From this use of the prayer theme Luke demonstrates that it is the entire life of Christ, not only his sufferings, that are important for our salvation (p. 336).

Thirdly, Feldkämper discovers extensive parallels between Jesus' prayers and those of the early church (pp. 306–333, 337). This is true not only of the frequency of prayer but also of their context: namely, that of wonder-working deeds and suffering. But the parallels are not perfect; Jesus is not simply a paradigm for Christian piety. Jesus' prayers are also unique, for: a) the prayers of the community are indebted to the prior prayers of Jesus (Lk. 6:12; 22:32); b) the community is only able to praise God through the Spirit given by the exalted Lord (Acts 2:4,11; 10:46; 19:6); and, c) the community prays to and worships Jesus (Acts 7:59f; Lk. 24:52). Consequently, the prayers of the church are mediated through the "true Pray-er" Jesus (p. 337f). Christian prayer is possible only insofar as Jesus has revealed the Father, and then mediated our salvation by the strength of his own prayer-life.

Feldkämper has broken important new ground in his study of Lukan prayer. He is a keen observer of the text, and even though he tends to run rather far afield in order to make his points, the present study has benefitted a great deal from his exegetical insights; certainly no one before him had discussed Lukan prayer and christology as he has. However, "breaking new ground" also describes the limitations of his study. There is a great deal which can yet be said in this area. The first major flaw in his work once again results from the influence of Conzelmann: he has ignored the Lukan birth narratives; in particular, he has overlooked Jesus' confession of God as his Father in Lk. 2:49. This omission seriously undercuts his dialogical thesis on prayer, which is crucial to so much of what follows in his work, concerning not only the nature of prayer itself but also the organisation of prayer texts in Luke's gospel.

But the most serious problem in Feldkämper's work is the absence of any definite relationship drawn between the fact of Jesus prayers and the theological themes which are regularly found in association with those prayers. Feldkämper waits until the last two pages of his book to make a few suggestive remarks about Jesus' prayers "mediating" certain benefits to the disciples, but at no point has he worked out exactly *how* or *where* that process has occurred. This omission becomes most noticeable as he discusses those characteristics of the gospel prayer texts which indicate various (and variable) parallel relationships (pp. 285–305). Here Feldkämper produces many interesting observations (not all of which are entirely convincing), but he is unable to offer any sort of explanation as to why these themes, ie. the power of Jesus' ministry and his suffering, are repeatedly associated with prayer. What is the exact nature of this relationship? The material cries out for some sort of inference to be drawn, but Feldkämper is silent. He does say that "Luke has developed the motif of Jesus' prayers into an extensive 'inter-locking' network" (p. 304), but this observation also points to the limitations of Feldkämper's analysis. For, in the absence of any causal/relational explanation, Luke's prayer texts simply become sign-posts pointing toward other important salvific themes; they serve as "pegs" which anchor the interrelated themes of suffering, etc., but there is no inherent reason why these points of contact need to be prayers. Some other theme might be just as suitable, for there is no causal explanation which might give prayer *per se* a generative, or even *a necessary* role in these connections. Feldkämper has begun to explain the literary significance of Jesus' prayers in Luke, but he has not offered any account of Luke's convictions regarding the actual significance of prayer in the life of Jesus. Consequently, Feldkämper has made a start in demonstrating that Luke's prayer theme has an important place in the development of his christology, but the precise nature of this connection has yet to be uncovered.

### 1.1.5 More Unpublished Dissertations: Wrestling with Ott and Harris

Several other Ph.D. dissertations[15] have been written on Lukan prayer, all of which make the work of Ott and Harris their point of departure. C. M. Fuhrman (1981) submitted *A Redactional Study of Prayer in the Gospel of Luke*, omitting any examination of the book of Acts. He unquestioningly endorses Conzelmann's eschatological programme and accepts Ott's view of prayer and the parousia delay. Although he correctly criticises Harris' heavy-handed pursuit of prayer and *Heilsgeschichte*, his own alternative suggestion that this theme was already present in Mark (1:35; 6:46; 15:34) and Q (Lk. 10:2, 21f) hardly carries conviction. Lk. 18:1 is made the organising principle of all Luke has to say about prayer, and the

---

[15] Fuhrman's work was submitted to Southern Baptist Theological Seminary, Louisville, Kentucky; Mobley's to Southwestern Baptist Theological Seminary, Fort Worth, Texas; and Plymale's to Northwest University, Evanston, Illinois.

concern to harmonise everything else with this statement leads Fuhrman to cast his thesis so all inclusively that virtually anything might fit within it, except the explicit contradiction, "do *not* always pray, and *do* lose heart!"

R. A. Mobley attempted to unite the various approaches to Lukan prayer in his work entitled *Structure and Significance in the Lukan Concept of Prayer* (1983). He essentially integrates the views of Ott and Harris, although he claims that it was not the parousia delay but the church's response to persecution which guided Luke's teaching on prayer. His conclusion concerning Luke's paranetic material is valuable: God is faithful to guide his people as he unfolds his plans for the world; such comforts are enjoyed by those who remain steadfast in prayer. But his exegesis makes the proposed *Sitz im Leben* of persecution no more obvious than Ott's ideas about Christ's belated return. Some reflection on the eschatological presuppositions involved in his endorsement of Ott might have proved helpful.

The most recent contribution to the study of Lukan prayer is *The Prayer Texts of Luke-Acts* by S. F. Plymale (1986). Plymale examines the content of nine prayer passages in Luke-Acts in order to establish that Luke was in step with the literary habits of his day by using prayers as a vehicle for conveying the cardinal concerns of his writings. While rejecting Harris' assertion that the content of a prayer is immaterial to Luke's view of its role in salvation-history, Plymale nonetheless accepts the basic tenets of Harris' argument. He does not explain the selection of his nine prayer texts; for example, why does he treat the Nunc Dimittis but not the Magnificat or the Benedictus? And his fundamental assumption about the place of literary prayers in the ancient world is never established. His discussion of the background material is confused by his failure to distinguish between the religious/psychological role of prayer within a society, and the literary/theological role of prayer texts within religious literature. This, combined with the injudicious description of virtually any superficial similarity as a "parallel," makes Plymale's work of limited value.

All of these works have at least three points in common. With only minor alterations, they accept the conclusions of Ott and Harris (and Conzelmann) as fundamental. In doing so, they unconsciously limit the scope of their own investigations, believing that these previous works have already drawn the basic parameters for future study of prayer in Luke-Acts. As a result, they focus exclusively upon Luke's paranetic concerns; the possibility of there being some christological significance to Jesus' prayer-life does not even arise.

## 1.2 The Proposal and Method of the Present Work

It should be clear by now that there is a great deal yet to be done in the study of Lukan prayer. But the present work cannot attempt a wholistic examination of all aspects of Luke's theology of prayer. Its goals are much more modest. Therefore, it may be useful to say at the outset what this study will not try to do and why. This work will not attempt any thorough study of prayer in the life of the church in Acts, which would include discussing the role of prayer in *Heilsgeschichte*. Nor will it exhaustively treat Luke's didactic prayer materials; similarly, it will not focus upon Jesus as the Paradigmatic Pray-er because this too would be to look primarily at an aspect of Luke's paranetic agenda. What this study does hope to do is to elucidate the christological significance of Jesus' prayer-life as portrayed in Luke's gospel and then show the significance of this presentation for the christology of the book of Acts. What does the content of Jesus' prayers tell us about his identity and his relationship with God? Of course, it has been observed *ad nauseam* that Jesus is revealed as the Son, but is there any additional significance in his being portrayed as the *praying* Son? Why does Luke consistently associate certain concepts and activities with Jesus' prayers? If it appears that Luke does have a particular reason for this, is it possible to determine the nature of the relationship between Jesus' prayer-life and these other themes? In the course of answering these questions other features of Luke's work – such as prayer in the book of Acts, *Heilsgeschichte* and paranesis – will be discussed insofar as they help to illuminate the central christological concerns.

The method to be followed will attempt to combine the insights of redaction and literary criticism.[16] However, the redactional study will serve the purposes of the literary analysis. Ideally, it should primarily function as a "short-cut" method of revealing features of the literary landscape which should be noticeable nonetheless in their own terms.[17] Interpretations which are derivable solely from redactional comparisons, in other words which are totally invisible before such com-

---

[16] Literary criticism is used here, not in the old sense of source analysis, but in the more contemporary sense of analysing the literary qualities of a document. Markan priority and the two document hypothesis are presumed in the redaction criticism.

[17] For an example of a similar "complementary" use of redaction and literary criticism see N. Petersen, *Literary Criticism for New Testament Critics*, (Philadelphia, 1978), p. 84.
The importance of such literary study is becoming increasingly recognized. For examples of how this approach is being applied to Luke-Acts see R. J. Karris, "Windows and Mirrors: Literary Criticism and Luke's Sitz im Leben" in *Society of Biblical Literature 1979 Seminar Papers vol. I*, (Missoula, 1979); *Luke, Artist and Theologian: Luke's Passion Account as Literature*, (New York, 1985); C. H. Talbert, *Literary Patterns, Theological Themes and the Genre of Luke-Acts*, (Missoula, 1974); W. C. van Unnik, "Eléments artistiques dans l'évangile de Luc" in *L'Evangile de Luc: Problèmes littéraires et théologiques*, (Gembloux, 1973); L. T. Johnson, *The Literary Function of Possessions in Luke-Acts*, (Missoula, 1977); J. B. Tyson, "The Problem of Food in Acts: A Study of Literary Patterns with Particular Reference to Acts 6:1–7" in *Society of Biblical Literature 1979; The Death of Jesus in Luke-Acts*, (Columbia, 1986), especially pp. 7–9 for a discussion for how the apparent insolvability of the details of source-criticism has heightened the awareness of the need for a complementary literary-critical method. For a general discussion of the need for and methodology of such work see N. Perrin, "The Evangelist as Author: Reflections on Method in the Study and Interpretation of the Synoptic Gospels and Acts," *BR*. 17 ('72) 5–18; D. Robertson, *The Old Testament and the Literary Critic*, (Philadelphia, 1977), (although the author's preoccupation with genre comparisons limits the value of this work for actually analysing the text); R. Alter, *The Art of Biblical Narrative*, (New York, 1981); R. M. Frye, "A Literary Perspective for the Criticism of the Gospels" in *Jesus and Man's Hope, II*, (Pittsburg, 1971); "The Jesus of the Gospels: Approaches through Narrative Structures" in *From Faith to Faith: Essays in Honour of Donald G. Miller on His Seventieth Birthday*, (Pittsburgh, 1979); "On the Historical-Critical Method in New Testament Studies," *Per*. 14 ('73) 28–33; N. Frye, *Anatomy of Criticism*, (New Jersy, 1957),

parison commences and swiftly vanish again as soon as it ends, are not legitimate readings of a gospel narrative. Each gospel was written to be read in its own terms, with its own plotting, its own time sequence, its own idiosyncrasies. By insisting upon a method which places final authority in the integrity of the individually received narrative a study makes itself *more* historically accurate and critically appropriate to the task at hand, ie. attempting to recover what an author intended to communicate to his audience through the final literary product which came from his hand.[18] Such an approach will reveal important insights not only into Luke's perception of Jesus, but also into Luke's ability as an author. The judgments of a previous generation which saw Luke as crude and unliterary have, thankfully, been laid to rest for some time now, and will, hopefully, be buried even deeper by the present work.[19]

The particular challenge facing a study such as this is the fact that over half of the prayer notices in Luke's gospel (3:21; 5:16; 6:12; 19:18, 28f; 11:1) are simply editorial comments,[20] containing no explicit information as to either the content or the significance of Jesus' prayer in that circumstance.[21] But does this mean that

---

especially his chapter on the "Theory of Symbols"; H. Frei, *The Eclipse of Biblical Narrative: A Study in Eighteenth and Nineteenth Century Hermeneutics*, (New Haven, 1974); R. Wellek and A. Warren, *The Theory of Literature*, (Middlesex, 1973, 3rd ed.).

[18] Cadbury (*Making*, p. 331) said this long ago: "I think it is quite wrong to suppose that Luke or even John in writing assumed in the readers a knowledge of earlier gospels. The new work was in each case intended to stand by itself. It is we moderns who make the comparison, and only too often we suppose that the author anticipated such comparison ... Each wrote a work to serve its own purpose independently and without regards to others. At most an ancient author could hope to be a supplanter." Also cf. B. S. Easton, *St. Luke*, (Edinburgh, 1926), p. ix: "... (Luke) meant his gospel to be interpreted on its own merits, not after comparison or harmonizing with other documents."

At numerous points throughout his career Cadbury sounded the alarm over the deficiencies of stylistic and linguistic analysis, and the uncertainty of their usefulness for source and editorial analysis. Unfortunately, many have not heeded his warnings; see Cadbury, *Making*, pp. 67–69; *The Style and Literary Method of Luke*, vol. I, (Cambridge, 1920), pp. 6f, 62 n. 78; *The Beginnings of Christianity*, vol. II, (London, 1922), p. 166.

[19] Cf. P. Schubert, "The Structure and Significance of Luke 24" in *Neutestamentlich Studien für Rudolf Bultmann*, (Berlin, 1954), p. 185 – Luke is "crude" and "naive"; C. K. Barrett, *Luke the Historian in Recent Study*, (London, 1961), p. 22 – Luke is "superficially clearer and simpler" than Mark; Cadbury, *Making*, p. 92 – Luke is "artless" and "untheological"; A. Schweitzer, *The Quest for the Historical Jesus*, (London, 1948, 2nd ed.), p. 6 – all the gospel writers "lacked literary gift."

[20] All redactional insertions into traditional material; cf. Feldkämper, *Betende Jesus*, p. 30.

[21] The variety of Luke's prayer vocabulary, its distribution, and its comparison with the vocabulary of the other gospels, the NT and the language of the ancient world have been analysed many times before. There is no need to repeat that work here; see Feldkämper, *Betende Jesus*, pp. 17f, 28–30; Monloubou, *La Prière*, pp. 101–132; Harris, *Prayer*, pp. 13–15, 19f; Hunter, *Prayers*, pp. 58–63; Mobley, *Structure*, pp. 205–208; Ott, *Gebet*, pp. 14–16, 95–97; Smalley, "The Spirit," p. 59; O'Brien, "Prayer," p. 113; Trites, "Prayer," p. 169; A. Hamman, "La prière chrétienne et la priere païenne, formes et différences", *ANRW*. II. 23.2, pp. 1193–1199; K. J. Scaria, "Jesus Prayer and Christian Prayer," *Bibl.* 7 ('81) 160; J. Michalczyk, "The Experience of Prayer in Luke-Acts," *RevRel*. 34 ('75) 790; W. H. Johnston, *A Historical and Theological Study of Daily Prayer Times in the Ante-Nicene Church*, unpublished Ph.D. dissertation, (Notre Dame, 1980), pp. 47–49.

no conclusions can be drawn about the import of these prayers? No. Luke had a reason for including these editorial statements, and while there may be little or no explicit information given, there is a great deal of implicit information readily available. Immediate context, the relationship to surrounding events, narrative structure, the recurrance of thematic elements and the distribution of such editorial comments throughout the framework of the complete story all provide important evidence for drawing reasonably secure conclusions about the meaning of such notices.

This aspect of literary investigation could be likened to detective work. If a detective were investigating a series of crimes and repeatedly came upon the same man holding the same smoking gun at the scene of each and every murder it would not require much imagination to draw the reasonably sensible conclusion that this man was the perpetrator. Of course, such circumstantial evidence alone (in the absence of an eye-witness) might not justify a guilty verdict beyond any shadow of a doubt, but it could well lead to a verdict beyond any reasonable doubt.

Similarly, while many of the situations in Luke also lack an "eye-witness," there is no lack of smoking guns! In fact, there are a great many of them, and it is the conviction of this study that enough of them point in the same direction to allow reasonably firm conclusions being drawn about the ways in which Luke elucidates his beliefs about the person and work of Jesus through his unique portrayal of Jesus' prayer-life.

But neither is Luke wholly devoid of "eye-witness" testimony. Several texts do relate the contents of Jesus' prayers and this material substantially endorses the intimations drawn from Luke's editoral work elsewhere. Specifically, this thesis will argue that Luke presents Jesus as the Chosen One of God, the final eschatological Prophet, who superintends the revelation of the Father, especially the revelation of his own messiahship/sonship; who extends God's call to the elect and relieves their spiritual blindness; who experiences God's guidance and the Spirit's power in his own ministry; and who preserves the discipleship of his followers through tribulation, all through the avenue of prayer. But beyond this, his efficacious prayer ministry on this earth is preparatory to his exercising a similar role in heaven as the church's exalted Intercessor.

## 1.3 Christ as Heavenly Intercessor in the New Testament

While the significance of Jesus' intercessory prayers comprises only one aspect of the many-sided picture of Jesus' prayer-life in Luke-Acts, its special place in the pre-and post-resurrection/ascension development of Lukan christology makes this facet of Jesus' prayer-life of particular importance. The fact that the idea of Christ offering heavenly intercessions is rare in the NT gives even greater significance to this dimension of Luke's portrayal; especially since Luke sustains a consistent development of this idea throughout his narrative, whereas elsewhere only brief and relatively undeveloped references are made in the course of paranesis. A better understanding of the importance of what Luke has done will be possible if the examination of Luke-Acts is prefaced by a brief look at the three other NT passages which discuss the heavenly intercession of Christ (Rom. 8:34; Heb. 7:25; I Jn. 2:1).

## 1.3.1 Romans 8:34

One of the first questions to be asked of Rom. 8:34 is precisely what activity is being referred to as Christ's "intercession for us"? Does it deal with the lasting effects of Christ's past work on the cross? Or does it concern actual prayers of intercession offered in heaven? And if it is the latter, does it describe a present, ongoing activity? Or is it a future work to take place at the last judgment?

The evidence points most strongly towards Paul's referring to real prayers of intercession.[22] Verse 34 describes a four-fold "unfolding" of new moments of salvific activity (death → resurrection → right hand → intercession). The last two, introduced as they are by ὃς καί, indicate that Paul is thinking of distinct, complementary activities, each predicated upon its antecedent. He is not simply unfolding the ongoing relevance of a single, past event.[23] Thus while the eternal value of the atonement is the presupposition to Jesus' heavenly intercession, it does not itself constitute such intercession.

The precise moment at which these prayers are offered continues to be a matter of debate. Many claim that Paul refers to the final judgment when Christ will rise to confess his elect before the Judge, and/or defend them against Satanic accusation (something thought to happen only at the final judgment).[24] The advocates of this view point primarily to the presence of the future tense throughout vv. 31–39 and the pervasive use of forensic (thus, eschatological) language.[25] Some also point out affinities with the synoptic Son of Man tradition where that eschatological figure is said to appear as an advocate for the faithful in the final judgment (Mk. 8:38; Mt. 10:32f).[26]

---

[22] See Margreth, Gebetsleben, pp. 81f.

[23] Cf. the otherwise excellent article of M. Mauchline, "Jesus Christ as Intercessor," ExpT. 64 ('52–3) 355–360, who after a good discussion of the relevant texts backtracks into explaining Jesus' heavenly "intercession" in terms of the "eternal value" of his work of atonement.

[24] C. K. Barrett, The Epistle to the Romans, (London, 1962), p. 173.

[25] Representative advocates of this position would be O. Michel, Der Brief an die Römer, (Göttingen, 1955), pp. 281f; E. Käsemann, Commentary on Romans, (Grand Rapids, 1980), p. 248 (although his interpretation is rather ambiguous); D. Hay, Glory at the Right Hand: Psalm 110 in Early Christianity, (Nashville, 1973), pp. 60, 130, 134; T. Priess, "The Inner Witness of the Holy Spirit," Int. 7 ('53) 268f; Barrett, Romans, p. 173 (ambiguous); for further references see, M. Gourgues, A La Droite de Dieu: Résurrection de Jésus et Actualization du Psaume 110:1 dans le Nouveau Testament, (Paris, 1978), p. 50 n. 9.

[26] Hay, Glory, pp. 40, 130f; E. Obeng, A Study of Romans 8:26f, unpublished Ph.D. dissertation, (Aberdeen, 1980), p. 49; J. Dupont, "'Assis à la droite de Dieu' L'interpretation du Ps 110,1 dans le Nouveau Testament" in Resurrexit: Acts du Symposium International sur la Résurrection de Jésus (Rome 1970), (Rome, 1974), p. 380.

However, as this study will demonstrate (chapter 7), Luke sees this aspect of the synoptic Son of Man tradition (Lk. 12:8f) as decidedly *un*-eschatological; it deals with a present day aspect of the Son of Man's activity. It will also become clear that forensic language can be used to describe Satanic activity (if, indeed, that is what Paul has in mind) in this life; it need not be eschatological.

There are also persuasive responses to the other main arguments.[27] Forensic language itself does not necessarily suggest the future judgment since Paul transforms it into a metaphor for the present struggles of Christian existence. His entire argument turns upon the justification of the believer's *present* security in the midst of tribulations. The future tenses posit hypothetical situations now made impossible by God's commitment to his elect. Therefore, just as Christ's past death and resurrection demonstrate God's commitment to his own, so too do Christ's present intercessions. Security in the future is founded upon the Christian's present position as one loved by God and prayed for by Christ.

Other important elements are Paul's combination of the language of the heavenly court (albeit with a this-worldly significance) with the reference to Christ's position at the right hand of God. Even though this is often categorised as an allusion to Ps. 110:1, this is not necessarily the case.[28] There is no reference to Christ's "sitting;" thus any similarity is limited to his position at "the right hand," which could as easily be derived from a judicial passage in the OT unrelated to Ps. 110 (see chapter 7).[29]

### 1.3.2 Hebrews 7:25

Only the epistle to the Hebrews unmistakably develops the idea of Jesus as our heavenly High Priest. His uniqueness as the only perfect High Priest contributes to an emphasis upon the finality of his sacrificial work (1:3f; 7:27; 9:12, 25–28; 10:12–14; 12:2). The author makes it plain that Christ's "sitting at the right hand of God" signifies, first of all, the completion of his work of atonement. However, there is a second train of thought in this letter, not restricted to 7:25, which also suggests that Christ's priestly ministry continues (cf. 2:17f; 4:14–16; 8:2; 9:24; 12:24). But how can our High Priest both have finished and be continuing his

---

[27] See the thorough discussion in Gourgues, *A La Droite de Dieu*, pp. 48–57. Other representatives of this position would be W. Sanday and A. Headlam, *A Critical and Exegetical Commentary on the Epistle to the Romans*, (Edinburgh, 1930), p. 221; N. Johansson, *Parakletoi, Vorstellungen von Fürsprechern für die Menschen vor Gott in der Alttestamentlichen Religion, im Spätjudentum und Urchristentum*, (Lund, 1940), p. 234; F. Leenhardt, *The Epistle to the Romans*, (London, 1961), p. 238; J. Murray, *The Epistle to the Romans*, (London, 1967), pp. 329f; Dupont, "Assis à la droite," pp. 379f; U. Wilckens, *Der Brief an die Römer (Röm 6–11)*, vol. 2, (Zürich, 1980), pp. 174f; A. T. Hanson, *The Image of the Invisible God*, (London, 1982), pp. 145f. However, not all would see it as an either/or proposition. Some, such as Dupont, Obeng and Wilckens, interpret it as a present activity which also has a future significance at the judgment.

[28] Gourgues, *A La Droite de Dieu*, pp. 49f.

[29] Cf. Zech. 3:1ff, a similarity also observed by Leenhardt, *Romans*, p. 238.

work? More specifically, why would he need to intercede for believers after offering the final sacrifice?

D. Hay has suggested that 7:25 represents an older tradition which has not been satisfactorily integrated into the author's theology of Christ's heavenly priesthood.[30] As with the interpretation of Rom. 8:34, there are also those who view Christ's heavenly intercession here in "static" rather than dynamic terms. For example, C. Spicq points to Ex. 28:29 where the priest's breastpiece, bearing the names of the tribes of Israel, constitutes his own person into "a living intercession."[31] Therefore, Christ's intercession consists in the entirety of his priestly work of death, resurrection and exaltation.

However, the phrase πάντοτε ζῶν εἰς τὸ ἐντυγχάνειν ὑπὲρ αὐτῶν does not readily justify this interpretation, which seems to be motivated by a desire to dissipate any apparent tension created by this text. The verb ἐντυγχάνειν concerns the activity of an "appeal."[32] This active meaning is underscored by the use of a purpose clause (an accusative articular infinitive) following the participle (ζῶν). Spicq's "passive" interpretation would require a different construction, such as ζῶν ὡς followed by the nominal form of the word (ἔντευξις). The meaning of the text is quite simply that the heavenly High Priest, having once offered the final sacrifice for our sins, continues to pray for his people in heaven.[33]

There is no suggestion here that this intercession results from any inadequacy in the sacrifice once offered, nor that God is somehow intransigent in begrudging his mercies.[34] God is amenable (cf. Rom. 8:32!) and Christ's sacrifice is sufficient; but whereas the atoning aspect of his priestly office is completed, the mediatorial aspect of his work continues. Thus this is not a contradiction in the theology of Hebrews, but a complementary development. For it is, in fact, the permanence of Christ's sacrifice which provides the justification for his intercession. His sacrifice need not be repeated because he alone is an eternal High Priest (7:23f); therefore, unlike his predecessors, he is able to completely save all those who turn to him (7:25a). But the fact that he lives forever also means that he is continually able to intercede for his own (7:25b). Though it is not explicit, this seems to imply that

---

[30] Cf. Hay, *Glory*, pp. 149f.

[31] C. Spicq, *L'Epitre aux Hébreux*, (Paris, 1953), vol. II, p. 198 ("une intercession vivante"); so too J. Wensley, "The Heavenly Intercession of Christ," *ExpT*. 40 ('28–9) 562 ("... the intercession of Christ is not 'verbal' but 'real'... [it] is not a prayer but a life.")

[32] See H. Braun, *An die Hebräer*, (Tübingen, 1984), p. 221; O. Michel, *Der Brief an die Hebräer*, (Göttingen, 1984); O. Bauernfeind, "τυγχάνω," *TDNT*. vol. VIII, p. 243. This evidence is similarly relevant to Rom 8:34.

[33] Margreth, *Gebetsleben*, p. 82; Michel, *Hebräer*, p. 277; Braun, *Hebräer*, p. 221; T. Robinson, *The Epistle to the Hebrews*, (London, 1933); Johansson, *Parakletoi*, p. 235; A. McNicol, *The Relationship of the Image of Highest Angel to the High Priest Concept in Hebrews*, unpublished Ph.D. dissertation, (Vanderbilt, 1974), pp. 200, 217–219. McNicol points out that the Jewish understanding of heavenly intercession included, not only prayer, but active advocacy on behalf of the oppressed.

[34] F. F. Bruce, *Commentary on the Epistle to the Hebrews*, (London, 1964), p. 155; P. E. Hughes, *A Commentary on the Epistle to the Hebrews*, (Grand Rapids, 1977), p. 270; *pace* the criticisms of Hanson, *Image*, pp. 156–163.

the content of Christ's heavenly prayers concern the effective application of the benefits of his atonement to all those who come to God through him. Therefore, Christ's final sacrifice not only provides the presupposition for his prayers, but their content as well.

Finally, Hebrews is also distinctive in its discussion of Jesus' earthly prayer-life (5:7–10). The fervency of his prayers on earth were a part of the process by which he was made a perfect High Priest. This is noteworthy, first of all, because Christ is seen to continue to do in heaven what he has already done regularly in his life here on earth.[35] Secondly, Jesus' earthly devotion to prayer is shown to be one of the factors contributing to his ability to offer intercession in heaven. This relationship between earthly piety and heavenly intercession is an important element in Luke's description of Jesus as well (see chapter 8).

### 1.3.3 I John 2:1

This text is different from the previous two in that Jesus' heavenly activity is not described by a verb but by a noun appropriate to his present status: he is our παράκλητος. The literature on the meaning of this word is expansive, but for the present purposes it is adequate to take account of the consensus regarding its use in I John. The majority of commentators agree that here it has the meaning of "Advocate." The specified situation of appealing to God on behalf of sinners guilty of transgressing God's law gives a judicial cast to the passage which is best respected by this particular interpretation.[36] Although some would deny that judicial ideas lie in the foreground of the text, arguing instead for a predominant image of priestly activity,[37] there is no reason for these two elements to be mutually exclusive.[38]

It is generally recognised that Christ acts as Paraclete by interceding with God on behalf of his people who fall momentarily into sin. Therefore, unlike the case of Rom. 8:34 and Heb.7:25, there is seldom an appeal to a "passive" understanding of this work. However, R. Bultmann has claimed that this text nevertheless contradicts the predominant theological line of thought in I John.[39] Elsewhere the forgiveness of sins is based upon the atoning death of Christ (1:7; 2:2; 4:10), whereas here it is the result of our having an Advocate with the Father. A. T.

---

[35] Bruce, *Hebrews*, p. 155 also points to Lk. 22:32 and Jn. 17, as do Michel, *Hebräer*, p. 277; Wensley, "Heavenly Intercession," p. 561; Braun, *Hebräer*, p. 221.

[36] Margreth, *Gebetsleben*, pp. 78f; C. H. Dodd, *The Johannine Epistles*, (London, 1946), p. 24; R. Schnackenburg, *Die Johannesbriefe*, (Freiburg, 1963), pp. 90f; C. F. D. Moule, *The Phenomenon of the New Testament*, (London, 1967), p. 91; J. Michl, *Die katholischen Briefe*, (Regensburg, 1968), p. 208; J. L. Houlden, *A Commentary on the Johannine Epistles*, (London, 1973), p. 64; H. Balz, *Die "Katholischen" Briefe*, (Göttingen, 1973), p. 169; I. H. Marshall, *The Epistles of John*, (Grand Rapids, 1978), p. 116; S. S. Smalley, *1, 2, 3 John*, (Waco, 1984), pp. 36f.

[37] Balz, *Katholischen*, pp. 169f; G. Johnstone, *The Spirit-Paraclete in the Gospel of John*, (Cambridge, 1970), p. 83.

[38] Schackenburg, *Johannesbriefe*, pp. 90f; Houlden, *Johannine*, p. 64.

[39] R. Bultmann, *Die drei Johannesbriefe*, (Göttingen, 1969), p. 29.

Hanson objects to the text as a crude reversion to "a primitive christology of celestial propitiation."[40]

However, the author of I John did not see these beliefs as contradictory, nor does he present any concept of propitiation in heaven. The linking καί of v. 2 indicates the relationship between Christ's advocacy and his sacrifice: Jesus is qualified to intercede because he has made atonement.[41] The atonement is not repeated in heaven. Because of its sufficiency it is continuously appealed to and applied in heaven. Jesus' advocacy is predicated upon the value of his sacrifice in a way similar to that in Heb. 7:25 (and perhaps Rom. 8:34).[42]

This appeal to the fundamentals of sacrifice may suggest that Christ's advocacy is performed in his capacity as High Priest. If so, the point is not made explicit as it is in Hebrews. A. J. B. Higgins has suggested that the language of expiation in I Jn. 2:1, combined as it is with the title Paraclete, provides the transition point between the simple presentation of Jesus as Intercessor in Rom. 8:34 and the idea of priestly intercession/sacrifice found in Heb. 7:25.[43] However, it could just as conceivably be argued that the increasing specification of the precise content of Christ's prayers, ie. appeal to his sacrifice as the basis of forgiveness (implicit in Heb. 7:25; explicit in I Jn. 2:1), demonstrates a development in the opposite direction. In any case, there is no evident reason to assume that heavenly intercession conceived of in exclusively priestly terms was thought to be the apotheosis of the NT teaching in this area.

The second foundation for Christ's ability to intercede for sinners is his own righteousness (δίκαιος). He alone may approach God on a sinner's behalf because he alone is without sin.[44] This too may point to an underlying belief in the need for priestly purity,[45] but once again the idea is not made explicit. However, this does have similarities with that facet of the book of Hebrew's estimation of Jesus' prayer-life, wherein his earthly piety is seen to be preparatory to his priestly work in heaven (cf. Heb. 5:7–10).

## 1.4 Conclusions

There can be no doubt that the early church distinguished itself from its Jewish heritage by asserting that Christ was the only intercessor in heaven. Why this distinctive attitude is not elaborated upon more extensively in the NT is a question

---

[40] Hanson, *Image*, p. 154.
[41] Smalley, *1, 2, 3 John*, p. 37.
[42] Cf. Michl, *Katholischen*, p. 208; Balz, *Katholischen*, p. 170.
[43] A. J. B. Higgins, "The Old Testament and Some Aspects of New Testament Christology," *CJT*. 6 ('60) 209.
[44] Schnackenburg, *Johannesbriefe*, p. 92; Schunack, *Johannes*, p. 31; Houlden, *Johannine*, p. 64; Michl, *Katholischen*, p. 208; Marshall, *Epistles*, p. 117.
[45] So Schnackenburg and Houlden.

more easily asked than answered.[46] Where it is mentioned in the epistles it appears
as the expression of a shared tradition, and serves as only one element in a wider
matrix of salvific activity. The exact content of Jesus' prayers, and the situations in
which they are elicited, are not always made clear. Paul appears to believe that
they are offered in a fashion commensurate with the individual needs of the
struggling believer. The writers of both Hebrews and I John associate them more
closely with the forgiveness of sin, and would seem to draw a connection between
the contours of Jesus' earthly piety and his heavenly intercession. All three writers
predicate Christ's ability to offer prayers in heaven, to a greater or lesser extent,
upon the sufficiency of his sacrificial death. This is one reason why he alone is able
to do this work.

Luke's portrait of Jesus as Intercessor shares points of common interest with
almost every element of this composite picture from the epistles. Only the cause
and effect relationship between sacrifice and intercession is lacking, although even
this is not wholly absent. However, Luke's estimation of the significance of Jesus'
prayer-life is also much more complex, for in his view Jesus' intercessions, both in
this life and in heaven, are at the heart of the manner in which he carries out his
past and present tasks as Saviour. Hopefully this will be demonstrated in the
course of this study by: first, examining both Luke's use of his editorial prayer
notices, and their relationship to those prayers of Jesus which have some content;
secondly, periodically correlating the results of this study of Jesus' own prayer
habits with both the didactic materials contained in the gospel and the various
prayer materials in the book of Acts; and finally, comparing this study of Luke-
Acts with the theology of heavenly intercession in ancient Judaism. This final
comparison will not only help to clarify the nature of the relationship between
Judaism and the NT doctrine in general, but will especially underline the forma-
tive convictions (both shared and distinctive) of Luke's peculiar contribution to
this aspect of NT christology.

---

[46] Wensley, "Heavenly Intercession," pp. 559f discusses some of the possible dangers inherent
in this idea which may have moderated its development, although it must be admitted that
neither is there much NT evidence to suggest that the ideas were wrestled with in these terms
either; also see D. R. de Lacey, "Jesus as Mediator," *JSNT*. 29 ('87) 101–121.

# Chapter 2

# Prayer and Jesus' Self-Revelation
# Part I

## Introduction

Luke associates the prayers of Jesus with the acquisition of spiritual insight at key locations throughout his gospel. There are at least three, and perhaps four, passages in which these prayers are directly related to the insight acquired by others into Jesus' true identity. Such a relationship is found in Peter's Confession (9:18–27), the Transfiguration (9:28–36), the Crucifixion Narrative (23:32–49), and perhaps the Journey to Emmaus (24:13–35).

The present chapter will deal with the first two of these passages, including a brief discussion of the way in which Luke expresses this revelation theme through a metaphorical use of the language of seeing and hearing. The basic argument of this entire study will be that Luke presents Jesus primarily, though not exclusively, as an Intercessor whose prayers on behalf of the disciples serve to accomplish all that is required for successful, obedient discipleship – including their calling, illumination and perseverance. Peter's recognition of Jesus as the "Christ of God" in Lk. 9:18ff recounts a turning point in Jesus' relations with his disciples since it is the beginning of their true appreciation of his identity. If this study's basic thesis is correct, then this is exactly the sort of insight which could only be had by the beneficiaries of Jesus' intercessory prayers. Therefore, this first confession of Jesus' messiahship is also a logical starting point for the search for evidence that it is in fact the prayers of Jesus which mediate such spiritual perception.

## 2.1 Jesus' Prayer and Peter's Confession (Lk. 9:18–27)

In fact, Luke is unique in associating Peter's christological confession with Jesus at prayer. Both his use of καὶ ἐγένετο plus a finite verb, and ἐν τῷ plus the infinitive for a temporal clause are characteristic of Lukan style.[1] It seems clear that this

---

[1] Both of these constructions have been variously identified as Hebraisms or Septuagintalisms. The fact that they occur less frequently in Acts (the first construction, *perhaps* in 10:25 only; the second in 2:1; 3:26; 4:30; 8:6; 9:3; 11:15; 19:1) than in Luke ( the first construction 22x; the second 32x) has been one of the mainstays to the argument that Luke has deliberately mimicked a Biblical" style of writing in the gospel. See J. Fitzmyer, *The Gospel According to Luke*, vol. I, (New York, 1985), pp. 118–120, 772; I. H. Marshall, *The Gospel of Luke: A Commentary on the Greek Text*, (Grand Rapids, 1978), p. 366; A. Plummer, *The Gospel According to St. Luke*, (Edinburgh,

introduction to the confession scene is the product of Luke's own hand, wherever the idea itself may have arisen.[2]

However, it may also be true that, at least structurally, the mention of prayer in Mk. 6:46 provides the "source" for Luke's phrase.[3] As the beginning of the Markan material left out by Luke's "Great Omission" (Mk. 6:45–8:26), Mk. 6:46 occupies the same relative location in Mark's gospel as 9:18a occupies in Luke's. But, as Marshall has pointed out, such dependence would have required Luke to "completely alter" the original setting of the prayer,[4] which in turn would also obscure the evidence needed to demonstrate such dependence. Actually, Luke's version of Peter's confession does not require any reference to this Markan text, even though the structural correspondence between Mark and Luke may have confirmed Luke in this particular mention of Jesus' prayer. The manifest absence of any grammatical evidence of a literary relationship between the two passages speaks loudly in favour of their independence. Luke's theology of prayer and revelation alone, as this is consistently worked out in his editorial prayer notices, is quite sufficient in itself to explain the origin of Lk. 9:18a.


## 2.1.1 The Significance of the Prayer: For Whom does Jesus Pray?

Since the work of O. G. Harris, it has generally been recognised that Luke's prayer theme highlights those events which he views as being particularly significant in salvation-history; and in the gospel such events have to do with new phases in the

---

1981), p. 45; M. Zerwick, *Biblical Greek*, (Rome, 1963), par. 387–389; *BDF*, par. 404; J. C. Hawkins, *Horae Synopticae*, (Oxford, 1899), pp. 15, 30, 32; H. F. D. Sparks, "The Semitisms of St. Luke's Gospel," *JTS*. 44 ('43) 132, 137; "The Semitisms of the Acts," *JTS*. ns. 1 ('50) 16–28.

[2] The similarity between the significance of this particular prayer (as shall be argued) and Jesus' congratulations to Peter in Mt. 16:17 could, perhaps, indicate the existence of a common non-Markan source/tradition lying behind this aspect of their two accounts. This would also add to the various reasons for rejecting O. Cullmann's suggestion that the tradition behind Mt. 16:17ff was originally associated with the events recorded in Lk. 22:31ff (see chapter 6); cf. R. Gundry, "The Narrative Framework of Matthew 16:17–19," *NovT*. 7 ('64) 1–9.

[3] Cadbury, *Style*, vol. II, p. 98; E. Klostermann, *Das Lukasevangelium*, (Tübingen, 1975), p. 106; D. M. Stanley, *Jesus in Gethsemane: The Early Church Reflects on the Suffering of Jesus*, (New York, 1980), p. 191; J. M. Creed, *The Gospel According to St. Luke*, (London, 1953, 4th ed.), p. 130; J. Schmid, *Das Evangelium nach Lukas*, (Regensburg, 1960, 4th ed.), p. 167; also see the discussion in Feldkämper, *Der betende Jesus*, pp. 105–108. For a discussion of how this suggestion of Luke's allusion to Mk. 6:46 relates to the question of the "Great Ommission" see, B. H. Streeter, *The Four Gospels: A Study of Origins*, (London, 1964 11th ed.), pp. 176–179; W. Grundmann, *Das Evangelium nach Lukas*, (Berlin, 1969), pp. 188f; H. Schürmann, *Das Lukasevangelium*, (Freiburg, 1969), pp. 525–527; C. H. Talbert, "The Lukan Presentation of Jesus' Ministry in Galilee: Luke 4:31–9:50," *RevExp*. 64 ('67) 495; Conzelmann, *Theology*, pp. 52–57; W. Wilkens, "Die Auslassung von Mark 6:45–8:26 bei Lukas im Licht der Komposition Luk. 9:1–50" *TZ*, 32 ('76) 195–197.

[4] Marshall, *Commentary*, p. 366.

ministry of Jesus.[5] However, to posit some significance to Jesus' prayer does not automatically explain how or why it is significant, especially when there is no explicit statement as to what Jesus was praying for. Why, precisely, should Lk. 9:18a be seen as a decisive point in *Heilsgeschichte*? This question presents a challenge to any interpretation which attempts to draw a specific correlation between this prayer and a particular aspect of the narrative. But this does not mean that such relationships do not exist, nor that answers cannot be suggested.

The majority of contemporary scholars would contend that Jesus's prayer primarily concerns a newly developed understanding of his mission.[6] They would contend that chapter nine begins a new phase, not only in Jesus' ministry, but also in Jesus' self-understanding. Just as it is frequently asserted that Jesus' baptism was the beginning of his messianic self-consciousness, so it is also maintained that this prayer is the means by which Jesus "came to an awareness of God's will for a new departure in his life," involving rejection, suffering, and death.[7] Can one find any real evidence of this in the text?

Harris provides the reasoning behind this interpretation. He contends that Jesus' prayer must be for himself since *he* is the one praying; the often suggested comparison with Mt. 16:17, which describes Peter's confession as a revelation from God, would work only if Peter had been the one praying. Furthermore, this prayer serves to introduce Jesus' first pronouncement of the necessity of his suffering and death (v. 22); and since the passion is God's plan for his Son it must have been revealed to the Son in his prayer (which is the way in which the Father and Son relate to each other).[8]

These standard arguments have a number of weaknesses:

1) The first argument assumes that a person may only pray for himself. But Jesus could and did pray for someone other than himself, as did Peter. To say that Peter would have had to be the one at prayer in order for there to be a similarity with Mt. 16:17 is a *non sequitur*.

2) It is quite likely that Jesus experienced an ongoing revelation of the Father's will for his life; and it would be expected that prayer played a large part in this

---

[5] Harris, *Prayer*, pp. 3, 116, 197f, 221. A comment such as H. Greeven's, that Lk. 9:18a is merely a literary invention intended to separate Jesus off from the crowds, would have difficulty finding support today; see *Gebet und Eschatologie im Neuen Testament*, (Gütersloh, 1931), pp. 18f. Harris himself has pointed out (*Prayer*, p. 59) that Lk. 4:42 demonstrates how Luke can show Jesus departing from the crowds without any mention of prayer (in fact, even while he omits a reference to prayer; cf. Mk. 1:35!).

[6] For example, Harris, *Prayer*, pp. 62f; Talbert, "The Way of the Lukan Jesus: Dimensions of Lukan Spirituality," *PRS.* 9 ('82) 243–245; Feldkämper, *Der betende Jesus*, pp. 120f, 123f.

[7] Talbert, "Lukan Spirituality," p. 243. Feldkämper is representative when he says (*Der betende Jesus*, p. 124): "The prayer of Jesus in 9:18 actualizes his unity with God in the acceptance of the divinely decreed necessity of his suffering and death ... in his prayer he makes the salvation-will of the Father his own ... In this sense his prayer here also makes salvation possible." (my translation).

[8] Talbert, "Lukan Spirituality", p. 243 produces the same argument concerning the role of Jesus' prayer in 9:28f. It will be similarly dealt with in the appropriate section of this chapter.

process. But the question now is not whether Jesus received new insights into the Father's will through prayer, but whether the narrative of 9:18–27 justifies the view that *this* was the particular moment at which Jesus first came to understand the necessity of his passion; and furthermore, whether *this* prayer was the means by which he arrived at this new insight. An examination of the passage will show that such is not the case:

a) There is no indication that the subject matter of v. 22 is new to Jesus. The prayer is not immediately associated with Jesus' teaching on suffering, but with Peter's christological confession. The main finite verb ἐπηρώτησεν connects Jesus' question, "Who do the crowds say that I am?", directly to the preceding participial clause (προσευχόμενον). The result is that Jesus' probe into the disciples' attitude towards him is linked with his prayer.[9] This connection indicates that Luke's interest in Jesus' prayer lies in its relationship to the disciples' answer to his question and the understanding of Jesus thereby revealed.

b) Furthermore, it is the resulting confession by Peter, not the prayer itself, which elicits Jesus' teaching on suffering. The ὁ δὲ of v. 21 places the teaching on suffering in antithesis to the confession, "the Christ of God."[10] What follows serves as a correction to the disciples' views;[11] it is new to them, but there is no indication that it is new to Jesus. The point of the narrative is the precise definition of the meaning of messiahship,[12] not the illumination of Jesus.

3) The evidence thus far indicates that Luke intends his reader to relate the effects of Jesus' prayer in 9:18, not to Jesus himself, but to the disciples; more specifically, the prayer concerns their understanding of Jesus' messiahship as he prepares them for the question he is about to ask.[13]

---

[9] J. Radermakers, "The Prayer of Jesus in the Synoptic Gospels," *LV.* 24 ('69) 567. Feldkämper, pp. 117f observes this connection as well, and even specifically associates it with Jesus' intention for the disciples. However, he then pursues the standard argument, ignoring the implications of such an association between this prayer and what Jesus anticipates in asking such a question of the disciples.

[10] H. Flender, *St. Luke: Theologian of Redemptive History*, (London, 1967), p. 31; also see *BDF.*, par. 447.

[11] *Pace* W. Dietrich, *Das Petrusbild der lukanischen Schriften*, (Stuttgart, 1972), pp. 96–103. Dietrich argues that Peter's confession already entails an understanding of the necessity of Jesus' death and resurrection. However, he confuses how the Christ-title can be seen by Luke's reader, who already knows the end of the story, with how it should be read with respect to Peter and his situation as a character at this point in the narrative.

[12] Fitzmyer, *The Gospel*, vol. I, p. 771.

[13] Of course, it might be said that the possible options have been needlessly restricted. Jesus could have been praying for something other than his own or the disciples' understanding of his person; cf. Marshall, *Commentary*, p. 366, who says that Jesus was praying "for *divine guidance* before making the decisive revelation which is to follow." (emphasis mine). However, two points are relevant with regards to this: 1) If "what follows" is meant to refer to Jesus' teaching about his passion, then perhaps an openness on the part of the disciples to what Jesus has to say about his suffering should also be included among this prayer's concerns. But if it is meant to refer to Peter's confession, then it is doubtful whether this can be seen as Jesus "making" a revelation to anyone;

Further evidence pointing in this direction is found in Luke's use of the paraph-rastic present articular infinitive. This phrase, composed of the temporal clause ἐν τῷ εἶναι αὐτὸν προσευχόμενον, is intended to show that the disciples were present with Jesus at the time of his prayer. This accounts for the apparent contradiction in the phrase κατὰ μόνας συνῆσαν αὐτῷ οἱ μαθηταί (praying "alone with his disciples"). Though it is possible to play down this tension,[14] it is perhaps better to allow it to stand and seek a possible explanation. J. Fitzmyer suggests that Luke "tolerates this inconsistency in his redaction" because of his desire to highlight the prayer motif.[15] But this only explains the retention of "while he was praying (alone)," it does not account for Luke's reticence to omit "his disciples were with him." Lk. 11:1 indicates that Luke is able to emphasise the prayer motif and relate it to the disciples without them being mentioned explicit-ly. Any solution for this problem, therefore, must focus not on the activity of prayer, but on the presence of the disciples.[16]

Since the reader is not told exactly what Jesus was praying about, it is necessary to look to the structure of the narrative for suggestive implications. Such structur-al indicators as are found in these previous observations indicate that Luke is emphasising *the presence of the disciples with Jesus at the time of his prayer.*

### 2.1.1.1 The Feeding Miracle

But there is yet another reason for viewing the disciples as the focal point of Jesus' prayer in 9:18. When the Twelve return from their mission (9:1–6) they report to Jesus all that they had done; Jesus then "took them and retired privately into a city called Bethsaida" (καὶ παραλαβὼν αὐτοὺς ὑπεχώρησεν κατ᾽ ἰδίαν κτλ.; 9:10). This verse has several interesting features:

---

rather, it is a revelation being "given" from elsewhere. It is the relationship outlined in 10:22 at work: the Father is revealing the Son; the Son does not reveal himself (see chapter 3).
2) When an alternative is drawn between prayer *either*-for-himself-*or*-the-disciples it is merely to emphasize who is *the main beneficiary* of this prayer according to the Lukan narrative.Certainly, a person at prayer may touch upon any number of subjects, and this could have been the case here. However, such historical questions are distinct from the questions of Lukan redaction. As far as Luke the author is concerned, possessing a tradition which indicated that Jesus was at prayer does not imply that he knew anything about the actual contents of that prayer (would an evangelist omit such precious information about the Lord's devotional life had it been known?). What is important for the present purposes is not what may have actually been prayed, but *how Luke treats that prayer in the telling of his story.* This literary study is what will reveal Luke's theology of prayer.
[14] Plummer, *Commentary*, p. 246 explains: 1) it means that Jesus was with his disciples in a solitary place; and 2) the disciples did not join in prayer with Jesus. S. Brown, *Apostasy and Perseverance in the Theology of Luke*, (Rome, 1969), p. 83 takes κατὰ μόνας quite literally and so interprets συνῆσαν αὐτῷ as the disciples' "solidarity" in faith with Jesus.This is doubtful. Harris, *Prayer*, p. 58 explains it in terms of a Lukan distinction between the circle of disciples and the crowds which follow Jesus (cf. 6:12; 9:28; 11:1; 22:39f; Mk. 4:10). This is more likely.
[15] Fitzmyer, *Commentary*, vol. I, p. 774.
[16] Alternatively, Luke could have omitted κατὰ μόνας. But it is difficult to speculate about why an author did not pursue what would appear to be alternative possibilities. It is more worthwhile to focus attention upon likely explanations for why he did what he actually did.

1) To begin with, the verb ὑποχωρέω occurs in the NT only in Luke's gospel (5:16; 9:10). Its other Lukan occurrence indicates that Jesus "retires" in order to pray. Retirement, of one sort or another, is a regular element of Jesus' prayer-life in Luke (cf. 4:42 [?]; 6:12; 9:28f; 22:39–41; cf. 21:37). However, it should also be observed that, in contrast to Markan tendency, Luke's Jesus does not necessarily retire into isolated places in order to pray (Mk. 1:35; 6:46; cf. in addition to the above, Lk. 11:1; 22:31). Therefore, his retiring into a city does not exclude the possibility that Jesus has gone there to pray; in fact, that Luke describes it as an ὑποχωρήσις might well suggest that this is exactly what Jesus intended to do in Bethsaida.

2) Jesus is also said to have retired to Bethsaida "privately" (κατ' ἰδίαν) with his disciples. This mention of privacy is also a regular feature of Jesus' prayer-life in Luke (cf. 6:12; 9:18; 11:1 [?]). It is noticeable that this situation of "retiring privately with the disciples" is very similar to the circumstances outlined in 9:18, of "being alone with the disciples." This parallel may explain why Luke chose to retain the troublesome κατὰ μόνας discussed earlier in v. 18; for he intended this text to resume his description of the situation already introduced in v. 10, and the κατὰ μόνας takes the reader back to the prior κατ' ἰδίαν. If this is correct, the interpretation of v. 10 carries with it several results:

Firstly, it re-emphasises the focus upon the disciples' presence with Jesus at the time of his prayer; in short, it offers another piece of structural evidence that Jesus is intentionally praying for their benefit.

Secondly, it indicates that Jesus had purposely withdrawn with the disciples in order to generate the situation seen in 9:18ff, where Peter's christological confession could come forth; this in turn further indicates that Jesus had already foreseen his destiny of suffering, and that this prayer specifically concerned itself with the disciples' confession and his subsequent teaching.

Thirdly, in Luke's view, then, the coming of the crowds (v. 11) interfered with Jesus' original intention for the disciples. The linking of the miracle of The Feeding (vv. 12–17) with v. 10, which is in turn connected to v. 18, means that The Feeding of the Five Thousand takes on an even more intimate relation to the events of Peter's confession than has previously been noted.[17] It most certainly is more than an accidental consequence of the Great Omission.

Various interpretations of this connection have been offered. A. Plummer states that no connection between v. 18 and the prior miracle is "either stated or

---

[17] This observation adds further evidence for the elaborate, premeditated structuring found in Luke nine; cf. Fitzmyer, "The Composition of Luke, Chapter 9" in *Perspectives on Luke-Acts*, (Danville, 1978); *The Gospel*, vol. I, p. 771; E. Ellis, "The Composition of Luke 9 and the Sources of Its Christology" in *Current Issues in Biblical and Patristic Interpretation*, (Grand Rapids, 1975); J. G. Davies, "The Prefigurement of the Ascension in the Third Gospel," *JTS.* ns. 6 ('55) 230f; Talbert, "Jesus' Ministry in Galilee," pp. 482–497; Wilkens, "Die Auslassung," pp. 193–200; F. Schütz, *Der leidende Christus: Die angefochtene Gemeinde und das Christuskerygma der lukanischen Schriften*, (Stuttgart, 1969), pp. 64f.

implied."[18] But surely the evidence produced thus far speaks to the contrary. More frequently it has been said that the Feeding Miracle serves, as do the pericopae which follow, as an answer to Herod's question in v. 9; thus forming part of a complex christological presentation organised by Luke throughout chapter nine.[19] While this may be a part of chapter nine's explanation, the next section will give reason to doubt whether the Herod pericope (vv. 7–9) serves thematically in this way to introduce the whole of the remaining chapter, or is more appropriately read in juxtaposition with Peter's confession. In any case, it must be admitted that the Feeding Miracle – at least when compared with the subsequent sections (vv. 18–20, 21–27, 28–36, 43b–45, 51–56, 57–62) – is among those which fits least comfortably into this suggested christological scheme (the same might also be said of vv. 46–50).

Others, noting the sequence of Feeding Miracle/Confession, have suggested a connection with the Johannine tradition found in Jn. 6:14, 68f.[20] This is an interesting observation, particularly since no one pursues its implications for Luke 9, which support the present thesis. Nevertheless an appeal to John does not uncover Luke's intention in this chapter. A more satisfactory understanding of its function in Luke is part and parcel of the particular significance of the Herod pericope suggested below and the correlation between vv. 10 and 18ff already proposed.

S. Brown believes that the Feeding of the Five Thousand fits into a pattern of miracles eliciting faith in Jesus,[21] pointing out that "the crowds" of v. 18 are the same as those who are fed in the preceding miracle. However, this identification of "the crowds" should not be taken for granted, especially since the confessions made by the crowds are shown to be inadequate, and therefore are not necessarily the evidence of faith or spiritual insight; further, their proper antecedent is to be found not in v. 11, but in the "some" (τινων) of v. 7, as is demonstrated by the paralleling of vv. 7f and 19.

### 2.1.2 Peter and Herod: The Confession as "Seeing"

Luke's handling of vv. 7–9 and 18–20 suggests that he intends these two sections to be read in conjunction with each other. Their close proximity, due to the Great Omission and Luke's deletion of Mk. 6:17–29 (cf. Lk. 3:19f), serve to give the two narratives a greater affinity than they would have otherwise had. Luke's omission of Mark's account of John's execution also alters the significance of Herod's perplexity (see below). Indeed, as Fitzmyer has said, "...one might wonder why the evangelist ever retained the episode itself, once he had decided to

---

[18] Plummer, *Commentary*, p. 245.

[19] Feldkämper, *Der betende Jesus*, p. 118; Stanley, *Jesus in Gethsemane*, p. 191; Fitzmyer, "The Composition of Luke 9".

[20] Fitzmyer, "The Composition of Luke 9," pp. 143f; Schürmann, *Lukasevangelium*, pp. 505f; Marshall, *Commentary*, p. 364.

[21] Brown *Apostasy*, p. 59; similarly Grundmann, *Das Evangelium*, p. 189.

transpose and curtail radically the more important story of the Baptist's imprison-ment."[22] The focus of the pericope is no longer the fate of John, but Herod's confusion over the ministry of Jesus. It is not a matter of omitting "more impor-tant" details, but of creating different emphases.

The result is a highlighting of parallels which indicate that Luke intended vv. 18–20 to be read in the light of vv. 7–9. The repetitions of the crowds' conjectures about Jesus' identity and the abbreviation of the Herod pericope both serve to emphasise this particular parallel. But beyond this, Luke has redacted each of these sections so as to make the connection even more explicit. First, he has altered Mark's ὅτι προφήτης ὡς εἷς τῶν προφητῶν (6:15) to ὅτι προφήτης τις τῶν ἀρχαίων ἀνέστη (Lk. 9:8). And, secondly, Luke has revealed his intentions by making the same modification in Mk. 8:28, par. Lk. 9:19: ὅτι εἷς τῶν προφητῶν is changed into 'ὅτι προφήτης τις τῶν ἀρχαίων ἀνέστη. The result is that an explicit connection is drawn between the scene portraying Herod's ruminations and that displaying the disciples' understanding, a connection not at all clear in Mark.

These observations alone are not new,[23] but the interpretation being placed upon them here is. This parallel has often been attributed to the "thematic" nature of Herod's question in v. 9. But beyond this, interpreters have not attempted to investigate the parallel; this seems to be a serious oversight. Luke has offered sufficient evidence to suggest that he did indeed intend the *entirety* of these two pericopes to be read in association with each other; through the linking of the central verses of each (vv. 8 and 19) he has subtly asserted that the reader is to work outwards from the centre of each pericope and discover important parallels in both the introductions and conclusions.

*9:7a, 18*: Herod is introduced as having "heard about" all the things which had been happening. Notice the second-hand nature of his information, as well as the confusion which it creates in his own mind. Herod is "hearing without under-standing," and it is clear that he has no one who is able to clarify the issue of Jesus' identity for him.

The disciples are introduced, on the other hand, by having their association with Jesus underscored (remember, even at the risk of a logical difficulty). They are not alone. In addition, the Jesus who accompanies them is a *praying* Jesus. This contrast between the isolated Herod "hearing" without understanding, and the disciples in the company of the praying Jesus is the key to what follows.

---

[22] Fitzmyer, "The Composition of Luke 9," p. 141. He further says (p. 151 n. 42): "...a nagging problem in this whole discussion is why Herod is made to ask the crucial question. Why would Luke assign such an important role to him?...[This] Herod episode merely fits the larger problem of the role Herod plays in the third Gospel as a whole. If that could be satisfactorily answered, then possibly this nagging problem would also be solved." The discussions of Herod in this and the following chapter will answer this question by showing that Luke uses Herod to amplify his belief in the revelatory significance of Jesus' prayers.

[23] Cf. Fitzmyer, "The Composition of Luke 9," pp. 145f; *The Gospel*, vol. I, pp. 757, 759, 771; Marshall, *Commentary*, p. 355, 363, 366; Harris, *Prayer*, p. 56.

*9:7b–8, 19*: Herod is "utterly perplexed" (διηπόρει) over the various explanations that he hears about Jesus. There is no corresponding verb at this point in Mark; therefore, it is reasonable to take this added bit of Lukan vocabulary (elsewhere only in Acts 2:12; 5:24; 10:17) as Luke's way of highlighting Herod's failure to understand. The disciples, on the other hand, display no confusion at all. They are familiar with the very same rumours as Herod, yet there is no hint of any uncertainty on their part.

*9:9a, 20a*: Herod asks the question (εἶπεν δὲ Ἡρῴδης [ἑαυτῷ ?]), "Who then is this that I hear such things about?" He remains uncertain, unlike the accounts in both Mark and Matthew where he concludes that Jesus must be John the Baptist come back to life (Mk. 6:16; Mt. 14:2). Once again, Luke highlights Herod's confusion, this time through his indecisiveness. But Jesus also asks a question (εἶπεν δὲ αὐτοῖς), "Who do *you* say that I am?" (Ὑμεῖς δὲ τίνα με λέγετε εἶναι;). The emphatic "you" serves to contrast the disciples' opinion not only with that of the crowds, but also with the confusion of Herod, since Herod's source of information and consequent uncertainty have served to include him within the same category as the crowds.

*9:9b, 20b*: Herod's question receives no answer. He reaches no conclusion. Just as he has heard without understanding, he is now left on his own to try and "see" Jesus, but as future events will tell, without any promise of real spiritual perception (cf. 23:8–12).[24] When Herod does finally meet Jesus there is a three-fold repetition of his interest in "seeing" him (23:8), which explicitly relates that meeting back to Herod's musings in 9:9. But it is also stated clearly in chapter 23 that Herod's interest in Jesus is primarily motivated by a desire to witness some miracle.[25] But Jesus neither speaks to Herod nor does he perform the desired sign. Thus Herod does not see what he is really interested in (a miracle), and what he should be interested in (Jesus' identity) is not revealed. Even after meeting Jesus, he remains in the dark and neither "sees" nor "hears" anything at all.

However, Jesus' question of the disciples does receive an answer. Peter, as the representative of the disciples, confesses him as "the Christ of God." Consequently, by means of the parallel between 9:9 and 9:18ff, Peter's confession is presented

---

[24] See D. Hamm, "Sight to the Blind: Vision as Metaphor in Luke," *Bib.* 67 ('86) 457–477. Hamm offers an excellent discussion, not only of the Herod material (p. 466), but of the idea of "seeing" as a metaphor for spiritual illumination all throughout Luke-Acts. When this article was published nearly identical conclusions had been reached simultaneously by myself, although Hamm does not relate his discussion to Jesus' prayers, nor is Herod juxtaposed with Peter. For a more general discussion see K. Lammers, *Hören, Sehen und Glauben im Neuen Testament*, (Stuttgart, 1966), pp. 37–48.

[25] The connection between τὰ γινόμενα (9:7) and σημεῖον γινόμενον (23:8) suggests a similar interest in both scenes. According to Luke, Herod's interest from the beginning had to do with sign-seeking, not the possibility of Jesus either continuing John's movement or actually being John raised from the dead; *pace* Plummer, *Commentary*, p. 242; J. B. Tyson, "Jesus and Herod Antipas," *JBL.* 79 ('60) 239f.

as a successful "seeing." He exhibits the spiritual perception which Herod lacks. He *does* "see" the very thing which Herod says he would like to see, ie. "Who is this man?"[26]

The incident in 23:8–12 extends the parallels even further. Peter has been with Jesus at prayer. Herod sees only the Jesus who will not speak. Jesus asks Peter a question about who he is. Herod asks Jesus a question about what he can do for him. Peter is committed to Jesus and has seen many signs. Herod has no commitment to Jesus and sees no sign. Peter is given insight through Jesus' prayer and so answers properly. Herod is not in the company of the praying Jesus, therefore he sees nothing and receives no answer. In short, the disciples with Jesus see and hear, Herod does not.[27]

Far from eliminating its "pivotal" role in the gospel story, as some have claimed,[28] Luke's rewriting of this chapter has simply redefined its role in terms of his own concern with prayer and revelation. Jesus' prayer in 9:18 is not only a watershed in the narrative structure of this section, it also lays the foundation for an understanding of the revelatory aspect of Luke's prayer theme. For here he provides the first, paradigmatic example of that dynamic at work. In Lk. 9 the dividing line between those who truly see and hear (the disciples) and those who are spiritually blind and deaf (represented in Herod) is graphically portrayed. If it is asked what has led the disciples to see Jesus in different terms than either Herod

---

[26] O'Brien, "Prayer," p. 115 suggests that this is the fulfillment of Jesus' words in 8:10: "to you it has been given." It is doubtful if a connection with this particular verse is in view, although O'Brien's understanding of the significance of 9:18 is certainly on the right track.

[27] Other comparisons have been suggested which relate Jesus' trial before Herod, not to Herod and the disciples in Lk. 9, but to trials before other "Herods" in Acts. Thus some have seen Paul's trial (Acts 25–26) so structured (Cadbury, *Making*, pp. 231, 310; J. Munck, *Acts*, [Garden City, 1967], pp. lxxvii-lxxviii; Flender, *St. Luke*, p. 131; cf. Conzelmann, *Theology*, p. 217 n. 2). Others, in a manner reminiscent of Dibelius' arguments concerning Lk. 23:8–12 and Acts 4:25–28, have suggested the opposite influence to be at work, moving from Acts 25–26 to Lk. 23 (cf. M. Dibelius, "Herodes und Pilatus," *ZNW*. 16['15]113–126, especially pp. 123ff, with P. Walaskay, "The Trial and Death of Jesus in the Gospel of Luke," *JBL*. 94 ('75) 89ff; Talbert, *Genre*, p. 22). Still others see a parallel with Peter's trial before Herod in Acts 12 (E. Buck, "The Function of the Pericope 'Jesus before Herod' in the Passion Narrative of Luke" in *Wort in der Ziet: Festgabe für Karl Heinrich Rengstorf*, [Leiden, 1980], pp. 173–175; G. W. H. Lampe, "Miracles in the Acts of the Apostles" in *Miracles: Cambridge Studies in their Philosophy and History*, [London, 1965], p. 176). However, it is not apparent that Luke would have felt himself under any particular pressure to ensure that Jesus appear before no fewer judges than his later apostles (as Walaskay, p. 89 implies). And the admission, by Buck, (p. 174), that such "parallels" are not "exact" is something of an understatement. In fact, aside from an Herodian being involved in each instance, there are no parallels at all between these various trial scenes. Peter is miraculously delivered, and never comes to trial before his Herod. Paul comes to trial, but his judge is always referred to as Agrippa, never as Herod. Even if legitimate, such observations *may* add to an understanding of the structure of Luke-Acts, but they usually contribute little to an understanding of the individual pericopae involved.

[28] Creed, *The Gospel*, p. 130.

or the crowds – why do they view him as something more than another OT prophet? – this is where the answer is to be found: the prayers of Jesus.[29] It was not what they had seen as much as it was what Jesus had prayed that made the difference.

As the climax to Jesus' ministry in Galilee, Lk. 9:18ff demonstrates that it is the prayers of Jesus which separate those who understand him as the Christ from those who do not. As Luke's prelude to the Travel Narrative, which largely concerns the demands and obligations of discipleship, it makes clear from the outset that while the charge to obedient self-sacrifice is incumbent upon all who wish to follow Jesus (9:23–25, 57–62; 14:25–35), those who travel this road with him do not do so through their own ability alone; the first steps of true discipleship are taken as a result of the illumination offered through the prayers of Christ. And before this study is complete it will be discovered that the prayers of Jesus concern themselves not only with the initiation of such enlightened discipleship, but its perseverance as well (see Lk. 22:31f).

## 2.1.3 In What Sense is This a "Revelation"?

This is not the place to discuss the precise meaning of Peter's confession, either within the context of first century Judaism, the early church or even Luke's gospel. Such an undertaking would require far more space than this study on prayer would allow. But there is a need to briefly anticipate one possible objection to the claim that Peter's confession constitutes a divine revelation. Pointing to the historical circumstances of Peter's confession, some have insisted that Peter must either have conceived of Jesus as a this-worldly messianic ruler, or his words would be the post-Easter confession of the church "in which the Χριστός-title . . . had become completely disassociated from the Jewish concept of the Messiah."[30]

There is no need to deal here with the second half of this alternative, but the first half should be addressed. It is not unusual to read that Peter's confession needs to

---

[29] Marshall, *Commentary*, p. 364 asks, "What had they seen that the people had not seen?" The answer is "not very much," if by "seen" is meant "witnessed with the physical sense of sight." But their spiritual perception, and the context established by vv. 10, 16, and 18, must cause the reader to look for an ingredient other than simple physical perception. The quandary being introduced here (why different people who "witness" the same events reach different conclusions about them) not only makes an important point about Luke's view of Jesus' prayers, but it also raises a significant question regarding Luke's perspective on miracles and faith. Is it really as obvious as most interpreters seem to suggest that Luke consistently offers a positive correlation between miracles and belief?

[30] E. Dinkler, "Peter's Confession and the 'Satan' Saying: The Problem of Jesus' Messiahship" in *The Future of Our Religious Past: Essays in Honour of Rudolf Bultmann*, (London, 1971), p. 184; so also Dietrich, *Petrusbild*, pp. 99f, 102f.

be understood in a typically Jewish political sense.[31] But, if this is true, in what respect may Peter's confession be called a "revelation",[32] particularly in light of the fact that Jesus must correct it and add his own instruction on suffering? Is it not, instead, merely the hopeful expression of Peter's nationalist yearnings? This is a legitimate question, but Peter's confession need not be fully "Christian" in order for it to be revelatory.

1) We remember that the tradition behind Mt. 16:17f (which has already been suggested as having connections with that behind Lk. 9:18ff) also describes Peter's confession as a "revelation" from the Father. Whatever else might be made of the distinctive wording used by Matthew – "the Christ, the Son of the Living God" – it entails no reference to future suffering. Yet, this shortcoming does not prohibit Matthew's Jesus from explicitly describing the confession as a revelation (Mt. 16:17).[33]

2) No matter how far short of the ultimate significance of the Christ-title Peter's confession may fall, it still expresses a more elevated conception of Jesus than those opinions held by the crowds. The popular attitudes expressed suggest that Jesus had not made any direct, public claims to messiahship; and his deeds up to that point may not have unequivocally exhibited the type of "messianic" qualities anticipated by the people. Yet, his even asking the question (v. 20) implies that Jesus considers the popular speculations about himself to be inadequate, even though they may have been quite reasonable deductions based upon the evidence and information which Jesus had provided about himself.[34] But this means not only that Jesus was dissatisfied with popular attitudes towards his ministry, but also that in expecting something more from the disciples he was waiting for *an evaluation which would go beyond what could be deduced from the objective evidence alone.* In asking the question "Who do you say that I am?" he simultaneously rejects the crowd's opinions and asks for a new trajectory from his own followers. It is a

---

[31] Fitzmyer, *The Gospel*, vol. I, 775; Stanley, *Jesus in Gethsemane*, p. 190 also says that Peter's confession shows the extent to which the "pre-resurrection view of the disciples" could not break out of traditional Jewish expectations. However, also note the opinion of Ernst, *Das Evangelium*, p. 295, who adopts a middle-ground and says that the title is not yet identical with the confession of the early church, "er sagt aber mehr als der herkömmliche jüdische Messiasname mit seines nationalistischen Implikationen." Also see O. Cullmann, *Peter: Disciple, Apostle, Martyr,* (London, 1962), pp. 178–180; and Dietrich, *Petrusbild,* pp. 94–104.

[32] If it is not true (that Peter's confession entails only Jewish political aspirations), is the present argument in favour of the activity of "divine revelation" adequate to meet the charge that what is really encountered in Lk. 9:18ff is the post-Easter faith of the early church? On its own, the answer is "No." But further discussion of this argument here is unnecessary since this writer tends to agree with the view which interprets Peter's pre-resurrection understanding of Jesus' messiahship in terms of contemporary Jewish expectations.

[33] Margreth, *Gebetsleben,* p. 228 also interpreted the use of Jesus' prayer here as Luke's way of reiterating Matthew's attitude on revelation. However, he and others like him, reach this important insight by importing their perceptions of Mt. into Lk., rather than by discovering how Lk. makes the same point in his own terms.

[34] Ellis, *The Gospel,* p. 139; W. Manson, *The Gospel,* pp. 106f; Fitzmyer, *The Gospel,* vol. I, p. 774; Marshall, *Commentary,* p. 366.

question which assumes both the need and the possibility of a revelation![35] Thus not only the answer but even the question itself is born of Jesus' prayer. When read in this light the question also strongly intimates Jesus' own messianic self-consciousness, in spite of the fact that there may be little explicit evidence up to this point for such self-awareness.

In addition, Peter's answer does present a more elevated view of Jesus' position than does the answer of the crowds. Peter conceives of Jesus as the awaited Messiah, his Deliverer. Thus there are at least three levels of messianic expectation at work in Lk. 9:18–27. There is the expectant but inadequate attitude of the crowds; there is the inadequately messianic understanding of the disciples; and then there is Jesus' fuller understanding of his own position, which includes his future road to death and resurrection. Neither the disciples nor the crowds are overtly wrong in what they confess;[36] as is shown by the Emmaus disciples, there were those even among Jesus' close followers who had primarily thought of him as a "prophet" (24:19). The significance of Peter's confession, then, lies in the fact that while he may still be thinking in terms of traditional, messianic categories, the disciples are at least distinctive in thinking of Jesus within that particular framework.

3) How else are Peter's words to be explained? As has already been pointed out, Peter and the other disciples have not witnessed anything more than the crowds. They have "seen and heard" exactly what the people at large have seen and heard, and yet they now show that they "see and hear" very much more. Such a situation suggests the operation of a revelatory process: the Father has effected a revelation through the prayers of the Son (cf. the discussion of Lk. 10:21–24 in chapter 3).

4) Fitzmyer has remarked that Peter's confession is not a particularly "new" insight within the context of the gospel (cf. 2:11; 4:41; 8:28; 1:32f and 4:34 could be added).[37] If this were true it could have grave consequences for any attempt to draw a paradigmatic, revelatory connection between Jesus' prayer and Peter's confession in 9:18ff. However, while this is the case for Luke's reader, it is not true for the disciples. All but one of these previous identifications of Jesus take place before the calling of the first disciples in 5:1–11. The remaining incident is related as a personal conversation between Jesus and a demon, so that the pronouncement of 9:18 still comes as a new insight *for the disciples*. In addition, each of these other instances of confession (1:32f; 2:11; 4:34, 41; 8:28) actually provide important evidence of the truly revelatory nature of such messianic insight. The first two are pronouncements made by an angel from heaven and the remaining three come

---

[35] *Pace* Schürmann, *Lukasevangelium*, p. 530, who in some sense understands the revelation to come with the question itself. The question shows the need for, and Jesus' expectation of, a revelation, but the revelatory *act* is connected not with the asking but with the praying.

[36] Cf. Dillon, *From Eye-Witnesses*, p. 121 n. 154 for bibliography and discussion pertaining to the partially correct nature of the crowd's and the disciples' views of Jesus. The cumulative answers of the crowds, the disciples and Jesus build "a climax-pattern" of Lukan christology; *pace* Schürmann, *Lukasevangelium*, p. 507 who discusses only the "fallacy" of the crowd's views.

[37] Fitzmyer, *The Gospel*, vol. I, p. 771.

from demons! In the final example, the demonic outcry of 8:28 answers the disciples' earlier question in 8:25, "Who is this?", underscoring the fact that it requires supernatural insight to know Jesus' true identity. Luke is emphatic: insight into the messianic status of Jesus is an exclusively supernatural phenomenon. How else could the disciples answer a question in 9:20 which they had unfruitfully asked themselves in 8:25? Luke has made it abundantly clear that even if Peter's confession were to consist of nothing more than a traditional Jewish expectation, such insight is not the result of any human ability alone; it is a supernatural knowledge.

### 2.1.4 Luke 9:18–27: Conclusion

While it is true that Luke says nothing explicit about the content of Jesus' prayer in this narrative, regardless of what may or may not have actually been said, Luke's own contextualisation and expression of the prayer notice point towards his own attitudes about its significance. Decyphering these contextual clues leads to a conclusion at variance with the modern consensus. Jesus' prayer does not, in this instance, relate to his reception of any new insight from God; rather, it is concerned with the disciples: it is their newly found insight into the person of Jesus which Luke wishes to highlight in this prayer context. Because of Jesus' prayer, they now see and hear what others have not seen or heard. Peter's confession becomes exemplary for all those who confess Jesus to be the Christ; such an acknowledgement is testimony to Jesus having prayed on their behalf.

## 2.2 Revelation and the Language of Seeing and Hearing in Luke-Acts

A major factor in the description of Peter's confession as a revelatory event was Luke's metaphorical use of the language of seeing and hearing. Although the second term was less relevant in this case than the first, subsequent discussion of this phenomenon will employ both with equal importance. Whilst the primary interest of this study is in the specific relationship between the process of revelation and the activity of prayer, it might be helpful to briefly examine, in more general terms, the way in which Luke uses the language of seeing and hearing to express the phenomenon of revelation before relating it any further to the specific activity of prayer. Prayer is not always associated with this language, but a broader familiarity with what Luke intends to convey by such metaphors will prove helpful to the proper understanding of Luke's meaning when prayer is involved.

## 2.2.1 "Seeing" as Spiritual Insight

Luke regularly uses verbs of seeing with a deliberate *double entendre* so that "seeing" includes the apprehension of spiritual realities.[38] This is true for Luke's use of βλέπω (14x Lk.; 14x Acts) and ὁράω (79x Lk.; 65x Acts; cf. their coordination in 10:24), as well as θεωρέω (7x Lk.; 14x Acts), θεάομαι (3x Lk.; 3x Acts) and ἀτενίζω (2x Lk.; 10x Acts). However, the various *ways* in which Luke uses this *double entendre* are not always adequately distinguished. For example, Harris observes that Luke's "predominant" use of ὁράω refers to "supernatural" rather than "ordinary" sight; "only three occurrences have the meaning of sense perception (Lk. 23:49; Acts 7:26; 20:25)."[39]

Harris' account of ὁράω is not as clearly defined as it might be. While it may be true that "supernatural vision" is not simply *ordinary* sight, it does not follow that supernatural vision necessarily excludes ordinary *sight*. Harris' not atypical contrast between supernatural and ordinary vision assumes that spiritual realities may not be perceived by the physical senses. But to say that the language of seeing may refer not only to an object's sensual perception, but also metaphorically to the "perception of that thing's inner significance," is a different type of *double entendre* than it would be to say that "seeing" language may refer to the actual sensual perception of a spiritual/supernatural object or reality. In fact, the latter usage would not constitute a *double entendre* at all, but simply be the attribution of objective, "sensual" reality to a supernatural entity. Luke uses seeing language in both of these ways and modernistic world-views must not be allowed to obscure that fact by failing to distinguish properly between these two uses of language.

A brief examination of βλέπω will confirm this statement. In fact, since it is usually admitted that βλέπω had traditionally been more closely associated with sense perception as a function of the eye, as compared with ὁράω which was used more flexibly and thus more regularly with the metaphorical sense of "intellectual perception,"[40] such a diversified use of βλέπω should highlight the significance of each of the two categories of usage being discussed here. One would expect a metaphorical usage to be well entrenched within all of Luke's seeing language if βλέπω is being harnessed for the task. Likewise, the concrete nature of supernatural vision must be taken very seriously if Luke does not hesitate to use even this verb with reference to it.

Βλέπω is used straightforwardly to refer to physical sight within the material realm alone in: Lk. 7:21 (Jesus gives sight to the blind);[41] 7:44 (Jesus asks, "Do you

---

[38] Cf. Flender, *St. Luke*, p. 154; Hamm, "Sight to the Blind," pp. 457ff.

[39] Harris, *Prayer*, p. 71. Harris defines the remainder of Luke's uses as referring to the perception of "a vision or some supernatural entity." However, room must also be made for the idiomatic use in Acts 18:15, which is in a different category altogether.

[40] W. Michaelis, "Ὁράω," *TDNT*. vol. V, pp. 316f, 324, 327; BDF., par.101. A lack of space prevents a similar study of Ὁράω, but a preliminary investigation indicates that the results would be the same.

[41] But cf. Hamm, "Sight to the Blind," p. 460 who argues for the metaphorical interpretation of this and other miracles.

see this woman?"); 24:12 (Peter sees the linen strips in Jesus' tomb); Acts 3:4 (Peter exhorts a man to "look at us!"); 4:14 (the Sanhedrin sees a healed man); 8:6 ( the crowd sees Philip's miraculous signs, though there may be a double meaning here); 13:11 (Elymas is blinded); and possibly 22:11 (Paul is blinded by the light; cf. 9:8?). The verb is used with a *double entendre*, to denote "insight" into the significance of what is "seen," in Lk. 6:41f (as a simile within a parable; so also 8:16; 9:62; 11:33); 8:10 (though seeing they do not see; also Acts 28:26); 21:8 (watch out not to be deceived); 21:30 (when the signs are right you may see the seasons); and perhaps also in an inverse sense in Acts 9:8f and 22:11 (where Paul's blindness may serve as a physical demonstration of his spiritual problems).[42]

Finally, there are also those instances where the word designates the actual physical sight of a supernatural reality and no metaphor for mere, subjective insight is intended: Acts 1:9, 11 (Jesus ascends into heaven in sight of the disciples; the phrase "from before their eyes" emphasizes the physical nature of their vision);[43] 2:33 (the manifestations at Pentacost were visibly seen; the coordination of sight with hearing highlights this fact, as will be pointed out below. Also, note the use of ὤφθησαν in 2:3); 12:9f (Peter "thinks" that he was "seeing a vision," a phrase included in order to clarify that he actually *physically* saw the angel).[44]

These brief observations form an adequate basis for making the following observations:

Firstly, when one speaks of "spiritual perception" in Luke-Acts it must be understood that two different, but equally legitimate, phenomena may be dealt with: one concerns the apprehension of significance through spiritual insight; the other deals with physically seeing some aspect of the supernatural world.

Secondly, it follows, therefore, that Luke makes no sharp distinction between the realms of the natural and the supernatural; the two not only meet, but actually inter-mingle so as to make it difficult, if not impossible, to separate them. To see the supernatural may require supernatural vision, but it can be a type of vision which is objectively no different from that employed to read a paper or watch a sunset.

## 2.2.2 To "See and Hear"

Many similar observations can be made about Luke's use of ἀκούω (60x Lk.; 89x Acts) as have been made for βλέπω. Obviously, this word can refer straightforwardly to the physical act of hearing (Lk. 1:56, 66; 2:18, 46f; 8:50; to list just a

---

[42] See Hamm, "Sight to the Blind," p. 461.

[43] Cf. the discussion of E. Epp, "The Ascension in the Textual Tradition of Luke-Acts" in *New Testament Textual Criticism, Its Significance for Exegesis*, (Oxford, 1981), pp. 131–145 which shows the tendency in D to "de-objectify" the ascension account through the elimination of details.

[44] T. Mullins, "New Testament Commission Forms, Especially in Luke-Acts," *JBL.* 95 ('76) 611f also points out that references to angels in Luke-Acts are intended to refer to such visions as objective events. John M. Hull, *Hellenistic Magic and the Synoptic Tradition*, (London, 1974), pp. 90–92, in his discussion of ὁράω, makes a very pertinent comment when he says that one should

few). But it may also carry a *double entendre*, signifying a "listening" which leads to a deeper understanding/acceptance/ belief. The programmatic statements of Lk. 8:8 and 14:35 make this clear: "The one who has ears to hear let him hear!" Further examples would be Lk. 5:15 (this text, along with others such as 6:18; 7:29; 19:48; 21:38, must be understood in light of Jesus' relationship with "the people," a topic to be discussed in a subsequent chapter); 6:27, 47f; 8:21; 9:35; 10:16, 24, 39; 11:28; 16:31; Acts 2:11, 37; 3:22f; 4:4, 20, 13:48; 16:14; 18:8; 19:5; 28:26f; and many others. Similarly, the inter-penetration of the natural and supernatural realms affects Luke's hearing language as it did his seeing, although in this instance it is not always easy to establish that the hearing is objective (ie., able to be heard by bystanders) rather than only subjective (heard only by the individual himself). In Paul's encounter on the road to Damascus the Lord's voice is portrayed as an objective spiritual reality (Acts 9:4, 7), indicating that the supernatural voice was heard with Paul's physical sense of hearing. Although later accounts may seem to prefer a more subjective/experiential interpretation of this "hearing" (22:7, 9), perhaps the more concrete view of supernatural involvement in the world seen elsewhere in Luke-Acts should at least make it possible to read this, as well as other less clear-cut examples (Acts 10:44. 46; 11:7; 26:14, 29), as the physical hearing of an objective voice as well.[45]

Luke's coordination of seeing and hearing language combines these categories in such a way as to show the significance of public "testimony." Every combined use of "see and hear" (or *vice versa*) refers to objective realities which were seen with the eyes and heard with the ears; no mere subjective visions or auditions were involved:

Lk. 2:20 – refers to the whole of the events related in vv. 8–18; the events in Bethlehem are obviously physical, while such features as ἐπέστη (v. 9), ἐγένετο σὺν (v. 13), καὶ ἐγένετο ὡς ἀπῆλθον ἀπ' αὐτῶν εἰς τὸν οὐρανὸν (v. 15), plus the fact that there is more than one shepherd involved, all serve to indicate the objective nature of the angelic vision as well.

Lk. 7:22 – in answer to their question, John's messengers are referred to the miracles and the preaching of the Kingdom performed by Jesus.

---

not over-emphasize the "visionary" nature of supernatural "appearances" in Luke-Acts since the word is consistently used with *physical* manifestations (Lk. 24:34; 9:31; 1:11; Acts 9:17; 3:31; 26:16a; 2:3; 7:2, 26; 11:13; 12:7). From this he concludes that Luke understands the word "appear/appearance" to designate a real, not simply a subjective, vision.

[45] H. R. Moehring, "The Verb ἀκούειν in Acts 9:7 and 22:9," *NovT.* 3 ('59) 80–99, especially pp. 95ff, has clearly demonstrated that the classical rule concerning genitive and accusative constructions following ἀκούειν was so regularly transgressed by the time of the NT as to hardly constitute a "rule" at all. Thus he concludes that the accounts of Acts 9:7 and 22:9 stand in irreconcilable contradiction to each other (p. 99). However, Moehring does not appreciate the fact that the very inconsistency which causes a rule to be broken may also occasionally cause it to be kept; to prove that a "rule" (which at one time it clearly was) is regularly transgressed is not necessarily to prove that it is never applied. The fact that Paul's friends too share in the initial impact of Christ's appearance to Paul (26:14) may also point indirectly to the objective nature of the voice which accompanied the light from heaven.

Acts 2:33 – the crowd is referred to the publicly witnessed phenomena of Pentacost (vv. 3–12) as evidence of the Spirit's dispensation.

Acts 4:20 – Peter believes that his status as an eye-witness to the public ministry, life, death, resurrection and exaltation of Jesus (vv. 13–15) compels him to witness to what he knows as a result.

Acts 8:6 – the people feel compelled to listen to Philip when they hear his preaching and see for themselves the miracles he performs.

Acts 19:26 – Demetrius claims that it is the very public nature of Paul's ministry which should make his threat to the silver-smiths' trade most obvious.

Acts 22:15 – this passage might be seen as providing the only exception to this argument; Paul's encounter with the exalted Christ is explained as his personal commissioning to be an "eyewitness" messenger of the gospel. The Lukan concern for the reality of that which is testified to by an eyewitness must, however, dispose the interpretation towards the view that this too is an example of real seeing and hearing.[46] Both the necessity and the objectivity of this criterion is established early on with Matthias (Acts 1:21–22; cf. also 13:31). Paul is distinguished from the Twelve in not having actually walked with the earthly Jesus, but he is qualified to be a "witness" (22:15; cf. 1:22) only because he has actually seen and heard Jesus himself.[47]

This phrase "seen and heard" consistently refers to phenomena which are *actual* events. In at least Acts 2:33 and 19:26 this is their sole significance; they speak of something's public accessibility. Beyond this, because such events are real, they may serve as evidence for the *truthfulness* of what is being said; this is why the language of "seeing and hearing" is so closely combined with that of being a

---

[46] *Pace* G. Lohfink, *The Conversion of St. Paul: Narrative and History in Acts*, (Chicago, 1976), p. 25; cf. pp. 37–46, 75–80.

[47] For Luke's idea of "witness" as "eye-witness," a concept which binds the work of the church together with that of the earthly Jesus, see Conzelmann, *Theology*, p. 216, n. 1; Hastings, *Prophet*, p. 142, n. 2; K. H. Rengstorf, *Die Auferstehung Jesu*, (Witten, 1960), p. 125; C. Talbert, *Luke and the Gnostics*, (Nashville, 1966), pp. 17–29; "The Lukan Presentation of Jesus' Ministry in Galilee: Luke 4:31–9:50," *RevExp.* 64 ('67) 490f, 495–497; G. Klein, *Die zwölf Apostel*, (Göttingen, 1961), pp. 203–208; R. Dillon, *From Eye-Witnesses to Ministers of the Word*, (Rome, 1978), pp. 8f; and U. Wilckens, "Kerygma und Evangelium bei Lukas: Beobachtungen zu Acts 10:24–42," *ZNW.* 49 ('58) 233, who says, "Der Gedanke der Zeugenschaft der Apostel als der von den Augen zeugen und zugleich ersten legitimierten Verkündiger ist bei Lukas besonders ausgeprägt und hat bei ihm besonderes theologisches Gewicht ... Man könnte sagen, nur auf Grund dessen, daß die Apostel 'Zeugen' waren, läßt sich eine 'Apostelgeschichte' im Sinne des Lukas schreiben ... Dieser Gebrauch von μάρτυς ist typisch lukanisch ..." Flender, *St. Luke*, p. 121, makes the same basic assertion, but attributes to Acts two conflicting view of "witness:" one concerned with Jesus' earthly life (Acts 1:15; 10:39, 41; 13:31); and the other focusing upon the resurrection (Acts 2:32; 3:15; 4:33; 13:31; Lk. 24:48). However, this is a false distinction since there is not a single text in the first category which does not share also in the second. Whether or not Jesus' life itself is mentioned, the focal point of the "testimony" always concerns the resurrection; cf. Talbert, *Gnostics*, p. 29.

"witness."[48] Elsewhere, however, the term also indicates that these real events may require spiritual discernment in order to plumb their deeper significance; a *double entendre* is intended. At least the suggestion that deeper spiritual insights await the witnesses of such events, as being in some way or another contained within the events themselves, may be found in Lk. 2:20; 7:22; Acts 4:20; 8:6; 22:15. Furthermore, ample encouragement along the present path of investigation is found in Lk. 2:20. As the first of these texts, and therefore as the example which may well be intended to paradigmatically define the scope and significance of this phrase, Lk. 2:20 clearly portrays "seeing and hearing" as the sovereignly bestowed benefits of divine intervention and revelation (ie. the angels provide spiritual insight to enable the shepherds to interpret the physical observation of the baby).[49]

### 2.2.3 Does "Seeing" take Priority over "Hearing?"

There is disagreement over the relative significance of the roles of seeing and hearing in the NT. It is generally contended that "hearing is a characteristic of Hebrew religion and seeing of Greek."[50] Therefore, it is implied that the way in which one views this matter indicates one's opinions concerning whether the influences exerted within the NT are primarily Hellenistic or Palestinian. For those who stress the connection between the Old and New Testaments, it is easy to assert that "the burden of proof surely lies on those who contend that seeing plays a prominent part in the synoptic Gospels."[51] However, this is exactly what

---

[48] Acts 19:26 may appear to be an exception to this. However, it is the only instance where the phrase "see and hear" is used by a non-believer in Luke-Acts, and so it cannot be used to testify to the truthfulness of the apostolic witness. However, Demetrius does use the phrase for the same purpose as do the other actors in Luke-Acts, which is to demonstrate the truthfulness of what he is saying himself, ie. his charges against Paul are obviously true since anyone else may see and hear Paul's behaviour for himself.

[49] Cf. Monloubou, *La Prière*, p. 188. The useful discussion on pp. 198–191 relates this "seeing/hearing" phenomenon to the illumination of the Spirit. This raises a point which will be increasingly relevant to the christological discussions of chapters 7 and 9. It is doubtful if Luke relates the work of illumination as rigorously to the Holy Spirit as Monloubou maintains. However, Luke does relate this work, at significant junctures, to the effects of Jesus' prayer-life. Thus there is an extent to which Luke's christology covers an area which other NT writers would include within their pneumatology.

[50] A. R. George, *Communion with God in the New Testament*, (London, 1953), p. 105. The same position is maintained by G. Kittel, "'Ακούω," *TDNT*. vol. I, 216–225; Michaelis, "'Οράω," pp. 315–367.

[51] George, *Communion*, p. 94. George's primary concern is to correct the mystical traditions of spirituality which conceive of "the vision of God" as the highpoint of Christian devotion. For this reason he places greatest stress, and rightly so, upon the OT/prophetic example of devotion which emphasizes hearing and obeying the Word. However, his corrective concern causes him to overlook the fact that when "seeing" is used of "spiritual insight" into the true nature or status of a person or event the language of sight is being employed in a qualitatively different fashion than when applied to the ecstatic vision of God himself.This, then, should significantly loosen the implication that "seeing" language necessarily indicates a Hellenistic perspective upon the divine-human relationship.

this study has begun to demonstrate; and even more explicit evidence will be forthcoming.

On the other hand, Conzelmann may be taken as an example of those who, without regard to any Greek/Hebrew debate, are able to assert that Luke considers "seeing more important than hearing, which corresponds exactly to the relative importance he attaches to Jesus' words and deeds."[52] He seems to suggest that an interest in "phenomena" causes Luke to give priority to what Jesus does rather than to what he says. As evidence he cites:[53] 1) the order of words in Acts 22:14f, which "is of real significance," even though he admits that firm conclusions cannot be drawn from word order; 2) Acts 13:12 virtually links seeing with believing; 3) significant results follow upon people's seeing (cf. Acts 2:7; 3:12; 4:13), and Luke often highlights seeing (Lk. 10:23; 19:37; Acts 8:6, 13; 14:11; 26:16); and, 4) Jesus' teaching merely interprets what he does; therefore, his action must precede his word.

However, several points may be made in response to this position. First of all, Conzelmann does not explain why the order of Acts 22:14f should have a greater significance than that of Lk. 2:20 or Acts 8:6. Acts 22 simply recounts the sequence of events in Paul's Damascus encounter, where he saw a light before he heard the voice. But there is no epistemological significance attached to this part of the sequence in v. 14; rather, if such significance is to be found, it is in the earlier section of the verse. There the statement that Paul has been "chosen to know" would actually give precedence to his hearing Christ's voice, since even after seeing Christ Paul still had to ask "Who are you?". Christ then *spoke* to Paul; this was the decisive element in the revelation (9:5f).

Secondly, Acts 13:12 does not link believing exclusively with seeing, but with *both* "seeing what had happened" as well as "being deeply impressed by the teaching about the Lord." In fact, if there is a difference to be noted, it may be that ἐκπλησσόμενος indicates that their belief had more to do with the teaching than with τὸ γεγονός.

Thirdly, for all of the examples which seem to highlight seeing there are as many others which do the same for hearing. And many of these, in fact, are due to Lukan redaction, which indicates that it is Jesus'. teaching that is of particular importance (cf. Lk. 4:18–27, 31f, 36, 43f; 5:1, 15, 17; 6:18; 7:29; 9:35, cf. Acts 2:22f; Lk. 10:39; 15:1; 19:48; 20:1; 21:37f; 22:53). As it is, not all of Conzelmann's own examples speak as clearly as he assumes (cf. Lk. 10:24; Acts 8:6; 14:11, here the inappropriate response to miracle alone requires verbal correction; cf. vv. 15ff; 26:16, Paul's vision requires verbal explanation).[54] Even while Conzelmann lays

---

[52] Conzelmann, *Theology*, p. 192.

[53] Conzelmann, *Theology*, p. 192, n. 2.

[54] Cf. Dillon, *Eye-Witnesses*, pp. 19, 27. Also see p. 127, n. 172 for a discussion similar to that being offered here. M. Rese *Alttestamentliche Motive in der Christologie des Lukas*, (Gütersloh, 1969), p. 152, n. 39 also critiques Conzelmann on this point; cf. Dietrich, *Petrusbild*, p. 280. P. J. Achtemeier, "The Lukan Perspective on the Miracles of Jesus" *JBL*. 94 ('75) 550f offers a good

stress upon the seeing element of Luke's picture, others have placed an equal emphasis upon Luke's highlighting of the "word" and "hearing" as a part of Luke's "Jesus as the final Prophet" theme.[55] Finally, the relationship existing between word and deed is open to an interpretation other than the one given by Conzelmann. The temporal priority of sight does not necessarily indicate an epistemological priority. It may simply be that, as in the OT, that which is revealed by sight is given so as to provide a framework for the cardinal revelation which follows with the word.[56] In this case seeing provides a context, but not the content, of God's communication.[57] In fact, this very thing has already been observed in several of Conzelmann's own examples.

In view of all this, it seems best to avoid exclusive claims of priority for either seeing or hearing in Luke-Acts. At different points each is be given priority over the other, yet rather than being taken as a contradiction, or an inconsistency within Luke-Acts, it would be more appropriate – and certainly more *apropos* the literary ability demonstrated by Luke elsewhere – to regard this as the result of Luke's viewing both as of equal significance, even though the two faculties may function differently in relationship to each other.

### 2.2.4 Seeing, Hearing and the Prayers of Jesus

In his stimulating investigation of Luke's metaphorical use of the language of sense perception, D. Hamm compares Jesus' healing of the blind, where he is the "enabler of vision," with other instances of seeing language, where Jesus is the "object of vision."[58] This study of Jesus' prayer-life has begun to reveal the point at which these two perspectives on Jesus converge. That point is Jesus at prayer. When the metaphorical use of the language of perception is encountered in association with Jesus' prayers he becomes, in one and the same act, both the enabler and the object of an individual's apprehension. Through his prayer Jesus enables those for whom he prays to perceive his true identity and to hear his teaching; he becomes the proper object of their spiritual aspirations and the authority to whom they listen. By his prayers Jesus causes people to see and hear.

---

discussion of the equivalent significance attached by Luke to both Jesus' teaching (what is heard) and miracles (what is seen); however, on pp. 559 ff he inexplicably arrives at a very different conclusion!

[55] G. W. H. Lampe, "The Lucan Portrait of Christ," *NTS*. 2 ('55–56) 169f; also, "The Holy Spirit in the Writings of St. Luke" (Oxford, 1955), pp. 173–181; H. Guy, "Matthew 11:25–27; Luke 10:21–22," *ExpT*. 49 ('37–38) 236–237; M. Boring, *Sayings of the Risen Jesus: Christian Prophecy in the Synoptic Tradition*, (Cambridge, 1982), pp. 41–43; Marshall, *Commentary*, pp. 210, 241; E. Prevallet, *Luke 24:26: A Passover Christology*, unpublished Ph.D. dissertation, (Ann Arbor, 1968), pp. 29f, 53–64; Fitzmyer, *The Gospel*, vol. I, pp. 213–215.

[56] Michaelis "'Ορἀω," p. 330.

[57] Kittel, "'Ακοὐω," pp. 218f.

[58] Hamm, "Sight to the Blind," p. 458.

## 2.3 Jesus' Prayer and the Transfiguration (Lk. 9:28–36)

Few gospel stories present as concentrated a mass of interpretive knots as does the account of the Transfiguration.[59]Fortunately however, they do not all need to be untied here. This material simply needs to be discussed insofar as it contributes to an unravelling of the significance of Luke's prayer notices in 9:28f. The relevance of the Transfiguration will become apparent as two issues are considered: first, the association of the disciples with Jesus as he prayed; and, second, the recurring themes of seeing and hearing which appear in the details of the narrative.

### 2.3.1 Jesus, the Disciples and Prayer

Luke not only adds the element of prayer to his version of the Transfiguration, he emphasises its importance by mentioning it twice in succession. First, Jesus goes up the mountain, with Peter, James and John, "in order to pray" (προσεύξασθαι; an infinitive of purpose). Then, by means of a present articular infinitive (ἐν τῷ προσεύχεσθαι αὐτὸν), Luke makes it clear that the Transfiguration takes place *while* Jesus is at prayer. Furthermore, the coordinating participle παραλαβὼν relates the disciples' presence with Jesus directly to his intention to ascend the mountain "in order to pray." While it may not be profitable to speculate about Luke's motives and/or sources for adding these prayer notices to his Markan material, it is possible to observe the consequences of his editorial work, the first of which is the clear linking of the presence of the three disciples with Jesus' intention to pray. The similarity between this situation and that found in 9:10–18 is clear.

It is generally recognised that the Transfiguration serves to confirm Jesus' intimate fellowship with the Father and encourage him along the new phase of his ministry which has just been disclosed to the disciples (9:21–27).[60] Jesus' prayer serves to highlight this intimacy, and present the means through which it is experienced. The proleptic experience of glorification must, at least partially, be interpreted as heavenly encouragement for Jesus as he begins his journey to the God-ordained city of eventual death and resurrection. Therefore, it becomes clear at this point, as it was not in 9:18, that this prayer concerns Jesus' understanding of himself and his relationship with God. It is difficult to believe that Luke would want to say that Jesus actually prayed for the experience of the Transfiguration *per se*; rather, it must be an instance of that communion with God whereby Jesus

---

[59] For bibliography on the Transfiguration and discussions of its various interpretations see, E. Nardoni, "A Redactional Interpretation of Mark 9:1," *CBQ.* 43 ('81) 365–384; J. Nützel, *Die Verklärungserzählung im Markusevangelium*, (Würzburg, 1973); Harris, *Prayer*, pp. 66–68; Fitzmyer, *The Gospel*, vol. I, pp. 795–797; Dietrich, *Petrusbild*, p. 104 f n. 187.

[60] Feldkämper is, once again, representative when he writes (*Der betende Jesus*, pp. 148, 150): "While praying he takes this fate upon himself and eventually walks this Way; he obtains his own glory . . . Jesus is able to work by God's power because he submits himself in prayer wholly to the will of the Father. By this prayer he expresses that he does not act in his own power, but his strength is power given to him by the Father." (my translation).

experiences the Father's encouragement, given to him in a manner which he determines to be appropriate to Jesus' needs (an idea to be discussed more fully in a later chapter).

However, it must be repeated that Lk. 9:28f does not mark the moment at which Jesus came to acquire new insight into his path of suffering. Conzelmann asserted that the Lukan Transfiguration marks the beginning of Jesus' "passion awareness," just as the baptism had marked the beginning of his messianic consciousness.[61] The resulting contradiction with 9:21f was explained as the result of Luke's clumsy redaction. Harris followed Conzelmann's line and so made the same mistake here as he made at 9:18, for he concludes that not only does 9:28 illustrate that God has guided the course of redemptive history at this moment through Jesus' prayer, but that Jesus also learned that "the cross was in God's plan when he was praying."[62] But whatever may be concluded about the confirmatory/guidance aspect of this prayer for Jesus, there is no more evidence here than there was in 9:18 that this prayer has served as an avenue for a new revelation to him. Encouragement, Yes. New revelation, No. Jesus has already demonstrated that he understands the nature of his destiny; and, for his part, Luke has demonstrated that he possesses more literary skill than to allow such an obvious contradiction to stand in his redaction. Clearly, Luke does not introduce prayer into the Transfiguration to say that it is the means by which Jesus acquired new insight into his mission.

But notice that once again, Jesus is not alone. There is an audience on hand for this event. Luke's introduction of the prayer motif here not only connects prayer with Jesus' transformation, but it again associates prayer with the disciples' witnessing an event pregnant with christological significance. I. H. Marshall has made the crucial observation:[63] "Prayer is the appropriate posture for a divine revelation, although here the revelation is *not to the One praying but to the accompanying disciples*" (emphasis mine).

It has already been seen that Luke's editing of chapter nine serves to highlight the christological significance of the successive pericopae.[64] The Transfiguration also fits within this pattern, serving to answer Herod's question (v. 9), as did Peter's confession. Consequently, it offers another revelation of who Jesus is, another opportunity "to see" Jesus, and in so doing also provides heavenly sub-

---

[61] Conzelmann, *Theology*, pp. 57f.

[62] Harris, *Prayer*, p. 232. He is on firmer ground when he earlier speaks of the Transfiguration's "confirmation" of Jesus' suffering messiahship (p. 64). D. Bock, *Proclamation from Prophecy and Pattern: Lucan Old Testament Christology*, (Sheffield, 1987), p. 116 draws upon the second Moses typology to suggest that Jesus here receives a revelation of his suffering and glory.But the appearance of Mosaic traits in Luke's description of the event does not require a revelation of suffering to Jesus at that moment.

[63] Marshall, *Commentary*, p. 383.

[64] Fitzmyer, "Chapter 9," pp. 146f; Ellis, "The Composition of Luke 9," pp. 121f, 124–127.

stantiation and expansion of Peter's new insight.[65] The true nature of Jesus' messiahship is elucidated; but, quite remarkably, it is again revealed by God to those disciples who are present with the praying Jesus.

While Luke does not explicitly say that Jesus' prayer was concerned with the disciples, neither does he say that Jesus was praying for himself. As usual, Luke says nothing at all about the content of Jesus' prayer. Yet, this does not undermine the value of those observations which see the Transfiguration as an encouragement to Jesus. Neither should it undercut the present proposal that Luke intends Jesus' prayer to be read in relation to the revelatory event witnessed by the disciples. The contextual clues may be fit into precisely the same scheme as was discovered in 9:18–27: Luke conceives of the prayers of Jesus as a catalyst for the reception of divinely bestowed insight into the person and character of Christ; once again, through the prayers of Jesus, the disciples see and hear something more about who Jesus is. While the common observation that Jesus is shown praying at "important moments" is not specific enough to explain either the role played by prayer itself or the particular importance of any such moment, it is now becoming clear that a dominant feature of such events is an expanding christological portrayal of Jesus; and prayer appears to be a means of opening a channel of communication between the divine and human realms whereby the power of God becomes operative among men.

## 2.3.2 The Transfiguration as "Revelation"

Attention has been given in a previous section to Luke's metaphorical use of seeing and hearing language to communicate the apprehension of spiritual realities. The relevance of this broader linguistic phenomenon to the specifics of Luke's prayer theme has already been advanced in the study of Lk. 9:7–27, where the illumination afforded Peter by Jesus' prayer is portrayed, via his juxtaposition with Herod, in terms of a successful seeing and hearing event. The validity of these interpretive observations is now reinforced by the recurrance of such language in connection with the prayer notice of 9:28f.

The Transfiguration narrative may be divided into two parts.[66] The first half

---

[65] Fitzmyer, *The Gospel*, vol. I, pp. 792f; Creed, *The Gospel*, p. 132; W. Manson, *The Gospel*, p. 112f; Prevallet, *Luke 24:26*, p. 82; Ellis, *Commentary*, p. 142: "The transfiguration is a prophetic preview of both the future glory and the true nature of Jesus' messiahship."

[66] Feldkämper, *Der betende Jesus*, pp. 131f, provides an interesting structural analysis which uses the contrasting figures of Jesus and the Disciples as the clues to his divisions:

A. vv. 28–34                      B. vv. 35–36
1. Jesus, vv. 28–32              1. Jesus, vv. 35–36a
2. Disciples, vv. 33–34          2. Disciples, vv. 36b

However, Jesus and the Disciples are not kept as distinct from one another in the narrative as this structure suggests.

(vv. 28–34) concerns what the disciples eventually see (but do not hear). The second half (vv. 34–36) concerns what they hear (but do not see):

In part I (vv. 28–34) Jesus' appearance is dramatically altered, τὸ εἶδος τοῦ προσώπου αὐτοῦ ἕτερον. Various suggestions have been offered for why Luke substitutes this phrase for Mark's μετεμορφώθη: perhaps he wished to avoid the connotations which the latter word may have had for Gentile readers;[67] or, he may have wanted to heighten the associations with Moses' experience on Mt. Sinai.[68] This alteration can also be explained by Luke's interest in presenting what the disciples "saw" during this revelatory experience. The word εἶδος, as the root indicates, has to do with that which may be seen, hence "appearance." Though less idiomatic, an equally legitimate translation of this phrase would be "the sight of him changed" (cf. especially II Cor. 5:7; also Jn. 5:37; I Thes. 5:22).[69] Luke's other use of εἶδος, to describe the descent of the dove at Jesus' baptism (3:22; σωματικῷ εἴδει), is employed for exactly the same purpose; it also emphasises the visible appearance of spiritual realities (see chapter 5).[70]

This quality in Luke's usage is important. By using this particular word Luke sustains his portrayal of the Transfiguration as an experience of seeing. Furthermore, the word's concurrent relationship to the temporal clause, in the present articular infinitive προσεύχεσθαι, is in line with and even underscores the prayer-revelation motif which it has been suggested is at work. Jesus is proleptically transformed by the glory he will enjoy as the resurrected and ascended Christ *while* he prays.

Furthermore, the summary description of these events in v. 36 as "what they had seen" (ὧν ἑώρακαν) complements v. 29 and forms an *inclusio* around the actual Transfiguration. Thus vv. 29 and 36 frame the narrative and together define it as a "seeing" event.

But Jesus is not the only one visibly transformed; the glorified figures of Moses and Elijah "appear" as well (v. 31; οἳ ὀφθέντες ἐν δόξῃ). The visible appearance of all three to the disciples is then reiterated in v. 32; "they saw his glory (δε εἶδον

---

[67] Plummer, *Commentary*, p. 251; Creed, *The Gospel*, p. 134; Klostermann, *Lukas*, p. 107; M. -J. Lagrange, *Evangile selon Saint Luc*, (Paris, 1921), p. 272; Leaney, *Commentary*, p. 167; J. Blinzler, *Die Neutestamentilchen Berichte über die Verklärung Jesu*, (Münster, 1937), pp. 41, 46; F. Neirynck, "Minor Agreements Matthew-Luke in the Transfiguration Story" in *Orientierung an Jesus: Zur Theologie der Synoptiker*, (Freiburg, 1973), p. 259.

[68] Schürmann, *Lukas*, p. 556 rejects the "Gentile misunderstanding" view (n. 19) and prefers to see an allusion to Ex. 34:29f; also see B. D. Chilton, "The Transfiguration: Dominical Assurance and Apostolic Vision," *NTS*. 27 ('81) 121, who cites Ex. 24:17 (LXX). However, while the Sinai experience is important for understanding the Transfiguration, it is doubtful whether this pro-vides an adequate explanation for Luke's use of εἶδος; see Fitzmyer, *The Gospel*, vol. I, p. 799.

[69] See *AGB.*, p. 220, definition 3.

[70] Neirynck, "Minor Agreements," p. 260, while not drawing out the implications for its usage, shows that there is no evidence of a variant tradition here. The appearance of τὸ εἶδος reflects Lukan usage.

τὴν δόξαν αὐτοῦ) and the two men standing with him."[71] The language of "appearance" is not uncommon in Luke-Acts (4x Lk.; 9x Acts, 4 of these being in Stephen's speech), and it is not infrequently used in connection with prayer related events (Lk. 1:11; 22:43; Acts 2:3 for ὤφθη; and Lk. 1:22; 3:21f; Ac. 2:17; 9:11; 10:3f, 9f, 30; 12:7; 16:27 for various descriptions of other "seeing" or "visionary" experiences in connection with prayer). While prayer is not always associated with appearances of this sort, such language as is now used in the Transfiguration is part of a Lukan tendency wherein prayer is often linked with the "reception of revelations" through supernatural visitation.[72] In this case, the disciples see a revelation of Christ's glory, a transformation of his person, which has occurred through the avenue of his prayer. Whereas in 9:18 Jesus' prayer served to effect a degree of spiritual illumination which allowed Peter to see more deeply into the identity of Jesus' person with his "inner eyes," now in 9:28f Jesus' prayer serves to effect an outward transformation which, being perceived by the disciples' physical eyesight, will likewise lead to a deeper appreciation of Jesus' identity.

But neither is the idea of spiritual perception wholly absent from this story. There is also a metaphorical seeing at work in the narrative together with the objective perception. Because the disciples were asleep during the conversation with Moses and Elijah about Jesus' ἔξοδος, they are not introduced to either the identity of these characters or their reflection upon Jesus' work in Jerusalem. Their sleep serves to focus the first half of the story exclusively upon the disciples' *seeing*, since they consequently fail to hear anything that has been said,[73] but it also serves

---

[71] The use of ὀφθέντες here indicates that the Transfiguration is presented as a real appearance rather than a dream; cf. Marshall, *Commentary*, p. 55; J. E. Alsup, *The Post-Resurrection Appearance Stories of the Gospel Tradition*, (London, 1975), pp. 60f; K. H. Rengstorf, *Die Auferstehung Jesu*, (Witten, 1960), pp. 117–127; Blinzler, *Verklärung Jesu*, p. 41; W. Prokulski, "The Conversion of St. Paul," *CBQ*. 19 ('57) 465. The idea that Jesus and the three disciples shared an identical ecstatic experience (as is suggested by Michaelis, "Ὁράω," p. 354, and W. Manson, *The Gospel of Luke*, [London, 1930], p. 115) is difficult to believe. More unbelievable is the suggestion of H. D. A. Major, *The Mission and Message of Jesus*, (London, 1937), pp. 113–115, that it was Peter's own crisis experience which was shared by Jesus. However, even setting aside the historical question, it is impossible to read *Luke's* account as anything other than an actual event; see A. Kenny, "Transfiguration and the Agony in the Garden," *CBQ*. 19 ('57) 449; and especially Hull, *Magic*, pp. 95f.

[72] G. W. H. Lampe, "The Holy Spirit in the Writings of St. Luke" in *Studies in the Gospels*, (Oxford, 1955), p. 169.

[73] It has also been suggested that the disciples' sleep contributes to Luke's "Passion Secret," since they miss the discussion about the work to be done in Jerusalem (so Harris, *Prayer*, p. 69). However, such an evaluation views Luke's secrecy theme in terms of the disciples' "misunderstanding" of the events, as the Messianic Secret has been discussed in Mark. Luke's fundamental redefinition of the Secret in terms not only of the Passion (if, in fact, this is an alteration of Mark's intent, which may be debatable), but also in terms of "divine concealment" rather than "misunderstanding," makes such an evaluation unfeasible (see the discussion in chapter 4). The disciples are not "caused" to sleep, and since this is the distinguishing mark of Luke's secrecy theme it is unlikely that their sleeping here can relate to it (cf. Lk. 9:45; 19:34; 24:16). It may draw an association with their behaviour on the Mount of Olives (22:45; so Conzelmann, *Theology*, p. 58; A. Kenny, "Transfiguration and the Agony in the Garden," *CBQ*. 19['57]444–452; Klostermann, *Lukas*, p. 107), but neither does the sleep there relate to the secrecy theme.

to highlight the spiritual insight which they acquire through the event. Peter may not have "known what he was saying" when he suggested building three tents in v. 33, but he did know what he was seeing! Without any introduction or explanation, Peter recognises the two figures for who they are – Moses and Elijah (v. 33). As Plummer has remarked, "The power to recognize them was granted with the power to see them . . ."[74] Without such insight the vision would have been meaningless; but with the experience also comes the spiritual perception needed to recognise what is being seen. Both levels of the "seeing" imagery are in operation. Consequently, the prayer which served as an avenue for the physical transformation also comes to supply renewed spiritual insight.

Part II of the Transfiguration (vv. 34–36) presents the divine response to Peter's suggestion, as is shown by the use of the present participle in the genitive absolute, δὲ αὐτοῦ λέγοντος. Peter's suggestion is countermanded by the voice from the cloud. Whatever the symbolism behind the cloud, and whoever is or is not included within the αὐτούς who enter, it serves to prevent the disciples from seeing what happens next; v. 36 makes this clear – the disciples cannot see into, or out of, the cloud. Jesus simply reappears "alone." Consequently the import of this part of the narrative is directed away from the heavenly figures and refocused upon that which is *heard*. Hearing is emphasised in v. 35 just as strongly as seeing was emphasised previously: "A *voice* (φωνὴ) came from the cloud *saying* (λέγουσα), 'This is my Son, the Chosen One, *hear him* (αὐτοῦ ἀκούετε).'" A divine voice is heard, which further elucidates the true identity of Jesus.

There is no reason to unravel here the full significance of each of the titles used in this verse. It is enough to note: 1) that they concern the fuller revelation to the disciples of who Jesus is; 2) the voice commands that the disciples listen to Jesus' teaching; this not only offers divine confirmation of Jesus' understanding of his mission (vv. 22–27), but also shows that a true understanding of Jesus' identity entails the proper appreciation of his authority to speak for God; and, 3) it is widely acknowledged that the words αὐτοῦ ἀκούετε allude to Dt. 18:15, thus presenting Jesus in terms of the eschatological Prophet-like-Moses (cf. Acts 3:22f; 7:37)[75] Consequently, the prophetic understanding of Jesus expressed earlier by the crowds is again corrected, not as being overtly wrong, but as simply inadequate. Jesus is a prophet of sorts. But he is a greater prophet than they have imagined; and

---

[74] Plummer, *Commentary*, p. 251.

[75] See Feldkämper, *Der betende Jesus*, pp. 143f; Fitzmyer, *The Gospel*, vol. I, p. 803; Schürmann, *Lukas*, p. 562; W. Manson, *The Gospel*, p. 115; Chilton, "Transfiguration," p. 121; Marshall, *Commentary*, p. 388; Ellis, *Commentary*, p. 143; Lampe, "The Holy Spirit," p. 174; F. Bovon, *L'Oeuvre de Luc: Etudes d'exégèse et de théologie*, (Paris, 1987), pp. 73–91, especially p. 78; Bock, *Proclamation*, pp. 115f. Others prefer to understand the voice as a retrospective divine confirmation of the teaching contained in vv. 21ff; so Grundmann, *Evangelium*, p. 193; Ernst, *Evangelium*, p. 306. But there is no reason that these two interpretations may not be combined; so Marshall, *Commentary*, p. 388; *pace* Prevallet, *Luke 24:26*, p. 82. Conzelmann's statement that *if* there is an allusion to Dt. 18:15 here "then there is admittedly a suggestion of typology; but Luke has simply taken it over from the tradition without reflecting on it" is interesting for what it assumes to know about Luke's inner thoughts; see *Theology*, p. 167 n. 3.

this deeper view of Jesus as the eschatological Prophet is also now linked with the task of suffering which was earlier used to explicate both Jesus' use of the Son of Man title (v. 22) and Peter's confession of Jesus as the Christ of God (v. 20).

### 2.3.3 Luke 9:28–36: Conclusion

Once again, as in 9:18ff, Luke has described the presence of the disciples with the praying Jesus as the occasion for their reception of a new revelation into the true meaning of Jesus' person and ministry. Suffering in Jerusalem, future exaltation, both of which will be fulfilled by Jesus as the eschatological, Mosaic prophet, are all a part of this revelation which comes to them, again expressed in terms of seeing and hearing, while Jesus prays. Also, as in 9:18ff, Luke does not relate the content of this prayer, although he does once again provide various indicators relating the prayer to the surrounding phenomena. He thereby allows the reader to draw certain conclusions, if not about the actual content, then about the general effects of Jesus' prayer and its relationship to the attendant circumstances. In this way Luke indicates:

Firstly, that prayer is a means of Jesus' communion with the Father; by it he finds divine confirmation of the course of his ministry.

Secondly, the prayer situation becomes an opportunity for the Father to communicate his encouragement to Jesus. Consequently, prayer becomes "the medium" of the Transfiguration,[76] an experience which is not specifically solicited. This type of phenomenon will be discussed more fully in a subsequent chapter; suffice it to say for now that prayer, as an avenue of communication with God, appears to provide an opportunity for him to "answer" in ways which he determines to be appropriate, but which may not have been specifically requested. Jesus' prayer has provided an opportunity for God to effect an unexpected element of his will.

Thirdly, Jesus' prayer, as the opportunity for the Transfiguration, also becomes the means of the attendant christological revelation to the disciples. Luke explicitly relates their presence with Jesus to his intention to pray on the mountain. Thus the disciples' seeing and hearing is referred back to their presence with the praying Jesus. In this way, the prayer and the resulting revelation of Jesus are correlated in the nature of a cause and effect relationship. The absence of an explicit content to the prayer is amended by Luke's redaction, which is as suggestive here of the prayer's import as it was in the earlier situation at 9:7–27. In any event, just as the lack of content does not undermine the apparent relationship between this prayer and the Transfiguration, it should not lessen the implied relationship between Jesus' prayer and the revelation received by the disciples. As in Peter's confession, Jesus prays and those who are with him receive new insight into who he really is.

---

[76] Stanley, *Gethsemane*, p. 191. Jeremias, "Gebetsleben," p. 138 says that the Transfiguration is being presented "as a result" of Jesus' prayer.

Chapter 3

# Jesus Rejoices and Thanks God for Hearing His Prayers (Luke 10:21–24)

## Introduction

The prayer of Jesus recorded in Luke 10:21–24, and its parallel in Matthew 11:25–30, have been called "the most important verses in the Synoptic Gospels."[1] To say that they have been extensively studied would be something of an understatement. Being the lengthiest of all Jesus' recorded, personal prayers is enough in itself to imbue this text with great significance, and this feature is the primary cause for its examination in the present study. It is also the only place in the NT where Jesus is said to rejoice.[2] But in addition to these traits, this prayer exhibits a distinctive Johannine character[3] which gives it special importance for understanding the development of NT christology. As a result, most studies have devoted their attention to the Matthean version, to the near neglect of the Lukan. This is because Mt. 11:27//Lk. 10:22 forms the heart of the Johannine material, and the lengthened Matthean text, which includes the promise of rest for the weary (Mt. 11:28–30), provides a logion unique to Matthew with a seemingly intrinsic connection to the important Father-Son material in the preceding verses.[4] The unfortunate result is that when reference is made to Luke's text the comment is often more appropriate to Matthew than to Luke; Luke 10:21ff is read through Matthean tinted spectacles.[5] This tendency is particularly evident by the way in

---

[1] A. M. Hunter, "Crux Criticorum – Matt. 11:25–30 – A Re-Ap-praisal," *NTS.* 8 ('62) 241.

[2] Plummer, *Commentary*, p. 281; J. Navone, "Prayer," *Scr.* 20 ('68) 117.

[3] The famous description of this passage as a "lightning bolt fallen from the Johannine heaven" (wie ein Aerolith aus dem johanneischen Himmel gefallen) was made by Karl von Hase in a series of lectures delivered in 1823/4, which were published in *Geschichte Jesu, Nach akademische Vorlesungen*, (Leipzig, 1876); see p. 422. For further discussion of the apparently Johannine character of this passage, see M. Sabbe, "Can Mt 11,25–27 and Lc 10,22 Be Called a Johannine Logion?" in *Logia: Les Paroles de Jésus – The Sayings of Jesus*, (Leuven, 1982); B. M. F. van Iersel, *"Der Sohn" in den Synoptischen Jesusworten*, (Leiden, 1964), pp. 150f.

[4] The precedent for this approach was set by E. Norden in *Agnostos Theos: Untersuchungen zur Formengeschichte Religiöser Rede*, (Leipzig, 1913), where he built his form-critical arguments concerning this passage upon an assumption of the original unity of Mt. 11:25–30. Subsequent discussions have continued to pursue Norden's Matthean agenda. See n. 48 for further discussion of Norden's work.

[5] Even Jeremias is guilty of this misreading of Luke; see *Prayers*, p. 78, where he says that "the only personal prayer of Jesus of some length from the time before the passion is a thanksgiving in spite of failure (Mt. 11:25 par. Lk. 10:21)." This assessment may be true for Matthew, where the

which Luke 10:23–24 is regularly excluded from structural analyses of the passage.[6] But these verses form as vital a link with Jesus' expression of thanksgiving in Luke as do "the rest for the weary" verses in Matthew. If Luke's meaning is to be understood aright then Lk. 10:21–24 must be examined as a whole on its own terms. The present study cannot discuss all of the issues in these verses which have been the subject of scholarly debate throughout the years. Primary attention will be given to answering the question of why Jesus offers this particular prayer at this particular point in Luke's gospel. What elicits this outburst of joyful thanksgiving? An examination of certain elements in the prayer's structure and vocabulary will indicate that, in Luke's view, Jesus is thanking his Father for hearing the prayers which he has offered on behalf of the disciples in 9:18 (and perhaps 9:28f). Jesus is prayerfully expressing his gratitude for the spiritual illumination given them by God in answer to his prayers.

## 3.1 What Does Jesus Thank His Father For?

Lk. 10:21–24 exhibits a poetic structure consisting of three four-line strophes, interspersed with two editorial comments (vv. 21a, 23a). Feldkämper provides a good analysis of the first two strophes (vv. 21–22), and since this investigator basically agrees with his observations there is no need to repeat that work here.[7] Therefore, the present structural analysis will deal with only two issues; firstly, its departure from the consensus concerning the presumed hypotactic logic of the two middle lines in strophes I and II; and secondly, the structural and thematic coherence of strophe III with the preceding material.

[Ἐν αὐτῇ τῇ ὥρᾳ ἠγαλλιάσατο [ἐν] τῷ πνεύματι τῷ ἁγίῳ καὶ εἶπεν]

(I)

| | |
|---|---:|
| Ἐξομολογοῦμαί σοι, πάτερ, κύριε τοῦ οὐρανοῦ καὶ τῆς γῆς, | 1 |
| ὅτι ἀπέκρυψας ταῦτα ἀπὸ σοφῶν καὶ συνετῶν, | 2 |
| καὶ ἀπεκάλυψας αὐτὰ νηπίοις· | 3 |
| ναί, ὁ πατήρ, ὅτι οὕτως εὐδοκία ἐγένετο ἔμπροσθέν σου. | 4 |

(II)

| | |
|---|---:|
| Πάντα μοι παρεδόθη ὑπὸ τοῦ πατρός μου, | 1 |
| καὶ οὐδεὶς γινώσκει τίς ἐστιν ὁ υἱὸς εἰ μὴ ὁ πατήρ, | 2 |

---

prayer follows immediately upon the condemnation of the unrepentant cities, but it is decidedly untrue for Luke, where the prayer not only follows the rejoicing of the seventy (two) after their successful mission, but (as this chapter will argue) also expresses Jesus' joy over the success of his intercessory prayers for the disciples.

[6] See Feldkämper, *Der betende Jesus*, p. 159ff for a recent example of how an otherwise fine analysis is flawed by this omission.

[7] Feldkämper, *Der betende Jesus*, pp. 159–162. Others have also recognized this repeated four line structure; see Norden, *Agnostos*, p. 285; C. F. Burney, *The Poetry of Our Lord*, (Oxford, 1925), p. 133; Jeremias, *The Theology of the New Testament*, (London, 1971), p. 57; M. Miyoshi, *Der Anfang des Reiseberichts*, (Rome, 1974), p. 127; J. Kloppenborg, "Wisdom Christology in Q," *LTP*. 34 ('78) 140. With the exception of Norden, these others restrict their analysis to v. 22.

καὶ                τίς ἐστιν ὁ πατὴρ εἰ μὴ ὁ υἱὸς                   3
                  καὶ ᾧ ἐὰν βούληται ὁ υἱὸς ἀποκαλύψαι.   4

[Καὶ στραφεὶς πρὸς τοὺς μαθητὰς κατ' ἰδίαν εἶπεν,]

(III)

Μακάρια οἱ ὀφθαλμοὶ οἱ βλέποντες ἃ βλέπετε            1
λέγω γὰρ ὑμῖν ὅτι πολλοὶ προφῆται καὶ βασιλεῖς ἠθέλησαν   2
ἰδεῖν ἃ ὑμεῖς βλέπετε καὶ οὐκ εἶδαν,                3
καὶ ἀκοῦσαι ἃ ἀκούετε καὶ οὐκ ἤκουσαν.            4

### 3.1.1 Does Jesus Thank God for Both His Hiding and Revealing?

Lines 2 and 3 of each of the first two strophes stand in a paratactic construction. This straightforward observation is usually accompanied by the interpretive assertion that the logic informing each pair of lines is hypotactic; in other words, the thought expressed in the second line is subordinate to that of the third. Thus the emphasis in the first strophe lies not upon God's "hiding these things from the wise and learned," but upon his "revealing them to little children."[8] The two lines should be translated as "... although you have hidden ... nevertheless you have revealed ..." According to this interpretation Jesus rejoices over God's revealing activity, but not his hiding. Similarly, in strophe II the emphasis would lie upon "only a son knows his father," not "only a father knows his son."[9]

The reasoning behind this interpretation, however ancient it may be, is not self-evident. It is not established on the basis of evidence by its advocates; it is simply asserted. Jeremias, for example, begs the question by stating his conclusion: "The thanksgiving in (Lk. 10:21) is not about the concealment of knowledge, but about its revelation."[10] He cites E. Norden as a supporting authority; but aside from the fact that Norden is discussing v. 22, not v. 21, a glance at his argumentation reveals the same procedure. Norden also states his conclusion without any supporting

---

[8] Margreth, *Gebetsleben*, pp. 127 f, traces this interpretation back to Chrysostom; Feldkämper, *Der betende Jesus*, p. 168 refers to Marcion, Tertullian and Clement; also see George, *Communion*, p. 38; Marshall, *Commentary*, p. 434.

[9] Jeremias' translation (*Prayers*, p. 50) is: "Just as only a father really knows his son, so only a son really knows his father." Also see, *Theology*, p. 59; Feldkämper, *Der betende Jesus*, p. 160. Jeremias simply asserts this conclusion on the basis of his analysis of the previous verse, which is here being critiqued.

[10] *Prayers*, p. 50. Similarly in *Theology*, p. 57; on p. 59, where this conclusion is repeated, he merely refers back to the argument presented on p. 57! In *Die Sprache des Lukasevangeliums*, (Göttingen, 1980), p. 65, Jeremias describes "grammatical parataxis in logical hypotaxis" as a pre-Lukan characteristic of "Q".
H. Conzelmann is also typical when, in his *TDNT* article on σύνεσις (vol. VII, p. 893 n. 46), the extent of his argumentation is to say that "Naturally thanks are not given because 'these things' are reserved ..."

evidence, aside from a reference to previous authorities,[11] namely H. Gressmann and P. Wendland,[12] whose remarks hardly endorse any foregone conclusions.

Gressmann says that such *parallelismus membrorum* may permit the subordination of one line to another in a limited number of cases (nur in geringem Umfang). Hebrew parallelism and Greek syntax counterbalance each other (schliessen sich aus) on this point, by which he seems to imply that such decisions rest, not upon firm grammatical evidence, but subjective interpretation.

Wendland is of even less help. When his work is consulted one discovers that he is not discussing hypotactic logic but the hyperbolic use of antithetical parallelism. He states that an understanding of syntactical subordination in this idiom can only be achieved through the "living recitation" (lebendige Vortrag) of the concepts involved in the parallelism. In other words, it depends upon a personal evaluation of the subject matter. He does not cite Lk. 10:21f//Mt. 11:25–27 as an example, and those examples which are discussed clearly illustrate the point being made: when such parallelism is intended the content alone makes the interpretation fairly obvious.[13] This latter point has also been clearly demonstrated by H. Kruse in his thorough study of the semitic idiom of dialectical negation.[14] Consequently, the presence of hypotactic logic in Lk. 10:21, 22 cannot be presumed, especially in the absence of some obvious indicator to this effect in the subject matter. Neither Gressmann nor Wendland establish its presence; Norden and Jeremias offer no evidence for it; and there is nothing in the text to require or even suggest it. For those who continue to insist upon it nonetheless, it is suggested that the text may now evoke a hypotactic meaning to its reader, not because it is inherent within Lk. 10:21f, but because it has become the presumed significance of the passage, deriving from the long-standing repetition of an unsubstantiated claim.[15]

One suspects that the appeal to hypotaxis results from an interpretive prejudice against the idea of Jesus rejoicing over God's hiding his revelation from "the wise and the learned." But this is to allow arbitrary theological presuppositions to

---

[11] *Agnostos,* p. 286, see n. 1. Norden writes: "Grammatisch ausgedrückt: die formale Parataxe von b und c ist logisch eine Hypotaxe, in der b dem c untergeordnet ist."

[12] "Die Oden Salomos," *Internationalem Wochenschr.* July 22, 1911, p. 5; and *Die Hellenistisch-Römische Kultur in ihren Beziehungen zu Judentum und Christentum: Die Urchristlichen Literaturformen,* (Tübingen, 1912), p. 285, respectively.

[13] Wendland mentions Mk. 4:30; 8:35; Mt. 10:32f//Lk. 12:8; Mt. 25:29//Lk. 19:26; Mt. 10:28//Lk. 12:4f; Mt. 10:27//Lk. 12:3; Mt. 7:7f//Lk. 11:9f; Mt. 11:7–9//Lk. 7:33–35; Mt. 5:46f//LK. 6:32f.

[14] H. Kruse, "Die 'Dialektische Negation' als Semitisches Idiom," *VT.* 4 ('54) 385–400. On p. 390 Kruse lists the three essential elements of this idiom: 1) an obvious truth which is so self-evident that it can be denied without fear of misunderstanding; 2) the affirmation of an opposite fact which underscores the previous negation; and, 3) a resulting synthesis which is not clearly articulated, but occurs intuitively in the mind of the hearer through analysing the contrast. In this case it is also evident that the interpretion of the idiom is not straightforward; it is a highly subjective procedure, requiring a subject matter which clearly predisposes one towards such conclusions.

[15] Cf. W. D. Davies' discussion of "epigonous" nuances in *The Setting of the Sermon on the Mount,* (Cambridge, 1964), pp. 44f.

muffle the text.[16] In any case, it would not alter the fact that God has hidden his revelation from some as well as revealed it to others, a two-fold activity which not only has a great deal of OT precedent[17] but is also suggested by other passages in Luke (Lk. 9:45; 18:34; 24:16; see chapter 4). As W. Grimm has said, there is no way to avoid the note of "theocentric determinism" in this text.[18]

Actually, the paratactic construction suggests that both lines are governed by Jesus' thanksgiving in line 1. And since there is nothing in the subject matter to indicate the subordination of one thought to the other, the two middle lines of v. 21 more naturally form a synthetic parallelism wherein each line is of equal value. Consequently, the οὕτως of line 4 finds its antecedent in the entirety of this middle distich (lines 2 and 3), there being nothing to suggest a reference to one part of the parallelism and not the other. Jesus is shown rejoicing over both God's hiding and revealing activities, each of which are the expression of God's "good pleasure."

*3.1.2 The Thematic Integrity of Verses 21–24*

Scholarly interest in Matthew's version of this material has meant that the peculiarities of Luke's version have not received the attention which they deserve. Their literary integrity is revealed by even a superficial examination of the text, which suggests that they too are composed of a four-line structure parallel to that in vv. 21–22. Regardless of the view taken towards the traditional relationship between the three main sections of this pericope (vv. 21, 22, 23 f), the literary unity acheived here in Luke's editorial work testifies to the vital part which vv. 23–24 must play in any proper understanding of Luke's meaning in vv. 21–22.[19]

---

[16] See Plummer, *The Gospel*, p. 281: "It is very arbitrary to confine the thanksgiving to ἀπεκάλυψας: it belongs to ἀπέκρυψας also. That God has proven his independence of human intellect is a matter for thankfulness." Also see F. Godet, *A Commentary of the Gospel of St. Luke*, (Edinburgh, 1870), vol. 2, p. 28; and E. Ellis, *The Gospel of Luke*, (Grand Rapids, 1974), p. 158: Jesus' thanksgiving concerns "the reversal of priorities in the coming age." G. Bertram ("νήπιος," *TDNT*. vol. IV, p. 922) refers to Marcion as one of "the many" who have tried to soften the meaning of Jesus' statement.

[17] See A. Oepke, "καλύπτω," *TDNT*. vol. III, pp. 556–92; "κρύπτω," *TDNT*. vol. III, pp. 957–78. Luke's treatment of God's hiding and revealing is entirely consistent with OT and Jewish conceptions of the subject. God controls his own revelation, and is hidden from men unless he reveals himself (Is. 29:10ff; 30:30). Nothing may be hidden from God in this life, and eventually he will uncover all secrets (Dan. 2:22; Jer. 16:17; 23:24; Sir. 39:19; cf. Lk. 8:17; 11:33; 12:2).

[18] W. Grimm, "Der Dank für empfangene Offenbarung bei Jesus und Josephus Parallelen zu Mt. 11:25–27," *BZ*. 17 ('73) 253; also see Hunter, "Crux," p. 244; Margreth, *Gebetsleben*, pp. 128f. But cf. Marshall, *Commentary*, p. 434; Godet, *Commentary*, vol. II, p. 29; and Plummer, *St. Luke*, p. 281, who emphasise the personal character traits which may contribute to determining whether or not one will benefit from God's revelation.

[19] A comparison of Luke's use of this tradition (10:23–24) with Matthew's (13:16–17) will be carried out in a later section of this chapter.

The traditional relationship between v. 22 and vv. 23 f has been discussed more extensively than that between v. 21 and v. 22 because of the significant divergence found in Mt. 11:28–30. Fitzmyer, *The Gospel*, vol. II, p. 866; Marshall, *Commentary*, p. 431; and Hunter, "Crux," p. 244 see vv. 21 and 22 as an original unity; further bibliography may be found in B. M. F. van Iersel,

The γάρ in the second line of this third strophe indicates that it is logically subordinate to line 1, which serves as the thematic statement to the whole. Lines 3 and 4 comprise a unit of synthetic parallelism, in a paratactic construction, which is logically subordinate to line 2, both lines expressing the desires of the many prophets and kings.

Line 1 corresponds to line 3 through the repetition of both βλέπετε and the relative pronoun ἅ. The reoccurence of this pronoun in line 4 also indicates the correspondence of line 1 with the entirety of the parallelism created by lines 3 and 4. The "blessed" of line 1 also corresponds to the verb ἠθέλησαν in line 2. In this way the "good fortune" of those who see is contrasted with the unfulfilled desires of the kings and prophets who did not.

The various parallel elements of lines 3 and 4 are obvious.[20] Worthy of special

---

*"Der Sohn" in den Synoptischen Jesusworten*, (Leiden, 1964), p. 147. Those such as R. Bultmann, *The History of the Synoptic Tradition*, (Oxford, 1968), p. 159; Jeremias, *Prayers*, 62; Kloppenborg, "Wisdom Christology," pp. 132, 135; N. P. Williams, "Great Texts Reconsidered: Mt. 11:25–27 = Lk. 10:211–22," *ExpT.* 51 ('40) 183; E. Percy, *Die Botschaft Jesu*, (Lund, 1953), p. 260; van Iersel, *Der Sohn*, p. 148; M. E. Boring, *Sayings of the Risen Jesus: Christian Prophecy in the Synoptic Tradition*, (Cambridge, 1982), p. 150; and P. Winter, "Matthew 11:27 and Luke 10:22 from the First to the Fifth Century: Reflections on the Development of the Text," *NovT.* 1 ('56) 120, n. 4, deny the original integrity of the two sayings. Concerning vv. 22 and 23f,Godet, *Commentary*, vol. II, p. 34; A. Harnack, *The Sayings of Jesus: The Second Source of St. Matthew and St. Luke*, (London, 1908), p. 306 f; T. W. Manson, *The Sayings of Jesus*, (London, 1949), p. 80; and Plummer, *Commentary*, p. 283 all affirm the original unity of these verses; while Bultmann, *History*, p. 109; Hunter, "Crux", p. 247; Kloppenborg, "Wisdom Christology," p. 135; and Klostermann, *Lukas*, p. 118 also all imply Lukan unity, but only through various critiques of Matthean unity. On the other hand, Marshall, *Commentary*, p. 431; Williams, "Great Texts," pp. 183, 216; Norden, *Agnostos*, p. 283; J. M. Creed, *The Gospel According to St. Luke*, (London, 1953), p. 150; M.Dibelius, *From Tradition to Gospel*, (London, 1971), p. 279, n. 2; and Fitzmyer, *The Gospel*, vol. II, p. 865, all believe that Luke's use of vv. 23f is the result of his editorial arrangement.
    The concurrence of Luke 10:21–22 and Mt. 11:25–27 (Matthew probably preserving the original wording; cf. Cadbury, *Style*, vol. II, p. 166; Harnack, *Sayings*, p. 274; J. M. Robinson, "Die Hodajot-Formel im Gebet und Hymnus des Frühchristentums" in *Apophoreta*, [Berlin, 1964], p. 228; W. Grundmann, *Das Evangelium nach Lukas*, [Berlin, 1979], p. 215), combined with both the stuctural and material integrity of the two stophes when taken together, and the absence of any editorial link between them, argue strongly for the original unity of these two strophes in "Q".The common objection that strophe I is a prayer addressed to the Father while strophe II is a didactic section addressed to the disciples is not very substantial. A brief look at the psalms will show that prayers of thanksgiving frequently contain discursive material which rehearses the reasons for the psalmist's rejoicing (Pss. 5; 20; 31; 40 and many more; cf. J. P. Audet, "Literary Forms and contents of a Normal Εὐχαριστία in the First Century," *SE. in TU.* 73 ('59) 644–648. This would be particularly true of psalms used in the cult, where the nation as the benefactor of God's deliverance would be audience to the leader's praise. In this way the psalm of thanksgiving also serves as a psalm of remembrance. Given the similarities between this pericope and the thanksgiving psalms of the OT (as well as Qumran; cf. Robinson, "Die Hodajot," *passim*) the mere presence of the disciples with Jesus provides an adequate explanation for why the discursive second strophe follows upon the thanksgiving of the first. Jesus is rehearsing, in his prayer, the reason for his rejoicing, for the benefit of the disciples.
    [20] The repetitive ἅ, καί, and οὐκ; the aorist active infinitives ἰδεῖν/ἀκοῦσαι, present active indicatives βλέπετε/ἀκούετε and aorist active indicatives εἶδαν/ἤκουσαν.

notice is the correspondence between the ὑμεῖς in line 3, and the ὑμῖν of line 2, both of which are contrasted to the πολλοὶ προφῆται καὶ βασιλεῖς in line 2. As a result of this comparison, the "blessed" group which is now able "to see and hear" is defined both exclusively, ie. it is not the prophets and kings, and inclusively, ie. it is rather the "you," which Luke's editorial introduction (v. 23a) has already defined as the disciples. The juxtaposition of these groups of people in v. 24 corresponds to that in v. 21, where the Father hides his revelation from the wise and learned but reveals it to little children. This correspondence is made especially evident by the paralleling of a two-fold subject in the first instance (wise and learned/prophets and kings) and a single subject in the second (children/you, the disciples). The result is not so much an identification of the wise and learned with the prophets and kings, or the little children with the disciples, as it is a comparison of the parallel activities of hiding and revealing. Just as the wise and learned had these things hidden from them, so many prophets and kings "wanted to see but could not see, and wanted to hear but could not hear." And just as the little children had "these things" revealed to them, so the disciples have "seen and heard."[21]

Similarly, the "you" who see and hear in line 3 not only corresponds to the little children to whom the Father reveals in v. 21, but also the "whomsoever" (ᾧ ἐὰν) to whom the Son reveals in v. 22. Conversely, this also indicates that the "not seeing/not hearing" in lines 3 and 4 (v. 24) corresponds to the fact that no one knows either the Father or the Son in v. 22, as well as the Father's hiding activity in v. 21.

The result is a parallelism between the final two lines of v. 24 which affirms God's sovereignty over the disposition of his revelation, the very point with which the pericope began in v. 21. These final two lines correspond perfectly with each of the concluding lines of the two preceding strophes. That those who wanted to see and hear have not been allowed to do so (v. 24) correlates with the fact that the Son reveals the Father to whomever he chooses (v. 22), and the demonstration of the Father's good pleasure in hiding as well as sharing his own revelation (v. 21).

Luke's third strophe gathers together the various elements of the previous two and offers a concluding benediction upon those who have seen and heard the Father's revelation. The "eyes which have seen" in line 1 refers back to the uses of revelation language in the two previous verses. Jesus congratulates his disciples for their good fortune, for the Father has allowed them to see and hear things which others have wanted to witness but been denied.

---

[21] For a discussion of the identification of the disciples as little children, see W. Grundmann, "Die ΝΗΠΙΟΙ in die Urchristlichen Paränese," *NTS.* 5 ('59) 201–204; J. Dupont, "Les 'simples' (petâyim) dans la bible et a Qumrân: A propos des νήπιοι de Mt. 11,25; L, 10,21" in *Studi sull'Oriente e la Biblia,* (Genoa, 1967); S. Légasse, "La révélation aux NEPIOI," *RB.* 67 ('60) 321–348; *Jésus et L'Enfant: "Enfants", "Petits" et "Simples" dans la Tradition Synoptique,* (Paris, 1969); Bertram, "νήπιος," pp. 914–922. This is typical of the Lukan theme of eschatological reversal; cf. Feldkämper, *Der betende Jesus,* p. 171.

*3.1.3 Is Jesus Thanking God for Responding to His Prayers in Chapter Nine?*

Important thematic similarities between the subject of Jesus' prayer in Lk.
10:21–24 and the events surrounding his prayers in 9:18 and 28f have emerged
from the study thus far. These are principally evident in the metaphorical use of
seeing and hearing language, which is used to describe the process whereby things
revealed by God to the disciples are simultaneously hidden from others. The
parallels between these features of Jesus' prayer in chapter 10 – features highlighted
through the Lukan connection of vv. 23f with vv. 21f – and the events surrounding Jesus' prayers in chapter 9 – which is also the result of Lukan redaction –
should not be overlooked. Since Jesus is thanking God for illuminating the
disciples' spiritual vision, and since this is exactly what has happened in response to
Jesus' prayers earlier in the gospel, would it not seem appropriate to ask whether
the revelatory activity over which Jesus rejoices now is the action taken by God in
revealing his Son to the disciples at Peter's confession and the Transfiguration?
Indeed, such a possibility would loom large at this point. But before such a
conclusion could be asserted with any confidence two further questions must be
answered: Firstly, in chapter 9 the revelation to the disciples concerned Jesus' true
identity; is there any indication that this is also the content of the revelation
referred to by Jesus in chapter 10? Secondly, in addition to this use of seeing/hear-
ing language, is there any other evidence in 10:21–24 to suggest that Jesus thanks
God for responding to his prayers?

### 3.1.3.1 What Does the Father Hide and Reveal?

In order to answer this question a decision must be made concerning the specific
referent of the indeterminate "these things" (ταῦτα/αὐτὰ) in v. 21. Usually commentators begin their search by looking to the prior events in the mission of the
seventy (two). Or, alternatively, a form-critical approach is adopted, searching for
a reconstructed *Sitz im Leben* suitable to the text. However, because there is no
clear antecedent to the "these things" in the first approach, and there are no
controls upon an interpreter's imagination in the second, a vast array of solutions
have been proposed for this question, most of which are equally convincing, or
unconvincing, since there are no clear criteria for discriminating among them. Just
a few of the proposed interpretations of "these things" have been: that it consists of
the knowledge of God's will;[22] the message about the Kingdom preached by the
seventy;[23] God's plans and purposes in Jesus;[24] the divine secrets revealed to Jesus at
that moment;[25] the reciprocity of the Father/Son relationship revealed in v. 22,
together with the fact that Jesus is mediator of the Father's revelation;[26] the

---

[22] Creed, *St. Luke*, p. 148.
[23] Plummer, *Commentary*, p. 281; Johansson, *Parakletoi*, p. 202.
[24] Marshall, *Commentary*, p. 434.
[25] Grimm, "Der Dank," p. 252f.
[26] P. Hoffmann, *Studien zur Theologie der Logienquelle*, (Münster, 1972), p. 120.

mystery of Jesus' death and resurrection;[27] eschatological secrets revealed to the church;[28] the secret of Jesus' unique sonship;[29] the disciples' successful mission;[30] their authority over demons;[31] the downfall of Satan;[32] the disciples' names being written in the heavenly books;[33] the whole theme of God's present victory in the world;[34] the disciples' successful mission, the fact that their names are written in heaven, the fall of Satan from heaven, the woes on the unrepentant cities, all the things which were not seen by the kings and prophets, and in fact any event of eschatological significance.[35]

How is one to discern the correct answer from such a wide range of options? In addition to the thematic indicators, which will help to answer this question more definitely, there is an internal logic to these four verses which narrows the range of possible answers considerably. A further look at the structural relationships within the text will provide some useful guidance in this direction.

To begin with, it should again be observed that there is a correspondence between God's hiding activity in v. 21 and the fact that no one knows the Son in v. 22. In both cases the significance of what is not known precedes the mention of what is revealed.[36] There is a chiastic relationship between the subject and the recipients of revelation throughout the two strophes. In v. 21 the subject of the revelation is left indeterminate (these things), while the recipients of the revelation are mentioned explicitly (not the wise and the learned, but little children). Conversely, in v. 22 this sequence is reversed. The recipients of the revelation are only mentioned indeterminately (whomsoever), while the subject of the revelation is mentioned explicitly (the Father is the subject of the Son's revelation; and, it follows therefore, that the Son is the subject of the Father's revelation).

This last conclusion is derived from the development of thought running from v. 21 through v. 24. It would seem clear from the structural parallels discussed above that the hiding and revealing processes in vv. 21 and 23f have the same audience in view. At least it would be difficult to see how the consistency found between the opening and the conclusion of the pericope could be maintained if v. 22 were to interject a distinct revelation addressed to yet another group of people.

---

[27] K. J. Scaria, "Jesus' Prayer and Christian Prayer (Lk. 10:21–22)," *Bibl.* 7 ('81) 164.

[28] Kloppenborg, "Wisdom Christology," p. 136

[29] J. Bieneck, *Sohn Gottes als Christus Bezeichnung der Synoptiker*, (Zurich, 1951), p. 85, calls it the "Sohnesgeheimnis"; also see Chapman, "Dr. Harnack", p. 566; Hunter, "Crux," p. 243.

[30] Monloubou, *La Prière*, p. 68.

[31] Grundmann, *Lukas*, p. 215.

[32] Stanley, *Gethsemane*, p. 192.

[33] J. Ernst, *Das Evangelium nach Lukas*, (Regensburg, 1977), p. 341.

[34] J. Nützel, *Jesus als Offenbarer Gottes nach den lukanischen Schriften*, (Würzburg, 1980), p. 159.

[35] W. D. Davies, "'Knowledge' in the Dead Sea Scrolls and Matthew 11:25–30," *HTR.* 46 ('53) 137.

[36] Feldkämper, *Der betende Jesus*, p. 161; J. Bieneck, *Sohn Gottes*, p. 85, also make this observation. However, neither of them develop the the two-fold parallelism between the two strophes as thoroughly as they might.

Such conceptual disjunction would not be conducive to the logical development already attested in the previous structural analysis.

Consequently, the recipients of revelation in v. 22, the "whomsoever" in line 4, correspond to the recipients of revelation in v. 21, the "children" in line 3. The Father/Son chiasm in v. 22 not only serves the purposes of Semitic idiom, as Jeremias has pointed out,[37] but also of the development of thought. Because "only the Son knows the Father" it follows that only the Son is able to reveal the Father (the unexpressed object in v. 22 line 4). By the same token, because "only the Father knows the Son" the object of the Father's revelation in the first strophe (indeterminately expressed as ταῦτα/αὐτά ) must be those things which concern the true nature of the Son.[38] The logic runs like this:

(v. 21 ) A. I thank you Father for *revealing* the nature of the
Son *to whomever you choose.*
(v. 22b) B. *Only the Father knows the Son,* and
C. therefore only the Father *can reveal the Son.*
(v. 22c) B'. Likewise, *only the Son knows the Father.*
A'. Therefore, only the Son *can reveal* the nature of the
Father *to whomever he chooses.*

While the grammar may also allow for an A/B/C/B'/C' structure, the thought content of these two verses supplies the structure outlined here. This internal logic leads to the conclusion that Jesus rejoices in prayer because the Father has revealed Jesus' true person and character to the disciples. Because the disciples have come to know Jesus in this way he is able, as the only one who knows the Father, to then reveal the Father to them as well.[39]

But there is further evidence suggesting that "these things" concern the revelation of the Son. Luke develops a consistent theme of hiddenness throughout his gospel wherein God actively obscures the significance of Jesus' messiahship and/or the necessity of his suffering and death in Jerusalem (9:45; 18:34; 19:42; 24:16). God's "hiding these things from the wise and the learned" (v. 21) fits perfectly within this scheme, especially when compared with 19:42; and his "revealing them to little children" finds a perfect echo in 24:31, as well as the revelation to the disciples in 9:18ff, 28ff. The hiding and revealing language in 10:21−24 unites Jesus' prayer with the subject matter of these other passages, in which case this internal logic further sustains Luke's emphasis upon the sovereignty of God's revelation.

---

[37] Jeremias, *Prayers,* p. 47; *Theology,* pp. 57f; following G. Dalman, *The Words of Jesus,* (Edinburgh, 1902), p. 283.

[38] This internal logic is also seen clearly by H. Schumacher, *Die Selbstoffenbarung Jesu bei Mat. 11,27 (Luc 10,22): Eine kritischexegetische Untersuchung,* (Freiburg, 1912), p. 159; and J. Chapman, "Dr. Harnack," p. 564f. The logic within the two strophes is, itself, a weighty argument in favor of the canonical order of lines 2 and 3 in the second strophe; cf. Harnack, *Sayings,* pp. 272ff.

[39] Grundmann, *Lukas,* p. 218.

Furthermore, while there must be some material connection between 10:21–24 and the preceding mission of the seventy (two), its precise nature is not self-evident; and any search for antecedents must be guided by the content of the verses themselves, not by theoretical *Sitze im Leben*. If one follows the flow of thought and action from chapter 9 through chapter 10, it would appear that the success of this mission serves to legitimate the truth of the Father's revelation of the Son.[40] The disciples are able to overcome the enemy (v. 19) only because the authority given to them by Jesus was effective; and Jesus is able to dispense such power only because he actually is the messiah, the Son of God, as confessed by Peter (9:18ff) and glorified by the Father (9:28ff). Thus verses 17–20 do not supply the content of "these things," but evidence for the truth of it.[41] Because the revelation made by the Father in response to Jesus' prayers is true, the disciples could be successful in their mission, and Jesus could rejoice at the vindication of his identity and the efficacy of his prayer-life, as well as the disciples' success.

The content of "these things" has now been defined as Jesus' identity as the messianic Son of God by way of: the logic inherent within the structure of vv. 21–22; the flow of thought through chapters 9 and 10; and the use of revelation/hiding language elsewhere in the gospel. In conclusion, it is interesting to observe that other interpreters have arrived at similar results simply by asking the question, "What is it in particular that requires a special revelation from the Father?" For example, J. Bieneck and others have argued that since Jesus only spoke of his unique knowledge of God as *Abba* with the disciples, that the reciprocal half of that special relationship must also be in view here.[42] A. M. Hunter, adopting a form-critical approach to the problem, asked what would have been the most likely *Sitz im Leben* for such a logion. He concluded that the likeliest setting would have been "after Peter's confession, when increasing evidence of the disciples' growing faith may have moved Jesus to draw back a corner of the veil which concealed the last secret of this own spiritual life."[43] Similarly, N. Johansson has written that the possiblilty of Peter's confession of Jesus' messiahship can be understood only in light of Lk. 10:21–22.[44]

Though Hunter's suggestion that this passage contains a prayer originally uttered immediately after Peter's confession is debatable, it is worth noting that these different approaches have led others to the same two conclusions proposed in this study: first, the revelation referred to in Lk. 10:21–24 concerns the nature of

---

[40] Chapman, "Dr. Harnack," p. 566, n. 1.

[41] Cf. Hamm, "Vision as Metaphor," pp. 469f.

[42] Bieneck, *Sohn Gottes*, p. 85f; for similar views see Fitzmyer, *The Gospel*, vol. II, p. 869; F. Büschel, "δίδωμι," *TDNT*, vol. II, p. 171.

[43] Hunter, "Crux," p. 243; so also T. W. Manson, *The Teaching of Jesus*, (Cambridge, 1951), p. 110; Chapman "Dr. Harnack," p. 566; Margreth, *Gebetsleben*, pp. 126f; Bertram, "νήπιος," p. 922; Schumacher, *Selbstoffenbarung*, p. 188.

[44] Johansson, *Parakletoi*, p. 202.

Jesus' sonship; and, second, Jesus' joyful prayer is motivated by the events recorded in Lk. 9.[45]

### 3.1.3.2 The Meaning of Ἀγαλλιάομαι and Ἐξομολογέω

It is now time to address the second question posed above: what further evidence might there be to suggest that Jesus is thanking God for answering his prayers? This section will answer that question by discussing the use of ἀγαλλιάομαι and ἐξομολογέω, first in the OT and then in Luke-Acts.

### 3.1.3.2.1 Ἀγαλλιάομαι and Ἐξομολογέω in the OT

Most instances of ἀγαλλιάομαι in the OT, and certainly the majority of the non-penitential occurrences of ἐξομολογέω, are concerned with thanksgiving over God's faithfulness in delivering the petitioner from some danger.[46] What is of particular significance in this definition is how often such rejoicing and praise explicitly describe God's action as *an answer to a prayer* for deliverance. This use of ἀγαλλιάομαι is found in Pss. 5:11; 20:5; 31:7; 40:16; 59:16; 70:4; and ἐξομολογέω is used this way in Pss. 7:17; 18:49; 28:7; 43:4, 5; 54:6; 57:9; 86:12; 88:10; 106:47; 108:3; 109:30; 138:1; 140:13; 142:7; Sir. 51:1, 12; Dan. 2:23.[47] In all of these examples of "joy" and "praise," God is being thanked *for answering the psalmist's prayer.* A brief look at Sirach 51 will serve to illustrate the point. This text has been chosen as an example because of the significance attached to it by both F. D. Strauss and E. Norden.[48] It *is* significant for a proper understanding of Lk. 10:21 ff,

---

[45] It would expedite the argument of this study if Lk. 10:21–24 did follow immediately upon Peter's confession, but there is no justification for such rearrangement. Luke 10:21 f (par Mt. 11:25–27) seems to have been linked with the Woes upon the Unrepentant Cities (Lk. 10:13–16; Mt. 11:20–24) in "Q." Jesus' prayer has been placed where it is in each gospel because of its relation with this passage; see Fitzmyer, *The Gospel,* vol. II, p. 865; Kloppenborg, "Wisdom Christology," p. 133.

[46] See S. Légasse, *Jésus et L'enfant,* pp. 148f; R. J. Ledogar, "Verbs of Praise in the LXX Translation of the Hebrew Canon," *Bib.* 48 ('67) 39–44; A. F. J. Klijn, "Matthew 11:25//Luke 10:21" in *New Testament Textual Criticism,* pp. 4f.

[47] The connection with prayer becomes noticeable within the context of the psalm as a whole; the entirety of each psalm must be read.

[48] F. D. Strauss was the first to argue for a parallel structure between Sir. 51 and Mt. 11:25–30 in "Jesu Weheruf über Jerusalem und die σοφία τοῦ θεοῦ. Matth. 23:34–39; Lk. 11:49–51; 13:34f. Ein Beitrag zur johanneischen Frage," *ZWT.* 6 (1863) 84ff (see H. D. Betz, "The Logion of the Easy Yoke and of Rest [Matt. 11:28–30]," *JBL.* 86 ('67) 11; pp. 10–24 of this article offer a good history of the debate). A. Loisy appears to have reached the same conclusion independantly in *L'Evangile et l'eglise,* (Paris, 1908, 4th ed.), pp. 77f (so T. Arvedson, *Das Mysterium Christi: Eine Studie zu Mt. 11:25–30,* [Leipzig, 1937], p. 6 n. 3; P. Hoffmann, "Die Offenbarung des Sohnes: Die apokalyptischen Voraussetzungen und ihre Verarbeitung im Q–Logion Mt. 11:27 par Lk. 10:22," *Kairos.* 12['70]270 n. 1). Norden acknowledged his debt to Strauss in *Agnostos,* p. 281 and described his own analysis of Mt. 11:25–30 and Sir. 51 as an attempt "seinen Nachweis zu wiederholen und zu ergänzen." Norden's description of Mt. 11:25–30 as a three-part Hellenistic ῥῆσις speech was artificial at best, even in its own day. The discovery of 11QPsaSirach has demonstrated what had already been indicated in R. H. Charles' edition of the text in 1913 (*The Apocrypha and Pseudepigrapha,* [Oxford], vol. I, pp. 514f): namely, that Sir. 51 was not an original

but not because it is in the form of a hypothetical three-part Hellenistic ῥῆσις speech, as Norden believed. Rather, its import lies in the cause-and-effect relationship demonstrated between prayer and thanksgiving. The opening verses express the author's grateful praise to God for rescuing him from a dangerous situation (vv. 2–7; ἐξομολογέω, 2x; αἰνέω 1x). He then reflects upon God's mercy (v. 8), which consists in his rescuing "those who wait upon him." Thus he "sends up his prayers" (vv. 9–10) and the Lord answers them; *because of this* (διὰ τοῦτο) he now "praises" God (vv. 11–12; ἐξομολογέω, 2x; ὑμνέω 1x; αἰνέω 1x; εὐλογέω 1x).

There is a similar pattern in the second half of the chapter (vv. 13–30). The praise which the author offers to God is elicited by His faithfulness *in answering the prayers* of the one who seeks wisdom.

Just as these two words may be used in other connections, so too additional words can be employed in association with answered prayer; for example, ὑμνέω (Ps. 22:22; Sir. 51:11), αἰνέω (Pss. 18:3; 22:23, 26; 56:10; 69:30, 34; 74:21; 102:18; Sir. 51:11, 12, 22; Dan. 2:23), εὐλογέω (Ps. 34:1; Sir. 51:12; Dan. 2:19, 20) and δοξάζω (Ps. 22:23; 50:15; 86:9). In fact, Sir. 51 has already illustrated this point. But it is worth noting that these other words do not appear in such contexts nearly as often:[49] αἰνέω, 10.5 percent; ὑμνέω, 6.7 percent; δοξάζω, 3 percent; εὐλογέω, 1.6 percent; while ἐξομολογέω is 23 percent; and ἀγαλλιάομαι is 10.5 percent.

This insight into the specific circumstances which motivate the writer's joy and praise is highlighted when those occasions are examined where ἀγαλλιάομαι and ἐξομολογέω occur together, as they do in Lk. 10:21;[50] 8 of 19 instances are psalms praising God for his faithfulness in answering prayer. Of those examples where this connection is not obvious, two more nonetheless imply a response to some unmentioned prior prayer (Ps. 9:1, 2, 14; Tob. 13:1ff); seven praise God for his greatness and faithfulness (Pss. 75:1, 9; 92:1, 4; 97:1, 8, 12; 33:1, 2; 89:5, 12, 16; 100:2, 4; 105:1, 43); one extols the righteous king (Ps. 45:7, 15, 17); and one thanks God for the Torah (Ps. 119:7, 62, 162).

Those psalms which do express joy and thanksgiving in response to God's answering of prayer do so in connection with the contemplation of God's faithfulness. It is only because God is faithful that prayer is not only possible but worth-

---

literary unity; cf. Jeremias, *Prayers*, pp. 48f, n. 93. This makes Norden's thesis untenable. For further critique of Norden see Kloppenborg, "Wisdom Christology," p. 134; N. P. Williams, "Great Texts Reconsidered," *ExpT.* 51 ('40) 182–186; 51 ('40) 215–220; Arvedson, *Mysterium*, pp. 6–9; J. Weiss, "Das Logion Mt. 11:24–30" in *Neutestamentliche Studien für Georg Heinrici*, (Leipzig, 1914); Hoffmann, "Offenbarung," pp. 275–277; and further bibliography to this effect in van Iersel, *Der Sohn*, p. 147 n. 2; Hoffmann, "Offenbarung," p. 270 nn. 2–3. Fitzmyer, *The Gospel*, vol. II, pp. 867f provides a current survey of the arguments.

[49] The basis for these statistics has not simply been the number of occurrances of a word, but the number of situations in which it appears. In other words, if the same word is used more than once in thanking God for answering a single prayer, then that has been counted as only one occurrence of that word. This ensures that the statistics reflect the number of times such language is associated with an answer to a prayer, rather than simply a psalmist's enthusiastic repetition of praise.

[50] Cf. Bultmann, "ἀγαλλιάομαι," *TDNT.* vol. I, p. 20.

while: Ps. 30:4, 5 rejoices over a deliverance which came as God's answer to the author's prayer (vv. 2, 8–10). The entirety of Ps. 35 is a prayer for rescue, with the notices of joy and praise coming in association with God's responding to the petitioner's requests (vv. 9, 18, 27). Psalm 42 is a song of hope expressing the author's belief that the Lord will answer his prayers in the future (vv. 5, 11). Similarly, Ps. 71 offers praise because the author knows that the Lord will be faithful in answering prayer (vv. 22, 23). The verb ἀνθομολογέω makes an appearance in Ps. 79:13, where the author promises to praise the Lord after he saves him in response to his prayers. A particularly clear example is found in Ps. 107. Here the oppressed are described as those who "cry out to the Lord in their trouble" (vv. 6, 13, 19, 28). The Lord answers their prayers and "delivers them from their distress" (vv. 6, 13, 19, 28). Consequently, the people praise the Lord and tell of his works with songs of joy (vv. 21, 22, cf. 1, 8, 15, 31). The close relationship between Ps. 118 and 107 is immediately evident by their identical openings in verse 1. God's enduring *ḥesed* is once again demonstrated by his faithful response to his peoples' petitions (v. 5, 21, cf. 1, 15, 19, 21, 28, 29). Ps. 145 praises God for his greatness and faithfulness, both of which are demonstrated in his "nearness to all who call on Him" (vv. 18–20, cf. 7, 10).

This brief study of the OT contexts in which ἀγαλλιάομαι and ἐξομολογέω occur reveals that these two words can hardly be called "technical terms." They do not appear exclusively in prayer contexts; there are other circumstances in which they describe joy and thanksgiving; and there are other words which can be used in relation to answered prayer. But the regularity of their association with prayer, particularly when the two words occur together, is such that their simultaneous appearance in Luke 10:21 should at least raise the strong possibility that this too is a prayer of thanksgiving elicited by God's faithfulness in hearing and responding to petitions previously offered by Jesus.[51] It should also be mentioned that Jesus' thanksgiving prayer is similar to the psalms of the Qumran Hodayot.[52] This observation is important in helping to identify the form of the prayer and setting it squarely within a Jewish milieu, but it does not necessarily circumscribe the parameters within which Lk. 10:21–24 must be interpreted. The precise *Sitz im Leben* of the Hodayot is still unknown. Therefore, the fact that the Qumran hymns do not express themselves as thanksgivings offered to God for his answers to prayer is not necessarily a hindrance to the present argument concerning the setting of Lk. 10:21ff. Apples and oranges should not be confused simply because they both fall under the generic heading of "fruit".

---

[51] O. Michel, "ὁμολογέω," *TDNT*. vol. IV, p. 214.

[52] Robinson, "Die Hodajot-Formel," pp. 194–198, 226–228; Grundmann, *Das Evangelium*, p. 214; Marshall, *Commentary*, p. 433. The thanksgiving in these hymns most frequently concerns the greatness of God's person and the goodness of his acts, particularly as this is seen in his imparting of divine revelation; see 1QH 2:20, 31; 3:19, 37; 4:5; 5:5; 7:6, 26, 34, 8:4; 11:3, 11, 15. This certainly has significance for the Father's disposition of "all things" to the Son in Lk. 10:22.

Similar remarks may be made regarding related work by W. Grimm.[53] He has argued that the thanksgiving prayer in Daniel 2:19–23 provides the formal paradigm for other thanksgiving prayers found in apocalyptic (I En. 39:9–11), Qumran (1QH 7:26f), and Josephus, (*War* 3.354), as well as Lk. 10:21f (par. Mt. 11:25–27). The common bond uniting each of these examples is that they are all offered in response to a divinely bestowed revelation. However, while this may be an adequate explanation of the prayers in I En., 1QH and Josephus, it fails to take account of the more fundamental connection between Daniel and Luke. It has already been shown that Daniel's prayer of praise was not simply offered in response to a divine revelation; it was offered because the revelation was given in response to Daniel's prayer (Dan. 2:17–20). God had "made known to (Daniel) *what (he) had asked" of him* (v. 23). The other thanksgiving prayers studied by Grimm may well be related to Dan. 2, as is Lk. 10:21f, for other reasons as well; and Luke, as a result, may well be similar to these other prayers in various respects. But concentration on this general similarity at one level may obscure the more basic connection between Daniel and Luke on another. A common OT tradition has manifested itself in different ways at different points.

### 3.1.3.2.2 Ἀγαλλιάομαι and Ἐξομολογέω in Luke-Acts

It has often been observed that joy is an important theme in the gospel of Luke.[54] The root ἀγαλλια- occurs 7 times in the Lukan corpus (Lk. 1:14, 44, 47; 10:21; Acts 2:26, 46; 16:34). While it must be admitted that most of these do not contribute to the present argument, the first instance is significant for the connection made between prayer and rejoicing.

Lk. 1:14 is a part of Gabriel's announcement to Zechariah concerning the birth of John the Baptist. This section is introduced by a discussion of both Zechariah's and his wife's piety (vv. 5–6) as well as Elizabeth's barrenness (v. 7). The introduction serves a two-fold purpose. It not only affirms that Elizabeth's childlessness is not the punishment for her sin, it also establishes that, as pious Israelites, daily prayer would have been a regular part of their lives. By mentioning Elizabeth's barrenness in conjunction with her piety in this way the reader is given a clear indication of what constituted at least a part of the couple's daily prayers to God – the request for a child. This is substantiated by Gabriel's words to Zechariah in the temple (vv. 13ff). According to the immediate situation, Gabriel's promise that "your prayer has been heard" (v. 13) appears to refer to the priestly prayer being offered by Zechariah in conjunction with the burning of incense (v. 10). But the

---

[53] Grimm, "Der Dank," pp. 249–256.

[54] Cf. I. H. Marshall, *Luke: Historian and Theologian*, (Grand Rapids, 1971), p. 202f. To supplement ἀγαλλιάομαι, the verbal and nominal forms of χαίρω, χάρα occur 30 times in Luke-Acts (verb: 11x Lk., 7x Acts; noun: 8x Lk., 4x Acts); as compared to 12x in Matthew (6 each) and 3x in Mark (the verb twice, and the noun once).

message that Gabriel actually brings (v. 13b) indicates that it is Zechariah's personal prayer for a son which God is now about to answer.[55]

The beginning of this narrative is also reminiscent of other miraculous births in the OT. The situations of Sarah (Gen. 16:1; 18:9–15; 21:1–7) and especially of Hannah (I Sam. 1:2ff, particularly vv. 3, 7) are very similar. As R. Brown has catalogued the parallels between these stories, there is no need to repeat that work here.[56] It simply remains to point out that Luke's emphasis upon Elizabeth's piety conjoins well with the central motif in the story of Hannah: Samuel is born in response to her diligent prayer (I Sam 1:10f, 12, 15f, 17, 20, 26f).

Consequently, the literary style of Luke's narrative brings the theme of God's operation in response to prayer to the fore in at least two ways. Firstly, the details of the narrative indicate that it is the couple's past prayers for a child which are now being answered, and these personal prayers have meshed with God's plans for the entire nation in a way which will thoroughly supercede their limited personal expectations. Secondly, the literary allusions to I Sam. 1 call to remembrance another mother, who was likewise given her child as God's gracious answer to her prayers.

The use of ἀγαλλίασις in Lk. 1:14, in the context of God's action in response to prayer, is entirely in keeping with the previously discussed OT evidence. Zechariah is told that the answer to his prayer, ie. his son, will bring him χαρά καὶ ἀγαλλίασις, that is the joy commonly elicited by answered prayer.

However, it must also be said that the other instances of ἀγαλλια- in the gospel are not supportive of this connection. Answered prayer is not mentioned as the occasion for Mary's joy in either Lk. 1:44 or 1:47. Acts 2:26 may be construed as describing an attitude characteristic of prayer, but the joy is elicited by the resulting intimacy with the Lord. Acts 2:46 may associate joy with prayer through the parallel with v. 42, but it is more joy in prayer than a joy over answered prayer. Finally, Acts 16:34 relates the Philippian jailer's joy to his conversion, and there is no mention of any prayers offered to this effect. Consequently, it must be concluded that there is no consistent usage of the root ἀγαλλια- in Luke-Acts which would relate it to answered prayer in particular, although its use in Lk. 1:14 would seem to support the arguments made concerning Jesus' attitude in Lk. 10:21.

The case is somewhat stronger with ἐξομολογέω. The predominant NT meaning of this word is "to acknowledge," either one's sin (Mt. 3:6; Acts 19:18; Ja. 5:16) or one's submission before God (Rm. 14:11, quoting Is. 49:18; 45:23). It is most

---

[55] This ambiguity in the annunciation, "your prayer has been heard," is deliberate. Zechariah and Elizabeth's personal prayers, without their knowing it, have been concerned with the same issues as Zechariah's priestly prayers for the nation. God's answering of the one is also his answering of the other. In this way Luke demonstrates that individual concerns may well be a part of God's broader work in the world, and personal prayers may serve unexpected purposes in salvation-history.

[56] R. Brown, *The Birth of the Messiah*, (London, 1977), pp. 268f, 273; cf. Fitzmyer, *The Gospel*, vol. I, p. 309.

frequently translated as "confession." But it may also mean "to consent, agree" (Lk. 22:6), or "to praise, extol" (Lk. 10:21 par. Mt. 11:25; Rom. 15:9, quoting Ps. 18:49). Thus the meaning of "praise" in the NT is unique to the present passage and Rm. 15:9, which is in fact a quotation from one of the OT thanksgiving psalms discussed in the OT section of this study. At that point it was observed that the author of Ps. 18 "praises" God because he has answered his cries for help and saved him (vv. 3f, 6ff).

Once more it is the opening chapters of Luke which provide a usage similar to that found in Jesus' prayer. At Jesus' presentation in the temple (2:21–40) the two figures of Simeon and Anna are depicted in a parallel manner. The devotion of each is emphasised (2:25a, 36f), as is their presence in the temple at the moment of their inspiration (2:27, 37b), and the eschatological hope for which they each await (2:26, 38b).

Anna, in particular, is said to have been devoted to prayer, and it was this prayer which oriented her towards awaiting, and thus seeing, the messiah when he came. Luke's emphasis here is not surprising, for requests that God send his messiah and redeem his temple, as well as his people, are included in both the Palestinian and Babylonian versions of the *Tephillah* (benedictions 10, 14 and 1, 10, 14, 15 respectively) as well as the opening section of the Kaddish.[57] The well recognised semitic character of Luke's opening chapters would place them within an original social milieu in which this connection would have been self-evident.

Anna's thanksgiving is especially significant because it expresses her awareness that the hope which has formed her prayers has now been answered. Therefore, she ἀνθωμολογεῖτο τῷ θεῷ. The ἀντι- in this form of the verb underlines the fact that Anna's praise is an answer to God's gracious action,[58] which is itself an answer to her prayers (cf. Ps. 79:13!). Anna's thanksgiving, which is the only other place in Luke-Acts where an -ομολογέω word is used to refer to praise, provides a particularly clear parallel to the opening line of Jesus' prayer: ἐξομολογοῦμαί σοι, πάτερ.

---

[57] J. Petuchowski and M. Brocke (eds.), *The Lord's Prayer and Jewish Liturgy*, (London, 1978), pp. 27–37. Though it is true that the present forms of these prayers were not fully developed until after the first century, it would be extremely unlikely for some version of these particular petitions not to have been a part of these prayers from their very earliest days; cf. Jeremias, "Gebetsleben," p. 123, especially n. 5; H. Greeven, "εὔχομαι," *TDNT.* vol. II, pp. 801f; J. Heinemann, *Prayer in the Talmud: Forms and Patterns*, (Berlin, 1977), pp. 22, 220–224.

[58] Michel, "ὁμολογέω," p. 213. This is the only NT occurrence of the form most common in the OT, where the verb is normally followed by τῷ θεῷ. Michel follows Bultmann in not giving sufficient attention to the role of prayer in this material. He writes, "Formally these are psalms of thanksgiving and hymns of praise in the strict sense, but in content they speak of eschatological fulfillment." This is only indirectly true since "fulfillment" is being described in terms of God's answer to prayer.

### 3.1.4 Conclusions Concerning Verses 21–22

None of the preceding evidence or arguments are conclusive in themselves, but there is a cumulative value to them which is increased when combined with both the internal and the narrative logic of Jesus' prayer itself. It cannot be decisively proven, but it has been shown to be very probable,[59] that Jesus rejoices in Lk. 10:21–24, and offers a prayer of thanksgiving, because he has perceived that his earlier prayers have been answered by his Father. Such a conclusion should not be surprising, since the only way available for discussing prayer with God is through another prayer. The medium through which requests to God are made must also be the medium through which appreciation is expressed when he responds. It follows that what Jesus thanks the Father for doing is also that for which he has prayed; the content of v. 21 is both the statement of what God has done and the restatement of Jesus' original prayer request. At this point something very important has taken place: observing the connection between the language of thanksgiving and prayer has allowed passage through a door which has otherwise been marked "Private." Something of the content and significance of those moments may be perceived which otherwise are only tantalizingly described as Jesus' "withdrawl to a solitary place to pray." Luke's careful redaction of 9:7–27, 28–36 has already intimated that Jesus' prayer concerned the Father's revelation of his true identity to the disciples. Now his thanksgiving prayer in 10:21–24, if the interpretation proposed here is correct, makes that explicit.

## 3.2 Whose Eyes See and Whose Ears Hear?
## Luke's Use of Verses 23–24

Understanding Luke's redaction of vv. 23–24 also is important to the proper interpretation of 10:21–22. Three aspects of these two verses will be examined, each of them peculiarly Lukan: 1) the location of these words after the prayer and explication of vv. 21–22; 2) the beatitude in v. 23; and, 3) the reference to "prophets and kings" in v. 24.

### 3.2.1 The Location of Verses 23 and 24

Matthew locates these two verses in his thirteenth chapter (vv. 16f) after Jesus has explained why he teaches in parables (vv. 11–15). There the saying makes two points. Firstly, the disciples are fortunate enough to live in the era of salvation-history which the prophets and righteous men of the past could only anticipate.

---

[59] See E. P. Sanders, *Jesus and Judaism*, (London, 1985), p. 326 for a ranking of interpretative conclusions as certain, highly probable, probable, possible, conceivable, and incredible. The present interpretaion of Lk. 10:21–24 should be rated as more than possible, but perhaps less than highly probable.

Secondly, this privileged position carries with it a great responsibility.[60] The disciples must be sure that they perceive the significance of Jesus' life and actions correctly; seeing and hearing alone do not ensure understanding. Their privileges must be supplemented by obedient faith. Matthew emphasises the responsibilities of faith through his frequent references to "understanding" (vv. 13, 14, 15, 19, 23), and the reference to Is. 6:9–10 (Mt. 13:14–15). Luke also uses this passage from Isaiah, but not in association with Jesus' beatitude; it appears at the end of Acts (28:26–27), where it serves the same purpose as for Matthew.

Luke places this "Q" passage in the position occupied by the Matthean offering of rest to the weary in Mt. 11:28–30. This different arrangement affects the saying's meaning by associating it, not with Jesus' kingdom teaching in this present age of salvation, but with the Father and the Son's mutual revelation.[61] A cause-and-effect relationship between Jesus' prayers and the "seeing and hearing" of such revelation has already appeared in chapter 9, as well as been implied by the present interpretation of 10:21–22. This also now becomes the significance of 10:23–24 as it stands in Luke's gospel. The disciples, the little children who have benefitted from Jesus' prayers, are blessed because they have been allowed to see Jesus as others have not.

The Matthean meaning of these verses cannot be read into Luke if Luke is to be understood correctly. The blessedness of occupying a particular location in salvation history is incidental for Luke. The disciples' blessedness now lies in the fact that they have been chosen as the recipients of a divinely bestowed insight into the character and nature of Jesus, by virtue of his electing prayers.[62] Salvation-history is pertinent only in a mediated fashion *vis à vis* prayer.

The second consequence of the way Luke uses these verses is that the implicit Matthean exhortation to be "perceiving" is lost. There is no indication that the disciples are to derive an ethical exhortation from this beatitude. Rather, it has become a simple blessing upon their good fortune in having been prayed for by Jesus. They truly are blessed because they are among those to whom the Father and the Son have been revealed.

Matthew underlines his sovereignty/responsibility tension in two ways. First of all, the immediate proximity of the woes upon the unrepentant cities to Jesus' prayer of thanksgiving contrasts the condemnation of stubborn unbelief (Mt. 11:20–24) with the affirmation that the Father and the Son are understood only as

---

[60] R. Gundry, *Matthew: A Commentary on His Literary and Theological Art*, (Grand Rapids, 1982), pp. 257f discusses how Matthew's handling of the entire section serves his interest to "emphasize human responsibility rather than divine intent."

[61] Cf. Barrett, *Holy Spirit*, p. 88.

[62] This investigator has yet to find a commentator who disagrees with the "eras of salvation history" interpretation of Luke's text, which only shows how difficult it is to read the gospels as they stand individually, without being unduly influenced, even unintentionally, by their parallels; for example, see Bultmann, *History*, p. 109; Creed, *St. Luke*, p. 150; Ernst, *Das Evangelium* p. 343; Fitzmyer, *St. Luke*, vol. II, pp. 869, 875; Grundmann, *Das Evangelium*, p. 220; Hoffmann, *Studien*, p. 105; Marshall, *Commentary*, p. 438; Manson, *Sayings*, p. 80; W. Manson, *The Gospel of Luke*, (London, 1930), p. 129; Miyoshi, *Der Anfang*, pp. 133, 140; Plummer, *Commentary*, p. 283.

they are revealed to men (11:25–27). In Mt. 11:25 Jesus praises the Father for hiding from men the very truths which they have just been condemned for not believing.

Matthew then reverses this contrast in verses 28–30. After emphasising the fact that a relationship with the Father and Son is only had by revelation (vv. 25–27) Jesus then goes on to call men to respond obediently to his message in order to enjoy just such a relationship (vv. 28–30). An affirmation of the sovereignty of God's revelation is sandwiched in between two affirmations of human responsibility.

However, Luke has eliminated this tension in two ways, each resulting from his treatment of the Matthean sections dealing with human response. Firstly, the thanksgiving prayer has been dislocated from the woes upon the cities by the intervention of two pieces of material: the "Q" logion in 10:16 (cf. Mt. 10:40), and the "L" section concerning the triumphant return of the seventy (10:17–20). Consequently, the responsibility/sovereignty contrast established by the juxtaposition of the woes and the prayer in Matthew is eliminated in Luke.[63]

Secondly, the absence of Matthew's "come unto me" saying has the same effect. Luke's version of the prayer, unlike Matthew's, is not calling for a response to Jesus; it is blessing those to whom Jesus has already been revealed. Luke's use of all the material held in common with Matthew (the woes upon the cities, the prayer itself, and the beatitude found in Mt. 13), as well as the absence of material unique to Matthew (11:27–30) all serve the same purpose: the Matthean election/obedience tension is replaced by a straightforward assertion of divine sovereignty and the blessedness of those whom it has benefitted.[64]

### 3.2.2 The Beatitude in Verse 24

A comparison of the Matthean and Lukan versions of this beatitude reveals several differences:

| Matthew | Luke |
|---|---|
| ὑμῶν δὲ μακάριοι οι ὀφθαλμοὶ ὅτι βλέπουσιν, καὶ τὰ ὦτα ὑμῶν ὅτι ἀκούουσιν | μακάριοι δι ὀφθαλμοὶ οἱ βλέποντες ἃ βλέπετε |

---

[63] Fitzmyer, *The Gospel*, vol. II, p. 865 says that Luke separates the woes from the prayer in order to make them a part of the mission charge. The separation certainly does accomplish this, but it also does much more.

[64] Michaelis, "ὁράω," p. 347 claims that Luke "seems to make 10:23f rather over-rich by combining it with 10:21", but without specifying what he means by this. He further states that Mt. 13:16f (par. Lk. 10:23f) emphasizes the "increased obligation to make a right decision in the light of (salvation history)." Statements such as this once again reveal the unstated conviction that Luke necessarily must conform to Matthew's intentions.

Firstly, while Matthew has a ὅτι clause, Luke has an articular participle. Secondly, Luke lacks Matthew's reference to "hearing ears." Thirdly, Luke has an expanded version of the "seeing eyes" portion of the blessing. Fourthly, Luke's expansion includes a relative pronoun which supplies the object of the seeing. Each of these points will be discussed in turn.

1) Once again the two distinct versions underline the differences in perspective between Matthew and Luke. Within the context of Matthew 13, to say that "your eyes are blessed because they see" is to draw attention to the fact that the disciples are among those who understand the teaching of the kingdom. The "*that* they see" highlights their responsiveness to Jesus' message, whereas Luke's participle, lacking as it does Matthew's specifying ὑμῶν, simply points out the blessedness of seeing eyes, whoever's eyes they may be.

2) Matthew's reference to hearing ears is important because of its association with the parables of the kingdom. The reference is to hearing and responding to the truths of Jesus' kingdom teaching. However, in Luke the primary reference is not to the hearing of teaching,[65] although the retention of this element in the second half of v. 24 is a reminder that it is still an element of their blessedness (cf. 9:22, 35). Rather, the primary emphasis lies upon the "seeing" of spiritual realities.[66] Once again, the disciples are not being exhorted to understand correctly, but are being congratulated for their good fortune.

3) Luke's expansion of the seeing element in the beatitude, by the relative clause, further underlines the previous point. *Seeing* is the issue. The reader is being emphatically referred back to those instances where the disciples "saw" the Father's revelation.

4) Again, the association of the disciples' seeing with Jesus' prayer is brought out by Luke's use of the relative pronoun. The neuter plural (ἅ), with an indefinite antecedent, is structurally parallel to the use of ταῦτα, which constitutes the αὐτά, "that are revealed" in v. 21. The previous structural analysis and exegesis of these verses have demonstrated the reciprocal nature of the Father's and the Son's revelation. The consistent flow of thought in these verses leads to the conclusion that the content of the "things which" are seen in v. 23 is the cumulative revelation of the Father and the Son discussed in vv. 21 and 22. The disciples are being congratulated not merely for seeing, but also for what it is they have seen,[67] ie. the Father and the Son.

---

[65] Nützel, *Offenbarer*, p. 173 suggests that this omission is due to Luke's portrayal of the disciples as "Proclaimers" rather than "Hearers."

[66] Cf. Michaelis, "ὁράω," p. 347; Marshall, *Commentary*, p. 438; Lammers, *Hören*, pp. 39f. Michaelis claims that Luke loses an important point of contrast with contemporary Judaism by this omission, since Judaism's "expectations of the age of salvation are always in terms of seeing," (as compared to Jesus, who uniquely co-emphasized hearing as the reception of his message). However, Luke's disinterest here in phases of salvation history explains why this comparison, or the lack thereof, does not concern him.

[67] Fitzmyer, *The Gospel*,vol. II, p. 867; Marshall, *Commentary*, p. 438. Fitzmyer does not specify the content of what is seen; Marshall identifies it as Jesus' "mighty works." Bultmann, *History*,

### 3.2.3 The Prophets and Kings

The third significant difference between the Matthean and Lukan versions of this passage, at least for the purposes of this study, is the appearance of Luke's "kings" in the place of Matthew's "righteous men." It has already been argued that the salvation-historical import of v. 24 has become secondary for Luke. While there is a definite salvation-historical contrast being made in this passage between men of the past who were unable to enjoy the benefits of Jesus' prayer-life and the disciples who now can,[68] Luke's phrase "prophets and kings" also makes it possible for Luke to have these ancient, historical figures represented typologically in a specific, contemporary prophet and king. Luke's paradigmatic use of Herod in chapters 9 and 23 has already made his representative role evident. Is it possible that he could represent, not only those who fail to see generally, but these kings as well? This question will be answered after discussing Luke's depiction of the representative prophet.

Jesus himself describes John the Baptist as the greatest of the prophets (7:26–27). And even though Luke provides more detail concerning the nature of John's ministry and message than do the other synoptics, it is significant that nowhere in Luke do Jesus and John ever meet. The one place where they do see each other in the other gospel accounts, at Jesus' baptism, is rewritten by Luke in such a way as to avoid this very thing (3:21–22)![69] Luke's use of the aorist infinitive βαπτισθῆναι suggests that Jesus was baptised after all the people.[70] Also, because Luke has already related John's imprisonment in the preceding pericope (3:19–20), his role in the baptism is conspicuously absent (cf. Mk. 1:9; Mt. 3:13f; Jn. 1:29–34). Though one might suspect that Jesus' baptism is distinguished from that of the

---

p. 109, identifies this element in Luke as being more original, saying that Matthew is "artificial" by comparison; but cf. Bernadicou, "The Spirituality of Luke's Travel Narrative," p. 462; and Grundmann, *Das Evangelium*, p. 220 who say just the opposite. According to Grundmann the emphasis in Matthew is different from that in Luke in that "... liegt nicht auf dem 'Dass,' sondern auf dem 'Was' des Sehens der Ton." This may be true of Matthew, but that would not make it untrue of Luke. Miyoshi, *Der Anfang*, p. 140, understands the pronoun to refer to Jesus' status as the exhalted "coming King." His conclusion is correct insofar as the "what" is comprised of Jesus' messianic identity, but his way to it, by means of comparing Jesus with "the kings" in v. 24, misunderstands the kings' role in that verse.

[68] In "Selige Augenzeugen, Luk. 10,23f. Alttestamentlicher Hintergrund und ursprünglicher Sinn," *TZ.* 26 ('70) 172–183, W. Grimm discusses the Jewish development of OT makarisms (especially see pp. 172–175). He points to various passages (Mek. on Ex. 19:11; 15:2; targum ps-Jon. on Num. 24:3) which refer to the blessedness of those who are able to witness the present revelation of mysteries which the OT prophets could only speak of in parables; the same relationship between Lk. 10:23f and Mek. on Ex. 15:2 is drawn independently by Davies, *Setting*, p. 42.

[69] "It is remarkable that ... so far as we know they (John and Jesus) come into actual contact only at one brief period, when the Forerunner baptized the Christ." This comment by Plummer (*Commentary*, p. 98) is true for every gospel except the one upon which he is commenting!

[70] Plummer, *St. Luke*, p. 98.

masses in order to present it as "the climax to the activity of John,"[71] John's absence from the scene actually creates more of an anti-climax where he is concerned. Rather, Luke has made John's imprisonment (3:19–20) the climax of his ministry. The resulting picture is not so much the highlighting of John as it is the lone presentation of Jesus baptised by himself; only the passive participle βαπτισθέντος remains to speak against Jesus actually performing his own baptism.[72] The questions that this raises – for the baptism of the people indicates what Luke must have known anyway, namely that John *was* present at Jesus' baptism – seem to cause no problems for Luke. The boldness of this apparent incongruity should cause John's absence from the baptism scene to be taken seriously; explanations which see it simply as Luke's way of rounding off his presentation of John before proceeding on to Jesus are certainly unsatisfactory.[73]

If Luke had actually intended to do what this study is suggesting, namely present John as a contemporary representative of all those OT prophets who had wanted to see the coming of the messiah but been denied that privilege, then he must be portrayed as a prophet "who wanted to see but did not see." And if, again, as is being suggested, Luke intended Jesus' prayers to be seen as the key to such spiritual insight, then John cannot be portrayed as deriving any spiritual illumination from Jesus' prayers. This is exactly what Luke has done, or rather has not done.

It has already been shown that part of the way in which Luke indicates, in chapter 9, that the disciples are the immediate beneficiaries of Jesus' prayers is their spatial proximity while he prays. The same motif was also used by Luke to explain Herod's spiritual blindness. The fact that only Luke portrays both Jesus as praying at his baptism *and* John as being absent from the baptism coincides with this spatial motif. Luke knows that, as the one who represents the prophets, John could not have enjoyed any illuminating benefits of Jesus' prayer in 3:21, unlike the crowds who were present, who witnessed the resulting revelation from heaven, and whom Luke consistently describes as eager to follow Jesus thereafter.[74] Through Luke's redaction, John neither sees Jesus nor hears him pray, and he fails to witness the heavenly confirmation of Jesus' sonship, which takes place by means of both an event to be seen (3:22a) and a revelation to be heard (3:22b; the baptism scene will be discussed further in chapter 5).

---

[71] Marshall, *Commentary*, pp. 150, 152.

[72] W. Wink, *John the Baptist in the Gospel Tradition*, (Cambridge, 1968), p. 83 claims that the participle is in the middle voice (n. 1) so that Jesus *did* baptise himself; Luke thoroughly eliminates John in order to prevent anyone from thinking that Jesus was John's disciple. However, the aorist middle of this verb would be βαπτισάμενος.

[73] *Pace* Talbert, *Genre*, p. 104; George, "Jésus fils de Dieu," p. 186. Wilson, "Eschatology," pp. 331f surveys the various suggestions for John's absence. Discussion of Conzelmann's "eras of salvation-history" explanation for this have become commonplace; cf. Conzelmann, *Theology*, pp. 18–27, especially p. 21; for various critiques see Oliver, "Birth Stories," pp. 202–226; Robinson, *Der Weg*; Wilson, "Eschatology," pp. 330–347; Marshall, *Luke*, pp. 144–147.

[74] This is not meant to imply that the crowds henceforth perceive Jesus' sonship.

John's status is also suggested by his query concerning Jesus in 7:18ff. This passage reiterates the fact that John has neither heard nor seen Jesus himself; even after his emissaries return, his information is still only second hand (7:22). In contrast to the Johannine tradition, Luke's John has not given any prior witness to his convictions concerning Jesus' identity;[75] his absence from the baptism has eliminated the testimony about Jesus found in Mark (1:9) and Matthew (3:13). Consequently, the doubts registered in Lk. 7:18ff do not contrast with any previously expressed convictions, and so the seeming incongruity of John's question in Matthew is absent from Luke.

Luke also fails to mention that John is imprisoned when he sends his delegation to Jesus (cf. Mt. 11:2). While this may be inferred from 3:19–20, its immediate absence from 7:18 nevertheless alters the implied motivation for John's question. According to Matthew, John wonders about Jesus' identity because he does not see him acting in power; more specifically, he wonders how he could possibly be imprisoned if Jesus were really the messiah.[76] However, Luke's version requires that one look elsewhere for the reasons behind John's doubts. This rendering of 7:18 is commensurate with the unique character of 3:21f: John is confused over Jesus' true nature because he has not benefitted from the illumination mediated through Jesus' prayers.

John is the greatest of the prophets (7:26). What better figure could be chosen to representatively depict the situation of God's prophets in the past? It was his unique task to prepare the way for the messiah (7:27) and preach the good news of the kingdom (3:18). He stands as a bridge between the era of the law and the prophets and the time of the preaching of the kingdom of God (16:16).[77] Therefore, he will enter into the kingdom of God, not only as a prophet (13:28), but also

---

[75] Marshall, *Commentary*, p. 288.

[76] A discussion of the various explanations suggested throughout the centuries for John's question is offered by J. Dupont, "L'Ambassade de Jean-Baptiste (Mattieu 11:2–6; Luc 7:18–23," *NRT.* 83 ('61) 805–821, 943–959. For a briefer survey see Fitzmyer, *The Gospel*, vol. I, pp. 664f, 673; cf. E. Hill, "Messianic Fulfillment in St. Luke," *TU.* 73 ('59) 194f.

[77] Conzelmann's reliance upon this text to exclude John from the era of Jesus' ministry is well know; see *Theology*, pp. 16, 20, 23ff. However, the meanings of both prepositions, μέχρι and ἀπὸ τότε are ambiguous, and almost every conceivable combination of meanings has been entertained by someone: a) inclusive "until" and exclusive "from then" – G. Schrenk, "Βιάζομαι," *TDNT.* vol. I, pp. 610, 612; E. Ellis, *The Gospel of Luke*, (Grand Rapids, 1974), p. 202; Flender, *St. Luke*, pp. 124f; b) inclusive "until" and inclusive "from then" – E. Bammel, "Is Luke 16:16–18 of the Baptist' Provenience?," *HTR.* 51 ('58) 103 n. 14; K. Chamblin, "John the Baptist and the Kingdom of God," *TB.* 15 ('64) 10–16; G. Braumann, "Das Mittel der Zeit," *ZNW.* 54 ('63) 123f; Minear, "Birth Stories", pp. 122f; D. Daube, *The New Testament and Rabbinic Judaism*, (London, 1956), pp. 185f. Daube also provides several examples of the inclusive use of *min*, which would supposedly lie behind the original saying; c) exclusive "until" and inclusive "from then" – E. Käsemann, "The Problem of the Historical Jesus" in *Essays on New Testament Themes*, (London, 1964), pp. 42f; d) both inclusive and exclusive "until" and inclusive "from then" – Fitzmyer, *The Gospel*, pp. 1116f. The wide range of opinion on this issue underscores the aptness of Minear's comment in "Birth Stories", p. 122:"...rarely has a scholar (ie. Conzelmann) placed so much weight on so dubious an interpretation of so difficult a logion." It is probably best to understand

as a preacher of the kingdom himself. John's similarity with Herod does not lie in his status or destiny within God's economy, but in the outworkings of Jesus' prayer-life. He is contrasted with Jesus' disciples as one who wanted to "see" the messiah, but who was denied this privilege, not because of God's judgment, but because he was the last and the greatest of the prophets.

The cue which initiated this figurative approach to v. 24 was Luke's reference to kings, compared to Matthew's righteous men, and the coincidence between Luke's depiction of Herod and the language used here to describe these men's fate. A closer look at the evidence indicates that just as John the Baptist represents the prophets who did not see, so Herod is intended to represent past rulers "who wanted to see what the disciples see but did not see it."

The OT antecedents for this verse are obscure at best. Both Is. 52:15 and 60:3 have been suggested,[78] but neither fits very well. The second text lacks any seeing or hearing language, while the first makes reference to Gentile kings (as does the second) who are taken by surprise at the work of the Suffering Servant. This, in fact, raises the main reason for each text's inappropriateness: in neither instance are the kings wishing to see anything, least of all the age of fulfillment. They are unexpectedly overrun by God's plans. But, according to Luke, this is the key issue in identifying these kings: they *wanted* to see (ἠθέλησαν ἰδεῖν), but in fact they were not allowed to see. It is an explicit denial of the kings' desires.

Secondly, it was previously pointed out that only Luke records Herod's particular interest in the identity of Jesus (9:9b) and his desire to see him (9:9c).[79] When Herod does eventually see Jesus in 23:8 the language used is identical with that found in 10:24 – Herod had been "wanting to see Jesus for a long time" – making the identification of Herod with the kings even more explicit. The way in which Luke relates Herod's position to Jesus' prayers has already been discussed in chapter 2. And even though Luke regularly calls Herod "tetrarch" rather than "king" (Lk. 3:1, 19; 9:7; cf. Mk. 6:14), this small obstacle is mitigated by the consistent presentational similarities noted above, together with the fact that the representational character of v. 24 would have been lost if Luke had written about "many prophets and tetrarchs."[80] Luke has clearly illustrated with this verse how different figures from the past, whose desires to see the age of fulfillment went

---

both prepositions inclusively (cf. Acts 10:30; Rm. 5:14; 15:19 for the inclusive use of both; as well as Mt. 11:23; 28:15 for the inclusive use of μέχρι, which would be the most debatable of the two).John is presented in the guise of a prophet; yet he is greater than the prophets, for he preaches the gospel (3:18) and marks the beginning of the ministry of the messianic kingdom (Acts 1:22). This evidence clearly prohibits an exclusive meaning for "from then." Fitzmyer nonetheless denies that Lk. 3:18 can mean that John preached the good news (*The Gospel*, vol. I, pp. 148, 174, 475; *pace* Wink, *John*, pp. 52–57), although he never justifies his claim that εὐαγγελίζομαι only means "to exhort" in Luke. Marshall's analysis (*Luke*, p. 146) is the most cogent. He concludes, "John is a bridge between the old and the new eras.He belongs to both, but essentially to the new one... He is portrayed both as a prophet and as the first preacher of the gospel."

[78] Marshall, *Commentary*, p. 439; Grimm, "Luk. 10,23f," pp. 175f, 178.

[79] Cf. Miyoshi, *Der Anfang*, p. 133.

unfulfilled, continue to find their counterparts in Jesus' contemporaries: the prophets in John the Baptist; the kings in Herod Antipas. The factor which now determines their blindness is not salvation-history, but the prayers of Jesus.

## 3.3 Conclusions: Jesus' Thanksgiving for Answered Prayer

A number of important conclusions have been reached in the course of this study of Luke 10:21–24. Most important is the clear statement of Jesus' status as the sole mediator of all knowledge of the Father. One must first know Jesus in order to know God. But the true knowledge of Jesus as the Son is also the exclusive possession of the Father and is only revealed to those whom he chooses. This unique, reciprocal relationship is self-evident in v. 22. But the new insight provided by this study is the light which has been shed upon the pivotal role played in this process by Jesus' prayers. The dispensation of the Son's revelation is effected, as is the ensuing revelation of the Father, through Jesus' prayer-life. Jesus' task as mediator of God's revelation is executed by means of his efficacy as Pray-er. Luke highlights this aspect of Jesus' prayer-life through his use of "seeing and hearing" language in the gospel. In Lk. 10:21–24 the wise and the learned, the disciples, Herod and even John the Baptist are all presented as different types of examples of the effectiveness of Jesus' prayers in hiding and revealing the Father's revelation.

Secondly, Luke's portrait of Jesus-at-prayer makes it clear that, in his view, the Lord's work as interceding mediator was already fully operative during his earthly ministry. It was not a new status bestowed upon him after the ascension, which is a point worth noting in the writings of Luke, who is so often credited with a predisposition for "exaltation christology."[81] The foundation of Jesus' work as intercessor does not lie in his exaltation but in his antecedent filial relationship with the Father. It is his status as the Son, not his subsequent role as risen Lord, which gives him the unique right to guide God's electing arm through prayer. Later on in this work it will be argued that one of the reasons for Luke's emphasis upon this facet of Jesus' earthly prayer-life is its place as the functional presupposition to his work as heavenly intercessor. But it is important to observe here that Luke's presentation of Jesus' earthly prayers undercuts anything like pure christological functionalism; their efficacy does not depend upon the completion of any prior task; Jesus is not an "intercessor-designate." The power of his prayer is solely dependent upon a unique status, an intimate relationship with God, which allows

---

[80] However, Buck makes several pertinent observations in "Jesus before Herod," p. 177. Firstly, Lk. 21:12b reverses the order of the figures in Mk. 13:9b (Mt. 10:18a) to "kings/governors." Secondly, this order agrees with that in Acts 4:27, where Herod and Pilate are portrayed as representative of "kings and rulers" (v. 26). In these subtle ways Luke not only *does* describe Herod as a king himself, but also depicts him as the king who was representative of all other worldly kings antagonistic to God's messiah.

[81] Cf. the discussion of Lukan exaltation christology in Fitzmyer, *The Gospel*, vol. I, pp. 22f, 194–197; for a seminal discussion of functional christology, as it is rooted in salvation-history, see O. Cullmann, *The Christology of the New Testament*, (London, 1959), pp. 3–6, 315–328.

Jesus an access and a hearing had by no one else. Consequently, neither is Jesus' role as exalted heavenly intercessor based exclusively upon functional considerations. He will be able to intercede in heaven, not only because he was a powerful pray-er during his life on earth (see chapter 8), but also because he is the ascended Son.

Thus, while it cannot be decisively proven, it is suggested as probable that Luke 10:21–24 is presented by Luke as a thanksgiving prayer offered by Jesus because he has seen God working in response to his obedient prayers. Luke uses this prayer to express both the content of the Father's revelation, and the aim of Jesus' prayers in chapter 9, thus explicating here what is only implied through editorial notices elsewhere: the Father hides and reveals as the Son prays.

Chapter 4

# Prayer and Jesus' Self-Revelation
## Part II

### Introduction

In chapter 2 the introductory discussion of the self-revelatory significance of Jesus' prayers suggested that there were at least three, and perhaps four, passages in which Jesus' prayers were portrayed as the means by which an individual received spiritual illumination into the true nature of Jesus' person. The Lukan passion narrative, with its two unique prayers offered by Jesus on the cross, is the third of these passages; while the less clear-cut example is found in Jesus' encounter with the disciples on the road to Emmaus. The present chapter will first discuss Luke's handling of the crucifixion story (23:32–49); it will then look at the relevance of the Emmaus Road encounter (24:13–35) for a correct evaluation of the revelatory significance of Jesus' prayer-life.

### 4.1 The Passion Narrative: Jesus' Prayers from the Cross (Lk. 23:32–49)

The question of the sources which lie behind Luke's passion narrative is still a matter of debate.[1] However, whatever his compositional method may have been, Luke wrote with a knowledge of Mark's account and so a comparison with Mark remains useful for highlighting the distinctive features of Luke's narrative, whether it is believed to illustrate why Luke did not use Mark, or how he edited his primary source. Consequently, this study will begin by observing the major differences between the two which will eventually prove significant. Minor distinctions will be noted later, as they become pertinent in the course of the investigation.

---

[1] Such scholars as V. Taylor, *The Passion Narrative of St. Luke*, (Cambridge, 1972); Grundmann, *Das Evangelium*, p. 431; and Ernst, *Das Evangelium*, p. 633, argue for Luke's dependence upon another source, into which he inserted Markan material. Others, such as Creed, *The Gospel*, 284f; Marshall, *Commentary*, p. 866; E. Schweizer, *The Good News According to Luke*, (London, 1984), pp. 354–356; and Fitzmyer, *The Gospel*, vol. II, pp. 1366, 1500 recognise the conflation of Markan with non-Markan elements (L? or Q?) without the express recognition of any independent, written passion source. Still others would argue for Lukan redaction of Mark alone; so A.

## 4.1.1 A Comparison of Luke 23:32–49 and Mark 15:21–41

One of the most noticeable differences is the contrast between Mark's single cry of despair (15:34b) followed by an inarticulate outburst at the moment of death (15:37), and Luke's two prayers of trust and surrender (23:34, 46).[2] Mark's single prayer has been omitted in conjunction with the following material concerning the misunderstanding about Elijah (15:35f). And Luke presents Jesus' second prayer (23:46b) as if it were the "loud cry" of Mk. 15:37. The result is that each of the two halves of Luke's crucifixion scene (vv. 32–43, 44–49) opens with a clearly articulated prayer from Jesus, the contents of which are unique to his gospel.

Luke also includes a distinctive section concerning the repentant thief (23:39–43). Mark makes two references to the two thieves crucified with Jesus (15:27, 32b). The result is a Markan *inclusio* around the general mockery of vv. 29–32a, with the second reference serving as the conclusion to the first half of Mark's narrative (15:21–32), stating that both of the thieves "reviled" Jesus (v. 32b). However, Luke inserts his own distinctive tradition at this very point, with the result that only one of the criminals mocks Jesus, and the first half of his narrative ends not with mockery, but with the second criminal's repentance and confession (vv. 41f).

In the second half of his account (15:33–41) Mark relates the tearing of the temple curtain (v. 38) in between Jesus' death cry and the centurion's confession. Luke places the veil's tearing together with the darkening of the sun (23:45) before Jesus' second prayer, which correlates to the death cry in Mark. In this way the centurion's confession is brought into immediate proximity with Jesus' prayer, and the second half of Luke's narrative is made to mirror the first: a prayer in the opening of the section is followed by a confession concerning Jesus (v. 47) and repentance (vv. 48f).

Finally, Mark offers two examples of the verbal mockery hurled at Jesus (15:29, 31f) and mentions four categories of people who participated in this derision: v. 29, passers-by; v. 31, chief priests and scribes; v. 32b, two thieves. Luke, on the other hand, describes three instances of verbal mockery (23:35b, 37, 39) and attributes each to one of three groups which taunt Jesus: v. 35b, the leaders; v. 36, the soldiers; v. 39, one criminal.

## 4.1.2 The Structure of Luke's Crucifixion Scene

As a result of this comparison with Mark, a number of structural features are discovered in Luke's narrative which are important for its interpretation. As already mentioned, the passage is divided into two parts (23:32–43, 44–49), as is

---

Büchele, *Der Tod Jesu im Lukasevangelium*, (Frankfurt, 1978); F. Matera, The Death of Jesus According to Luke: A Question of Sources," *CBQ*. 47 ('85) 469–485. See Fitzmyer, vol. II, pp. 1365f for a survey of scholars and their opinions.

[2] See pp. 79–85 for a discussion of the textual debate surrounding Lk. 23:34.

indicated by the two-fold pattern of "Prayer/Repentance-Confession."[3] Luke's unifying of Mark's disparate parts concerning the criminals and the signs further allows each of the two sections to be subdivided into four parts each:

| | |
|---|---|
| Intro – Two Criminals (32f) | Intro – Signs (44f) |
| Jesus' Prayer (34a) | Jesus' Prayer (46) |
| Spectators (mock) (35b–39) | Conversion (47) |
| Conversion (40–43) | Spectators (repent) (48f) |

The chiastic reversal of the second two elements (conversion/spectators), together with the opposite attitudes expressed by the two groups of spectators, will later be used as evidence to show that the first prayer for "forgiveness" (v. 34) does not function solely within the first half of the narrative but does double duty as the thematic introduction to the entire scene. Likewise, the final element of repentance does not relate only to Jesus' second prayer but functions as the corresponding conclusion to the whole narrative.

But there are other parallels and points of connection interrelating the two sections. In the first instance, the three-fold mockery is balanced by a three-fold mention of those who do not mock Jesus:

| Mock | Do Not Mock |
|---|---|
| 1. The Leaders (35b) | 1'. The People (35a, 48) |
| 2. The Soldiers (36) | 2'. The Centurion (47) |
| 3. A Criminal (39) | 3'. A Criminal (40–43) |

The correspondence between these two sets of groups is clear. The people dissociate themselves from their leaders.[4] The centurion and the second criminal dissociate themselves from their compatriots (had the centurion participated with the soldiers earlier?), and they are each related as doing so *subsequent* to Jesus' praying. Jesus prays and the attitudes of others change. The people watching are also indirectly related to this prayer dynamic in the second half of the narrative, as will be shown below.

Other features serve to integrate the two halves of the narrative, forging a thorough thematic unity throughout the whole scene. The "watching" (θεωρῶν) of the people (v. 35) in the first half is again emphasised by the three "watching" words in vv. 48f (θεωρίαν, θεωρήσαντες, ὁρῶσαι). The four-fold use of οὗτος,

---

[3] Feldkämper, *Der betende Jesus*, p. 252 has also recognized this two-fold pattern in the narrative, although he has not drawn the same interpretive conclusions. Grundmann's four-fold multiplication of a three part structure (vv. 33–34, 35–43, 44–46, 47–49; see *Das Evangelium*, p. 431) is a bit forced, particularly in the first and last sections. It also fails to appreciate the import of the structural elements as outlined here. Büchele, *Der Tod*, pp. 70–75, argues for a three-fold structure influenced by Dt. 19:15 and the legitimatising effect of "2 or 3 witnesses;" this is properly critiqued by Tyson, *The Death of Jesus*, pp. 116f.

[4] For a discussion of λαός and ὄχλος see pp. 85 nn. 37, 38, and 150–151 especially nn. 139, 141.

twice used by mockers (vv. 35b, 38) and twice in statements of vindication (vv. 41b, 47), as well as the ironic interplay between the use of δικαίως in the criminal's self-accusation (v. 41) and the δίκαιος of the centurion's confession (v. 47) also serve to unify the narrative. These observations do not exhaust the structural features of the narrative, but these elements are already sufficient to justify Taylor's description of Luke's crucifixion scene as "a well-conceived narrative, surely a product of conscious art."[5]

### 4.1.3 "Father, forgive them . . ." (Lk. 23:32–43)

The textual question concerning v. 34a remains troublesome for commentators.[6] Since this text plays a significant role in the present argument some attention should be devoted to the text-critical question.

#### 4.1.3.1 The Textual Problem of Verse 34a[7]

Arguments against authenticity:

1) External evidence: The mss evidence against the text is early and weighty: p75 א[a vid] B D* W Θ a,d syr[s] sa, bo [mss] 38 0124 435 579 1241 Cyril.

2) Internal evidence:

a) If the text were original it would be difficult, if not impossible, to account for its omission since it so clearly conforms to the early Christian view of Jesus.

b) The prayer interrupts the connection between vv. 33 and 34b.

c) This prayer that the Jews be forgiven conflicts with their condemnation in vv. 28–31.[8]

---

[5] Taylor, Passion Narrative, p. 97.

[6] Accept as Lukan: F. H. A. Scrivener, A Plain Introduction to the Criticism of the New Testament, vol. II, (London, 1894, 4th ed.), pp. 356–358 (a most thorough discussion of the external evidence); A. Harnack, "Probleme im Texte der Leidensgeschichte Jesu," SPAW. 11 ('01) 255–261; Streeter, The Four Gospels, pp. 138f; Büchele, Der Tod, p. 46, especially n. 157; Schmid, Das Evangelium, p. 348; Ellis, The Gospel, pp. 267f; ; Dibelius, Tradition, p. 203 n. 2; Harris, Prayer, pp. 113f; H. Surkau, Martyrien in jüdischer und frühchristlicher Zeit, (Göttingen, 1938), p. 67; Fitzmyer, The Gospel, vol. II, p. 1503, and Feldkämper, Der betende Jesus, pp. 257f (these two both offer a good response to the most common arguments against authenticity); Grundmann, Das Evangelium, pp. 432f. See Marshall, Commentary, pp. 867 for a typically succinct summary of the evidence, arguments and their proponents.
Reject as Non-Lukan: Plummer, St. Luke, p. 531 (quoting Westcott and Hort, vol. II, appendix, p. 68, in favour of a non-Lucan, but possibly dominical, tradition); B. Metzger, A Textual Commentary on the Greek New Testament, (London, 1971), p. 180 (non-Lucan, dominical tradition); Jeremias, "παῖς θεοῦ," TDNT. V, p. 713 n. 455 ("an ancient addition resting on solid tradition"); Creed, The Gospel, p. 286; A. H. Dammers, "Studies in Texts, Luke xxiii, 34a," Th. 52 ('49) 138–139; W. Soltau, "Die Herkunft der Reden in der Apostelgeschichte," ZNW. 4 ('03) 143;Ott, Gebet, p. 96 n. 14. These last four scholars reject the passage outright.
Undecided: Conzelmann, Theology, pp. 89f, who limits his remarks to the internal evidence (undecided, but probably yes); D. Daube, "'For they know not what they do:' Luke 23:34," SP. in TU. 79 ('61) 58–70.

[7] This is not a complete listing of the external evidence; see the standard critical editions.

[8] Büchele, Der Tod, p. 46 n. 157.

d) The text may be explained as an interpolation modelled upon Is. 53:12, the teaching in Lk. 6:28, Stephen's prayer in Acts 7:60, or even Hegesippus' account of the martyrdom of James.[9]

e) The idea of forgiveness for acts committed in ignorance could easily be derived from Greek and Latin sources,[10] and such an ignorance motif is also found in Acts (3:17; 13:27; 17:30) from where it might have been read back into the gospel.[11]

Arguments in favor of authenticity:

1) External evidence:

a) The mss evidence which includes the text is early and diverse; ℵ*,c A C Db L f¹ f¹³ 28 33 565 700 (with numerous other miniscules) aur,b,c,e,f,ff²,l, r¹ vg syr (c),p,(h,h mg),pal bo mss Marcion, Tatian, Hegesippus, Justin, Irenaeus, Clement of Alexandria, Origen, Eusebius and many other of the Fathers.

b) The combination of B and D is usually supported by the early Fathers. The lack of such support in this instance makes their agreement less decisive than usual.[12]

c) F. H. Scrivener dates the corrector of Db to the ninth century.[13] However, the addition of this verse resulted from the transcription of the Ammonian sections in the margins of D. Jesus' prayer from the cross was required in order for the successive Ammonian enumerations to remain correct.[14] This not only indicates that Jesus' prayer was present in the exemplar from which this scribe was adding the Ammonian sections, it also shows that the prayer had been present in the copy of Luke used in the composition of the Ammonian gospel harmony.[15] Thus the evidence of Db may actually point back to as early as the 3rd century.

d) C. S. C. Williams has observed that Tatian had displaced this prayer until after Jesus' self-surrender to God from the cross (v. 46). Such a rearrangement

---

[9] See the critique of these arguments as presented by Holtzmann in Margreth, *Gebetsleben*, p. 249. The story of James' martyrdom is recorded in Eusebius, *H.E.* 2.23.16.

[10] Creed, *The Gospel*, p. 286; Daube, "Luke 23:34," pp. 58ff; but cf. Harris, *Prayer*, pp. 113f.

[11] Fitzmyer, *The Gospel*, vol. II, p. 1503.

[12] Harnack, "Probleme," pp. 257f.

[13] F. H. Scrivener, *Bezae Codex Cantabrigiensis*, (Cambridge, 1864), p. xxvii; cf. the facsimile plate III, no. 11; also see the commentary on p. 437.

[14] See T. Prior, *Codex Bezae Cantabrigiensis*, vol. II, folio 278b for the facsimile showing the marginal addition together with the notations for the Ammonian sections.

[15] The Ammonian sections are derived from a gospel harmony credited by Eusebius of Caesarea to Ammonius of Alexandria (3rd century) who became bishop of Thumis in Lower Egypt. Eusebius mentions this harmony in his Letter to Carpianus, in which he explains his own list of gospel canons; see H. H. Oliver, "The Epistle of Eusebius to Carpianus: Textual Tradition and Translation," *Nov T.* 3 ('59) 138–145; H. K. McArthur, "The Eusebian Sections and Canons," *CBQ.* 27 ('65) 250–256; Scrivener, *Criticism*, vol. I, pp. 59–63; B. M. Metzger, *Manuscripts of the Greek Bible: An Introduction to Palaeography*, (Oxford, 1981), p. 42. On Ammonius of Alexandria, see O. Bardenhewer, *Patrology: The Lives and Works of the Fathers of the Church*, (Freiburg, 1908), pp. 60, 153; F. L. Cross and E. A. Livingstone, *The Oxford Dictionary of the Christian Church*, (Oxford, 1974), p. 45; K. Aland, *The Text of the New Testament*, (Grand Rapids, 1987), p. 171.

could possibly account for the verse's omission from some of the Western witnesses.[16]

e) p75 ℵ (in the gospels) and B, as significant as they each are individually, all represent the same Alexandrian textual family. In fact, it is highly likely that p75 represents, if not the actual examplar, then at least the archetype for the gospel tradition found in B.[17] Their combined testimony may, therefore, only be counted as a single witness. The question of this passage's omission from B actually becomes, then, a question of its absence from p75 (see below).[18]

f) The significance of this Alexandrian association is increased by the certainty of ℵ and B sharing in the same scribal tradition.[19] K. Lake suggested that these two mss may have actually been produced in the same scriptorium. In any case, the main scriptorium corrector of ℵ (identified as ℵ^a)[20] was quite likely to have also been involved in the production of B. Consequently, there can be no confidence

---

[16] *Alterations to the Text of the Synpotic Gospels and Acts*, (Oxford, 1951), pp. 8f. Williams raises this suggestion in discussing the work of F. H. Chase, *The Syro-Latin Text of the Gospels*, (London, 1895); cf. Williams, pp. 19–24 on the widespread influence of Tatian's text.

[17] See V. Martin and R. Kasser, *Papyrus Bodmer XIV–XV, Evangiles de Luc et Jean*, (Geneva, 1961), vol. I, p. 29; C. L. Porter, "Papyrus Bodmer (P75) and the Text of Codex Vaticanus," *JBL*. 81 ('62) 364f; K. W. Clark, "The Text of the Gospel of John in Third-Century Egypt," *NovT*. 5 ('62) 24; G. Fee, "P66, P75 and Origen: The Myth of Early Textual Recension" in *New Dimensions in New Testament Study*, (Grand Rapids, 1974), pp. 30f, 44; Aland *The Text of the New Testament*, pp. 14, 57.

[18] In any case, the unstated tendency, which has continued since Hort, to trust B above all other witnesses needs to be moderated; see Scrivener, *Criticism*, pp. 284–297, 302–311, for a critique of Hort on this point and a list of instances where Scrivener claims B does not preserve the original text; also see H. C. Hoskier, *Codex B and Its Allies*, 2 vols., (London, 1914) for a thorough, though sometimes polemical, discussion of the weaknesses of B.

[19] Constantin von Tischendorf was the first to suggest a relationship between these two mss by identifying the NT scribe in B with the scribe known as "D" in ℵ. This scribe in Sinaiticus wrote large sections of the OT, several cancel-leaves in the NT, added the NT superscriptions, and was the primary corrector of the NT in the scriptorium. Though Tischendorf's idea was repeated by Westcott and Hort (see *The New Testament in the Original Greek: Introduction, Appendix*, vol. II, [Cambridge, 1881], pp. 213f), his particular identification of scribes has since been rejected; cf. Helen and Kirsopp Lake, *Codex Sinaiticus Petropolitanus*, vol. I, (Oxford, 1911), p. xix; H. J. M. Milne and T. C. Skeat, *Scribes and Correctors of the Codex Sinaiticus*, (London, 1938), pp. 89f (the reader can reach his own decision by comparing the scripts of plate III in vol. I of Lake's facsimile edition). However, Lake did not exclude all possibility of connection, and even stated that there was "a high probability for the view that the two codices came from the same scriptorium" (vol. II, p. xv). Milne and Skeat simply re-identified the nature of the connection between ℵ and B. According to them, the scriptorium corrector of ℵ (scribe "D") was probably the main OT scribe in B (pp. 87, 90); the resemblance is "striking in the activities of the two hands as correctors . . . it would be hazardous to argue identity of the two hands . . . but the identity of the scribal tradition stands beyond dispute." That this scribe (if it was an individual) may have been involved in the production of different testaments in B and ℵ does not nullify the point being made, since there would still have been an accepted scribal standard within the scriptorium, to which individual scribes would have adhered. The discrepancy between ℵ* and ℵ^a shows an individual's divergence being brought into line with that standard.

[20] B. Metzger, *The Text of the New Testament, Its Transmission, Corruption, and Restoration*, (Oxford, 1964), p. 46; "a" designates the work of a "proof-reader" in the scriptorium. For the identification of this as the "D" scribe in ℵ see Lake, *Codex Sinaiticus*, vol. I, pp. xix-xxi, xxiii.

in asserting ℵ<sup>a</sup> and B as independent witnesses for the omission of Lk. 23:34.[21] There combination here is no weightier than ℵ* alone.

g) The omission of Jesus' prayer from p75 (and so from B) is, no doubt, a significant piece of evidence. However, several factors moderate its import.

Firstly, M. Parsons has recently sounded a warning against automatically accepting the readings of p75 simply because of the age of the papyrus.[22] More importantly, he has observed a tendency for the text to be altered in the interests of a "higher" christology. The following discussion of the relation of this prayer to the destruction of Jerusalem (point 2b below) certainly indicates that such christological concerns would have been current at the time of this document's transcription.

Secondly, the age of p75 (175–225 AD.) is significantly counter-balanced by the equally great, and in some instances even greater, age of several of the Fathers who are witnesses in favour of the prayer (Hegesippus, Marcion, Tatian, Justin, Irenaeus, Clement of Alexandria).[23]

Thirdly, there is no reason to suppose that p75 exhibits the "standard" text of 2nd century Egypt. While this papyrus is the earliest fragment to contain the gospel of Luke, other equally early papyri exhibit widely differing types of text, some of which relate to later text-types which do contain Jesus' prayer. For example, p66 (appr. 200 AD.) exhibits a mixed text containing a combination of Western (cf. the old Latin and old Syriac) and Alexandrian (cf. ℵ* A C L 33 bo) readings; furthermore, when ℵ and B diverge p66 tends to follow ℵ (cf. ℵ*).[24] Similarly, the text of p45 (200–250 AD.) is even more mixed, and if it exhibits any "family" affinities at all it is with the Caesarean text-type,[25] a group in which the majority of relevant compatriots witness to the originality of Lk. 23:34

---

[21] Scrivener, in critiqueing Hort's consistent dependence upon the combined testimony of ℵ B, alluded long ago to the undermining effect of this scribal relationship (admitted by Hort) between the two codices; see *Criticism*, vol. II, pp. 289f.

[22] M. Parson, "A Christological Tendency in P75," *JBL*. 105 ('86) 468. Parson is primarily discussing the testimony of this papyri against the Western non-interpolations. He concludes that the evaluative conflict in textual decisions is now between the witness of the Alexandrian text-type and the principle of *lectio brevior potior*; cf. pp. 465ff. G. Fee gives a telling defense of how the longer text may be original in more instances than are often admitted; see "'One Thing is Needful'?, Luke 10:42" in *New Testament Textual Criticism*, pp. 61–75.

[23] Scrivener, *Criticism*, vol. II, p. 289. Hegesippus, Marcion, Tatian, and Justin were at their height in the early to mid second century; Irenaeus was slightly later; Clement lived into the third century.

[24] V. Martin, *Papyrus Bodmer II: Evangile de Jean chap. 1–14*, (Geneva, 1956), pp. 17f, 151f; A. F. J. Klijn, "Papyrus Bodmer II (John I–XIV) and the Text of Egypt," *NTS*. 3 ('56–67) 329–334; F. G. Kenyon, *The Text of the Greek Bible*, (London, 1975, 3rd ed.), p. 74.

[25] F. G. Kenyon, *The Chester Beatty Biblical Papyri: Descriptions and Texts of Twelve Manuscripts on Papyrus of the Greek Bible*, (London, 1933, 1934), vol. I, pp. 6, 16f, vol. II.1, pp. x–xx; R. V. G. Tasker, "The Chester Beatty Papyrus and the Caesarean Text of Luke," *HTR*. 29 ('36) 345–352; C..C. Tarelli, "The Chester Beatty Papyrus and the Caesarean Text," *JTS*. 40 ('39) 46–55; "The Chester Beatty Papyrus and the Western and Byzantine Texts," *JTS*. 41 ('40) 253–260; Klijn, "Bodmer II," pp. 329, 331.

(cf. f¹ f¹³ 28 565 700). Admittedly, these are arguments from silence, but given the random manner in which the evidence of papyrus fragments has been preserved their cummulative effect is worth noting.

h) The fact that most of the old Latin and Syriac versions, which also represent the Western tradition, together with Marcion, Tatian, Justin and Irenaeus, who had all spent some time in Rome, include the reading strongly counteracts the combination of D and ℵᵃ.[26]

2) Internal evidence:

a) The omission of this text can be readily explained. Anti-Judaic polemic is widespread and consistently pursued throughout D.[27] The Jewish ignorance motif, for example, is regularly softened or eliminated altogether, and the relevant Acts passages all occur in speeches comparable to Jesus' own direct speech in this verse (Acts 3:17; 13:17; 17:30).[28] The elimination of Jesus' prayer would be entirely in keeping with this *Tendenz* of a text in which "words, clauses, and even whole sentences were changed, omitted, and inserted with astonishing freedom, wherever it seemed that the meaning could be brought out with greater force."[29]

b) Even if one is not convinced that the early church's anti-Judaic prejudice is sufficient to account for the omission of this text, it does argue strongly against the later insertion of such a prayer. This would especially have been the case after A.D. 70, when the destruction of Jerusalem would have made it apparent that God had *not* forgiven the Jews, and therefore had not answered the Lord's prayer. Not only would this situation have made it unlikely for such a prayer to be added to the tradition, the theological difficulty involved could even have supplied a motivation for the pious excision of Jesus' apparently unanswered prayer. Its continued retention in another sector of the mss tradition is most explicable as the faithful recording of dominical tradition.

d) Jesus' prayer (v. 34a) does not interrupt the connection between vv. 33 and 34b any more than does the statement about the location of the two thieves in v. 33c, yet it has never been suggested that this part of the text is an interpolation.[30]

e) The condemnation in vv. 28–31 concerns the Jews in Jerusalem, especially as they are represented by their obstinate leaders. However, Jesus' prayer relates to

---

[26] Cf. Harnack, "Probleme," p. 258.

[27] E. Epp, *The Theological Tendency of Codex Bezae Cantabrigiensis in Acts*, (Cambridge, 1966), p. 166; especially see pp. 41–64. Also see G. Rice, "The Anti-Judaic Bias of the Western Text in the Gospel of Luke," *AUSS*. 18 ('80) 51–57; "Some Further Examples of Anti-Judaic Bias in the Western Text of the Gospel of Luke," *AUSS*. 18 ('80) 149–156. Schweizer also argues strongly for this point; see *Luke*, pp. 359f.

[28] E. Epp, "The 'Ignorance Motif' in Acts and Anti-Judaic Tendencies in Codex Bezae," *HTR*. 55 ('62) 51–62; Harnack, "Probleme," pp. 259–261; J. Harris, "New Points of View in Textual Criticism," *Exp*. 8,7 ('14) 325–333; Streeter, *The Four Gospels*, pp. 137f.

[29] Westcott and Hort, *New Testament*, vol. II, p. 122. A reapplication of the dictum that "knowledge of documents should precede final judgment upon readings" (p. 31) may be pertinent at this point.

[30] See Feldkämper, *Der betende Jesus*, p. 257.

everyone, Jews and Gentiles, who are associated with the Passion (see below). Thus there is no contradiction between these two elements.

f) There are no parallels to this sort of prayer in Jewish literature, where martyrs only abuse their executioners.[31] Thus there could be no influence from Jewish sources, and the coincidence of Jesus' behaviour with Greek or Latin ideas hardly demonstrates later borrowing.

g) It is more likely that Stephen's prayer, and James' for that matter, would be modelled on Jesus' than vice versa.[32] There is no verbal similarity between Jesus' prayer and Stephen's, which would be surprising if Lk. 23:34a were a scribal gloss derived from Acts 7:60. However, one would expect conceptual similarity, expressed through just such verbal differences as these, if Luke were the author of both.[33] In the same way, Lk. 6:28 more readily proves the authenticity of the prayer, especially in the light of Luke's reflection in Acts 1:1 to have recounted "all that Jesus began to *do* and teach."

h) Similarly, Jesus' prayer serves as the presupposition for the ignorance motif to follow in Acts. It is more likely that Luke's development of this theme presumes Jesus' prayer than that the prayer was added later by a perceptive scribe.

i) The prayer is not based on any OT text (see the following discussion concerning Is. 53:12), and there is no mss evidence to suggest any such interpolation into the Passion narratives of either of the other synoptic accounts.[34] Why should such a scribal addition only appear in Luke's gospel?

j) The language and thought of the prayer are thoroughly Lukan: πάτηρ,[35] cf. Lk. 2:49; 10:21; 11:2; 22:42; 23:46; ἀφὲς αὐτοῖς..., cf. Acts 3:17; 7:60; 13:27; 17:30; τί ποιοῦσιν, cf. Lk. 6:11 (diff Mk. 3:6; Mt. 12:14); Lk. 19:48 (diff Mk. 11:18); also observe Jesus' teaching about loving and praying for one's enemies (Lk. 6:28; 11:4), and the appearance of prayer at significant events in Luke's narrative. It is much easier to account for these coincidences by assuming the text's authenticity than it is by postulating a clever scribe who later mimicked Luke's style.

The external evidence regarding Lk. 23:34a is far from clear, but the greater weight of evidence lies in favour of the text's authenticity. The combination of this external evidence with the very weighty internal arguments decisively tips the balance in favour of this prayer being an original part of Luke's gospel. In fact, the structural analysis previously offered in this study has begun to elucidate yet

---

[31] Surkau, *Martyrien*, p. 97.

[32] Margreth, *Gebetsleben Jesu*, p. 249.

[33] Cf. H. Cadbury, "Four Features of Lucan Style" in *Studies in Luke-Acts*, p. 92: "Variation of expression in *Luke* and *Acts*..indicates rather unity than diversity of authorship."

[34] Harnack, "Probleme," p. 258. Though it may be replied that Mark lacks the Q teaching on forgiving one's enemies, this still leaves Matthew to be accounted for. The possibility of influence from Stephen's martydom has already been eliminated.

[35] The fact that πάτηρ has also been identified as a mark of authentic Jesus material simply demonstrates Luke's faithfulness to the tradition.

another such internal argument. Without v. 34a the two-fold "Prayer/Confession" motif discussed above is eliminated, and the symmetry of the narrative significantly weakened. Furthermore, the theology of prayer which is being unravelled in Luke's gospel would expect just such a prayer to be found at this point in the story, as it is hoped this chapter will demonstrate.

### 4.1.3.2 Forgive Whom?

The exact "target" of Jesus' prayer has occupied much of the textual discussion, and the different answers are seen to variously affect the possibility of the later addition or excision of v. 34a. To whom does the ἀφὲς αὐτοῖς refer? To the Jews or to the Gentiles?[36] It is possible to arrive at a correct answer to this question only when one realises that it is not enough to read this prayer, as is usually done, as though it pertained only to those thought responsible for Jesus' prior sentencing (cf. Lk. 23:18, 21, 23). It must also be read within its immediate context. When viewed in this light several important points emerge:

First of all, Luke emphasises that the λαός stand "watching" Jesus, but do not mock him. The adversative effect of δὲ καὶ οἱ ἄρχοντες contrasts their behavior with that of the leaders.[37] In addition, Luke does not follow Mark in having οἱ παραπορευόμενοι blaspheme Jesus (Mk. 15:29); instead, they become the group (οἱ συμπαραγενόμενοι ὄχλοι) which later turns in remorse (v. 48) after initially watching.[38]

Secondly, the dividing of Jesus' cloak by the Roman soldiers is not related as the conclusion to the act of crucifixion, as in Mark (15:24). In Luke, it immediately follows Jesus' prayer for forgiveness.[39] Furthermore, Luke's use of δέ, rather than Mark's καί, gives an explanatory force to the clause.[40] Thus the prayer is as closely

---

[36] See Conzelmann, *Theology*, pp. 89f; J. Wilkinson, "The Seven Words from the Cross," *SJT*. 17 ('64) 69–82; Schmid, *Das Evangelium*, p. 348; D. Flusser, "The Crucified One and the Jews," *Immanuel*. 7 ('77) 25–37; Daube, "They Know Not," pp. 58–60; Fitzmyer, *The Gospel*, vol. II, pp. 1503f. An appeal to Luke's ignorance motif does not settle the question, though it is usually seen to do so in favor of the Jews, since Luke presents both Jews *and* Gentiles as being ignorant (cf. Acts 3:17; 13:27; 17:23, 30).

[37] J. Neyrey, *The Passion According to Luke: A Redaction Study of Luke's Soteriology*, (New York, 1985), p. 130; Flusser, "The Crucified," pp. 26 n. 3, 27f; J. Crowe, "The Laos at the Cross" in *The Language of the Cross*, (Chicago, 1977), p. 78. Luke alters the Mark's antagonistic understanding of the people, derived from Ps. 22:7f; see A. Rose, "L'influence des Psaumes sur le annonces et les récits de la Passion et de la Résurrection dans les Evangiles" in *Le Psautier*, (Louvain, 1962), pp. 316f.

[38] B. Beck, "'Imitatio Christi' and the Lucan Passion Narrative" in *Suffering and Martyrdom in the New Testament*, (Cambridge, 1981), p. 32; *pace* Plummer, *St. Luke*, p. 532; Crowe, "The Laos," p. 91.

[39] Feldkämper says it serves as the "conclusion" to the prayer; *Der betende Jesus*, pp. 264f.

[40] Zerwick, *Biblical Greek*, para. 467.

linked to the callous actions which follow as it is to the act of crucifixion which precedes it (cf. ὁ δὲ Ἰησοῦς ἔλεγεν, v. 34a).[41] The δέ plus imperfect highlights that Jesus prayed for them *"while* they crucified him." Consequently, Luke understands Jesus' prayer to be intended for the Roman soldiers just as much as the Jewish sector of the crowd responsible for his death.

Thirdly, the three-fold mockery extends both the offenses for which one might need forgiveness as well as the classes of people who stand in such need, for now the thief is included together with the leaders and the soldiers. Since the action which precipitates Jesus' prayer is left indeterminate, ie. "For they know not what they do"... "in trying me"?, "in crucifying me"? "in mocking me"?, the prayer serves to cover any actions in the narrative which would require God's forgiveness.[42] Consequently, the entire scene and all its actors stand under the shadow of Jesus' petition that God forgive them.[43] The relevance of this point is highlighted when one recalls that Luke describes the thief's mockery as "blasphemy" (v. 39; cf. Mk. 15:29). Jesus' prayer for forgiveness relates both structurally to the immediate confession of the repentant criminal, and thematically to the following confession of the centurion. Even though neither is depicted as mocking with their fellows, their lone testimonies stand starkly against the backdrop of Jesus' prayer.

Elsewhere it has been shown that Luke relates Jesus' prayers to the reception of insight by others into his true identity. Luke's juxtaposition of two prayers with two confessions in the passion narrative should strike the reader as laden with implication. Although the second prayer is not intercessory, the first plainly is. This first prayer serves as a thematic introduction to the whole of the crucifixion scene where at least some of those present express appropriate misgivings over Jesus' treatment, while the second prayer not only relates Christ's trust in God, but also functions structurally to carry on the prayer-revelation theme. Jesus is presented as an Intercessor before the Father, pleading on behalf of the various groups of sinners now scattered before his cross. This image, combined with Luke's use of Jesus' prayers elsewhere in the gospel, implies that Luke intends that a direct connection should be drawn between these two prayers of Jesus and the subsequent confessions made by repentant sinners. But there is even further evidence of this connection.

---

[41] Plummer, *St. Luke*, p. 531.

[42] The fact that the mockery is related after the crucifixion does not affect this observation. The limitations of the written, as opposed to a visual, medium requires that even simultaneous events be recorded consecutively. There is nothing in the tenses used which would necessarily restrict the prayer's reference to only those events prior to v. 34.

[43] Some would see evidence here pointing to an allusion to Is. 53:12: Feldkämper, *Der betende Jesus*, pp. 260, 266; Plummer, *St. Luke*, p. 532; Bock, *Proclamation*, pp. 145f; Ernst, *Das Evangelium*, p. 635; Wilkinson, "The Seven Words," p. 71; Grundmann, *Das Evangelium*, p. 433; Jeremias, "παῖς θεοῦ," pp. 710, 713. This might be possible with reference to the "counted among the transgressors" phrase of either the LXX or Hebrew texts (cf. Lk. 22:37). However, Luke's regular use of the LXX makes it unlikely that he is using the Hebrew version to attribute an intercessory function to the prayer (*pace* Feldkämper, p. 266; cf. Grundmann, p. 433). Jeremias admits this point (pp. 706f, 715), seeing it as evidence of a primitive, pre-synoptic tradition

## 4.1.3.3 "Save yourself..."

The three-fold mockery in the passion story connects this scene to Jesus' three-fold temptation in the desert.[44] These jibes are offered as a resumption of that particular Satanic attack (cf. 4:13; 22:3, 53).[45]

Satan's first set of temptations concerned who Jesus really was: the Son of God (4:3–12). In the same fashion, Luke employs the titles thrown at Jesus in derision at his passion as ironic ascriptions of his real identity. These mockers speak more truly than they realise, as the reader of Luke's gospel knows. This Jesus *is* the Christ (cf. 2:11, 26; 4:41; 9:20; 23:2f; 24:26, 46), the Chosen One (cf. 9:35), the King of the Jews (cf. 19:12–27, 38; 23:2f).

The mockery of Jesus' work is as ironic as that of his identity. They taunt him to "save himself" (cf. 4:9–12) as "he saved others" (cf. 7:50; 8:48, 50; 17:19; 18:42). However, if Jesus is the Christ, it is precisely by not saving himself that he will ultimately save both himself and others, for "the Christ must suffer" (9:22; 17:25; 24:7, 26, 46). Finally, one criminal even cries out (with more cause than the others!) "save yourself *and us.*" Though these hecklers may have no expectation of such a thing actually happening, this is exactly what Luke intends the reader to understand Jesus as presently doing: saving others![46] Luke's context makes it clear that the two conversions recorded at the cross are to be read as *Jesus' acts of salvation.*

However, salvation comes as the consequence of a confession concerning Jesus' true identity. The criminal not only recognises his own guilt and Jesus' innocence (v. 41), but also that mocking this innocent man is somehow incommensurate with the proper fear of God (v. 40). He further realises that Jesus exercises the kingly authority necessary to show him mercy and allow him entrance into the

---

interpreting Jesus' death in terms of the Suffering Servant. This may be correct, but it does not necessarily explain *Luke's* use of the prayer. In addition, even though such an argument would assist the present thesis, the same conclusion may be reached through the internal argument of the narrative itself, without recourse to hypothetical traditions.

[44] Neyrey, *The Passion*, pp. 180f offers a good examination of the parallels leading to this conclusion; also, J. Calloud, *Structural Analysis of Narrative*, (Philadelphia, 1976), p. 71; and Talbert, "The Way of the Lukan Jesus," p. 244.

[45] Which is not to imply that there have been no Satanic attacks during Jesus' ministry; *pace* Conzelmann. See chapter 6.

[46] Cf. Fitzmyer, *The Gospel*, vol. II, pp. 1501, 1515; Ernst, *Das Evangelium*, p. 639; Hamm, "Vision as Metaphor," p. 473. Neyrey, *The Passion*, pp. 133–155 provides a fine discussion of the Lukan soteriology revealed in these verses. However, as is typical, the salvific "power" is related solely to Jesus' death. This is correct as far as it goes, but such an analysis needs to be supplemented by the soteriological significance of Jesus' prayer.

Karris, *Luke*, p. 90, draws an important connection between this criminal and Lk. 4:16–30, which is also relevant to John's query in 7:19ff. This is the only example in Jesus' ministry where he "liberates" a prisoner (cf. 4:18), indicating not only the spiritual dimensions of the deliverance brought by Christ, but also the fact that it is effected by his death.

kingdom (v. 42), which is in essence a confession of Jesus' messiahship.[47] This criminal is saved because he suddenly comes to *recognise who Jesus is.*

Fitzmyer remarks that, "To ask how the man knew all this about Jesus is to miss the point of the story."[48] But actually, it is in *not* asking this question that the point of the story is missed. Usually, Jesus' prayer is analysed with respect to what it reveals of his attitudes at the time of death,[49] or as an expression of his "Solidarität mit den Sündern."[50] The criminal's confession is regarded as his response to Jesus' deportment on the cross.[51] In this way the confessing criminal becomes paradigmatic for Christian conversion.[52] Such analyses are unable to answer the obvious question which forces itself upon the reader: how does Luke account for the criminal's sudden, new insight? Yet, when this question is viewed within the framework of Luke's ideas about Jesus' prayer and his self-revelation, it becomes apparent that Luke has deliberately arranged his narrative in order to answer this very question. It is Jesus' intercessory prayer for forgiveness which is now answered as the Father reveals his Son to this criminal and so makes way for his salvation. To miss this connection is to ignore the function of the narrative's form when viewed in light of Luke's unfolding theology. This thief is contrasted as one who *does* "know what he is doing" by placing his faith in Jesus. Jesus' prayer makes way for the illuminating operation of God's elective revelation by which he discloses his Son to those whom he chooses (10:21–24).[53]

---

[47] Grundmann, *Das Evangelium*, p. 434; Crowe, "The Laos," p. 95; Marshall, *Commentary*, p. 872; Fitzmyer, *The Gospel*, vol. II, p. 1508.

[48] Fitzmyer, *The Gospel*, vol. II, p. 1508.

[49] For example, it expresses Jesus' faith in God (Neyrey, *The Passion*, pp. 142f); it presents him as the Righteous Sufferer (Büchele, *Der Tod*, pp. 81–84); Jesus is portrayed as the paradigm for Christian martyrs (Surkau, *Martyrien*, pp. 97, 99;Ernst, *Das Evangelium*, p. 635). The prayer is derived from Ps. 31:5, which was used as a part of the daily evening prayer; see Jeremias, "Gebetsleben," pp. 126, 140.

[50] Feldkämper, *Der betende Jesus*, p. 283.

[51] Talbert, *Luke and the Gnostics*, p. 76. F. Wulf, "'Jesus, gedenke meiner, wenn du in dein Königtum kommst," *GL.* 37 ('64) 1–3, especially p. 2.

[52] Büchele, *Der Tod*, p. 86; Rese, *Altestamentliche Motive*, p. 159; Neyrey, *The Passion*, pp. 135f. Feldkämper, *Der betende Jesus*, p. 267 approaches the correct conclusion when he writes, "So verstanden ist nicht nur Jesu Tod heilswirksam, sondern auch sein Gebet: Denn dieses verhilft den Ubeltätern angesichts seines Todes zur Busse und damit zur Sündenvergebung und zum Heil." He understands this "help" to occur as the criminal himself responds to Jesus' "solidarity with sinners" displayed through his prayer (pp. 254–256). However, this argument requires Mark's prayer of dereliction, not Luke's prayer of intercession; cf. also K. Scaria, "Jesus' Prayer and Christian Prayer," *Bibl.* 7 ('81) 174; Büchele, *Tod Jesu*, p. 50.

[53] Others have perceived Jesus' intercessory role in this prayer.Wilkinson, "The Seven Words," p. 69 calls Jesus the "High-Priest" offering "pardon." D. Henry, "'Father, forgive them; for they know not what they do' (Luke xxiii.34)," *ExpT.* 30 ('18–19) 87, calls Jesus the "Divine Advocate" pleading for the people. Jeremias, "παῖς θεοῦ," p. 715; *Theology*, p. 298 relates this prayer to the practice of Jewish martyrs interceding on behalf of Israel; Jesus "applies the atoning power of his death to others..." However, none of these discussions have yet perceived the *effective* relationship between *the prayer itself*, as distinct from Jesus' death, and subsequent insight into Jesus' messiahship.

## 4.1.4 "And Jesus cried out . . ." (Lk. 23:44–49)

Jesus' second prayer on the cross offers Luke's interpretation of the "loud cry" found in Mk. 15:37.[54] Luke's rearrangement of the tearing of the temple veil, placing it before the prayer, has already been observed. Together, these two Lukan alterations have several effects.

Firstly, whereas in Mark the centurion confesses after Jesus dies (15:39), and in Matthew he does so after an earthquake (27:54), in Luke the confession is brought into immediate proximity with Jesus' prayer.[55]

Secondly, both Mark and Matthew present the tearing of the temple veil as one of several events following Jesus' death; Luke focuses the reader's attention upon only one consequence of Jesus' death/prayer: the centurion's confession.[56] In a narrative which proceeds under the shadow of Jesus' prayerful intercession for sinners, Luke again purposefully highlights the prayer/ recognition relationship. Jesus prays and the centurion "sees". Thus, even though this second prayer is not itself intercessory, the theme continues: first, the organisation of the material points strongly to this conclusion; secondly, earlier Luke relates his revelation theme to prayer itself, whether or not the content of that prayer is said to be intercessory (cf. 9:18, 28f); and thirdly, vv. 44–49 continue to develop under the thematic auspices of the intercession made in v. 34a. Jesus' second prayer does not alter this; rather, its inclusion simply underscores the "causative" nature of prayer being presented. A second confession is thus preceded by a second prayer.[57]

### 4.1.4.1 "Seeing what had happened . . ."

The proliferation of seeing language in Luke's narrative (5 times in Luke 23, as compared to twice in Mk. 15:39f) is itself good reason for suspecting that Luke's revelation theme is in operation. When it is remembered how the language of seeing/hearing, prayer and confession/illumination has functioned elsewhere, finding all of these elements together here, whatever their original source, suggests that they have been arranged for similar purposes.

The centurion responds after "seeing what has happened" (ἰδὼν τὸ γενόμεν-

---

[54] Harris, *Prayer*, p. 115; Scaria, "Christian Prayer," p. 177; Feldkämper, *Der betende Jesus*, p. 274.

[55] Cf. J. Michaels, "The Centurion's Confession and the Spear Thrust," *CBQ.* 29 ('67) 107.

[56] M. Kiddle, "The Passion Narrative in St. Luke's Gospel," *JTS.* 36 ('35) 278; Matera, "The Death of Jesus," pp. 472–475; F. Weinert, "Luke, the Temple and Jesus' Saying about Jerusalem's Abandoned House," *CBQ.* 44 ('82) 70 all discuss this rearrangement with regard to its effect upon Luke's view of Jesus' death and the temple; cf. Fitzmyer, *The Gospel*, vol. II, p. 1519 for its further effects upon the place of the centurion. Also cf. Stanley, *Gethsemane*, p. 196; and D. Sylva, "The Temple Curtain and Jesus' Death in the Gospel of Luke," *JBL.* 105 ('86) 242ff.

[57] J. Bligh, "Christ's Death Cry," *HeyJ.* 1 ('60) 144 approaches this understanding of the redactional significance of Jesus' second prayer. He argues that Luke inserts this prayer in order to explain the centurion's confession; Jesus' words "forced his divine sonship upon the centurion's attention." To this telic understanding of the relationship only needs to be added the spiritual/ causitive dynamic.

ov). But what exactly has he seen? Being singular, τὸ γενόμενον cannot refer to a multitude of events.[58] It cannot possibly mean the tearing of the temple veil. Luke's uniting of the veil tradition with that of the sun's darkening, and his distancing of the darkness further from the prayer by inserting the veil's tearing in between the two, indicate that the darkness is not being referred to either.[59] The only event remaining is Jesus' death,[60] which Luke has united with his prayer. The coordination of the participle plus finite verb, εἰπὼν ἐξέπνευσεν, links Jesus' prayer and death together as a single event.[61] Therefore, it is seeing Jesus pray at the moment of death which elicits the centurion's confession.

The centurion joins the growing list of seeing/hearing figures who are interrelated to the praying Jesus. We remember that Herod heard τὰ γινόμενα about Jesus and from that point on ἐζήτει ἰδεῖν αὐτόν (9:7, 9). When he finally did manage to meet Jesus he hoped ἰδεῖν ὑπ' αὐτοῦ γινόμενον (23:8). The centurion now offers another comparative figure. Seeing Jesus at prayer leads him to confess his true identity; obviously seeing is being used here with both a literal and metaphorical significance.[62] He sees Jesus pray, and by means of Jesus' prayer he truly does "see" and so also comes to confess. Luke intends his reader to understand Jesus' prayer, not simply his death,[63] which has at any rate been indissolubly linked with the prayer, as the effective means of the centurion's spiritual illumination. And even though "seeing Jesus pray" is rather different from being supernaturally influenced by God's answer to Jesus' prayer, the structure of the passage and the content of Jesus' first prayer suggest that this is indeed the connection Luke intends to make.

However, the centurion is not alone in seeing and responding. The watching crowd does the same. Luke emphasises the similarity of their response through the precise way in which v. 48 is made to parallel v. 47a.[64] Each sentence is composed of: 1) a subject (a centurion/the crowd); 2) an aorist participle of seeing (ἰδών/θεωρήσαντες); 3) "what happened" (τὸ γενόμενον/τὰ γενόμενα); 4) a reaction (ἐδόξαζεν/ὑπέστρεφον); 5) a subordinate participial clause elucidating the response (λέγων/τύπτοντες). The things which the crowds see is plural (τὰ γενόμενα) because they have been watching since v. 35; the process of their illumination has taken place over the period of both prayers and confessions.

Though the crowds do not make a verbal confession, their turning and beating their breasts is meant to be understood as a description of remorse, if not of

---

[58] *Pace* Karris, *Luke*, p. 110; Feldkämper, *Der betende Jesus*, p. 280, who relate τὸ γενόμενον to everything prior to Jesus' death.

[59] *Pace* Schneider, *Das Evangelium*, p. 487.

[60] Beck, "Imitatio Christi," p. 46 n. 58; Fitzmyer, *The Gospel*, vol. II, p. 1519; *pace* Plummer, *St. Luke*, p. 539.

[61] Feldkämper, *Der betende Jesus*, p. 280.

[62] Büchele, *Tod Jesu*, pp. 54f also points out the role which this language plays in Luke's "witness" theme; cf. the discussion in chapter 2.

[63] *Pace* Büchele, *Tod Jesu*, p. 68.

[64] Feldkämper, *Der betende Jesus*, p. 280.

repentance (cf. 18:13).[65] Though a rather pedestrian word, elsewhere it can be argued that Luke uses ὑποστρέφω to describe "a reversal" of life made in response to God's revelation/intervention (2:20; 17:15, 18). It has already been suggested that the first passage (2:20) is paradigmatic for Luke's use of seeing/hearing language elsewhere; now it also shows itself to be exemplary of the response required to God's revelation. It is equally significant that both of these passages associate this "turning" with "glorifying God," a feature which knits the crowd's response even more closely to that of the centurion, the one complementing the other. And, of course, the crowd's remorse echoes the repentant criminal's confession of guilt.

By paralleling vv. 47a with 48 as he does, Luke ties the people's turning to the centurion's confession. This not only strengthens the reading of ὑποστρέφω with repentant overtones, but also presents this repentance as a further consequence of Jesus' prayers on the cross. Together with the watching disciples (v. 49), who are already committed to Jesus, the reactions of the crowds and the centurion form a fitting conclusion to the whole narrative. The fact that these individuals "see" Jesus while the whole land is covered in darkness (vv. 44f),[66] a darkness which effectively engulfs the nation's leaders, further highlights the spiritual import of their perception. Just as Jesus' first prayer set the tone for what Luke wants his reader to understand as happening throughout the course of the story, so this final scene provides the proper corollary: the Father has indeed offered forgiveness, as seen in confession and repentance. Jesus' intercessory prayer has been answered. Sinners have been saved.

### 4.1.4.2 "Surely this was a righteous man."

How the centurion's confession is interpreted will have a bearing upon the present argument, for if it does in fact issue as the result of Jesus' prayer then it should manifest a distinctive insight into the nature of Jesus' true identity. It is, first of all, important to notice that the statement is described as an expression of glory to God (ἐδόξαζεν τὸν θεὸν λέγων).

This is an expression characteristic of Luke which he uses to conclude sections which portray the manifestation of God's salvific activity in Jesus or through the kerygma (Lk. 2:20; 4:15; 5:25, 26; 7:16; 13:13; 17:15; 18:43; Acts 4:21; 11:18; 21:20).[67] Luke both introduces (2:14) and concludes (23:47) Jesus' life with glory

---

[65] Plummer, St. Luke, p. 540; Surkau, Martyrien, p. 99; Matera, "The Death of Jesus," p. 484; Grundmann, Das Evangelium, pp. 435f; Ernst, Das Evangelium, p. 640; Fitzmyer, The Gospel, vol. II, pp. 1515, 1520; Feldkämper, Der betende Jesus, p. 281 n. 106; Büchele, Der Tod, p. 55; Karris, Luke, p. 112; but cf. Marshall, Commentary, p. 877.

[66] Karris, Luke, p. 88.

[67] Creed, The Gospel, p. 288; Cadbury, Style, p. 107; Matera, "The Death of Jesus," pp. 480, 483; R. Glöckner, Die Verkündigung des Heils beim Evangelisten Lukas, (Mainz, 1975), p. 188; Feldkämper, Der betende Jesus, p. 281; Büchele, Der Tod, p. 54 n. 231.

being given to God.[68] In the first instance, this glorifying concerned God's gift of a Saviour (2:11). In the last instance, it concerns the death of this same Saviour (cf. 23:35b, 37, 39!). Thus by introducing the centurion's confession with this particular phrase Luke is telling his reader that it is an expression by one who has experienced the power of God's salvation himself.[69] As the final instance of this construction in Luke's gospel, it is also a premonition of the fact that two of its three uses in Acts will concern the extension of the gospel to the Gentiles (11:18; 21:20).[70]

The centurion's use of δίκαιος must be read in light of the foregoing discussion.[71] The main issue at stake is whether this word should be translated as "righteous" or "innocent."[72] Does the centurion merely make a judicial statement, or does he say something concerning Jesus' standing with God? Perhaps too strong a contrast here should not be drawn. Luke's use of οὗτος compares this confession with both the criminal's earlier acknowledgement of Jesus' innocence (v. 41), and the mockery of Jesus as Christ and King (vv. 35, 38). This redactional word may serve as a mediator between the two competing translations of δίκαιος. For, on the one hand, it contrasts the centurion's confession with the criminal's admission that he is being punished δικαίως. But, on the other hand, it

---

[68] Feldkämper, *Der betende Jesus*, p. 281.

[69] Glöckner, *Verkündigung*, p. 188.

[70] Some would claim this as justification for the idea that Luke thus presents this man as if he were a "good christian"; Fitzmyer, *The Gospel*, vol. II, pp. 1515, 1520; so also Neyrey, *The Passion*, p. 101. Jesus is presented as "a light for revelation to the Gentiles" (2:32); cf. Lampe, "The Holy Spirit," p. 179; Ellis, *The Gospel*, p. 270; W. Manson, *The Gospel*, 262.

[71] The relationship of Luke's δίκαιος to Mark's υἱὸς θεοῦ, and which would have been the earlier tradition, is not under discussion here. See J. Pobee, "The Cry of the Centurion – A Cry of Defeat" in *The Trial of Jesus*, (London, 1970), p. 91; Michaels, "The Centurion's Confession," p. 106; Fitzmyer, *The Gospel*, vol. II, p. 1515; Creed, *The Gospel*, p. 288. Bligh's comment ("Death Cry," p. 145), "Whatever the explanation, the substitution is much to be regretted, since . . . it obscures the immense dogmatic value of this passage" is already seen to be inappropriate.

[72] For the various arguments see: Loisy, *Luc*, p. 562; "Innocent" – G. D. Kilpatrick, "A Theme of the Lucan Passion Story and Luke xxiii. 47," *JTS*. 43 ('42) 34–36; R. Bratcher, "A Note on υἱὸς θεοῦ (Mark xv. 39)," *ExpT*. 68 ('56) 28; J. C. O'Neill, *The Theology of Acts in its Historical Setting*, (London, 1961), p. 142; G. Schrenk, "δίκαιος," *TDNT*, vol. II, p. 187; Ellis, *The Gospel*, p. 267; Schmid, *Das Evangelium*, p. 351; W. Manson, *The Gospel*, p. 262. Klostermann, *Das Lukas*, p. 226; Neyrey, *The Passion*, p. 100; Marshall, *Commentary*, p. 876; Grundmann, *Das Evangelium*, p. 435; G. Rice, "The Role of the Populace in the Passion Narrative of Luke in Codex Bezae," *AUSS*. 19 ('81) 152; D. Schmidt, "Luke's 'Innocent' Jesus" in *Political Issues in Luke-Acts*, (New York, 1983), pp. 117f.

"Righteous" – H. Dechent, "Der Gerechte – eine Bezeichnung für den Messias," *TSK*. 100 ('27–28) 440f; R. P. C. Hanson, "Does δίκαιος in Luke XXIII. 47 Explode the Proto-Luke Hypothesis?," *Hermathena*. 60 ('42) 74–78 (a pointed response to Kilpatrick); A. Descamps, *Les justes et la justice dans les évangiles et le christianisme primitif hormis la doctrine proprement paulinienne*, (Louvain, 1950), p. 84; Lagrange, *Luc*, p. 593; Matera, "The Death of Jesus," pp. 479–483; E. Franklin, *Christ the Lord: A Study in the Purpose and Theology of Luke-Acts*, (London, 1975), pp. 62f; Büchele, *Der Tod*, p. 54 (who sees a dual reference); Beck, "Imitatio Christi," pp. 41–44; Fitzmyer, *The Gospel*, vol. II, p. 1520.

also compares the centurion's sincere declaration to those earlier derisive applications of messianic titles.[73]
If a decision must be made, it should be in favour of righteous. Those who favour innocent primarily argue that it continues Luke's martyrdom theme,[74] and that a confession of righteousness would have been meaningless on the lips of a Gentile.[75] However, J. Neyrey has shown that the frequent emphasis upon martyrology, usually offered *in lieu* of any Lukan soteriological understanding of the cross, has been overestimated in past studies.[76] Also, Luke never uses δίκαιος for forensic innocence elsewhere in his writings.[77] And the real issue is not what would have been historically feasible on the lips of this centurion, but how Luke uses the man and his words in the course of his story.[78] Luke's description of the confession as "glory to God" has already indicated that more than mere innocence is intended. Jesus is proclaimed a Just Man, who is right with God.[79] Although the absence of a definite article prevents the present ascription from becoming a title itself, it does prepare the way for the use of ὁ δίκαιος as a messianic title later in the book of Acts (3:14; 7:52; 22:14).[80] Just as it will later be revealed to Paul that he was chosen by God ἰδεῖν τὸν δίκαιον καὶ ἀκοῦσαι φωνὴν ἐκ τοῦ στόματος αὐτοῦ (Acts 22:14), so now God also chooses this centurion, in response to Jesus' intercession, to see his Righteous One and hear words of effectual prayer from his mouth. This man stands with the repentant criminal as having been given true insight into the character of Jesus and his relationship with God. Luke intends his reader to see them both as having been touched by the prayers of the Righteous One.

---

[73] But for this man to even call Jesus innocent is no small claim. If he is innocent, then the Jews are guilty, and Jesus is indeed the Son of God and King of the Jews (22:66–23:3); see T. Geddert, *Mark 13 in its Markan Interpretive Context*, unpublished Ph.D. dissertation, (Aberdeen, 1986), p. 293 n. 91.

[74] Dibelius, *Tradition*, p. 203; Surkau, *Martyrien*, p. 99; Ernst, *Das Evangelium*, p. 639; Flender, *Luke*, p. 54; Talbert, *Gnostics*, p. 73; E. Lohse, "Lukas als Theologie der Heilsgeschichte" in *Die Einheit des Neuen Testaments*, (Göttingen, 1973) p. 162.

[75] Kilpatrick, "A Theme," pp. 34f.

[76] Neyrey, *The Passion*, pp. 129–155; see Marshall, *Historian*, pp. 92ff for a discussion of Lukan soteriology.

[77] Hanson, "δικαιόω in Luke," p. 76; Beck, "Imitatio Christi," p. 42.

[78] "The centurion is a character in Luke's story whose word, on a literary level, says more than we would expect from such a person." (Matera, "The Death of Jesus," p. 483 n. 49).

[79] Cf. L. Ruppert, *Jesus als der leidende Gerechte?*, (Stuttgart, 1972), especially pp. 48–58; J. Kilgallen, *The Stephen Speech: A Literary and Redactional Study of Acts 7,2–53*, (Rome, 1976), pp. 98–100.

[80] Matera, "The Death of Jesus," p. 481; M. Simon, *St. Stephen and the Hellenists in the Primitive Church*, (London, 1958), pp. 64f; Glöckner, *Verkündigung*, p. 190; Dechent, "Der 'Gerechte'," pp. 439–443; Jeremias, "παῖς θεοῦ," pp. 707, 710; R. Longenecker, *The Christology of Early Jewish Christianity*, (London, 1970), pp. 46f; Bock, *Proclamation*, p. 190 n. 112; Descamps, *Les justes et la justice*, p. 84 writes, "Il s'agit bien, dans les Actes, d'une véritable épithete messianique . . ."O'Neill, *Theology of Acts*, pp. 141, says that only Acts 22:14 intends the noun in a titular sense, but offers no convincing reasons.

*4.1.5 "You will not see me again . . ."*

Luke's crucifixion narrative is prefaced by one of the three addresses to Jerusalem recorded in this gospel (13:34f; 19:41–44; 23:27–29).[81] The first is a "Q" tradition which records both a lament over the city and the prophecy, "For I tell you, you will not see me until you say,'Blessed is he who comes in the name of the Lord!'" Matthew relates this material some time *after* Jesus' entry into the city, and so quite appropriately adds an "again" (ἀπ᾽ ἄρτι) to the saying (23:37–39).[82] The second lament is a tradition unique to Luke included in his Jerusalem Entrance material, thereby aligning it with the shared Markan tradition, "Blessed is the One who comes in the name of the Lord" (Mk. 11:9f; Mt. 21:9). The third lament is also a unique Lukan saying.

In addition to the obvious interest Luke displays in the fate of Jerusalem, the results of this treatment are several-fold.

Firstly, the prophecy, which in Mt. 23:37–39 is an unambiguous reference to the parousia,[83] in Luke becomes a premonition of his entrance into Jerusalem.[84]

Secondly, Luke does not talk about seeing Jesus "again", whenever that may be; he speaks of seeing Jesus *at all* (οὐ μὴ ἴδητέ με ἕως; 13:35).

Thirdly, the events at the crucifixion are explicitly related to both Jesus' preceding judgment oracles and his prophecy about not being seen again. What does all this mean? Especially when Jesus is standing very visibly before their eyes?

Marshall correctly says that Lk. 19:38 does not constitute the fulfillment of 13:35;[85] this prophecy continues to look towards a future day. But Jesus' entry into Jerusalem did offer *the opportunity* for its fulfillment. If the leaders and people of Jerusalem had glorified God for Jesus' salvific work (19:37) together with the disciples, if they too would have cried out, "Blessed is the king who comes in the name of the Lord!", then they would have "seen" Jesus for who and what he truly was, and come to realise on this day (ἐν τῇ ἡμέρᾳ; 19:42a) where their peace could be found (v. 38b; 2:14).[86] However, by their hard-heartedness (19:39) they missed

---

[81] For a discussion of the exact form of these pericopae, and how they relate to the *rîb* patterns of the OT, see Weinert, "The Temple," pp. 72ff; Neyrey, "Jesus' Address to the Women of Jerusalem (lk. 23.27–31) – A Prophetic Judgement Oracle," *NTS.* 29 ('83) 80ff, especially the bibliography in n. 34; and C. Giblin, *The Destruction of Jerusalem According to Luke's Gospel*, (Rome, 1985), pp. 37–43, 55f, 96–104.

[82] Fitzmyer, *The Gospel*, vol. II, p. 1037; Gundry, *Matthew*, p. 473; cf. Mt. 26:29, 64.

[83] D. Hill, *The Gospel of Matthew*, (London, 1972), p. 316; Gundry, *Matthew*, p. 474; F. Beare, *The Gospel According to Matthew*, (Oxford, 1981), p. 461.

[84] Giblin, *The Destruction*, p. 43; Hamm, "Vision as Metaphor," p. 471.

[85] Marshall, *Commentary*, pp. 577, 715; Bock, *Proclamation*, p. 121; *pace* F. Danker, *Jesus and the New Age According to St. Luke: A Commentary on the Third Gospel*, (St. Louis, 1974), p. 162; Fitzmyer, *The Gospel*, vol. II, pp. 1037; Conzelmann, *Theology*, pp. 75f, especially n. 4, but cf. the seemingly contradictory statement on p. 110.

[86] Cf. Giblin, *The Destruction*, p. 42; also Hamm (p. 471), "To 'see' Jesus in 13:35, then, means to perceive him as do the disciples of 19,37–38 . . ."

their opportunity, and as a result from now on the truth about Jesus will be "hidden from their eyes" (νῦν δὲ ἐκρύβη ἀπο ὀφθαλμῶν σου; 19:39b). The whole of the following sequence of events in the city take place under the shadow of this divinely induced epistemological darkness, a situation reminiscent of the programmatic words of Lk. 10:21–24. The leaders would neither believe Jesus' own testimony nor confess him themselves (cf. 22:67f!; diff Mk. 14:61f; Mt. 26:63f). Consequently, Luke (22:69) omits Mark's (14:62) phrase about the leaders seeing the Son of Man at the right hand of God. Due to their spiritual blindness, they will not be allowed to see any such thing.[87]

By introducing the passion with Jesus' final lament, which is also a prophetic judgment oracle over the city,[88] Luke indicates that the expectations raised in 13:35, and only partially fulfilled by the disciples at 19:38f, receive an incremental further fulfillment in the scene at the cross.

First of all, Luke portrays Jesus' death, and thus also his final intercessory prayer, as the concluding fate and work of a suffering prophet (cf. 4:24; 22:64; 13:33f).[89]

Secondly, all of the trial and subsequent mockery (22:66–23:3; 23:35, 37f, 39), with its callous rejection of Jesus' true status, falls under the rubric of God's judgment (19:42b; Acts 28:26f). This judgment immediately manifests itself in the divine withholding of spiritual insight.

But finally, even in his last moments, the praying Jesus continues to mediate the Father's revelation. The otherwise all pervasive spiritual gloom is pierced by two shafts of light. There are a few more who will yet "see" Jesus (vv. 35, 47, 48f; cf. 13:35). There is still another voice to "glorify God" (v. 47; cf. 19:37); someone else to recognise his kingship (v. 42; cf. 19:38). While the leaders of the nation stand in the darkness and remain blinded, a condemned criminal and a Roman soldier see Jesus. Once more the Father has exhibited his good pleasure in "hiding these things from the wise and the learned (cf. 19:39b) and revealing them to little children" (10:21).[90]

---

[87] Since Luke's version of this logion has only to do with Christ's heavenly session, having omitted those Markan details referring to the parousia (see chapter 7), he is not denying that the leaders will one day see Jesus' parousia as the Son of Man, only that they will not perceive his present exaltation and interim reign at God's right hand.

[88] Klostermann, *Lukas*, p. 227; Neyrey, *The Passion*, p. 109 (see pp. 108–121); F. Schnider, *Jesus der Prophet*, (Göttingen, 1973), pp. 74f.

[89] See Büchele, *Der Tod*, pp. 88–96; Rese, *Altestamentliche Motive*, pp. 66–71; U. Wilckens, *Die Missionsreden der Apostelgeschichte*, (Neukirchen-Vluyn, 1974, 3rd ed.), pp. 37–44, 210–212, 214–224; A. George, "Le sens de la mort de Jésus pour Luc," *RB*. 80 ('73) 207–209. It is important to note the association of Jesus' role as prophet with that of the Son of Man (cf. 9:22, 44; 18:31–33). The importance of this connection will become apparent in the discussion of Stephen's vision in Acts 7.

[90] Brower, "Mark 9:1," p. 39 sees the same dynamic at work in Mark.

### 4.1.6. Conclusion

In his book on the literary reading of biblical texts, entitled *The Art of Biblical Narrative*, Robert Alter has written:[91]

The Bible ... constantly insists on parallels of situation and reiterations of motif that provide moral and psychological commentary on each other ... No act or gesture is incidental and the sequence of events is never fortuitous.

Though Alter may have over-stated his own case, it is not accidental that Luke's deliberate paralleling of two scenes, each organised around the common denominators of Jesus' prayer and a subsequent revelation, has led to the further development of the mediatory significance of Jesus' prayer-life. Luke's narratival parataxis serves to underscore this very point. Also, in calling God Father (vv. 34, 46) Jesus recalls the unique relationship wherein, as the one given all authority, he exercises the prayerful disposition of the Father's revelation (10:22f). The new factor introduced into Luke's prayer-revelation equation by the passion story is the idea that perceiving Jesus' true identity results in an individual's salvation (v. 43, 47). In mediating his self-disclosure, Jesus' prayers also mediate God's salvation.

## 4.2 Luke's "Passion Secret": Is it Due to Human Misunderstanding or Divine Concealment?

Before discussing the Emmaus story (4.3) it may be useful to indicate why it is included in a discussion of the revelatory significance of Jesus' prayers. The disclosure of Christ to the disciples at Emmaus is the final instalment in what has come to be called Luke's "passion secret," a feature of this gospel which is integrally related elsewhere to Luke's perception of the significance of Jesus' prayers. It is the climactic role which the Emmaus story plays in resolving Luke's secrecy theme which initially suggests its relevance to the study of the revelatory significance of Jesus' prayers.

It has become commonplace to read that Luke "turns Mark's Messianic secret into a misunderstanding of the Passion."[92] But there are two points requiring clarification in this statement. Firstly, what is the precise nature of this misunderstanding? And, secondly, is Luke's secret concerned exclusively with the passion as is so often implied?

The divine necessity of the disciples' blindness, interjected by Luke into the

---

[91] (New York, 1981), pp. 91f, 112.

[92] Conzelmann, *Theology*, p. 56; also see Grundmann, *Das Evangelium*, p. 189; Brown, *Apostasy*, p. 61; Dillon, *Eye-Witnesses*, p. 24; Schütz, *Der leidende Christus*, p. 65; Glöckner, *Verkündigung*, pp. 157f; J. Wanke, *Die Emmauserzählung: eine redaktionsgeschichtliche Untersuchung zu Lk. 24:13–35*, (Leipzig, 1973), p. 88; "'... wie sie ihn beim Brotbrechen erkannten' zur Auslegung der Emmauserzählung Lk. 24, 13–35," *BZ.* 18 ('74) 190; and W. Wrede, *The Messianic Secret*, (London, 1971), p. 171 n. 29, who made this observation long before Conzelmann.

passion predictions at 9:45 and 18:34, has been frequently noted,[93] but it necessitates an important modification in Conzelmann's statement. Luke's misunderstanding of the passion must be read rather as the divine concealment of the passion. This shift from misunderstanding to hiddenness is pursued more consistently throughout Luke than is suggested by these two verses alone.

1) Luke omits any Markan material which even suggests that the disciples misunderstood something. Mk. 4:13 and 7:17 contain reproaches against the disciples for not understanding Jesus' parables, and Mk. 6:52 for not understanding the miracle of the feeding of the five thousand. Luke edits the first rebuke out of his version of the parable of the sower (8:11), and both the second and third disappear as a part of the Great Omission (cf. Mk. 6:45–8:26). Similarly, the disciples' hard-heartedness and misunderstanding concerning the yeast of the Pharisees (Mk. 8:17–21) is omitted from Luke (12:1), as is Peter's misunderstanding of the first passion prediction and the resulting rebuke by Jesus (Mk. 8:32f).[94]

2) Luke retains one Markan statement of misunderstanding, but modifies it in order to bring it into line with his own thematic emphasis by adding that "it was hidden from them so that they could not understand it" (Mk. 9:32; cf. Lk. 9:45).

3) Luke adds his own explanation of how God hides information from the disciples to Markan material which otherwise had no suggestion of the disciples' misunderstanding at all. Mk. 10:33f contains nothing suggesting that the disciples' misunderstood Jesus' third prediction of the passion, but cf. Lk. 18:34!

4) Luke adds non-Markan material which mentions God's direct action in preventing the disciples, as well as others, from being able to understand who Jesus is (Lk. 19:42; 24:16).

5) The only possible exception to this transformation of Mark's "messianic-secret via human misunderstanding" into Luke's "passion-secret via divine concealment" is in the introductory "L" material, 2:50. There Luke says that Mary and Joseph did not understand Jesus' question concerning his need to be ἐν τοῖς τοῦ πατρός μου. However, several factors prevent this exception from being particularly blatant.

Firstly, Jesus' response to his parents' question is itself extremely cryptic. The

---

[93] Wrede, *Secret*, pp. 95, 167, 172; Cadbury, *Style*, p. 107. The divine agency is made clear through the passive verbs and the ἵνα clause in 9:45; see George, "la mort de Jésus," pp. 206f; Schurmann, *Lukas*, p. 573; also Loisy, Rengstorf, Grundmann, Schmid, and Ernst on 9:45 and 18:34.

[94] Numerous explanations have been offered for the omission of Mk. 8:32ff: to improve the portrayal of the disciples (Cadbury, *Style*, p. 95; R. Brown [ed.], *Peter in the New Testament*, [Minneapolis, 1973], p. 111; Franklin, *Christ the Lord*, p. 59); because Jesus' ministry is a "Satan-free" period (Conzelmann, *Theology*); to diminish Peter's role and highlight the christological identification (E. Prevallet, *Luke 24:26: A Passover Christology*, unpublished Ph.D. dissertation, [Ann Arbor, 1968], p. 80). Wrede, *The Secret*, pp. 168f also observed Luke's omission of Peter's reproach; and while he did not make the connection explicit, he certainly made the proper implication by associating Luke's less reproachful treatment of the disciples with the "hiddenness" of the secret.

ambiguous nature of ἐν τοῖς τοῦ πατρός μου provides its own explanation for why Mary and Joseph fail to understand Jesus' meaning.[95] He is deliberately obscure.

Secondly, the meaning of at least half of the ambiguous phrase's interpretation, ie. "about my Father's business," while not referring exclusively to the necessity of Jesus' passion, does at least partially concern his future work at Calvary.[96] Thus even though Luke does not explicitly say that the meaning of Jesus' reply was hidden from his parents, both elements of Luke's divine concealment theme are nevertheless implied in the narrative: Jesus obscures the meaning of a reply which deals, in part, with his identity as the one who must suffer.

It becomes apparent that Luke has thoroughly reworked his material so as to eliminate all traces of merely human incomprehension from his secrecy theme. But this analysis has also shed light upon the second issue raised earlier: does Luke's secret concern only the passion? The answer is, No. Luke has introduced material which adds two further elements; firstly, the blindness of those other than the Twelve (19:42; 24:16); and secondly, it is not only the theological truth that the Christ must suffer which is hidden from individuals, but also the recognition, or identification, *of Jesus himself* as this messiah. This second level in Luke's treatment of his secrecy theme, which plays a pivotal role in the Emmaus story (Lk. 24:16, 19–27, 31), immediately recalls the connection forged elsewhere by Luke between God's work of hiding/revealing through Jesus' prayer-life on the one hand, and the unfolding presentation of Jesus' prayers as the means by which an individual acquires insight into the nature of his messiahship on the other. Since the meal at Emmaus constitutes the resolution of this theme in Luke's gospel, or at least it is the final occurrence of the language of divine concealment, it must be asked whether Jesus' prayer is involved here as it has been elsewhere?

## 4.3 The Meal at Emmaus and the Unveiling of the Secret (Lk. 24:13–35)

It is generally admitted that the recognition motif, framing the narrative as it does in vv. 16 and 31, is the central concern of the Emmaus story; and since this theme finds its resolution in the meal, vv. 29f are most commonly seen as the centre-

---

[95] Henk J. de Jonge, "Sonship, Wisdom, Infancy: Luke II. 41–51a," *NTS*. 24 ('78) 331–335 provides a good discussion of the deliberate ambiguity contained in Jesus' reply. The phrase probably means both "in my Father's house" and "about my Father's business." Also see F. D. Weinert, "The Multiple Meanings of Luke 2:49 and their Significance," *BTB*. 13 ('83) 19–22.

[96] de Jonge, "Sonship," p. 333.

piece of the story.[97] However, the means by which this motif is resolved is not so readily agreed upon. Some, following Wrede's discussion of the messianic secret, have assumed that a "secrecy theory" swept away by the resurrection characterises all of the gospels.[98] But whatever the implications for the other three gospels, this is not the case with Luke. The story of the empty tomb (24:1–12) underscores Luke's opinion that the fact of the resurrection does not of itself end the secret.[99] The Emmaus disciples, who had heard the women's report of the empty tomb and of the angels' words (vv. 9–11, 13), walk with the resurrected Jesus and are still prevented from recognising him. That Luke does not understand the resurrection, either as an event in itself or as the turning point between two eras, to be the significant factor in the unveiling of the secret is also indicated by his omission of Mk. 9:9 (cf. Lk. 9:36). For Luke, the disciples remain silent not out of obedience but out of divine concealment, and neither the resurrection alone nor its "evidences" are the conveyors of new insight.

Luke's reticence to attribute such an enlightening function to the resurrection has been perceived by others, who have offered a variety of alternative explanations. Thus the secret is alleviated by: the ascension;[100] Jesus' exposition of the

---

[97] This is generally true no matter what source, form, tradition, redactional, or structuralist techniques are used in analysing the pericope. See P. Schubert, "The Structure and Significance of Luke 24" in *Neutestamentliche Studien für Rudolf Bultmann*, (Berlin, 1954), pp. 173–176; Dillon, *Eye-Witnesses*, pp. 69–155; F. Schnider and W. Stenger, "Beobachtungen zur Struktur der Emmausperikope (Lk. 24, 13–35)" *BZ*. 16 ('72) 109f; X. Leon-Dufour, *Resurrection and the Message of Easter* (London, 1974), p. 163; J. Alsup, *The Post-Resurrection Appearance Stories of the Gospel Tradition*, (London, 1975), p. 196; B. van Iersel, "Terug van Emmaüs," *TijT*. 18 ('78) 294–323; O. K. Walther, "A Solemn One Way Trip Becomes a Joyous Roundtrip," *AshTJ*. 14 ('81) 65f; A. Delzant, "Les Disciples D'Emmaüs," *RSR*. 73 ('85) 177–186. After his thorough redactional analysis Wanke concludes that it is impossible to reconstruct the traditional sources for Luke's narrative; *Emmauserzählung*, pp. 23–126, especially pp. 109–114; "Brotbrechen," p. 181. Also see the discussion in Marshall, "The Resurrection of Jesus in Luke," *TynB*. 24 ('73) 75–91 showing the problems of the various source analyses.

[98] Wrede, *The Secret*, pp. 95, 184–220; J. Robinson, "On the 'Gattung' of Mark and John" in *Jesus and Man's Hope*, (Pittsburgh, 1970), pp. 108f; Franklin, *Christ the Lord*, p. 59; P. Minear, *To Heal and to Reveal: The Prophetic Vocation According to Luke*, (New York, 1976), p. 136; Conzelmann, *Theology*, p. 64, but cf. the statement concerning faith on pp. 93f n. 2. Conzelmann, "Gegenwart und Zukunft in der synoptischen Tradition," *ZTK*. 54 ('57) 295 has said that the secrecy theory, and by implication its resolution in the resurrection, is the "hermeneutische Voraussetzung" of the gospel genre.

[99] Dillon, *Eye-Witnesses*, pp. 18f, 25f; J. Kremer, *Die Osterbotschaft der vier Evangelien*, (Stüttgart, 1969), p. 60; Marshall, *Commentary*, pp. 888f; H. Anderson, "The Easter Witness of the Evangelists" in *The New Testament in Historical and Contemporary Perspective: Essays in Memory of G. H. C. Macgregor*, (Oxford, 1965), pp. 47f.

[100] Robinson, "Gattung," p. 113; Franklin, *Christ the Lord*, p. 31. Robinson is correct in perceiving that the secret persists even after the resurrection, but it is resolved, at least for the disciples, *before* the ascension.

Scriptures;[101] the personal presence of the risen Lord;[102] the willingness to pursue true discipleship;[103] or, finally, the meal shared with the disciples. Of all these alternatives only the last takes the role of vv. 30f, 35 seriously enough. These verses make it clear that *the meal* is the point at which the secret is revealed, and this would be the majority opinion among scholars today. But this then raises the further question of what it was about the meal which facilitated the disciples' insight. Some have said it was a unique feature of Jesus' mannerism, or the wording of his prayer at the table which sparked the disciples' recognition.[104] However, this explanation continues to misinterpret the issue as one merely of human incomprehension.[105] In addition, it is difficult to believe that such an important theological theme as this would find its resolution in the peculiar mannerisms of Jesus' eating habits; and if mannerisms were the real issue, it is strange that Jesus was not recognised earlier during the journey.

More frequently Luke's use of the phrase "the breaking of the bread" has led to a eucharistic explanation of the passage.[106] That is, Luke intends his reader to see in this shared meal a representation of the spiritual encounter which takes place between Christ and the Christian each time one participates in the church's

---

[101] Schubert, "The Structure," pp. 176f; B. Koet, "Some Traces of a Semantic Field of Interpretation in Luke 24, 13–35," *Bijdragen.* 46 ('85) 60, 70f; Fitzmyer, *The Gospel,* vol. II, p. 1558; Hamm, "Vision as Metaphor," p. 475. However, Luke has made it clear that the blindness in not an issue of incomprehension in need of clarification through instruction (*pace* Fitzmyer); note that the disciples do not even reflect upon the significance of Jesus' instruction until *after* the revelation. Those explanations which would want to associate the instruction with Jesus' actions at the meal – Jesus revealed in "word and act," perhaps articulated in the light of early church liturgy – suffer at this very point; for example see W. Manson, *The Gospel,* p. 268; R. Orlett, "Influence of the Early Liturgy upon the Emmaus Account," *CBQ.* 21 ('59) 212–219; P. Hebblethwaite, "Theological Themes in the Lucan Post-Resurrection Narratives," *ClRev.* 50 ('65) 365; Marshall, "The Resurrection," p. 81; *Last Supper and Lord's Supper,* (Exeter, 1980), p. 126.

[102] Plevnik, "Easter Faith," p. 504; Dillon, *Eye-Witnesses,* pp. 133f. Plevnik argues for this interpretation in light of v. 24. However, this is clearly impossible in light of vv. 15ff! These two disciples, even though they "see" Jesus, *still* do not "see" him any more than did the women!

[103] J. Gibbs, "Luke 24:13–35 and Acts 8:26–39: The Emmaus Incident and the Eunuch's Baptism as Parallel Stories," *BangTF.* 7 ('75) 22, 29. In addition to the weakness of the parallel with Acts 8, upon which this interpretation is based, also observe that the revelation does not take place while the disciples are "walking in the Way."

[104] T. Schermann, "Das 'Brotbrechen' im Urchristentum," *BZ.* 8 ('10) 46; Plummer, *St. Luke,* p. 557; G. Dalman, *Jesus-Jeshua,* (London, 1929), p. 136; Lagrange, *Luc,* p. 609; Audet, "Literary Forms," p. 651; Hunter, *The Prayers of Jesus,* p. 101.

[105] Cf. Schmid, *Das Evangelium,* pp. 356, 359; Ernst, *Das Evangelium,* pp. 659, 663f.

[106] The literature is immense; see J. Dupont, "Les pèlerins d'Emmaus (Luc XXIV, 13–35)" in *Miscellanea Biblica B. Ubach,* (Montserrat, 1953), pp. 349–374; an English translation is found in "The Meal at Emmaus" in *The Eucharist in the New Testament,* (London, 1964), see especially pp. 116ff; "Le Repas D'Emmaüs" *LumV.* 31 ('57) 87ff; H. Betz, "The Origin and Nature of Christian Faith According to the Emmaus Legend," *Int.* 23 ('69) 39; P. Benoit, *The Passion and Resurrection of Jesus Christ,* (New York, 1969), pp. 279–281; Dillon, *Eye-Witnessess;* J. Wanke, *Beobachtungen zum Eucharistieverständis des Lukas auf Grund der lukanischen Mahl Berichte,* (Leipzig, 1973), pp. 31–44, especially p. 41; *Emmauserzählung,* p. 116; "Brotbrechen," pp. 183f.

memorial celebration at the common meal. The strength of this interpretation is that it gives proper place to the pivotal role of bread-breaking in the narrative. But would it not be strange for this event to be reminiscent of the Last Supper, a meal at which these two disciples were not present, a fact which again eliminates the possibility of their recognising some unique mannerism, when the following pericope concerning the eleven who *were* present at the Last Supper has absolutely no hint of any eucharistic significance?[107] This dislocation is particularly odd in light of the emphasis upon recognition in the Emmaus pericope. Neither is there any indication in Luke that Jesus' frequent meals with sinners, at which his habits might have been observed, were important for an understanding of the significance of either the Lord's Supper or the appearance stories.[108] Thus the question poses itself, is it really so clear that Luke intends the Emmaus story to be read eucharistically?

### 4.3.1 "We Recognised Him in the 'Breaking of the Bread'..."

Most advocates of the eucharistic interpretation would argue that the Emmaus meal simply portrays Luke's eucharistic reinterpretation of what was originally a simple supper. It need not be read as Jesus' repetition of the Last Supper; rather, Luke has taken the language of the Last Supper, which in Acts eventually becomes the technical designation for the Christian eucharist (Acts 2:42, 46; 20:7, 11; 27:35), and projected it back into this event so as to communicate what he perceives to be the theological significance of the eucharist, ie. the presence of Christ in the breaking of the bread.[109] Since Jeremias' investigations into the Rabbinic uses of the phrase "the breaking of the bread" have established, or so the argument goes, that this term refers only to the opening ceremony of the common meal and was never used to designate the meal in its entirety,[110] and since it clearly does have such a wholistic meaning in Luke-Acts, it therefore cannot carry the customary Jewish

---

[107] Alsup, *Post-Resurrection*, p. 198 n. 566 calls this "something of a riddle to the Eucharistic position:" also cf. Lagrange, *Luc*, p. 609; B. P. Robinson, "The Place of the Emmaus Story in Luke-Acts," *NTS.* 30 ('84) 487.

[108] Alsup, *Post-Resurrection*, p. 199; Bowen, "Emmaus Disciples," p. 239. The arguments of those such as E. Lohmeyer, *Galiläa und Jerusalem*, (Göttingen, 1936) and H. Lietzmann, *Mass and Lord's Supper*, (Leiden, 1979), pp. 204–215, in favour of a continuity between the meals of the earthly Jesus and the eucharist depend upon conceptual arguments concerning the tradition; there are, however, no obvious linguistic associations made within Luke-Acts. For a discussion of Cullmann's thesis ("Lord's Supper") connecting the Lord's Supper with Jesus' post-resurrection meals, see Marshall, *Last Supper*, pp. 131–133.

[109] C. Bowen, "The Emmaus Disciples and the Purposes of Luke," *BW.* 35 ('10) 239; O. Cullmann, "The Meaning of the Lord's Supper in Primitive Christianity" in *Essays on the Lord's Supper*, (London, 1958), pp. 12f, 19; R. Orlett, "The Breaking of Bread in Acts," *BT.* 1 ('62) 108–113; Fitzmyer, *The Gospel*, vol. II, p. 1559; cf. also Marshall, *Commentary*, p. 900; Dupont, "The Meal," p. 121.

[110] J. Jeremias, *The Eucharistic Words of Jesus*, (London, 1966), pp. 109, 174 n. 3, 4; "..(this phrase) never refers to a whole meal but only (a) the action of tearing the bread, and (b) the rite with which the meal opened..." (p. 120). This claim shall be investigated later in this study.

sense. In determining an alternative meaning the real question then becomes, what would the expression have meant to Luke and his Gentile audience when used in a Christian setting?

In spite of its popularity, this eucharistic interpretation of the Emmaus meal faces substantial difficulties:

1) The cardinal theme of the narrative is not "presence" but "recognition" (cf. v. 16 μὴ ἐπιγνῶναι αὐτόν; v. 31 καὶ ἐπέγνωσαν αὐτόν; v. 35 ὡς ἐγνώσθη αὐτοῖς).[111] This fact is highlighted by the continued employment of Luke's seeing motif, evident in v. 24. The irony of this statment makes the significance of the eventual recognition unavoidable. Though this observation may not seem pertinent for those who make no connection between the eucharist and the presence of Christ, it is very relevant for those (largely Roman Catholic) scholars who do.

2) If Luke were trying to illustrate a connection between the meal and Jesus' presence, he has certainly gone about it in an unconvincing manner. For Jesus is present with the disciples *before* the meal, and then *leaves* them quite abruptly at the beginning of the meal, just at that point where one would expect some reference to meal fellowship. When he is present he is unrecognised; and when he is recognised he is no longer present. Such a vanishing Christ is a strange way to show his presence at the eucharist![112]

3) In light of this, what if the Emmaus story *did* concern itself with the meaning of the eucharist? What would it then mean? It would have to be saying that the eucharist leads to the recognition of Jesus' true identity. But is this possible?

First of all, there is no indication of such an appreciation of the eucharist anywhere else in Luke-Acts:

a) At the Last Supper the disciples still fail to recognise the role which Jesus is undertaking; and what little understanding they may already possess has not been brought to them through the meal (cf. Lk. 9:18ff).

b) Similarly, those instances in Acts which might be amenable to a eucharistic interpretation (2:42, 46; 20:7, 11) describe the assembling together of those who

---

[111] This point is well argued by Schnider and Stenger, "Beobachtungen," pp. 107–112; though their explanation of the meal as being symbolic of "fellowship within the community of Jesus" (cf. vv. 13–15, 29f, 31b) falters upon the absence of any obvious communal emphasis in these verses. Also see Dodd, "The Appearances of the Risen Christ" in *Studies in the Gospels*, (Oxford, 1957), p. 14; Marshall, "The Resurrection," p. 82; Alsup, *Post-Resurrection*, p. 196.

[112] Dupont ("The Meal") betrays his own awareness of this difficulty when he initially emphasises the moment of Jesus' recognition, ie. "... here is where we find the *theological intent* of the story" (pp. 110, 116, emphasis mine), but then inexplicably shifts the point to presence in his final conclusion. Attempts to find refuge in an "invisible presence" are merely reading ideas into the text; for example see J. Mouson, "Présence du Ressuscite: Les récits évangéliques d'apparitions," *CMCSE*, 54 ('69) 178–204, especially p. 198; F. Wulf, "Sie erkannten ihn beim Brechen des Brotes (Lk. 24,35)," *GL.* 37 ('64) 81f. Plummer's observation (*St. Luke*, p. 559) that it is the breaking, and not the partaking, which occasions their recognition should be remembered; *pace* Betz, "The Origin and Nature," p. 37.

have already recognised Jesus as the Christ; they are clearly instances of fellowship among the brethren.[113]

c) The one possible exception to this observation (Acts 27:35) gives no hint of any crew-members recognising Christ through the meal. In fact, there is no

---

[113] Contrary to strict Rabbinic usage, there are instances in Acts where "breaking bread" refers to the entire process of sharing a meal together. A Rabbinic sense in 2:42 would give the redundant meaning of "they devoted themselves to the apostles' teaching and the fellowship, to 'prayer' and to prayer." "Sharing food" in 2:46 requires the same extension of meaning there, designating the whole of a common meal; cf. Haenchen, *Acts*, pp. 191f; C. Callewaert, "La synaxe eucharistique a Jérusalem, berceau du dimanche," *ETL*. (Feb.,'38) 56ff.

Similarly in Acts 20:7 and 11, the church's gathering "on the first day of the week" to "break bread" does not necessarily refer to more than a particular instance of what was otherwise done regularly (καθ' ἡμέραν) in individual homes (κατ' οἶκον; 2:46). The description of Paul κλάσας τὸν ἄρτον καὶ γευσάμενος would suggest either: a) breaking bread is being used in its traditional sense of "saying the blessing," ie. Paul blessed the meal and ate it; or b) the two participles are placed in apposition, the second making clear what has already been established as the meaning of bread breaking, ie. they ate a meal together. Pace F. F. Bruce, *The Acts of the Apostles*, (Grand Rapids, 1951), p. 372, the presence or absence of the article (τὸν ἄρτον) does not appear to be significant to Luke (cf. Lk. 22:19; Acts 2 :46; 20:7 where it is absent; and Lk. 24:30, 35; Acts 2:42; 20:11 where it is present). To read the second clause as descriptive of the agape meal, while the first describes the eucharist, is overly subtle. If ἐφ' ἱκανόν (v. 11) may be taken with γευσάμενος rather than ὁμιλήσας, thus forming a structural parallel with κλάσας τὸν ἄρτον, and reading "breaking the bread and eating sufficiently," then this would offer further, though not essential, proof that the blessing precedes a fellowship meal. Such a translation hinges upon the position of the enclitic τε. Though a correlative τε would normally appear in second position, there is a clear example of its being misplaced and appearing first in Acts 26:22. Could it also be "misplaced" here? Cf. N. Turner, *A Grammar of New Testament Greek*, (Edinburgh, 1963), vol. III, p. 339. In addition, the way in which the eating is decidedly overshadowed by Paul's teaching, as if the breaking bread were incidental, and the fact that Paul's participation in the meal receives only a passing mention also make a eucharistic interpretation rather dubious; cf. Schermann, "Brotbrechen," p. 172; Robinson, "Emmaus Story," p. 492. Note also that γεύομαι is never used elsewhere, either by Luke or Paul, of the Lord's Supper (cf. I Cor. 11: 26f).

Didache 10:1 indicates that the common meal remained a *prior* part of the eucharistic celebration (*pace*, Lietzmann, *Mass*, pp. 189f), demonstrating that the phrases περὶ δὲ τοῦ κλάσματος (Did. 9:3) and τὸ κλάσμα (Did. 9:4) refer, not to the elements proper, but to *the entirety of the shared meal before the Lord's Supper* (so also G. H. Box, "The Jewish Antecedents of the Eucharist," *JTS*. 3 ('02) 366f, 389; even though he also places the eucharist proper before the agape meal, Box understands Did. 10:1 to refer to the entirety of both the agape and eucharist). In the absence of any compelling evidence to the contrary, it is reasonable to assume that in Acts the phrase either retains its more original and more limited Jewish sense, or the sense found in the Didache, rather than the later sacramental specification. The above arguments indicate why it is a mistake to identify κοινωνία in Acts 2:42 with the agape, as Jeremias does, and conclude from this that the final separation between agape and eucharist had occurred by the time of Acts (cf. *Eucharistic Words*, pp. 120f). Schermann, "Brotbrechen," pp. 166–169 rightly argues that it is the breaking of bread, ie. eating together, and the prayers which constitute the "fellowship" enjoyed.

Did. 14:1 (κατὰ κυριακήν δὲ Κυρίου συναχθέντες κλάσατε ἄρτον καὶ εὐχαριστήσατε), particularly in light of the previous discussion concerning Did. 9:3f and 10:1, probably refers to the agape meal, regardless of whether it preceded the eucharist, which had become regularly held on Sunday; cf. J. Behm, "κλάω," *TDNT*. vol. III, pp. 730f.

indication anywhere in Luke-Acts that the eucharist was ever used evangelistically by the early church.[114]

d) It also needs to be asked if the presence of Christ ever constitutes the significance of the eucharist elsewhere in Luke-Acts? This is doubtful. There may be room for such concepts as remembrance, fellowship, or expectation, but there appears to be little if any evidence for mystical presence.[115]

Secondly, elsewhere Luke has consistently associated his recognition theme with prayer. This important observation should be kept in mind as the present argument progresses towards the alternative interpretation of the breaking of bread to be discussed below. The pertinent question at this point becomes one of whether there is any reason to suspect that the prayers of Jesus are operative in the story?

It must be concluded that, whatever else one decides about the use of the phrase "the breaking of bread" in Acts, its use in Lk. 24:30, 35 does not require that the narrative be read eucharistically; in fact, there are some very reasonable arguments against it.

### 4.3.2 The Jewish Sense of "Breaking" and Luke 24

At several points there has been occasion to refer to the traditional Jewish meaning of the phrase "the breaking of bread." What was that meaning?

The Jewish ritual for opening a meal was a well established rite.[116] Though there was some discussion as to which blessings should be offered on which occasions (m. Ber. 6:1; Tos. Ber. 6.14,15), and the exact moment at which the bread was to be broken (b. Ber. 39a, b), the general outline of the proceeding was consistent. The host took the loaf of bread in his hands and offered a prayer of thanksgiving to God. The guests participated in this blessing by responding with a communal "Amen," which bound the group together in table fellowship under God. Only

---

[114] Cf. Didache 9:5, where it is evident that the early church limited attendance at even the agape meal. The arguments of B. Reicke, "Die Mahlzeit die Paulus und der Wellen die Mittelmeeres," *TZ.* 4 ('48) 409; Ph. H. Menoud, "Les Actes des Apôtres et l'Eucharistie," *RHPhR.* 33 ('53) 33; D. M. Stanley, "Liturgical Influences on the Formation of the Four Gospels," *CBQ.* 21 ('59) 33; and Wanke, *Eucharistieverstandnis*, pp. 28–30, in favour of a eucharistic "prefiguration" in preparation for future Christian discipleship are not justified; cf. Haenchen, *Acts*, p. 707; Marshall, *The Acts of the Apostles*, (Grand Rapids, 1980), p. 413; Bruce, *Acts*, p. 465; Robinson, "Emmaus Story," p. 492.
Actually, the three-fold process of (1) λαβὼν ἄρτον, (2) εὐχαρίστησεν τῷ θεῷ, (3) κλάσας simply designates the traditional ceremony which begins a Jewish meal (thus ἤρξατο ἐσθέειν, v. 36). The emphasis upon subsequently "eating until they were full" (vv. 36, 38) substantiates this.

[115] *Pace* P. Benoit, *The Passion and Resurrection of Jesus Christ*, (New York, 1969), p. 279. Marshall, *Last Supper*, pp. 128f discusses (the possibility of) "presence," but only in light of the Emmaus story, which has already been shown to be impossible.

[116] See Dalman, *Jesus-Jeshua*, p. 135–137; Jeremias, *Eucharistic Words*, pp. 175ff, 232; K. Kuhn, "The Lord's Supper and the Communal Meal at Qumran" in *The Scrolls and the New Testament*, (London, 1958), p. 81; also Lietzmann, *Mass*, pp. 168–170 for a discussion of the similarities between the Christian Agape and Jewish common meals.

then would the host break the bread and distribute the pieces (b. Ber. 47a). The guests would not begin to eat until the host had taken a bite of his bread (b. Ber. 47a). Then, at the end of the meal, one of those present would be called upon to offer a concluding prayer (b. Ber. 46a). The term consistently used to describe this opening ritual was "the breaking;" a reference to the bread was optional. By a process of metonymy this final action in the series came to designate the whole procedure; but since the whole was understood as a single act of prayer, "breaking the bread" was synonymous with pronouncing the prayer of blessing.[117] One of the clearest examples of this is found in b. R. H. 29b, a section discussing the proper recitation of the meal blessing: "Our Rabbis taught: A man should not break (bread) for visitors unless he eats with them..." It is clear that what is actually being referred to is the prayer which the host would normally offer before a meal with his guests. The language of "breaking"[118] is being used *in lieu* of an expression such as "to recite the blessing." The ruling is that a host may not *pray* over a meal in which he will not participate (an exception being the meals of household members, at which he may pray for the purposes of religious instruction).

The scene at Emmaus fits this custom exactly. Verse 30 says that as Jesus sat at the table with the two disciples:

$$λαβὼν τὸν ἄρτον$$
$$εὐλόγησεν$$
$$καὶ κλάσας (αὐτὸν)$$
$$ἐπεδίδου αὐτοῖς$$

This is a description of the typical opening of a Jewish meal. Two conclusions follow:

1) Here is evidence for both the Palestinian origin of the tradition lying behind Luke's Emmaus pericope, and his faithfulness to at least this element of that source.

2) The summary phrase used by the disciples in v. 35, ἐν τῇ κλάσει τοῦ ἄρτου, must then be read as referring back to this ceremony, which was understood as *a single act of prayer*. The breaking is the recitation of the meal blessing, together with the act of breaking. In other words, for these disciples to say that they were

---

[117] Schermann, "Brotbrechen," p. 42: "Mag mit dem Worte 'Brotbrechen' in jüdischer Zeit der Brotsegen als untrennbar gedacht worden sein..." (It seems to me that in Jewish times the words of 'breaking bread' were thought to be inseparable from the meal blessing...); Behm "κλάω," p. 729 n. 7: "As a term the breaking of bread may cover both the distribution *and the preceding grace* (cf. j. Ber. 10a, 12a)." (emphasis mine); Jeremias, *Eucharistic Words*, p. 109: "... we know, from rabbinical literature (these words) as technical terms for the *grace at table before the meal*." (emphasis mine); 176 n. 3: "He gave him a loaf of bread that he might break it. He said, 'Take (the bread) and *say grace*.'" (j. Ber. 8.12a, 45) (emphasis mine); p. 174 n. 3: "He takes the bread and pronounces the blessing over it." (j. Ber. 6.10a, 9; 6.10a, 45).

[118] Notice that the object "bread" is simply understood; for the Hebrew text see L. Goldschmidt, *Der Babylonische Talmud*, (Berlin, 1897–1909), vol. III, p. 378. Goldschmidt's translation also interprets "the breaking" (Brot anbrechen) as "zum Segenspruch."

caused to recognise Jesus "in the breaking of the bread" is tantamount to saying that he was made known to them *while he was at prayer.*

### 4.3.3 "He was made known to us as he prayed"

The controlling dynamics of the Emmaus story are in perfect accord with reading the resolution of Luke's secrecy theme as having taken place in an act of prayer. The disciples do not recognise Jesus because they are prevented from doing so (ἐκρατοῦντο τοῦ μὴ ἐπεγνῶναι αὐτόν, v. 16).[119] When they do "see" it is not through their own perception, but by God's revelation (αὐτῶν δὲ διηνοίχθησαν οἱ ὀφθαλμοί, v. 31; ὡς ἐγνώσθη αὐτοῖς, v. 35). What it is that they come to recognise offers the unification of the two levels of Luke's secrecy theme, discussed earlier in this chapter.

Firstly, they receive instruction from the Resurrected One about the necessity of his suffering and death. Previously, this has been hidden from the disciples (9:45; 18:34); and even now remains temporarily hidden from these two. They do not even reflect upon the effect of Jesus' teaching along the way, let alone understand its relation to him, until after they recognise him. Once the teaching has become clear to them, however, they find that, rather than deny their prophetic understanding of the messiah (v. 19), it merely clarifies that the messiah must be the final, *suffering* Prophet.[120]

Secondly, these two disciples have also been prevented from recognising Jesus himself. This blindness in the face of the "obvious" does not serve the purposes of some dogma concerning the transformation of the resurrection body; it once again presents, in paradigmatic form, the blindness concerning Jesus' true identity, which has characterised numerous figures throughout Luke's gospel: John the Baptist, Herod, the crowds, the disciples, the pharisees and other leaders of the nation. Elsewhere, the solution to this blindness has been Jesus' prayers.

Consequently, both levels of Luke's passion secret are illuminated at Emmaus. The disciples are allowed to "recognise" Jesus, and in so doing they also come to recognise exactly who he is as the messiah.[121] It is at this point, in the sovereign lifting of the veil of secrecy, that they also perceive the significance of Jesus'

---

[119] Plummer, *St. Luke*, p. 552.

[120] Dillon, *Eye-Witnesses*, pp. 122f. Luke confirms the legitimacy of their expectations elsewhere in Acts; cf. the language in Lk. 24:19 with similar expressions in Acts 7:22, 25, 27, 35, 37; and Acts 2:22 with 7:36. Also see chapter 7.

[121] The passion secret is not completely resolved at Emmaus. It is the first time that the Father has allowed the disciples to understand Jesus' instruction about the scriptural necessity of a suffering messiah. At this level, then, Wrede's idea that the secret finds resolution after the resurrection is correct; and this is why the language of "it was hidden from them" disappears from Luke's second volume. But the second, historical/existential level of Luke's passion secret, wherein an individual comes to perceive *Jesus of Nazareth* as this messiah, continues to operate in the book of Acts. The metaphorical use of seeing/hearing language demonstrates its presence, especially in such features as Paul's blindness (9:8, 17f), Paul's selection "to see" God's Son (22:14),

teaching from the Scriptures (v. 32). It is not the opening of the Scriptures which opens their eyes; it is the opening of their eyes which causes them to perceive the meaning of the Scriptures (ὡς διήνοιγεν ἡμῖν τὰς γραφάς, v. 32), just as they have come to perceive Jesus.

At every point, the movement of the Emmaus story relates to those very issues which have been shown to be essential to the proper understanding of the revelatory role of Jesus' prayers in the gospel of Luke: in connection with one of his prayers, Jesus' true messianic identity is revealed to men. The fact that the prayer was one of thanksgiving over a meal, rather than petitionary or intercessory, is not an insurmountable obstacle. Luke has already demonstrated that God is able to sovereignly respond to prayer in the way which he deems proper whether or not this action was specifically requested (Lk. 9:28ff); and elsewhere contentless prayer notices have been used to depict the revelatory significance of Jesus' prayer. If, as will be argued more extensively in a later section of this work, Luke understands prayer as an open channel of communication between God and man whereby God can fulfill his own purposes in the world, and if, as is clear in Luke elsewhere, one of God's chief purposes for Jesus' prayer-life is to use it as a means of revealing his messianic identity to men, then the interpretation suggested here for the Emmaus story is in perfect keeping with Luke's overall theology of prayer. Consequently, it may even be possible that Luke intends his reader to understand the ἐν plus the dative in v. 35 both temporally, on a historical level, and instrumentally, on a literary level. In other words: "Jesus was revealed to us ... while he 'prayed'/by means of his 'prayer.'"

Of course, one might want to ask why Luke does not make this point more explicitly. However, for these two disciples to have openly referred to Jesus' prayer would have misplaced the focal point of their new understanding. What Luke can say and what the characters in his story can say are two different things. They have come to understand *who* Jesus is, but they do not perceive *how* this new insight has been achieved. This confusion is evident in the bewildered musings of v. 32. The revelatory effect of Jesus' prayer-life is not perceived by any of the disciples in the gospel; it would have been out of place for Luke to write, "we recognised him ἐν τῷ προσεύχεσθαι αὐτόν." But once the prior unfolding of Luke's secrecy and prayer themes, together with their interrelationships, are understood what Luke has actually written serves admirably. "In the breaking of bread" is an appropriate expression for these disciples to make in this context. It is an adequate description of what has happened to them; and, for the perceptive reader, their simultaneous penetration of the messianic secret is pregnant with additional significance.

---

and the description of Paul's ministry as one of "opening the eyes of the Gentiles" (26:18). For an individual "to see" that Jesus of Nazareth is the messiah is as much a result of divine revelation in Acts as it is in the gospel (cf. Acts. 13:48; 16:14; 26:16).

## 4.4 Conclusion

One of the commendable aspects of the eucharistic interpretation of the Emmaus story is the motivation often lying behind it to relate the gospel narratives to the present experience of the church.[122] Rejecting the eucharistic understanding of Lk. 24:13–35 does not devalue this concern. The challenge of recognising Jesus as the messiah, and the means by which such spiritual illumination can take place, are ever contemporary concerns. Luke's solution, found in the prayers of Christ, implies the continuing relevance of his prayers long before the reader comes to Luke's story of the church's experience in Acts.

The scope of these prayers' influence is also expanding. Jesus' prayers have been found to mediate the revelation of his messiahship (Lk. 9:18 ff; 28 ff; 10 f:21–24; 23:34 ff; 24:13 ff), but now they are also seen to effect the forgiveness of sin, the salvation of God and the resulting promise of a future life with Christ in paradise (Lk. 23:34–49). To this list the Emmaus story now adds the illumination of the Scriptures. Luke is attaching an ever-widening range of spiritual activity, all of which is essential for Christian discipleship, to the revelatory significance of Jesus' prayer-life.

---

[122] Cf. R. F. O'Toole, "Activity of the Risen Jesus in Luke-Acts," *Bib.* 62 ('81) 482f.

Chapter 5

# The Phenomenon of Prayer and the Experience of Jesus

## Introduction

Now that we have completed the discussion of those passages in Luke which attach a self-revelatory significance to Jesus' prayers, attention should be turned to two other important features of Jesus' prayer-life. Firstly, prayer as an avenue for the experience of spiritual realities. Secondly, and more specifically, prayer as a guiding element in the course of Jesus' ministry. With only one exception (Lk. 22:31 f), all of the remaining prayer texts in Luke relate to one or the other, or even both, of these issues. A good deal of the material in Acts is relevant as well; why the experience of Jesus and the early church should coincide at these points will be discussed at greater length in a later section of this chapter.

The point of departure for the present discussion will be, appropriately enough, the baptismal scene in Lk. 3:21–22, which presents not only the first of Luke's redactional notices portraying Jesus' prayer habit, but also expresses both of the themes at issue in this chapter. The goal of the discussion will not be a thorough explanation of the whole of the passage, but only a look at the role played by prayer.

## 5.1 Prayer and the Experience of Spiritual Communication

### 5.1.1 Jesus' Baptism (Lk. 3:21–22)

It would be difficult to overlook the striking differences between Luke's account of Jesus' baptism and that of Mark.[1] The presence of all the people, the addition of Jesus' prayer, and the bodily descent of the dove are all unique to Luke, and each of them has a role to play in defining the theological significance of the scene. How Jesus' baptism relates to that of all the people (v. 21) is not easily decided, although

---

[1] As noted elsewhere, source considerations need not detain the progress of this literary analysis. Comparison with Mark is simply useful for highlighting Luke's distinctiveness. However, for the sake of discussion, it does appear more likely that Luke heavily redacted Mark than to posit a separate baptismal narrative in "Q": 1) Caird's argument from Lukan doublets may not be so confidently extended as to justify hypothetical doublets elsewhere (G. B. Caird, *St. Luke*, [Middlesex, 1963], pp. 24 f); 2) the small agreements betweem Luke and Matthew against Mark may be explained as simply coincidental (G. O. Williams, "The Baptism in Luke's Gospel," *JTS* 45['44]32); cf. Schürmann, *Lukas*, p. 197; *pace* Grundmann, *Das Evangelium*, pp. 106 f).

the weight of the grammatical arguments tilts the balance towards Jesus' being baptised after the people.[2] However, what is more clear is that Luke's use of the aorist articular infinitive (ἐν τῷ βαπτισθῆναι) followed by two genitive absolutes, one in the aorist ('Ιησοῦ βαπτισθέντος) and the other in the present tense (καὶ προσευχομένου), achieves several important ends.

Firstly, the focus of the story is no longer Jesus' baptism alone, but also the accompanying prayer which was ongoing after the baptism.[3]

Secondly, this places the opening of heaven (ἀνεῳχθῆναι τὸν οὐρανὸν) and the subsequent phenomena – the descent of the Spirit (καταβῆναι τὸ πνεῦμα) and the voice from heaven (φωνὴν ἐξ οὐρανοῦ γενέσθαι) – at the heart of the scene's activity.[4]

Thirdly, it emphasises that these phenomena are correlated with Jesus' prayer rather than only his baptism.[5] In fact, the realignment of the narrative is so complete that Lk. 3:21f is no longer an account of Jesus' baptism at all, but a portrayal of what God does as Jesus prays.[6]

The obvious question becomes, why does Luke mention prayer at this juncture in his story? But this question is subsidiary to the larger question concerning the entirety of Luke's pericope and its relationship to subsequent material in the gospel. The characteristics which make Luke's story *Luke's*, and not Mark's or Matthew's, are all of one piece. Therefore, how one answers the question about prayer will be related to how one answers these other questions concerning the narrative as a whole. One thing is certain, however. Luke's version of the baptism has done more than simply introduce prayer into a "significant" point in Jesus' life; it has forged a direct relationship between the act of prayer and the following events, for it was "while Jesus was praying that the heavens opened, the Holy Spirit descended bodily . . . and a voice came from heaven . . ."

This connection raises a further question about the nature of the relationship between Jesus' prayer and these subsequent events. It has been shown that, at least

---

[2] Cf. the discussion in chapter 3; Plummer reaches this conclusion after surveying Luke's use of the aorist elsewhere; *St. Luke*, p. 98. S. Case, "The Circumstances of Jesus' Baptism: An Exposition of Luke 3:21," *BW*. 31 ('08) 301 f concludes that the time element cannot be determined. E. D. Burton says that while the aorist tense prevents the baptisms from being coterminous, the preposition prevents them from being distinctly separated; *Syntax of the Moods and Tenses in New Testament Greek*, (Edinburgh, 1898), p. 51 para. 109; but cf. *BDF*. para. 404 (2). Thus is remains possible to think of John as absent from the prayer scene.

[3] L. Keck, "Jesus' Entrance Upon His Mission," *RevExp*. 64 ('67) 427; Plummer, *St. Luke*, p. 98; I. de la Potterie, "L'onction du Christ. Etude de théologie biblique," *NRT*. 80 ('58) 225–232, 234.

[4] Case, "The Circumstances of Jesus' Baptism," pp. 301 f; Feldkämper, *Der betende Jesus*, p. 39; Williams, "Luke's Baptism," p. 34.

[5] Creed, *The Gospel*, p. 57; Harris, *Prayer*, pp. 37–39. This remains true even if one insists that Luke does not temporally separate the reception of the Spirit from the baptism; cf. M. Turner, "Jesus and the Spirit in Lucan Perspective," *TB*. 32 ('81) 11 n. 39.

[6] Schweizer, *Luke*, pp. 79f. Case, "The Circumstances of Jesus' Baptism," p. 302 shows that the import of προσευχομένου is not that Jesus prayed during his baptism, but that he was at prayer at the time of the vision.

at some points, Luke understands prayer to be an avenue through which spiritual insight and/or revelation is received. Furthermore, the exact nature of this insight, at least where Jesus' own person is concerned, has to do with his messianic status as the final, suffering Prophet and Son of God. The association of prayer with supernatural phenomena in 3:21f is commensurate with this Lukan tendency. Being the first example of Jesus at prayer, it is not unreasonable to expect that this account will exhibit some relevance to the function of Jesus' prayers elsewhere in Luke. To what extent are these already elucidated functions to be found in Lk. 3:21–22?

### 5.1.1.1 "Seeing" and "Hearing" at the Baptism

It is generally recognised that Luke has objectified the various events associated with Jesus' baptism, the point being that this was not merely a subjective, vision-ary experience on Jesus' part, but a real, observable event.[7] Luke's omission of Mark's εἶδεν, which could perhaps suggest that only Jesus saw these phenomena, and his inclusion of the Spirit's descent σωματικῷ εἴδει make this plain. And whatever the possibility of an adverbial meaning being attached to ὡς περιστερ-ὰν in Mark (1:10), there can be little doubt that Luke's phrasing entails a clearly adjectival sense.[8] Although it has been suggested that Luke introduces the element of Jesus' prayer as his own way of retaining the event's subjective nature,[9] this does not deal adequately with the force of the bodily form of the dove. In fact, Luke's objectivisation of this event is so thorough that this itself should be understood as the explanation for his use of ὡς περιστερὰν ἐπ' αὐτόν rather than the Markan εἰς αὐτόν. Whatever the explanation for Matthew's coincidental agreement here it would have been clear to Luke that doves in bodily form do not enter into people! Alighting upon Jesus is exactly what a real dove would be expected to do.[10]

In view of this visual objectivisation of spiritual realities, there is nothing standing in the way of understanding the voice from heaven as equally objective; indeed, the context in no way excludes the possibility of this and even seems to

---

[7] F. Lentzen-Deis, *Die Taufe Jesu nach de Synoptikern*, (Frankfurt, 1970), p. 51; R. Collins, "Luke 3:21–22, Baptism or Anointing?," *BT.* 84 ('76) 825; H. Braun, "Entscheidende Motive in den Berichten über die Taufe Jesu von Markus bis Justin," *ZTK.* 50 ('53) 40f; Marshall, *Commentary*, p. 152; Fitzmyer, *The Gospel*, vol. II, p. 481; Schürmann, *Lukas*, p. 190. Turner disagrees, arguing that the bodily descent of the Spirit is no more in view here than is a physical sheet in Acts 10:11. This might be true of the common phrase "the heavens opened" were all that was said in Lk. 3:21f. But Acts 10:11 has no counterpart to the σωματικῷ in Lk. 3:22; see Turner, "Jesus and the Spirit," p. 12; "Spirit Endowment in Luke/Acts: Some Linguistic Considerations," *VE.* 12 ('81) 50.

[8] Schürmann, *Lukas*, p. 190; Marshall, *Commentary*, p. 153. The possible theological signifi-cance of the dove remains a mystery for interpreters, and in any case need not be decided for the progress of this study. For a discussion of the problems and the history of interpretation see L. Keck, "The Spirit and the Dove," *NTS.* 17 ('70–71) 41–67; Lentzen-Deis, *Die Taufe*, pp. 170–183; A. Feuillet, "Le symbolisme de la colombe dans les récits évangéliques du baptême," *RSR.* 46 ('58) 524–544.

[9] Greeven, *Gebet*, p. 21.

[10] *Pace* Lentzen-Deis, *Die Taufe*, p. 51.

suggest it. There is nothing intrinsic to an address in the second person which would prevent it from being overheard. The descent (καταβῆναι) of a visible dove in fact creates the expectation of the utterance (γενέσθαι) of an audible voice. The scene, then, describes both a seeing and a hearing event as Jesus prays.

Whether or not every aspect of this event was witnessed by all, it was both a seeing and hearing event for Jesus, and it would at least have been visible, even if not audible, to the bystanders. Luke's specific mention of ἄπαντα τὸν λαὸν, whether Jesus was baptised with or after them, places "the people" at the scene, just as Luke's omission of John the Baptist's role in the baptism serves to remove him from the scene (see chapter 3). Thus it is the people who have come to be baptised and are filled with messianic expectation (3:15), not their leaders or even John, who are made witnesses of Jesus' heavenly confirmation.[11] Luke's location of "all the people" at the place of Jesus' prayer should be kept in mind as the popularity of Jesus' ministry is later investigated, for here lies an integral part of its explanation: the crowds who will later embrace Jesus have been prepared to recognise him, not only through their baptism by John, but also by their presence at the scene of Jesus' baptismal prayer. They have witnessed a revelation of the praying Jesus' character just as the twelve disciples will later.

Without considering conjectural, cultural reasons for Luke's objectivisation of this narrative, there are sufficient literary hints within Luke-Acts itself to provide an explanation for what Luke has done.[12]

First of all, it has already been shown that Luke has a tendency to highlight the reality of spiritual phenomena through the language of seeing and hearing.

Secondly, prayer has been presented as a channel for the communication of spiritual "vision." More support for this is forthcoming, but this study has already amply demonstrated Luke's tendency to shape other prayer situations so as to present them as "seeing/hearing" events. Thus, far from being a detail which "defies explanation,"[13] Luke's use of σωματικῷ εἴδει in 3:22 coincides with his use of τὸ εἶδος in 9:29; and like the Transfiguration, is explicable in relation to Jesus' prayer.[14] Prayer provides a situation in which revelation may occur. It is only fitting that Jesus receive the first heavenly confirmation of his calling while at prayer; and it is not surprising that it should take a form perceptible to those

---

[11] Cf. E. Schweizer, "πνεῦμα," TDNT. vol. VI, p. 406 who also notes the public accessibility of this event.

[12] These characteristics are generally attributed to Luke's Hellenizing tendencies; see Lentzen-Deis, Die Taufe, pp. 51, 284–286; Talbert, Genre, p. 116; Schweizer, "πνεῦμα," p. 357; S. Schulz, "Gottes Vorsehung bei Lukas," ZNW. 54 ('63) 114; Jeremias, Theology, p. 52. However, Schweizer also points out that, in the rabbinic view, an appearance of the Spirit was seldom unaccompanied by external phenomenon (p. 381); also cf. Lampe, "The Holy Spirit," p. 168.

[13] Hull, Magic, p. 94.

[14] Others, such as H. Schlier, "Die Verkündigung der Taufe Jesu nach den Evangelien," GL. 28 ('55) 417, have related Jesus' baptism to the transfiguration via Jesus' prayer; but the full signifi-cance of this prayer-connection is missed if the visual similarities are not noted. Jeremias, "Gebetsleben," p. 138 argued that this pericope was evidence of Jesus' pneumatic experience in prayer, since here Jesus' prayer is seen "to produce physical and perceptible experiences."

around him. This is not yet a complete account of why Luke may have introduced prayer into Jesus' baptism. For this, its role as a messianic anointing will also need to be examined. But it does consistently explain the objectivisation of the attendant events in terms of Luke's belief, demonstrated elsewhere, in prayer as a means of spiritual communication.

### 5.1.1.2 Is Jesus' Prayer "Answered"?

As often happens in Luke-Acts, the actual content of Jesus' prayer is not related. However, it is common in the literature to read that the heavens open and the Spirit descends as God's answer to this prayer.[15] But, in the absence of an explicit request, it is difficult to speak about "answered prayer," since this implies a direct correlation between some petition and the consequent events.

Prayer notices devoid of any content are common in Luke-Acts (Lk. 1:10–13; 2:37; 3:21 f; 5:16; 6:12; 9:18, 28 f; 11:1; Acts 1:14; 2:42; 6:4, 6; 9:11, 40; 10:2, 9, 30 f; 11:5; 12:5, 12; 14:23; 16:25; 20:36; 21:5; 22:17; 28:8). It may be possible, in some of these examples, to infer the content of the prayer from its context (Lk. 1:10–13; 9:18, 28 f; Acts 9:40; 12:5, 12; 14:23; 20:36). There are also instances where a prayer's content is specifically related, either verbally (Lk. 2:28–32; 10:21 f; 22:42; 23:34, 46; Acts 1:24; 4:24–30; 7:59 f), or by implication through summary statements (Acts 8:15; 26:29; 27:29; 28:15).

There are many possible solutions to why Luke might not relate the specific concerns of any individual prayer. They may simply have been unknown to him, for any number of historical reasons. Or he may not have been interested in including such information in his story, due either to simple literary considerations, or to some more deep-seated theological interest. It may also be erroneous to assume that Luke viewed all prayer as either petitionary or intercessory. Prayer might also be seen as a means of personal communion with God, in which case a search for "answers" would be inappropriate. This feature of Jesus' own prayer-life has already been seen in Lk. 9:28 ff and 10:21 f (chapters 2 and 3).

Those who would make a panacea-like appeal to simple logistical/historical difficulties to explain why Luke so often mentions contentless prayer must face the obstacle presented by Lk. 22:42. Here is a situation where, even in Mark, there is every reason for no one to have ever known what Jesus prayed.[16]But Luke has complicated the situation further by not only preserving Jesus' prayer, but redac-

---

[15] Plummer, *St. Luke*, p. 100; Stanley, *Gethsemane*, p. 189; Collins, "Anointing," p. 828; Feldkämper, *Der betende Jesus*, p. 50; J. McPolin, "Holy Spirit in Luke and John," *ITQ*. 45 ('78) 117–131; Harris, *Prayer*, p. 42; Schurmann, *Lukas*, p. 197; Grundmann, *Das Evangelium*, p. 108; Conzelmann, *Theology*, p. 180; F. Hauck, *Das Evangelium des Lukas*, (Leipzig, 1934), p. 55. H. von Baer, *Der heilige Geist in den Lukasschriften*, (Stuttgart, 1926), p. 61 even goes so far as to say that the Spirit's coming demonstrates that this must have been what Jesus was praying for.

[16] D. Daube, "A Prayer Pattern in Judaism," *SE. TU.* 73 ('59) 545, attempts to explain the source of this knowledge about Jesus' prayer by comparison with traditional Jewish forms of death-bed prayers, which show a pattern of acknowledgment-wish-surrender. But Luke, alone among the synoptic accounts, does not follow this pattern, (see below) and so again undermines attempts at purely historical explanation.

tionally eliminating every remaining possibility that someone might have over-heard him, ie. Jesus leaves *all* the disciples behind, withdraws to pray alone, and returns as in Mark to find the disciples sleeping (22:39ff). Whatever the explana-tion of Mark's account, Luke has made it clear that the details of historical necessity are not always as important to him as the final shape of his narrative. Unless Luke believed Jesus to have engaged only in silent prayer, none of the other prayer notices (excepting perhaps 5:16) offers a comparable situation. In other words, in the vast majority of instances it could have been historically possible for a traditional account of the prayer to have survived (as in 10:21f); or, lacking this, an appropriate prayer could easily have been supplied by Luke without doing violence to the purported situation, *if* it were thought to be important or neces-sary. Luke's ability to compose appropriate remarks for speakers in Acts, remarks for which it is highly unlikely that there be any historical record (25:13–22; 26:30–32),[17] indicates that he would have been quite capable of producing an appropriate prayer for a given situation, if knowing the content of that prayer were important for understanding the situation and the role played by prayer. However, given that more often than not such content is lacking, one can only assume that the specifics of any particular prayer are not necessarily germane to Luke's overall attitude towards the relationship between human prayer and the divine response.

Studies into the epiphanic commissioning stories of Luke-Acts yield further evidence substantiating this conclusion. B. Hubbard has identified prayer as one of the themes of Luke's epiphany narratives;[18] the individual who receives such an epiphanic vision is often praying when it takes place (Lk. 1:10; Acts 9:11; 10:2, 9, 30; 11:5; 12:5, 12; 13:2f; 22:17). Even though the baptismal narrative may not fall into the formal category of commissioning narrative, what all of these instances have in common is that none of them records the content of the introductory prayer. Thus divine instruction is given from heaven in connection with prayer, but not necessarily in "answer" to prayer. The validity of this observation is greatly strengthened when one includes in the discussion those instances where the content of a prayer is given, yet what is prayed hardly appears congruous enough with the subsequent events as to warrant the language of answered prayer (so Lk. 22:42;[19] 23:46; 24:30; Acts 4:24–30). The result is that, while Luke does maintain a strong correlation between the act of prayer and subsequent revelatory/epiphanic

---

[17] See Marshall, *Acts*, pp. 41f; "This does not mean that the speeches are his own undisciplined inventions" (p. 42).

[18] B. Hubbard, "Commissioning Stories in Luke-Acts: A Study of their Antecedents, Form and Content," *Semeia*. 8 ('77) 103–126, especially pp. 121f; "The Role of Commissioning Accounts in Acts" in *Perspectives*, pp. 189, 193f; also T. Mullins, "New Testament Commission Forms, Especially in Luke-Acts," *JBL*. 95 ('76) 603–614.

[19] This does not contradict the earier observation made on this verse. Jesus' prayer on the Mount of Olives operates on both levels, where on the one hand the content is important to understanding his relationship with the Father, but on the other it is not so related to the immediate, attendant circumstances as to justify the language of "answers" to prayer, as will soon be shown.

events, he does not show such an overwhelming interest in the content of those prayers as to warrant an indiscriminate use of the language of answered prayer. For these reasons it would be better to speak about prayer as an activity in and of itself, that is as either communion or petition/intercession, as being preparatory to, or being the means through which, two-way communication between the earthly and the divine spheres becomes possible. G. W. H. Lampe recognised this aspect of Lukan prayer long ago:[20]

Prayer is . . . the point at which the communication of divine influence becomes effective for its recipients.

The key here is the unpredictability of divine influence. Prayer itself, irrespective of what is actually said, is communication with the divine realm. As such it places one in the ideal position to receive whatever God may have to give. Thus prayer opens up a doorway between earth and heaven, but once that door is opened only God himself knows what may pass back through it from heaven to earth. This is a part of the significance of "the heaven's opening while Jesus prayed" in Lk. 3:21; through prayer Jesus not only spoke with the Father, but also made himself susceptible to the communication of the divine will, whatever that might entail. The Spirit does not descend because there is a unique relationship between prayer and the Spirit in particular, as even Lampe lapses into saying elsewhere.[21] Luke does not say that Jesus prayed specifically for the Spirit, whether or not he may have actually done so historically. And there is not the sort of consistent, particular relationship between prayer and the Spirit which one would expect elsewhere in Luke-Acts if such were the case (see the following discussion).[22] The Spirit descends in Lk. 3:21 f because filling Jesus with the Spirit was the Father's particular will for him at that particular point in time. Though, technically, the absence of any specific prayer may be due to Luke's adherence to Mark, the resultant theological payload is consistent with the rest of Luke-Acts; and it has to do not with a Lukan disinterest in the formal characteristics of personal piety,[23] nor even an exclusive emphasis upon prayer as the identifying landmark of decisive salva-

[20] Lampe, "The Holy Spirit," p. 169. Also see Braun, "Entscheidende Motive," p. 40; J. Navone, "Prayer," *Scr.* 20 ('68) 116; Hubbard, "The Role of Commissioning Accounts," p. 193 for more accurate descriptions of the relationship between prayer and spiritual events in Luke.

[21] *Pace* Lampe, *The Seal of the Spirit*, (London, 1951), p. 44, who writes that "the grand object of prayer is the gift of the Spirit." Also see Harris, *Prayer*, p. 239; Ott, *Gebet*, p. 131; Monloubou, *La Prière*, pp. 60, 140. For a discussion of how the explanation offered here deals with Lk. 11:13 and Jesus' own experience as prayer, see below.

[22] *Pace* Conzelmann, *Theology*, pp. 175 n. 1, 180.

[23] *Pace* Harris, *Prayer*, pp. 201–220, although Harris' generalisations on this point can only be made at the expense of Lk. 18:9–14. This weakness in Harris' treatment of Luke's (dis)interest in the specifics of personal piety has been addressed by Plymale, *The Prayer Texts of Luke-Acts*, pp. 12–15.

tion-historical events.[24] Rather, it has to do with Luke's theology of divine providence and the unveiling of that providence through prayer.

### 5.1.2 Prayer and Divine Communication in Luke-Acts

It would now be appropriate to briefly survey this phenomenon of divine-human interaction as it occurs throughout Luke-Acts. The ways in which Luke highlights the objective reality of spiritual events have already been investigated. That analysis need not be repeated. Also, three passages which seem to come closest to presenting examples of answered prayer (Acts 1:24–26; 9:40; 12:5–17) will be reserved for a following section. At issue now is the question of what happens when people pray.

#### 5.1.2.1 Prayer and Spiritual Manifestations in the Experience of Jesus (Lk. 3:21 f; 9:28 f; 22:43 f)

A feature of prayer in Luke-Acts which is shared by the experience of both Jesus and the disciples is the perception of supernatural phenomena. The explanation for this common ground has already been proposed: prayer is not simply man's address to God; it is also one of the ways in which individuals open themselves to God's address to them. Prayer creates a channel for discourse between heaven and earth. The appearance of such things as visions and angels during prayer illustrate this dynamic interaction.

Jesus is portrayed as experiencing heavenly interaction after his baptism (3:21 f), at the Transfiguration (9:28–36) and on the Mount of Olives (22:43 f). The first two instances have been discussed elsewhere. Concerning the second of these, Moses and Elijah appear as messengers of encouragement. As such they are heaven's response to the channel opened by Jesus' prayer, but the Father sends them as the answer which *he* has determined to be the most appropriate for Jesus at that moment. They have not been requested. Rather, they provide a heavenly confirmation of Jesus' decision "to suffer many things."

The final example of such an experience in the gospel (22:43–44) is complicated by a textual question which demands attention before any interpretation is attempted.[25]

---

[24] Keck, "Jesus' Entrance," p. 473 n. 31: "Luke is not interested in the content of these prayers... but in the fact that prayer was a part of 'decisive events'... (Luke) does not want to suggest that at the baptism Jesus received the Holy Spirit because he prayed for it..." In the light of this Harrisian language it is interesting to note that O. G. Harris' dissertation was submitted in the same year (1967) that his supervisor, Keck, wrote this article.

[25] A representative listing of those for and against the text's authenticity would be: Against – Westcott and Hort, *New Testament*, vol. II, appendix, pp. 64–67, who called the text "a fragment from the traditions... rescued from oblivion by the scribes of the second century"; Plummer, *St. Luke*, pp. 509, 544; Easton, *Luke*, p. 320; Kiddle, "The Passion Narrative," p. 275; Metzger, *Commentary*, p. 177 (following Hort); Hauck, *Das Evangelium*, p. 269; Stanley, *Gethsemane*, pp. 205–209, 219 ("an inspired addition"); B. Ehrman and M. Plunkett, "The Angel and the Agony: The Textual Problem of Luke 22:43–44," *CBQ* 45 ('83) 401–416; Fitzmyer, *The Gospel*, vol. II,

### 5.1.2.1.1 The Textual Problem of Lk. 22:43–44

Evidence against authenticity

External Evidence:

a) These two verses are omitted in p69ᵛⁱᵈ p75 ℵᵃ A B T W 579 1071* numerous lectionaries, f syrˢ sa bo armᵐˢˢ geo Marcion, Clement, Origen, Athanasius, Ambrose, Cyril, and John-Damascus.

b) They are marked with asterisks or obeli in Δᶜ Πᶜ 892ᶜ 1079 1195 1216.

c) They are transposed after Mt. 26:39 by f¹³ and several lectionaries, which also transpose v. 45a. The sum of this evidence provides strong and diverse testimony against the authenticity of the text, indicating Western interpolation.[26]

Internal evidence:

a) Fitzmyer cites the principle of *lectio brevior potior* in favour of the verses' omission.[27]

b) There are no counterparts to this tradition suggested in the synoptic parallels.[28]

c) They introduce emotional details into the account which are otherwise contrary to Luke's dispassionate portrayal of Jesus.[29] This is the strongest of the stylistic arguments against authenticity.

d) When the verses are omitted a chiastic structure emerges which focuses upon Jesus' prayer in v. 42.[30]

e) The appearance of a strengthening angel seems to be poorly timed, coming

---

p. 1444; K. Aland, "Neue Neutestamentliche Papyri II," *NTS.* 12 ('65–66) 199, 203; *The Text of the New Testament*, p. 305.

For – Scrivener, *Criticism*, vol. II, pp. 353–356 (a very thorough discussion of the external evidence); Harnack, "Probleme im Texte," pp. 251–255; Leaney, *Luke*, pp. 272f; Creed, *The Gospel*, p. 273; Streeter, *The Four Gospels*, pp. 137f; Lagrange, *Luc*, pp. 561–3; Surkau, *Martyrien*, p. 93 n. 57; Loisy, *Luc*, pp. 526f; J. Holleran, *The Synoptic Gethsemane: A Critical Study*, (Rome, 1973), p. 98; Harris, *Prayer*, p. 110; Grundmann, *Das Evangelium*, p. 410; J. Schmid, *Das Evangelium nach Lukas*, (Regensburg, 1960), pp. 336f; Rengstorf, *Lukas*, p. 251; A. Schlatter, *Das Evangelium des Lukas*, (Stuttgart, 1960), p. 433; Ernst, *Das Evangelium*, p. 607; G. Schneider, "Engel und Blutschweiss (Lk. 22,43–44) 'Redaktionsgeschichte' im Dienste der Textkritik," *BZ.* 20 ('76) 112–116; H. Aschermann, "Zum Agoniegebet Jesu, Luk. 22, 43–44," *TV.* 5 ('53–4) 143–149; L. Brun, "Engel und Blutschweiss, Lc 22, 43–44," *ZNW.* 32 ('33) 275f; K. Kuhn, "Jesus in Gethsemane," *ET.* 12 ('52–53) 268; T. Lescow, "Jesus in Gethsemane bei Lukas und im Hebräerbrief," *ZNW.* 58 ('67) 217; Marshall, *Commentary*, p. 832; Schneider, *Das Evangelium*, vol. II, p. 459; Jeremias, *Sprache*, p. 294; Schweizer, *Luke*, p. 343.

[26] J. Fitzmyer, "Papyrus Bodmer XIV: Some Features of Our Oldest Text of Luke," *CBQ.* 24 ('62) 170–179; Holleran, *Gethsemane*, pp. 93f.

[27] Fitzmyer, *The Gospel*, vol. II, p. 1444.

[28] Fitzmyer, *The Gospel*, vol. II, p. 1444.

[29] Stanley, *Gethsemane*, p. 206; Ehrman, "Luke 22:43–44," p. 411; Hauck, *Das Evangelium*, p. 269.

[30] Stanley, *Gethsemane*, p. 213; Ehrman, "Luke 22:43–44," p. 413; both of whom admit to following M. Galizzi, *Gesù nel Getsemani (Mc 14,32–42; Mt 26,36–46; Lc 22,39–46)*, (Zürich, 1972), p. 138: A) 40, B) 41, C) 42, B') 45, A') 46. However, Galizzi actually divides the text: A) 41ab, B) 41c–42, C) 43, C') 44a, B') 44b, A') 45.

as it does after Jesus has already yielded himself to the Father in v. 42, and before the intensification of his anguish in v. 44.[31]

f) Aside from this single instance, Luke elsewhere agrees with the synoptic pattern, wherein angelic appearances occur only in the birth narratives and post-resurrection scenes.[32]

g) Harnack's linguistic arguments in favor of the verses' authenticity have been challenged by L. Brun.[33]

h) In view of all this, it is argued that vv. 43f are a later interpolation added as anti-docetic polemic or, considering Luke's martyrdom motif, inserted for encouragement at a time of persecution.[34]

Evidence in Favour of Authenticy
External Evidence:

a) The verses are included in $\aleph^{*,b}$ D K L X Δ* Θ Π* Ψ f¹ many miniscules, several lectionaries, a,aur,b,c,d,e,ff²,i,l,q,r¹ vg syr^{c,p,h,pal} arm eth Diatessaron, Justin, Irenaeus, Hippolytus, Dionysius, Arius (according to Epiphanius), Eusebius, Hilary, Caesarius-Nazianzus, Gregory-Nazianazus, Didymus, Ps-Dionysius, Epiphanius, Chrysostom, Jerome, Augustine, Theodoret, Leontius, Cosmos, Facundus. This is hardly an insignificant array of witnesses.

b) Lagrange points out that the reading is not exclusively Western since Dionysius of Alexandria did not use a Western text; this gives some diversity to the patristic testimony.[35]

c) Lagrange and Harnack both agree that the witnesses which omit the text represent hardly any geographical region other than Egypt, and even then not all of Egypt (ie. $\aleph$*).[36]

d) The strength of the p75 B combination is not as impressive when it is recalled that they represent the dual testimony of only a single, Egyptian textual tradition, p75 perhaps being the archetype of B (cf. pp. 81–82).[37]

e) The testimony of several of the Fathers in favour of the text is as early as p75 (Tatian, Justin, Irenaeus, Hippolytus); also the earlier discussion concerning the variety of Egyptian textual traditions and Lk. 23:34 is equally relevant here (cf. pp. 82–83).

f) The evidence of $\aleph^a$ B against the text versus $\aleph^{*,b}$ in favour of the reading also looks very much like the situation with Lk. 23:34, where the strong possibility of a

---

[31] Cf. Loisy, *Luc*, p. 526.

[32] Brun, "Lc 22, 43–44," p. 266.

[33] Brun, "Lc. 22, 43–44," pp. 266–269; Holleran, *Gethsemane*, pp. 95f; cf. Harnack, "Probleme im Texte," pp. 251–255.

[34] Ehrman, "Luke 22:43–44," pp. 408–410.

[35] Lagrange, *Luc*, pp. 562f.

[36] Harnack, "Probleme im Texte," p. 253.

[37] This shared tradition between B and p75 is demonstrated by Fee, "P66, P75 and Origen," pp. 30f, 44; also see n. 17 chapter 4.

common scribal tradition was seen to be in operation between ℵ* and B (cf. pp. 81–82).

g) Scrivener points out that at the end of v. 42 the original scribe of A had affixed the correct Ammonian and Eusebian numerals for vv. 43 f,[38] demonstrating that he was familiar with the passage, perhaps from his exemplar.

Internal evidence:

a) The principle of *lectio brevior potior* is not fool-proof, witness the growing consensus together with p75 in favour of reading the longer text of Lk. 22:19b–20.[39]

b) Luke diverges from the synoptic parallels at numerous points throughout his story; surely "variant" traditions are no less credible for being such.[40]

c) The unusual emotions of v. 44 could perhaps be explained by the uniqueness of the situation; in fact, without the intense emotion and resolution depicted on the Mount it becomes difficult to explain the confidence exhibited by Jesus at the passion (23:34, 46). These verses are almost required as the presupposition and explanation of Jesus' deportment in the following events.[41]

d) It is not incumbent upon every pericope to exhibit a chiastic outline! But if one insists, a telling outline is just as possible with these verses as without (also see chapter 6).[42]

e) The apparently ill-timed appearance of the strengthening angel speaks loudly for the authenticity of the text, not against it. Surely, any scribe creative enough to insert such a scene, and do it with thoroughly Lukan vocabulary, would also have been adept enough to ensure its reading more smoothly.

f) An angelic appearance here indicates the significance of the relationship between prayer and spiritual realities for Luke, a thematic note which is consistent throughout Luke-Acts. The support for that thematic note provided by this text speaks loudly in its favour. Luke is no more required to limit his angelophanies to the birth and post-resurrection narratives than he is to limit his prayer notices only to those found in Mark (cf. point b above).

g) Harnack's stylistic arguments have recently been extensively reaffirmed, in

---

[38] Scrivener, *Criticism*, vol. II, pp. 353f.

[39] See Jeremias, *Eucharistic Words*, pp. 139–159; for other presentations of how unreliable the principle of *lectio brevior potior* may be see Fee, "'One Thing is Needful?'," pp. 61–75; Parsons, "A Christological Tendency," pp. 468–469.

[40] The question is, variant with respect to what? The jury is still out on whether or not Mark formed the basis of Luke's passion narrative. It could just as easily be that, in Luke's mind, Mark contained the variant tradition.

[41] Cf. Holleran, *Gethsemane*, p. 98.

[42] For those so disposed, a chiasm is still not out of the question: A) 40; B) 41; C) 42a; D) 42b; D') 43; C') 44; B') 45; A') 46. See Feldkämper, *Der betende Jesus*, pp. 228f, 232 for another suggested outline.

light of Brun's criticisms, by J. Green.⁴³ For example, Brun's objection that an angel "from heaven" was without parallel in Luke-Acts ignores the fact that ἀπ' οὐρανοῦ is found in Luke (9:54; 17:29; 21:11), οὐρανός is at times used as a circumlocution for God (15:18, 21), and Luke does say elsewhere where his angels come from (Lk. 1:26; Acts 12:11) and go to (Lk. 2:15). Also, προσεύχομαι, καὶ ἐγένετο and ὡσεί are typical of Luke's redactional vocabulary; as is the use of simile (cf. Lk. 10:18; 11:44; 22:31), the appearance of physical manifestations at extramundane events (Lk. 1:20; 3:22; Acts 2:2f; 9:18), ὤφθη (Mt. 1x, Mk. 1x, L–A. 13x), ἄγγελος (Lk.12:8f; 15:10; 24:23; Acts 5:19; 8:26; 10:3, .7, 22; 11:13; 12:7, 23; 23:9; 27:23), θεὶς τὰ γόνατα (Acts 7:60; 9:40; 20:36; 21:5), ἐνισχύω (Acts 9:19), ἐκτενῶς (Acts 12:5; 26:7); while ἀγωνία, ἱδρώς, and θρόμβος are all *hapax legomena*.

h) It is easier to explain the omission than the addition of this text:

i – Epiphanius (*Ancoratus* 31.4–5 [GCS 25.40]) mentions the difficulties caused by these words of distress for some orthodox theologians of his own day.⁴⁴ In fact, some of them even omitted these verses from their own mss.⁴⁵

ii – He also mentions the attention given these verses by the Arians which would have helped make them suspect, something also suggested by an ancient scholium.⁴⁶

iii – It makes better sense to understand the martydom features as part of the consistent portrayal by the original author than a later interpolation by a clever scribe.⁴⁷

iv – An interpolator would have been required to make the insertion very early on, by at least the middle of the second century (cf. Justin, *Dial.* 103.8; Irenaeus, *Adv. Haer.* III. xxii. 2, xxxv. 3), and been clever enough to compose in a thoroughly Lukan style (cf. point e above).⁴⁸

v – At a later period an addition would not have been made which depicts the divine Christ in overwhelming distress and in need of angelic assistance. As M.

---

⁴³ J. Green, "Jesus on the Mount of Olives (Luke 22. 39–46): Tradition and Theology," *JSNT.* 26 ('86) 29–48. Green has significantly added to Harnack's earlier observations, offering good evidence for Luke's having used Mark together with his own special source material.

⁴⁴ Fitzmyer, *The Gospel*, vol. II, p. 1443.

⁴⁵ Scrivener, *Criticism*, vol. II, pp. 270, 355 f.

⁴⁶ ὅτι τῆς ἱσχύος τοῦ ἀγγλέου οὐκ ἐπεδέετο ὁ ὑπὸ πάσης ἐπουρανίου δυνάμεως φόβῳ καὶ τρόφῳ προσκυνούμενος καὶ δοξαζόμενος. The angel is interpreted as declaring Jesus to be strong; see D. F. Strauss, *Life of Jesus Critically Examined*, (London, 1973), p. 638. Also see Lagrange, *Luc*, pp. 562f; Streeter, *The Four Gospels*, pp. 137 f; Harnack, "Probleme im Texte," pp. 253 f; Brun, "Engel und Blutschweiss," pp. 276. J. Duplacy, "La préhistoire du texte en Luc 22:43–44" in *New Testament Textual Criticism, its Significance for Exegesis*, (Oxford, 1981), pp. 77–86 offers a discussion of the various doctrinal debates in which this text has played a part.

⁴⁷ This is the original thrust of Aschermann's arguments ("Zum Agoniegebet," pp. 146f), which are then unconvincingly used in a contrary fashion by Ehrman and Plunkett, "Luke 22:43–44," p. 410; cf. Dibelius, *Tradition*, pp. 201 f; Flender, *St. Luke*, p. 54; Ernst, *Das Evangelium*, p. 607; Surkau, *Martyrien*, pp. 93 f.

⁴⁸ See Neyrey, *The Passion*, p. 55; Holleran, *Gethsemane*, pp. 94 f; Schneider, "Engel und Blutschweiss," pp. 112–116.

Goguel has observed, at least one sector of the mss evidence against the text is Alexandrian; such an omission in this region could have been influenced by the spread of Athanasian orthodoxy.[49]

i) The similarity of this material to Mk. 14:33f, combined with Luke's tendency to avoid doublets and replace Markan omissions with similar material from his own special source(s), could explain the inclusion of vv. 43f in a way entirely consistent with Luke's compositional habits elswhere.[50]

j) The scene is so dispassionate as to become pedestrian in the absence of vv. 43f.

k) In addition, the disciples going to sleep "out of grief" becomes very difficult to explain without the extended prayer and lengthy struggle found in these verses.

Consequently, though it is impossible to be dogmatic, it is possible to be fairly confident in asserting that the weight of the internal evidence more than answers the objections made against these verses, and tips the scales very strongly in favour of the authenticity of Lk. 22:43–44.

### 5.1.2.1.2 The Strengthening Angel of Lk. 22:43–44

The form and function of 22:39–46 will be examined in more detail in chapter 6, but for now it is sufficient to observe that the relationship between prayer and spiritual phenomena detected elsewhere continues. As in the baptism, it is not unusual to read that the angel appears in answer to Jesus' prayer.[51] However, such language is less justifiable here than in 3:22, for now the content of Jesus' prayer *is* given and it does not include the request for a strengthening angel. It would be more accurate to say that once again prayer has been instrumental in opening the channel whereby God may respond in the way in which he deems most appropriate.[52] An angel is sent from heaven because this is how the Father has determined to meet Jesus' need; through this strengthening Jesus is enabled to persevere in obedience to the will of God. In fact, the prayer itself is the articulation of this very attitude. "Not my will but thine be done" expresses the reality which Luke sees repeatedly brought to expression in prayer: as the pray-er opens himself to speak with God, God's will is enacted.

---

[49] See Williams, *Alterations*, p. 7. However, E. C. Colwell has pointed out that the discovery of p75 has weakened this line of argument; see *Studies in Methodology in the Textual Criticism of the New Testament*, (Leiden, 1969), p. 151 n. 1.

[50] Brun, "Engel und Blutschweiss," pp. 275f; Green, "The Mount of Olives," p. 33. Of course, this assumes that Luke was adding to the Markan framework; cf. Taylor, *The Passion Narrative*, p. 69.

[51] Grundmann, *Das Evangelium*, p. 412; Brun, "Engel und Blutschweiss," p. 271; Schneider, *Das Evangelium*, p. 115; Feldkämper, *Der betende Jesus*, pp. 242, 244; Stanley, *Gethsemane*, p. 219; Harris, *Prayer*, pp. 112, 233. Beck, "'Imitatio Christ'," p. 38 has explained the appearance in terms of the Jewish concept of guardian angels; Surkau, *Martyrien*, p. 94 maintained that the angel brings Jesus the revelation of the Father's will.

[52] Cf. J. Neyreŷ, "The Absence of Jesus' Emotions – the Lucan Redaction of Lk. 22,39–46," *Bib.* 61 ('80) 166; R. S. Barbour, "Gethsemane in the Tradition of the Passion," *NTS.* 16 ('69–70) 246; J. Edmonds, "The Lucan Our Father: A Summary of Luke's Teaching on Prayer?," *ExpT.* 91 ('79–80) 143.

Luke highlights this aspect of Jesus' prayer. The agony prayers in both Mark and Matthew consist of: 1) a statement concerning what is possible for God; Mark being the stronger of the two; 2) followed by a request that the cup be removed; and, 3) the decisive, concluding provision that such occur only if it is the Father's will. However, Luke has eliminated the first of these clauses and written instead, "if you are willing, remove this cup from me."[53] Matthew also has an if clause, but it serves to modify Mark's first statement so that it remains the entertainment of alternative possibilities, "if it is possible..." As a result of Luke's alterations, Jesus does not concern himself with theoretical possibilities, but only the actualities of God's determination. As far as Luke is concerned, it is only possible for the will of God to be fulfilled.[54] In a sense, then, the two parts of Jesus' prayer are simply variations on the same theme for according to Luke's perspective on divine sovereignty, if it *were* God's will that this cup pass from Jesus, *it would do so*. For Jesus to say εἰ βούλει is tantamount to him saying πλὴν μὴ τὸ θέλημά μου.[55] This surrender of Jesus' θελήμα to the Father's βούλη is in agreement with the essence

---

[53] D. Daube's analysis of the Gethsemane prayer, seen in light of Jewish death-bed prayers, fails to shed light on Luke simply because he also fails to note this important difference; see "A Prayer Pattern," pp. 539f.

[54] At the same time, Luke yet retains something of the intractable tension between divine sovereignty and human responsibility; see Lk. 3:7–14; 7:29–30; 10:10–16; 13:1–5; Acts 7:39–43, 51–53; 13:46; 18:6, 10 (!); 28:25–28. Also note the way in which the sermons in Acts lead to a call for repentance; cf. Conzelmann, Theology, pp. 227; J. Dupont, "Repentir et conversion d'apres les Actes des Apôtres," ScEccl. 12 ('60) 137–173. Schulz, "Gottes Vorsehung," pp. 105–116 has rightly emphasized God's sovereignty in Luke-Acts, but has been injudicious in overstating much of the evidence. For example, it simply is not the case that Luke comes to root God's βούλη in his "own Being" and not in Scripture (pp. 105f). It is, in any event, artificial to hang such an interpretation upon what is simply a phenomenological distinction between God's revealed and his as-of-yet unrevealed will. Nor is Schulz's description of the OT idea of election, upon which so much of the motivation for his appeal to Roman and Hellenistic influence depends, a fair presentation of the data (p. 110). For a good critique see Marshall, Historian, pp. 105f, 111–115; also cf. Flender, St. Luke, pp. 143f.

[55] The etymological distinction between βούλομαι (deliberation, resolve) and θέλω (spontaneous desire) is of doubtful significance here, for Luke's usage does not permit their conveying any technical distinction between God's will and human decision, respectively; pace Holleran, Gethsemane, pp. 88–90; cf. Creed, The Gospel, p. 273; Stanley, Gethsemane, pp. 216f; Neyrey, "Jesus' Emotions," p. 159. ἀλλὰ τὸ σὸν requires a supplied θελήμα of God, not βούλει, showing that the two may be used interchangeably. Their use elsewhere agrees with this (cf. θελήμα/θέλω of God's predetermined will in Acts 13:22; 18:21; 21:14; 22:14; Lk. 12:47 [?]). In Acts βούλομαι is always used of man's decision, never God's, although this is not the case in the gospel (Lk. 10:22; 22:42). βούλη may also refer to human decision (Lk. 23:51; Acts 27:12, 42), and Acts 5:38 clearly shows the word's applicability to either divine or human resolve. However, there are also those instances where the noun is an important expression of God's foreordained plan (Acts 2:23; 4:28; 13:36; 20:27; cf. also Lk. 22:22; Acts 1:7; 10:42; 17:26, 31; 22:14; 26:16). Only once is this βούλη described as resistable (Lk. 7:30); however, Luke so circumscribes this idea that even such resistance is brought under God's sovereign control (Lk. 10:21; 19:42; Acts 2:23; 3:17–18; cf. 26:14). It is clear that Luke's usage must determine his meaning; neither word is a technicus terminus; pace the implication of Feldkämper, Der betende Jesus, p. 239. However, when used of God's counsel, both words do entail the meaning of sovereign predetermination, indicating that it is the Lukan concept of the divine will and not etymology which determines either words' meaning.

of Lk. 10:21–24. This is why the Son is able to reveal the Father "to whomever he wills"; his will is identical with the Father's εὐδοκία. By rewriting Jesus' prayer and introducing the angel as he has, Luke expresses in both speech and event the same perspective concerning individual prayer and the will of God.[56]

### 5.1.2.2 Prayer and Spiritual Manifestations in the Experience of Others

Others beside Jesus experience the open door effect of prayer. In Lk. 1:10ff Zechariah undergoes an angelic visitation at the hour of prayer (v. 10), and is told that the angel comes to announce the answer to his own request (v. 13, δεήσις). Of course, there is no question of either the crowds or Zechariah praying for an angel to appear in the temple, and when the angel tells Zechariah not to fear for "his prayer has been heard" the subsequent promise of a son makes it thoroughly ambiguous as to which prayer the angel refers. Is it his and Elizabeth's personal prayers for a child? Or is it Zechariah's priestly prayers just now offered in the temple? This deliberate ambiguity has been touched upon in chapter 3, but now its acceptability to Luke becomes clear. It is not necessary for Luke to specify exactly *what* prayer is at issue, for all prayer gives opportunity for the expression of God's purposes.

The prayers in Acts continue this trend. The events which transpire on the Day of Pentecost are associated with prayer via Acts 1:14, which is a summary statement describing not just one particular prayer meeting but the continual attitude of the early, pre-pentecost community.[57] The similarity in language makes the connection plain enough; there is no need for Luke to reintroduce prayer in 2:1:

1:14     οὗτοι πάντες ἦσαν προσκαρτεροῦντες
         ὁμοθυμαδὸν τῇ προσευχῇ

(v. 15)  ἦν τε ὄχλος ... ἐπὶ τὸ αὐτὸ ...

2:1      καὶ ... ἦσαν πάντες ὁμοῦ ἐπὶ τὸ αὐτό

Communal prayer forms the implied background to the descent of the Holy Spirit, although it is never said that the early church specifically requested that they be given the Spirit.[58] That they probably prayed with such an expectation may be implied in Acts 1:4–5, 8. But such evidence makes it all the more significant that Luke nowhere links an explicit prayer, ie. "constantly in prayer awaiting the Spirit," or "praying for the promised Spirit," with the events at Pentecost.

Once again, Luke also describes the attendant events in suitably objective language. Admittedly, the descriptions are offered as analogies: v. 2, "a sound like

---

[56] For a discussion of how this complete surrender to the divine will, and the consequent surrender of one's own petition, differs from Jewish petitionary prayer see Heinemann, *Prayer in the Talmud*, pp. 185f; "The Background of Jesus' Prayer in the Lewish Liturgical Tradition" in *The Lord's Prayer and Jewish Liturgy*, (London, 1978), pp. 86f.

[57] O. Bauernfeind, *Die Apostelgeschichte*, (Leipzig, 1939), p. 24; Marshall, *Acts*, p. 62; Conzelmann, *Die Apostelgeschichte*, (Tübingen, 1972), p. 27.

[58] Feldkämper, *Der betende Jesus*, p. 307.

(ὥσπερ) a mighty, rushing wind;" v. 3, "dividing tongues like (ὡσεὶ) fire." However, they are not analogies offered in *lieu* of actual events, but of describable events. This is demonstrated when "the sound like wind" proceeds to "fill the whole house" (ἐπλήρωσεν ὅλον τὸν οἶκον), something more easily said of a real wind than a mere sound. Similarly, the "divided tongues" may only be "like fire," but they are actually seen by all those present (ὤφθησαν αὐτοῖς). Prayer has once again preceded a revelatory seeing/hearing event in which an unpredictable inter-action between heaven and earth has taken place.

This pattern is repeated in Acts 4:29–31. The community gathers together for prayer (vv. 24, 31) and requests numerous things (vv. 29f). But they do not pray for the Holy Spirit, since the Spirit has obviously already been given. While God does answer the specifics of this prayer, for they do continue to speak the word with boldness (v. 31b), he does so by once again giving what they have not specifically requested, the Holy Spirit. And once again, the Spirit comes with objective phenomena.

The single exception to the pattern being described is found in Acts 8:14ff. There Peter and John do specifically request that the Holy Spirit be given to the Samaritans (v. 15). However, once the Spirit arrives Luke suddenly shifts from associating it with the apostles' prayer to linking its descent exclusively with the laying on of hands (v. 17, τότε ἐπετίθουν τὰς χεῖρας ἐπ᾽ αὐτούς, καὶ ἐλάμβανον πνεῦμα ἅγιον).

If this observation seems facile, then simply note the way in which Luke reiterates the point in v. 18, "when Simon saw that the Spirit was given *through* (διὰ) the laying on of the apostles' hands;" and then again in v. 19, ". . . so that everyone on whom I lay my hands may receive the Holy Spirit."[59] It would have been easy enough for Luke to have written "through prayer" or "through prayer and the laying on of hands" in each instance if he had liked.[60] And if he were as persuaded of the close association between the Spirit and prayer, as is often attributed to him, then Luke certainly might be expected to have done exactly this. But this is precisely what he does not do. Luke simply will not draw a direct cause-and-effect relationship between a specific petition in prayer and the response

---

[59] Bauernfeind's (*Apostelgeschichte*, p. 126) proposal that vv. 18–19 offer only Simon's misunderstanding of the phenomenon, and not the proper Christian interpretation, cannot stand in view of v. 17. N. Adler also critiques Bauerfeind on this point; see *Taufe und Handauflegung, Eine Exegetisch-Theologische Untersuchung von Apg 8,14–17*, (Münster, 1951), p. 74. Adler, too, is emphatic that the Spirit's descent is connected with the laying on of hands and not the prayer itself; see pp. 60, 70f, 73f.

[60] Prayer and the laying on of hands are simultaneous in Acts 6:6; 13:3 and 28:8. The first two describe the commissioning of Christian workers, all of whom already possess the Spirit; it is significant that in neither instance is there any mention of the "coming of" or "filling by" the Spirit. Acts 28:8 relates a healing, again with no mention of the Spirit. In Acts 9:17–19 Ananias lays his hands upon Saul and speaks of the filling of the Spirit, but there is neither a prayer nor any description of the Spirit's coming. Instead, Luke immediately relates the relief of Saul's blindness and his baptism. Only 19:6 again actually relates the Spirit with the laying on of hands, but as in 8:17–19 there is no mention of prayer! And Paul's action there would be subject to the limitations established by Luke here (see n. 62).

given by God. Even if one were to say that prayer and the laying on of hands forms a distinct "package", Luke is quite clear about which part of that package he is willing to associate with the Spirit's coming. Thus when the Spirit does come in association with prayer there is either no content given to that prayer, or the content does not concern the Spirit. Where the tradition has related a specific request for the Spirit, Luke associates the Spirit's coming not with the prayer, but with the related action of the laying on of hands (cf. 19:6)![61]

In fact, the whole of the following narrative dealing with Simon the magician (vv. 20–24) serves this very purpose. Having first distanced the coming of the Spirit from any specific petition for it, Luke now ensures that his replacement (ie. the laying on of hands) cannot be interpreted in terms of a simple cause-and-effect relationship either. Simon's request becomes a foil to emphasise the independence of the Spirit, and to eliminate all possibility of the sort of magical thought arising which could easily attach itself to any action, whether that be prayer or something else, yielding predictable results. Prayer is not magic. Neither is there any way in which one may control the dispensation of God's Spirit, for it is his gift (Acts 8:20; cf. 2:38; 10:45; 11:17; 15:8).[62]

The remaining examples of this revelatory effect of prayer may be summarised as follows: God's communication through prayer in Acts often takes the form of visions, angelic appearances or other obviously supernatural phenomena (9:11; 10:2f, 9f, 30f; 11:5; 12:5ff, 12; 16:25f; 22:17f). The objectivity of these events is not always clear, though it certainly is intended in 12:9f and 16:26. But Luke's use of visionary language elsewhere does not necessarily mean that he intends to exclude the possibility of an objective event having occurred. For evidence of this one need simply compare the initial description of Cornelius' vision in 10:3 (εἶδεν ἐν ὁράματι φανερῶς) with Cornelius' own account in 10:30 (καὶ ἰδοὺ ἀνὴρ ἔστη ἐνώπιόν μου ἐν ἐσθῆτι λαμπρᾷ).[63]

---

[61] *Pace* Haenchen, *Acts*, p. 306; also cf. J. H. E. Hull, *The Holy Spirit in the Acts of the Apostles*, (London, 1967), pp. 104f.

[62] Thus the Simon material is intended not only to portray the superiority of the church's power over magical power, perhaps reflecting a situation where competition with magical wonder-workers was an issue (see Haenchen, *Acts*, p. 308; Conzelmann, *Apostelgeschichte*, p. 62; *pace* H. Gunkel, *Influence of the Holy Spirit*, [Philadelphia, 1979], p. 64), but also to circumscribe the nature of prayer and its relation to the Spirit. Likewise, it would ensure that no magical significance be read into Acts 19:6; see Adler *Handauflegung*, pp. 73–75. As C. K. Barrett has said in "Light on the Holy Spirit from Simon Magus (Acts 8,4–25)," in *Les Actes des Apôtres: Tradition, rédaction, théologie*, (Gembloux, 1979), p. 294: "(This) is not a victory of superior magic over inferior, but of a non-magical view of the Gospel over a magical..."

[63] The situation of Peter's vision is an interesting one. It is difficult to believe that even Luke could have conceived of *this* as an actual event. However, given the extent to which Luke has heightened the objectivity of the events accompanying Jesus' baptism, could "the heaven's opening" before Peter (θεωρεῖ τὸν οὐρανὸν ἀνεῳγμένον, Acts 10:11) possibly be understood as an attempt to lend at least the aura of reality to these events via association with the baptism (cf. ἀνεῳχθῆναι τὸν οὐρανὸν, Lk. 3:21)?

### 5.1.2.3 Divine Revelation Given Independently of Prayer

In the foregoing examples supernatural events have taken place unexpectedly through prayer, but never in "answer" to prayer. The guiding principle throughout has been the independence of the divine will. This independence is also exhibited by the fact that not all revelatory events in Acts are associated with prayer, many occur without any prayer connection at all, ie. angelic appearances (5:19; 8:26, 29; 12:23; 23:11; 27:23), visions (9:3 ff; 16:9 f), and even the appearance of the Holy Spirit (4:8; 10:44; 11:15; 13:52; 16:6; 19:6; 20:23; 21:4). Though on the surface this seems to present an obstacle to the present thesis, that prayer is a means of divine communication in Luke-Acts, it actually offers further evidence for the particular manner in which this argument is being articulated. Prayer is one of the channels for the realisation of God's will among his people, but he is not limited to it. This, in fact, is the obvious significance of the absence of any prayer on Peter's part in Acts 11:15 ff. The dispensation of the Spirit takes place at God's instigation, and his alone (11:17). At times prayer serves to make God's will plain to the prayer, but his working need not be restricted by such acts of piety. God's plan is already in motion. Prayer does not change or affect that fact, it simply opens a window through which man may "see" God's activity and, perhaps, become a part of it.

The failure to perceive this nuance of the relationship between prayer and divine activity is responsible for the fundamental flaw in the now widespread thesis of O. G. Harris. Prayer is *not* the "means by which God guides the course of redemptive history."[64] The numerous examples listed above demonstrate that *Heilsgeschichte* may proceed, just as the Spirit may be bestowed, quite independently of the prayers of the church. In addition, the fact that not all prayer notices may convincingly be described as turning points, and that the essential dynamics of prayer continue to operate long after Acts 13, which marked the conclusion of Harris' study since he believed there were no more turning points for Luke after the Gentile mission had begun, also show that the "divine guidance of salvation-history" is not an accurate description of how Luke employs his prayer theme.[65] It would be more accurate to say that prayer is *a* means by which individuals discover God's will revealed to them so that they may become attuned to it and participate in its continuous unfolding. And even though this alone is not an adequate description of the role played by prayer in Jesus' own life, it certainly is an experience in which he shared.

---

[64] Harris, *Prayer*, p. 3; also Smalley, "The Spirit," pp. 60, 68; O'Brien, "Prayer in Luke-Acts," pp. 112, 127; Trites, "The Prayer Motif, " pp. 185 f.

[65] Without interacting specifically with Harris, Hubbard ("The Role of Commissioning Accounts in Acts") has offered another challenge to this thesis. He has convincingly argued that the commissioning narratives in Luke-Acts identify "decisive places throughout the narrative in such a way that God's hand is continually seen . . ." to be guiding the course of salvation-history (p. 198). Yet, prayer plays a part in only 8 out of 19 such accounts in Acts (p. 193). This hardly

5.1.2.4 Prayer and Spiritual Illumination

Prayer is not only related to supernatural manifestations in Luke-Acts but also to the interior dynamics of spiritual illumination. Of course, it is possible that new levels of personal insight may be derived from visionary experiences, but this is to be distinguished from the personal illumination which results immediately from prayer itself. It will also be important to distinguish whether such insight results from one's own prayer for oneself or whether it comes in response to another's intercession. The manner in which Jesus' prayers effect spiritual insight in others has already been discovered in Luke's gospel (9:18; 28f; 23:34, 46; 24:30, 35). Likewise, the generally loose relationship between the specifics (if any) of a prayer and the resulting insight has also been discussed. But there are several additional observations which still require formulation.

1) All of the explicit examples of the prayers of one person resulting in the spiritual illumination of another occur in Luke's gospel; there are none in Acts. Of course, people do pray for each other in Acts but the significance of these prayers is never directly tied to spiritual perception. The church commissions its new leaders with prayer (Acts 6:6; 13:3; 14:23); Paul prays with, and presumably for, his fellow believers as he leaves them for the last time (Acts 20:36; 21:5); but there is no revelatory effect recorded in any of these instances. It is interesting, too, that when Simon asks Peter to pray for him (Acts 8:24) it seems to be implied that Peter refused to do so (cf. Acts 8:22), since forgiveness comes in response to one's own repentance, not another's intercession (cf. Acts 2:38). Consequently, it appears that the prayers of disciples do not of themselves mediate spiritual life/perception to other individuals (on the church's prayer for Peter in Acts 12:5 see section 5.1.4 below).

2) How is this important difference between the gospel and Acts to be accounted for? An answer to this question is suggested by the obvious fact that the gospel prayers of illumination are all prayers of Jesus, whereas Acts records the prayers of disciples. Some might object that such a conclusion was tautologous, since only Jesus is seen to pray in Luke's gospel anyway. But this simply is not true (see the discussion of Zechariah and Anna below). The resulting implication is that revelatory prayers which are effective on another's behalf are Jesus' exclusive domain, and this obviously explains why they are limited to the gospel. There are examples in Acts of individuals having visionary experiences in response to their own prayers (Acts 4:31; 9:11f; 10:3, 9f, 30; 11:5), but this simply substantiates the point being made: the revelatory phenomenon is self-referential; the prayer does not mediate spiritual illumination or experience to anyone other than the pray-er.

Neither are there any clear instances of disciples specifically praying for unbelievers that they might come to understand Jesus' messiahship. In Acts only 26:29 could conceivably challenge this conclusion. Yet this is only an indirect reference;

---

gives prayer a premier role in the guidance of *Heilsgeschichte*. Of course, one may propose some sort of distinction between major and minor turning points, but even this sort of retrenchment admits to a significant weakening of Harris' thesis.

there is no prayer explicitly mentioned; and there are no results recorded among Paul's listeners, something which is totally unlike the situation when Jesus prays.

Similarly, Acts 16:25 relates prayer to the following miraculous phenomena, not the jailer's conversion.[66] It is the desperate situation created for the jailer by these events which elicit his willingness to hear and believe. In this respect, Paul's prayer is indirectly related, but it is vis-à-vis the sovereignly bestowed supernatural manifestations; there is no direct prayer-perception relationship.

Of course, one might say that texts such as Acts 2:42 and 6:4 describe prayer as an ubiquitous activity, overarching the whole ministry of the early church. And this would certainly be true. But it does not change the fact that there is not a single text in Luke-Acts where a disciple's prayer, whether it be explicitly intercessory or a redactionally placed prayer notice, is presented as the effective means of an unbeliever's receiving spiritual illumination into the status of Jesus. It is a long journey from the generalised picture offered in Acts 2:42 and 6:4 to this specific association.

The only possible exceptions to this rule in the gospel, that is where someone other than Jesus participates in a prayer-perception dynamic, are found in the figures of Anna (Lk. 1:37–38) and, possibly, Simeon (Lk. 1:25–33). However, once again in both instances the prayer dynamic is self-referential. And, at least in Simeon's case, the revelation of Jesus' identity is specifically mentioned, not as the result of any personal prayer, but as the fulfillment of a previously offered promise given through divine initiative. When these observations are combined with the fact that both Simeon and Anna meet the infant Jesus, who is unlikely to have already begun his own prayer ministry (!), it is seen that the basic observation is unaffected: whenever people are presented as perceiving Jesus' true identity in association with prayer, it is *only in connection with Jesus' own prayers*, no one else's.

3) The final observation to be derived from this evidence has already appeared in the previous section. When another person does receive some spiritual insight from these illuminating prayers it always concerns the nature and status of Jesus himself. This has already been amply demonstrated throughout the gospel.

### 5.1.3 Experience and Instruction in Luke

Even though this thesis is not a study of Luke's parenetic material, a brief look at how he handles Jesus' teaching on prayer will demonstrate how thoroughly Luke's attitudes towards the sovereignty of God have shaped his treatment not only of the actual phenomenon of prayer, but also of Jesus' instruction about the practice of prayer. Luke handles his source materials in such a way that what Jesus says about prayer aligns perfectly with the "open door" dynamic between heaven and earth illustrated through the practice of prayer in Luke-Acts.

---

[66] Cf. O. Weinreich, *Gebet und Wunder*, (Stuttgart, 1929), p. 322. Weinreich also observes that the content of the prayer is not given (p. 321).

### 5.1.3.1 "Praying with Faith": Luke's Use of Mark (Mk. 9:28f; 11:22–24)

Most of Mark's prayer material, and Luke's use or rearrangement of it, has already been discussed incidentally at some point in the course of this study (Mk. 1:35; 6:46; 14:32, 35f, 38f; 15:34). It only remains to comment upon the Markan material which Luke chooses to omit from his gospel. Mark 13:18 may fit this category, although Lk. 21:36 is probably intended as a preferred equivalent, in which case it should be categorised as a Lukan alteration. This leaves two texts with no equivalent in Luke, and their absence is extremely significant.[67] For both (Mk. 9:28f and 11:22–24) link the efficacy of prayer with the quality and/or quantity of one's faith, promising that the requests of believing prayer will always be granted.

Luke's version of Jesus' healing of a demon-possessed boy (Lk. 9:37–43) omits Mark's promise concerning the efficacy of prayer (Mk. 9:28f). Mark's story highlights the value of faith (vv. 19, 23–24), an issue for both the boy's father, who wrestled with unbelief, and the disciples, who lacked the faith necessary for success. The story-line progresses from Jesus' promise that "everything is possible for him who believes" (v. 23), to the disciples' question concerning their failure, "Why could we not drive it out?" (v. 28), and concludes with Jesus' reply that "this kind can come out only by prayer" (v. 29). Thus Mark associates the necessity of prayer with the promises of faith; by doing this he indicates that the solution to the disciples' dilemma was prayer offered in genuine faith.

Matthew's version of this story eliminates Jesus' words concerning prayer, as does Luke. But Matthew then elaborates upon the "faith" aspect of the story (Mt. 17:17–20) by adding the "Q" saying concerning faith "the size of a mustard seed." Luke's equivalent to this "Q" logion is found in Lk. 17:6,[68] where it concerns not the faith required to perform miracles as in Mark and Matthew, but the faith necessary for limitless forgiveness (cf. the difference in Mt. 18:21f). The results of Luke's rearrangement are two-fold.

---

[67] Very little attention has been given to Luke's treatment of Mark's prayer material. Only one attempt has really been made to explain the motives behind Luke's editorial work, particularly his omission of Markan material, and this by J. Dupont, "La Prière et son Efficacité dans L'Evangile de Luc," *RSR.* 69 ('81) 45–56; reprinted in *La Parole de Grâce: Etudes lucaniennes à la mémoire d'Augustin George,* (Paris, 1981). Dupont reaches the correct conclusions ("Prière," pp. 54f), but his treatment of individual passages (Mk. 9:28f; 11:24f) is not always as germane to the conclusions derived from them as one might hope. Dupont acknowledges a debt to the work of A. George, who discusses Lukan prayer in *Etudes sur L'Oeuvre de Luc,* (Paris, 1978), pp. 395–427. But George's work is cursory; Luke's redaction is not discussed in any detail; and George never examines Luke's omissions of Markan material. Fuhrman, *A Redactional Study of Prayer in the Gospel of Luke,* who appears to be unfamiliar with either Dupont or George, gives attention to Luke's use of Mark but his proposed thesis prejudices his analysis from the start. Consequently, while observing Luke's omissions (pp. 121–123, 126f), he is unable to attempt any explanation beyond admitting that they are "puzzling" and "obscure."

[68] Marshall, *Commentary,* p. 643; Fitzmyer, *The Gospel,* vol. II, pp. 1141f.

Firstly, Mark's teaching on the efficacy of the prayer offered in faith disappears from Luke. Luke does more than simplify the issues of the story.[69] He explicitly eliminates any possibility of finding there the promise that all things are possible for those who pray with enough faith.

Secondly, Luke's down-playing of the role of faith in this miracle combines with his distinctive use of the "Q" tradition concerning faith so that he nowhere makes the kind of "anything is possible if you believe" statements that are found in Matthew and Mark. His single logion to this effect (17:6) has been carefully circumscribed by the demands of forgiveness; it is not an open promise to the possibilities of the miraculous.

The other piece of Markan prayer material omitted from Luke is related to Jesus' withering of the fig tree (Mk. 11:24; par. Mt. 21:22). There Jesus says, "Whatever you ask for in prayer, believe that you have received it, and it will be yours." It is unlikely that Luke's omission of the cursing of the fig tree (Mk. 11:12–14, 20–23) can account for his omission of Mk. 11:24–25, for, as Dupont points out, these later verses are too tenuously related to the preceding material to have required excision along with the cursing narrative.[70] He suggests that Luke's aversion to doublets may explain the omisson of Mk. 11:25, since it is very similar to Lk. 11:4. This could well be; and the principle might be extended even further. Mk. 11:23 also may have been omitted as a doublet of the "Q" logion preserved in Lk. 17:6 (cf. the doublet in Mt. 17:20; 21:21). But be this as it may, it still fails to account for Luke's omission of Mk. 11:24. The only doublet to this statement is found in Mk. 9:23, 29, which is also the other Markan prayer passage omitted by Luke! This coincidence must strike the reader as more than accidental. In the first place, by excising these two texts Luke has eliminated the only two pieces of parenetic prayer material found in his Markan source. And, secondly, both of these texts convey an identical attitude towards prayer, namely that prayer requests are inevitably granted when they are made with enough faith.

It should be evident that Luke omits both of these passages for the same reason: they convey an attitude towards prayer which is at odds with the rest of his theology. For Luke it is not the will of the individual, but the will of God which is decisive in how prayer is answered. Prayer is not a means of instructing God, but of being instructed by God. Prayer opens an avenue for the individual to be incorporated into God's plan as the divine will becomes actualised in his or her life, whether or not the details of that will have been requested or anticipated. God cannot be coerced, nor may ideas which fall outside of his will be grafted onto his plan by any degree of faith.

---

[69] *Pace* Dupont, "Prière," pp. 47f, who believes Luke is merely highlighting Jesus' power to perform miracles (cf. especially v. 43).

[70] Dupont, "Prière," p. 48; *pace* Fuhrman, *Redactional Study*, pp. 126f.

5.1.3.2 "Persistent" Prayer and the Will of God (Lk. 11:5–13; 18:1–8)

It is increasingly recognised today that what has traditionally been labelled Luke's parable of the "Importunate Friend" (11:5–8) does not concern itself with persistence in prayer at all. There is no need to rehearse here the lexical debate surrounding ἡ ἀναιδεία in v. 8, which holds the key to a proper interpretation of the parable.[71] For the purposes of the present argument it is enough to note that, depending upon whom the quality of "shamelessness/boldness" is referred to, the petitioner or the householder, this parable deals with either the faithfulness of God in hearing prayer, or the confidence with which the praying disciple may approach God, or both.[72] All suggestions of "persistence" in the interpretation are totally unwarranted. Luke is not teaching that one may bend God's will by first bending his ear. Prayer offered repeatedly enough is no more guaranteed to effect the desired result than is prayer offered faithfully enough.

Having once eliminated ideas of persistence from the interpretation of Lk. 11:5–8 it becomes even easier to see them as rightly excluded from the interpretation of the Parable of the Unjust Judge (Lk. 18:1–8).[73] The concern over "justice" (vv. 3, 5, 7, 8) and anticipated-yet-delayed retribution (vv. 4a, 7f) indicate, first of all, that the scope of this instruction concerns perseverance amidst oppression; it does not offer generalised teaching on all petitionary prayer. Secondly, Luke's

---

[71] See N. Levison, "Importunity?," *Exp.* 9/3 ('25) 456–460; A. Fridrichsen, "Exegetisches zum Neuen Testament," *SO.* 13 ('34) 38–46, esp. 40–43; Harris, *Prayer*, p. 86; J. D. M. Derrett, "The Friend at Midnight – Asian Ideas in the Gospel of St. Luke" in *Donum Gentilicium: New Testament Studies in Honour of David Daube*, (Oxford, 1978), pp. 79–85; J. Jeremias, *The Parables of Jesus*, (New York, 1972), pp. 158f; K. E. Bailey, *Poet and Peasant: A Literary Cultural Approach to the Parables in Luke*, (Grand Rapids, 1976), pp. 119–133; R. R. Rickards, "The Translation of Luke 11.5–13," *BT.* 28 ('77) 239–243; A. F. Johnson, "Assurance for Man: The Fallacy of Translating ANAIDEIA by 'Persistence' in Luke 11:5–8," *JETS.* 22 ('79) 123–131; D. R. Catchpole, "Q and 'The Friend at Midnight' (Luke xi. 5–8/9)," *JTS.* 34 ('83) 407–411 (but cf. p. 413, where "persistence" is seen to enter in by way of Luke's redaction). The evidence for ἀναιδεία meaning something akin to "shamelessness/boldness" is overwhelming. It is surprising, therefore, to find the "persistence" interpretation continuing to be repeated by commentators: cf. Ellis, *The Gospel*, p. 166; Monloubou, *La Prière*, p. 78; A. Wurzinger, "'Es komme Dein Königreich' zum Gebetsanliegen nach Lukas," *BL.* 38 ('64–65) 94; Fitzmyer, *The Gospel*, vol. II, p. 910. Ott tries to have it both ways by recognising the linguistic arguments in favour of "audaciousness," but insinuating "persistence" by means of a comparison with Lk. 18:1–8, which is necessary for his overall thesis; thus he combines the two different definitions without explaining why; see *Gebet*, pp. 29–31.

[72] For the arguments of those who prefer the first option see Marshall, *Commentary*, p. 465, but also cf. pp. 462ff; Manson, *Mission and Message*, pp. 559f; Grundmann, *Das Evangelium*, pp. 228, 235; Feldkämper, *Der betende Jesus*, p. 188; Bailey, *Poet*, p. 133; Ernst, *Das Evangelium*, p. 366. J. Heinemann, *Prayer in the Talmud*, p. 245 provides some illuminating rabbinic parallels to both Lk. 11:5–8 and 18:1–8.

For the arguments of those who prefer the second option see Harris, *Prayer*, pp. 87f; A. D. Martin, "The Parable concerning Hospitality," *ExpT.* 37 ('25–26) 411–414; Derrett, "Asian Ideas," pp. 83–85.

[73] For example, cf. Ott's reciprocal interpretation of these two texts as a "parable-pair"; *Gebet*, pp. 71ff, 23–25; also Monloubou, *La Prière*, p. 78; Catchpole, "The Friend," pp. 411–413.

introduction (v. 1) is therefore concerned with bolstering belief in the value of prayer itself, not enjoining repetition of the same prayers over and over to achieve a desired end.[74] This repetitive approach to prayer has already been made by the oppressed, without success (v. 7). Indeed, it is the fact that repeated prayers for justice are *not* immediately answered (v. 7) which gives this parable its pastoral relevance. According to Luke, the timing of God's will does not ignore the disciples' prayers, but it is established independently of such prayers. It is the crisis of faith which may result from this collision between divine sovereignty and a naive belief in the immediate efficacy of persistent prayer that elicits Luke's exhortation to "always pray and not give up" so as to "be found faithful" by the Son of Man (v. 8). Thus this second parable not only does not teach that God's intentions may be immediately influenced by persistence in prayer, but it actually addresses the pastoral problems which may result when persecuted Christians approach God with just such ideas about prayer in mind.[75] The Parable of the Unjust Judge promises that God does answer prayer, but also warns of the dangers inherent in believing that prayers offered often enough will invariably be answered as and when requested.

The unifying theme throughout all of this material is that God is faithful to hear prayer *and* faithful to work his own good will. Lk. 18:1–8 checks inappropriate interpretations of Lk. 11:5–8, just as a proper understanding of ἀναιδεία (11:8) prepares the way for a clearer understanding of Luke's charge "to always pray" (18:1). The fact that the householder in chapter 11 gives his friend exactly what he asks for when he asks for it is not intended to mean that God can always be counted on to do the same for his disciples. Such a positive-answer-guaranteed interpretation would be as inappropriate as the element of persistence was seen to be earlier. Luke's use of the following "Q" material (11:9–13), with its distinctive Lukan features, is intended to circumvent just such thoughts as these before they are able to develop.

The first indication of Luke's purposes for this pericope is found in his pairing of fish/serpent, egg/scorpion (vv. 11f; cf. Mt. 7:9f, bread/stone, fish/serpent).[76] Luke contrasts two requests for food with two harmful alternatives. It has frequently been suggested that the point of Luke's two comparisons is the assurance that God will not deceive his children, references being made to serpents which look like

---

[74] Ott, *Gebet*, pp. 68f, reaches essentially the same conclusion. Luke uses ἐκτενῶς (Lk. 22:44; Acts 12:5) to refer to "persistence;" πάντοτε answers the question "How long?" by replying, "All the time."

[75] Note how the haggadic stories quoted by Heinemann (*Prayer in the Talmud*, p. 245), concerned as they are not with the efficacy of prayer techniques but with the faithfulness of God in hearing prayer, include parallels to both of these parables, indicating that each may be interpreted quite easily without any overtones of "persistence."

[76] The question of the original "Q" form of these pairings is interesting but not germane to answering the more important question of how Luke's (or Matthew's) pairs function within his gospel.

fish[77] and rolled up scorpions resembling eggs.[78] However, this "trickery" approach to understanding these pairs seems rather far-fetched. Surely the point being made is more straight-forward: God can be counted upon not to give his disciples harmful things, but to give them only good things.[79]

Luke's parable then finds its force through an *a fortiori* comparison with God (v. 13). If human fathers can be counted upon not to give harmful things to their children when they ask for good things, how much more may God be counted upon to do the same.[80] So far so good. But a final Lukan distinctive requires that this *a minori ad maius* argument be drawn out even further. Whereas Matthew promises that the Father may be counted upon to give his children "good things" (Mt. 7:11) in general, Luke specifies this good thing to be the Holy Spirit (Lk. 11:13).[81] The answer which God has to make to Christian prayer becomes very particular, resulting in the restriction of those things which may fall within the category of "good gifts." That which is considered to be "good" is no longer determined by the request of the petitioner, but by the will of the one petitioned. Consequently, Luke suggests that the *a fortiori* nature of the argument be extended, ie. if God will not give you harmful things when you knowingly ask for good things, is he any more likely to give you harmful things when you unwittingly ask for harmful things?[82]

By specifying the best gift Luke indicates that prayer is not a guaranteed means of acquiring whatever one asks for; it is the means by which God gives what he determines to be good. Luke does not say that the Father gives the Holy Spirit to "those who ask for it." He says that he gives the Spirit to those who pray. The verb

---

[77] Ott, *Gebet*, pp. 104–106; B. Hjerl-Hansen, "Le rapprochement poisson-serpent dans la prédication de Jésus (Mt. VII, 10 et Luc. XI, 11)," *RB.* 55 ('48) 195–198.

[78] H. Pegg, "'A Scorpion for an Egg' (Luke xi. 12)," *ExpT.* 38 ('26–27) 468–469; Plummer, *St. Luke*, p. 300.

[79] So too Bailey, *Poet*, p. 139; Marshall, *Commentary*, p. 466; Ott, *Gebet*, p. 110. Feldkämper, *Der betende Jesus*, pp. 197–201, following Miyoshi's analysis of Lk. 10:19 (*Der Anfang*, pp. 102–107), concludes that the serpent and scorpion represent demonic powers, the meaning being that God gives the Holy Spirit not simply as a "good gift" but as that power needed to overcome the demonic opponents of the coming Kingdom; cf. also P. Grelot, "Etude critique de Luc 10,19" in *La Parole de Grâce*, pp. 87–100, especially pp. 92–96. However, whatever one thinks of Miyoshi's arguments, Feldkämper's application of his conclusions to Lk. 11:11–13 is unacceptable. Would Luke have even considered it worth mentioning that, "If you ask God for something to eat you can count on him not to give you a demon"? The point of the parable is "God will not give you 'A' but will give you 'B';" *not* "God will give you 'B' in order to combat 'A'."

[80] Jeremias, *Parables*, p. 159.

[81] The debate concerning which version constitutes the original "Q" tradition continues; however, the answer is irrelevant to the present argument.

[82] At this point is should be clear that Matthew's bread/stone pair would not adequately fit Luke's purposes. Whichever evangelist preserves the original "Q" pairings (if either of them do), the present argument supplies the "motive" which Marshall (*Commentary*, p. 469) considers lacking in others' attempts to explain Luke's form as a deliberate alteration of "Q". In addition, Ott's suggestion (*Gebet*, pp. 109–112) that Luke regards all earthly gifts as harmful is seen to be wanting. The point is not that earthly gifts are harmful, but that God will not give his children harmful things even if they inadvertently ask for them.

αἰτέω serves not only as a catchword, providing a verbal link between the various pieces of tradition brought together by Luke in 11:1–13, but in so functioning it also acquires the connotations of the verb προσεύχομαι itself. Thus by the time Luke has unfolded his argument and reached the end of v. 13, τοῖς αἰτοῦσιν αὐτόν cannot mean "those who ask him (for the Holy Spirit)," for also observe the absence of any indirect object, but merely "those who pray." Furthermore, since the emphasis throughout has been upon the dependability of God's giving good things to all, it would seem unlikely that the conclusion be intended to suddenly circumscribe this promise with the proviso that God will only give his best gift to those who consciously ask for it.

It becomes apparent that, even in the handling of his parenetic tradition, Luke is guided by the conviction that prayer is a channel through which God reveals his will to men; neither faith, nor persistence, nor even specific requests for apparently good things may guarantee that the pray-er will receive exactly what he asks for. Such "positive" answers to prayer are instances where the individual's request coincides with the Father's will, which is the ideal situation of all prayer, and which is exactly why Jesus' prayer-life is seen to be so effective: he always prays according to the will of his Father (10:21–22). True prayer involves learning from God as much if not more than asking of God.[83] .

### 5.1.3.3 "Exceptions" and Conclusions: Prayer and Divine Sovereignty

Apparent exceptions to these conclusions about prayer and divine sovereignty disappear upon closer examination. The fact that Luke presents the Spirit as the best answer to prayer does not contradict the earlier observation that there is no exclusive connection between prayer and the Spirit. The point in Lk. 11:13 is not that God will always give the Spirit in answer to every prayer ever prayed; it is rather that God responds to prayer according to his own higher determinations, the best of which is the gift of the Spirit.

The apostles' prayer for Matthias (Acts 1:24) might also at first appear to be an exception. After all, does not God answer according to the request? But this story actually has less to do with Luke's theology of prayer than with his view of the integrity of the original circle of the Twelve. Consequently, it confirms the observation that prayer offered according to the will of God will always receive a "positive" response. Perhaps the same could be said about Peter's prayer in Acts 9:40. The context may suggest that he prayed for Tabitha's resurrection, but no

---

[83] Though Dupont ("Prière," pp. 54f) also becomes entangled in considerations of "persistence," his final evaluation of Luke's theology of prayer is correct: "... ne doit pas être regardée comme un moyen de faire pression sur Dieu et d'obtenir qu'il cede devant des désirs humains. Il n'y a de priere authentique que celle qui ouvre l'homme a l'action de l'Esprit une action qui le conformera aux désirs de Dieu et aux exigences de son Regne."

such words are stated. The impression, again, is that prayer allows the will of God to be realised through the pray-er.

The story of the church's prayer for the imprisoned Peter (Acts 12:5–17) raises numerous questions, but also falls short of contradicting these conclusions.[84] The mystery of divine sovereignty is highlighted by the fact that James is martyred (12:2), for whom there is no mention of the church praying, while Peter is delivered. Perhaps this itself reflects the conviction that prayer may reveal God's will but not alter it. In any event, the praying church's surprise at Peter's release (vv. 13–15) hardly testifies to the power of their faith; at the very least it indicates that God answered their prayer in a fashion which was wholly unanticipated by the prayer itself. Overall, the picture in Acts is more that of the church's prayer being in general agreement with God's plan, rather than God's action being determined by the prayers of the church.

Similarly, in the case of Zechariah and Elizabeth (Lk. 1:13), in addition to the ambiguity of the angelic announcement, Zechariah's response (v. 18) makes it clear that he had stopped believing in the value of his prayers, and so had probably stopped praying for a son, long ago. God had not been compelled by either Zechariah's faith or persistence.

Luke is consistent throughout all the various strata of his two-volume work: God enlists human prayer in the outworking of his plan, but the efficacy of prayer is not determined by anything which the pray-er brings, except agreement with the will of God.[85] It would be difficult to find a more non-magical view of prayer than that presented in Luke-Acts. The distinctive feature of magical thought, wherein one seeks to control or compel divine forces to operate in a desired fashion through the careful use of specific techniques, is far removed from the

---

[84] A good discussion of the issues in this passage is contained in I. H. Marshall, "Apg 12 – ein Schlüssel zum verständnis der Apostelgeschichte" in *Das Petrusbild in der neueren Forschung*, (Wuppertal, 1987), pp. 192–220.

[85] Heinemann also observes this as an aspect of Jesus' prayer-life, although his observations come from the gospels generally, not Luke in particular. He identifies this as one of the points of significant difference between Jesus and early Judaism. Judaism acknowledged the sovereignty of God but never abandoned a belief in the power of petition to influence His will; see *Prayer in the Talmud*, pp. 185f; "The Background of Jesus' Prayer," pp. 86f. However, there were elements within Judaism which were not very different from the attitudes expressed here in Luke; cf. for example the story of Ḥanina ben Dosa, who said of his prayers for healing, that "if I have freedom in prayer, I know that it is accepted; if not, I know that it is rejected"; see G. F. Moore, *Judaism in the First Centuries of the Christian Era*, vol. I, (Cambridge, 1957, 7th ed.), p. 377; also cf. vol. II, p. 236; m. Ber. 5:5; b. Ber. 34b. According to R. Isaac (b. R. H. 16b) praying in the belief that God is required to answer as requested ("the scrutinizing of prayer") is a sinful presumption. Particularly interesting is Ex. R. 31:5 on 22:24, which comments upon Solomon's prayer of dedication at the Temple; it describes Solomon as praying that God answer a man's request for money only if He knows that it will not bring harm to the man. This is precisely Luke's view of prayer and sovereignty. For further discussion of how Judaism related petitionary prayer to divine sovereignty see G. Harder, *Paulus und das Gebet*, (Gütersloh, 1936), pp. 133ff.

attitudes expressed by Luke.[86] The peculiar power of Jesus' prayer experience, which set him apart as unique,[87] is not explicable in magical categories. It must be viewed within an eschatological framework. Luke presents Jesus as the final Prophet, the Son of God and messiah, who pursues his ministry of teaching and healing in perfect obedience through the guidance and power of God, which was made available to him through prayer. The second half of this chapter will now develop this aspect of prayer in the ministry of Jesus.

## 5.2 Prayer and Jesus' Messianic Mission

### 5.2.1 Jesus' Baptism: The Inauguration of His Messianic Task

Luke's baptismal scene is different from Mark's in that it no longer serves as an introduction to the gospel. Through his birth narratives Luke has already given his reader much of the same information, so that a good deal of the significance of Mark's baptismal narrative has been fulfilled long before Lk. 3:21. This raises the

---

[86] This observation is particularly important in light of Hull's claim that Luke's portrayal of Jesus is one of the most magical of all the gospels; cf. *Magic*, pp. 87ff. Of course, the distinction between magic and religion may not always be rigidly defined, and thus, perhaps not always as definitely excluded from consideration as it is in Luke. However, M. Smith's attempt to eliminate the differences altogether by saying it is a "cliche that the religious man petitions the gods while the magician tries to compel them" has not met with general acceptance; see his *Jesus the Magician*, (London, 1978), p. 69. Smith tries to use Jesus' prayer-life as an argument for his status as a magician, saying that "Prayer was a specialty of ancient magicians. An early Greek term for 'a man who can get what he wants from the gods' – who will later be called 'a magician' – is 'a prayer,' namely, one who can pray effectively" (p. 130). This statement is interesting for two reasons: 1) it implicitly admits to the particular character of magic, generally accepted by scholars, yet earlier rejected by Smith; and, 2) it has been shown that this is exactly how Luke does not describe either Jesus' prayer-life or his teaching on prayer. M. Nilsson's comment is significant in this regard (*Greek Piety*, [New York, 1969], p. 175): "Magicians do not pray but compel gods or daimones by their potency."
For a good critique of Hull and Smith see Achtemeier, "Lukan Perspective on the Miracles," pp. 556–558; H. C. Kee, *Miracle in the Early Christian World: A Study in Sociological Method*, (New Haven, 1983), pp. 211ff, 288; *Medicine, Miracle and Magic in New Testament Times*, (Cambridge, 1986), pp. 112–115; also E. Yamauchi, "Magic or Miracle? Diseases, Demons and Exorcisms" in *Gospel Perspectives: The Miracles of Jesus*, Vol. 6, (Sheffield, 1986), p. 154 n. 61 for a list of reviews. For a discussion of magic in general, and the features marking it as an attempt to gain control over spiritual forces, see Kee, *Medicine*, pp. 95–121; Yamauchi, "Magic," pp. 131f; Hamman, "La Prière," pp. 1230f; E. M. Butler, *Ritual Magic*, (Cambridge, 1949), pp. 3, 14f; E. R. Dodds, *Pagan and Christian in an Age of Anxiety*, (New York, 1965), p. 125, n. 5; T. W. Davies, *Magic, Divination and Demonolgy among the Hebrews and their Neighbours*, (London, 1898), pp. 1–24, 59–64; J. Bergmann, "Gebet und Zauberspruch," *MGWJ*. 74 ('30) 457–463, who discusses five important differences between prayer and magic (pp. 462f); and D. Aune, "Magic in Early Christianity," *ANRW*, II.23.2, pp. 1515–1518, 1522, 1538, 1551, who draws upon the important work of W. J. Goode, "Magic and Religion: A Continuum," *Ethnos*. 14 ('49) 172–182.

[87] As already observed, there are points at which Jesus' experience is identical to that of the disciples: God answers even the Son's prayers according to His own will; and, prayer is regularly the point at which even Jesus receives his revelatory experiences; cf. George, *Etudes*, p. 415.

question of exactly what significance Luke attached to this pericope. Fitzmyer observes, "The only distinctive Lucan element in it is the notice that the heavenly identification of Jesus took place while he was at prayer . . ."[88] While prayer is not the only distinctive element, its distinctive importance has already been introduced. Now it is time to complete the discussion of how this baptismal prayer fits into Luke's unfolding portrayal of Jesus' ministry.

### 5.2.1.1 Lk. 3:21–4:44: The Beginning of the Messiah's Ministry

Arguments for a thematic unity in the material covering Lk. 3:21–4:44 do not stand or fall with adherence to any particular outline of Lukan structure.[89] Thematic development may easily transcend structural considerations; indeed, this is one of the complicating factors which makes the identification of any readily agreed upon "outline" so difficult. This material is the key to the correct interpretation of Jesus' baptism. Luke makes it plain that he is presenting the beginning (ἀρχόμενος, 3:23) of Jesus' ministry.[90] This means that the qualities which characterise this beginning are not unique to the beginning, but are presented as characteristic of the whole of Jesus' ministry. The things which are discovered here may be presumed for Jesus throughout the remainder of Luke.

### 5.2.1.1.1 The Messiah is Sent to Preach with the Spirit

Jesus' sermon in Nazareth "ostensibly defines the purpose of Jesus' Spirit-anointing."[91] He explains it as the necessary equipment for his being sent out to preach in both the Nazareth synagogue and later to the following crowds (εὐαγγελίσασθαι... ἀπέσταλκέν με κηρύξαι..., ἀποστεῖλαι... κηρύξαι..., 4:18–19,

---

[88] *The Gospel*, vol, I, p. 481.

[89] For a presentation of the various ways in which different outlines deal with this material see Fitzmyer, *The Gospel*, vol. I, pp. 135–142; Marshall, *Commentary*, pp. 131, 175; and Ernst, *Das Evangelium*, pp. 135, 165f: Preparation of the Ministry, John and Jesus (3:1–4:13), Galilean Ministry (4:14–9:50).Schurmann, *Lukas*, pp. 146–148: Beginnings in Galilea (3:1–4:44); Ellis, *The Gospel*, pp. 32–36: Inaugurating the Mission (2:41–4:30), Acts of the Messiah (4:31–6:11). Grundmann, *Das Evangelium*, pp. v–vi: John and Jesus (3:1–4:30), Jesus in Galilee (4:31–9:50). Danker, *New Age*, pp. 42, 54: John and Jesus (3:1–38), Outreach to Israel (4:1–9:50). J. H. Davies, "The Lucan Prologue (1–3): An Attempt at Objective Redaction Criticism," *TU*. 112 ('73) 78–85: Gospel Prologue (1:1–3:38).

[90] Cf. 4:21; B. Chilton, "Announcement in Nazara: An Analysis of Luke 4:16–21" in *Gospel Perspectives: Studies of History and Tradition in the Four Gospels*, (Sheffield, 1981), p. 160.

[91] Turner, "Jesus and the Spirit," p. 14. After examining Luke's redaction at 4:1, 14 Turner concludes that "we can be virtually certain that Luke intends us to interpret Jesus' baptismal experience in the light of what Jesus is reported to have said in 4:18–21." Also see "The Significance of Receiving the Spirit in Luke-Acts: A Survey of Modern Scholarship," *TJ*. ns. 2 ('81) 157.

43–44).[92] The Isaianic figure with whom Jesus identifies is himself a prophetic character, even a figure of the Mosaic Deliverer (cf. Is. 49:1–13; especially cf. v. 6 with Lk. 1:30–32).[93] The frequency with which the outpouring of the Spirit is associated with the work of the Isaianic servant easily explains the genetic connection made by Luke between the descent of the Spirit in 3:22, (cf. also Is. 42:1 ἐπ' αὐτόν, LXX; ἐπ' αὐτόν Lk. 3:22; also see Is. 11:2; 44:2f), and Jesus' exposition of Is. 61:1–2 at Nazareth.[94] And the use made of this passage in 11QMelch indicates

---

[92] The nature of the Spirit of prophecy and the role of the Spirit in the unique messianic status of Jesus are closely related but distinct issues; on the importance of this distinction see M. M. B. Turner, "Jesus and the Spirit," pp. 3–42. On the Spirit of prophecy see E. Pollard, "The Prophetic Activity of Jesus," BW. 24 ('04) 94–99; H. Cadbury, "Jesus and the Prophets," JR. 5 ('25) 607–622; C. H. Dodd, "Jesus as Teacher and Prophet" in Mysterium Christi, (London, 1930), pp. 53–66; P. Davies, "Jesus and the Role of the Prophet," JBL. 64 ('45) 241–254; F. Young, "Jesus the Prophet: A Re-Examination," JBL. 68 ('49) 285–299; Lampe, "Holy Spirit in Luke," pp. 173–180; F. Gils, Jésus prophète dans les evangiles synoptiques, (Louvain, 1957), pp. 45, 164; Barrett, The Holy Spirit, pp. 21, 94–99; Schweizer, "πνεῦμα," pp. 382, 400–407; G. Friedrich, "προφήτης," TDNT. vol. VI, pp. 843–847; F. Schnider, Jesus der Prophet, (Göttingen, 1973).

[93] R. Bloch, "Quelques Aspects de la Figure de Moïse dans la Tradition Rabbinique in Moïse L'Homme de L'Alliance, (Tournai, 1955), pp. 149–156; W. Brownlee, "Messianic Motifs of Qumran and the New Testament," NTS. 3 ('56–7) 18; Turner, "Jesus and the Spirit," pp. 25–27; A. Bentzen, King and Messiah, (Oxford, 1970, 2nd ed.), pp. 48–70; also cf. the discussion and review of the German edition of Bentzen's work (Messias – Moses redivivus -Menschensohn, [Zurich, 1948]) by R. Hicks, "Messiah, Second Moses, Son of Man," ATR. 33 ('51) 24–29, especially pp. 26f. Some, such as H. M. Teeple, The Mosaic Eschatological Prophet, (Philadelphia, 1957), pp. 56–60, and Bock, Proclamation, pp. 109f, have argued against this view, saying that the Isaianic Servant is depicted as both prophet and king (but especially as king; so Bock), and therefore cannot be a "New Moses" figure. However, W. Meeks has conclusively demonstrated that the eschatological New Moses was consistently portrayed as both prophet and king; see The Prophet-King: Moses Traditions and the Johannine Christology, (Leiden, 1967).

[94] Thus even though it is debated whether Is. 61 deals with the Isaianic Servant, the association of the role played by that figure and the task initiated by Jesus' baptism, which is related to the Servant, is made clear. In any case, Luke would have only been thinking in terms of a single, pneumatic figure described by the different Isaianic songs, being free of the various modern speculations regarding "deutero" Isaiahs. For a brief discussion of the various positions in the debate with bibliography see J. Sanders, "From Isaiah 61 to Luke 4" in Christianity, Judaism and Other Greco-Roman Cults, (Leiden, 1975), pp. 80–82, especially p. 80, notes 9–11; also S. Mowinckel, He That Cometh, (Oxford, 1959), pp. 254–255; for a discussion of the Servant-as-Prophet see Mowinckel, pp. 190–196, 214–233. The Qumran text 11QMelch. indicates that, in at least some quarters of Judaism, Is. 61 was understood as a pivotal text in the expectation of a Spirit-endowed, heavenly figure who would come as God's eschatological messenger in the last days. See M. de Jonge and A. S. van der Woude, "11Q Melchizedek and the New Testament," NTS. 12 ('66) 306–310; M. de Jonge, "The Use of the Word 'Anointed' in the Time of Jesus," NovT. 8 ('66) 141–142; J. Fitzmyer, "Further Light on Melchizedek from Qumran Cave 11," JBL. 86 ('67) 34; D. Hill, "The Rejection of Jesus at Nazareth (Luke iv 16–30)," NovT. 13 ('71) 179; J. Sanders, "From Isaiah 61," pp. 90–91, 103. The targum Ps-Jonathan also identified the Is. 61 figure as a prophet with respect to the song of Is. 42; see A. Finkel, "Jesus' Sermon at Nazareth (Luk. 4, 16–30)" in Abraham unser Vater: Juden und Christen im Gespräch über die Bibel, (Leiden, 1963), p. 109; Sanders, "From Isaiah 61," pp. 85–88. De Jonge and van der Woude further suggest that the Anointed Prophet in 11QMelch. may be synonymous with the prophet-like-Moses referred to in 4QTest. ("11QMelchizedek," p. 307). The relevance of these materials to Lk. 4:16ff is discussed by Turner, "Jesus and the Spirit," pp. 18–22.

that proclamation was an expected part of the messianic Deliverer's work when he arrived.[95] Jesus' explanation that "Today this scripture is fulfilled," indicates his adoption of a decidedly eschatological attitude towards himself; *he* is now this Spirit-anointed figure, by virtue of his baptism. Perhaps Luke presents the masses as unsure of Jesus' identity, wondering if he is "a" prophet, but it is clear that Luke presents Jesus as looking upon himself as *the* final Prophet, from the very beginning of his earthly ministry.[96]

Now that Jesus has received the necessary equipment, he sets about his task: he has been "sent" by God and so he "goes" (cf. 4:1, 14, 16, 30, 31, 34, 38, 42);[97] he is responsible for proclaiming God's word and so he teaches (4:15, 17–27, 31, 32, 36, 43–44); he has been sent to deliverer God's people, and so he heals (4:39, 40) and casts out demons (4:35–36, 41).[98]

Luke presents the beginning of Jesus' ministry with a flurry of activity, but he lays special emphasis upon his proclamation and the power of his word. By repeating the issues at both the beginning and the end of this section, in something of a three-fold conceptual *inclusio*, Luke highlights three points. Firstly, Jesus is anointed with the Spirit so as to be sent out as God's Deliverer (cf. v. 32b). Secondly, he pursues an itinerant ministry, teaching and healing throughout the entire countryside (cf. v. 31). Thirdly, his enthusiastic reception by all the people bears witness to his success (cf. v. 32a).

1. Jesus goes in the power of the Spirit to preach
a) v. 14a ὑπέστρεψεν ὁ Ἰησοῦς ἐν τῇ δυνάμει τοῦ
    πνεύματος εἰς τὴν Γαλιλαίαν
a') v. 43b ὅτι ἐπὶ τοῦτο ἀπεστάλην (cf. vv. 1, 18)

2. He pursues his ministry throughout the countryside
b) v. 15a καὶ αὐτὸς ἐδίδασκεν ἐν ταῖς συναγωγαῖς
    αὐτῶν
b') v. 43a καὶ ταῖς ἑτέραις πόλεσιν εὐαγγελίσασθαί με
    v. 44 καὶ ἦν κηρύσσων εἰς τὰς συναγωγὰς τῆς
    Ἰουδαίας

---

[95] R. Sloan, *The Favorable Year of the Lord: A Study of Jubilary Theology in the Gospel of Luke*, (Austin, 1977), pp. 51, 71f.

[96] So also Sanders, "From Isaiah 61," p. 93, 96; G. Beasley-Murray, "Jesus and the Spirit" in *Mélanges bibliques en hommage au R. P. Béda Rigaux*, (Gembloux, 1970), pp. 473–474; Sloan, *The Favorable Year*, pp. 47f. Consequently, this also indicates that *Luke* presents Jesus as the final Prophet from the beginning of his ministry; *pace* Moule, "Christology," pp. 162f.

[97] Even though Lk. 3:21–22 does not, strictly speaking, have the form of an OT "prophetic calling" narrative, when 3:21–4:44 are taken together the material does show those traits which one would expect as *the result* of such a call experience; see Dodd, "Jesus, Teacher and Prophet," pp. 58, 63; N. Habel, "The Form and Significance of the Call Narratives," *ZAW*. 77 ('65) 297–323; K. Baltzer, "Considerations Regarding the Office and Calling of the Prophet," *HTR*. 61 ('68) 567–581; Davies, "Jesus' Role," p. 251; Higgins, "Jesus as Prophet," p. 293.

[98] de la Potterie, "L'Onction du Christ," pp. 231, 235, 239, 250; Feldkämper, *Der betende Jesus*, p. 35.

3. He is popular with the people

c) v. 14b καὶ φήμη ἐξῆλθεν καθ' ὅλης τῆς περιχώρου
    περὶ αὐτοῦ
   v. 15b δοξαζόμενος ὑπὸ πάντων

c') v. 42b καὶ οι ὄχλοι ἐπεζήτουν αὐτόν, καὶ ἦλθον
     ἕως αὐτοῦ, καὶ κατεῖχον αὐτὸν τοῦ μὴ
     πορεύεσθαι ἀπ' αὐτῶν

In this way the important issues in 3:21–4:44 are highlighted. But the material concerning Nazareth is not only programmatic for the future course of Jesus' ministry;[99] Luke also offers it as being exemplary of what Jesus regularly taught "in their synagogues." Several conclusions result from this observation.

First of all, Jesus is presented as consistently offering himself as the Spirit-filled, messianic Deliverer throughout the whole of the Jewish territory.[100] This explains the introduction of τῆς Ἰουδαίας in v. 44. The example of Jesus' synagogue teaching in Nazareth represents an important ingredient of Jesus' message all throughout his ministry.

Secondly, this explains why Luke does not specify the content of Jesus' teaching in v. 15 ( diff. Mk. 1:14–15). Partly, it may be because it is supplied by the parallel with v. 43 (εὐαγγελίσασθαί με δεῖ τὴν βασιλείαν τοῦ θεοῦ). But, more importantly, it is the Nazareth pericope as a whole which is offered in lieu of Mark's briefer kerygmatic statement. Similarly, Jesus' presentation of himself as God's eschatological prophet, anointed to bring deliverance, is to be implicitly understood as the content of his synagogue teaching elsewhere (4:31, 43–44, 6:6; 13:10).[101]

Finally, Jesus is shown to be faithful to his calling. He has been anointed by the Spirit, and thus equipped to go forth to preach and heal. This is exactly what he does.

---

[99] Fitzmyer, The Gospel, vol. I, p. 529.

[100] Reading Ἰουδαίας (diff. Mk. 1:39) as a theological rather than merely a geographical reference; see G. Lohfink, Die Sammlung Israels: Eine Untersuchung zur lukanischen Ekklesiologie, (München, 1975), p. 40; Davies, "Lucan Prologue," p. 83; Marshall, Commentary, pp. 198f; Fitzmyer, The Gospel, vol. I, p. 558.

[101] Sloan, The Favorable Year, pp. 112f, 174f. The implications of this observation are significant for understanding the relationship between the preaching of Jesus and that of the early church. Bultmann's dictum that "The proclaimer became the proclaimed" (Theology of the New Testament, vol. I, [London, 1952], p. 33) is inadequate, at least for Luke-Acts. According to Luke, Jesus did speak extensively about himself, his calling, and the nature of his mission as an integral part of his proclamation of the Kingdom of God. Beasley-Murray, "Jesus and the Spirit," p. 465 n. 2, points out that a similar observation was made by J. Wellhausen in Das Evangelium Lucae, (Berlin, 1904), pp. 9f, who wrote, "The programme of Mk. 1:15 is quite deliberately omitted by Luke (4:15) and a wholly different one is set in its place." But Beasley-Murray then rejects Wellhausen's position (p. 473). However, this is unnecessary if Jesus' self-definition is integrated as a part of Luke's kerygma, rather than being seen as a wholesale substitution of Mark's.

### 5.2.1.1.2 Messianic Authority and the Praying Jesus

Jesus' baptism, or more accurately, his heavenly confirmation, introduces the unveiling of his messianic role in the gospel. But this new beginning for Jesus is also made the scene of Jesus' first prayer in the gospel. The possibility of there being an effective connection between this prayer and the attendent phenomena which endow Jesus with the Spirit and confirm him as God's Son has already been suggested. If such were the case, it would not only illustrate the way in which Jesus participated in the common human experience of prayer, but it would also illustrate what was distinctive about his prayer experience. Prayer becomes one of the means by which the Father both led the Son into and equipped him for his messianic ministry. It is a channel for divine communication, as it is for all other men, but what God communicates to Jesus is as unique as is his role as Saviour. Here is the last factor in understanding Luke's redaction in 3:21 f. Jesus is endowed with the Spirit *as* the One who prays. He is not only the final Prophet, he is the final Praying Prophet. The birth of his ministry is marked by the same prayer dynamic which will come to characterise it throughout.

The close association of Jesus' prayer with his messianic work is not unique to Luke. It is also found in a rudimentary fashion in the tradition. Mark 1:35, 38 link Jesus' prayer in the desert with his ministry of itinerant preaching. But Mark does not develop the connection. Luke, on the other hand, has turned Mark's single, undeveloped reference into a fundamental principle. This explains Luke's omission of this particular prayer reference from his Markan source.[102] The reference in Lk. 3:21 has taken its place. The transposition of this prayer from the end of Jesus' ministry in Capernaum to the inauguration of his life's ministry at the baptism makes Mark's later reference superfluous, and the role of prayer is made integral to all the various aspects of Jesus' ministry which follow.

The ongoing significance of prayer is further insinuated through the language of "power and authority" (Lk. 4:32, 36). This is closely related to Jesus' possession of the Spirit, for δύναμις and the Holy Spirit are often associated in Luke-Acts (Lk. 1:17, 35; 4:14; 9:1, cf. 11:20; 24:49; Acts 1:8; 6:8, cf. 6:3, 5; 8:13, cf. 6:3, 5; 10:38).[103] Jesus also begins exercising ἐξουσία as a part of his new ministry.[104] The crowds marvel because his λόγος has ἐξουσία (4:32, 36). But Jesus' λόγος comes as the prophetic word offered in the δύναμις of the Spirit, and both of these things, the prophetic commission and the Spirit's anointing, have come to Jesus as he prayed.

Here is the central issue in Luke's baptismal prayer notice. It is not the first revelation of Jesus' sonship,[105] nor does it offer Jesus as the proto-type of Christian

---

[102] Feldkämper, *Der betende Jesus*, pp. 37f. An equally important reason for Luke's omission of this reference is pointed out in the discussion of Lk. 6:12 below.

[103] See Barrett, *The Holy Spirit*, pp. 76f.

[104] Cf. F. F. Bruce, "The Holy Spirit in the Acts of the Apostles," *Int.* 27 ('73) 169f.

[105] *Pace* Harris, *Prayer*, p. 230.

baptism,[106] discipleship[107] or even the post-Pentecostal filling with the Spirit.[108] Luke is presenting Jesus as the Praying Prophetic Deliverer, who receives his commission and is anointed with the Spirit as he prays.

### 5.2.2 Luke 5:16: Jesus Also Fulfills His Commission Through Prayer

The next mention of Jesus' prayer is found in the redactional notice of Lk. 5:16.[109] Mark's mention of Jesus' going out to ἔρημος τόπος (1:45) is adequate in itself to explain why Luke might have considered prayer an appropriate addition to this verse (cf. Mk. 1:35; also Lk. 9:10, diff. Mk. 6:31, where once again Mark's ἔρημος τόπος elicits Luke's addition of ὑποχορέω; see the discussion in chapter 2).[110] This observation, combined with the preceding discussion of Lk. 4:42 (par. Mk. 1:35) with respect to Lk. 3:21 f, is sufficient to show that the prayer notice in Lk. 5:16 is not derived from Mk. 1:35,[111] but is Luke's independent addition.

Luke's reworking of the text results in a significant alteration of Mark's original meaning. In Mark Jesus goes into the desert, not because he chooses to, but in an unsuccessful attempt to avoid the great crowds seeking him in the cities. In Luke, who also shows Jesus being sought by large crowds, Jesus goes into the desert

---

[106] *Pace* A. Loisy, *The Origins of the New Testament*, (London, 1950), pp. 151f; Klostermann, *Lukas*, p. 55 (referring to Acts 8:15). It has already been shown that Luke does not actually relate Jesus' baptism, only that which follows. This would be inexplicable in an episode "paradigmatic" for Christian baptism.It has also been demonstrated that Acts 8:15 makes no connection between baptism and the Spirit, and militates against an association of prayer with the reception of the Spirit, thus obviating any purported parallel with Lk. 3:21 f.

[107] *Pace* Greeven, *Gebet*, pp. 21 f. Jesus certainly is presented by Luke as a model for Christian piety, but asserting this generally does not prove its particular relevance here. It has already been shown that the parallels between Jesus' experience at prayer and that of the early church have as much to do with Jesus' participation in the spiritual dynamics of human prayer as they do with any paradigmatic significance of the prayers themselves. There may be some merit to this point insofar as Jesus' "prophetic" experience is shared by the post-Pentacostal church, but even then the parallels are only partial for the distinctiveness of Jesus as *the* final, eschatological Prophet must circumscribe the language of proto-types.

[108] *Pace* Lampe, *Seal of the Spirit*, p. 44; Harris, *Prayer*, p. 239, who writes that "the connection of prayer with the Spirit provides the unifying principle in Luke's theology of prayer."(Here are the undeveloped roots of the triadic relationship prayer/Spirit/salvation-history, which Harris did not develop, but which would be enlarged upon by Smalley in "The Spirit, Kingdom and Prayer in Luke-Acts"). However, it has already been shown that Luke relates prayer with revelation in general, and not always the Spirit in particular. In fact, there are numerous instances where the Spirit is not related to prayer (see the previous discussion).

[109] Feldkämper, *Der betende Jesus*, p. 51 surveys the Lukan stylistic characteristics.

[110] Greeven *Gebet*, p. 16 also suggests Lukan redaction of Mk. 1:45, although he does not elaborate upon the suggestion.

[111] *Pace* Cadbury, *Style*, vol. II, p. 113; Feldkämper, *Der betende Jesus*, p. 52; Schurmann, *Lukas*, p. 278, n. 35; R. Pesch, *Jesu ureigene Taten? Ein Beitrag zur Wunderfrage*, (Freiburg, 1970), p. 106; Stanley, *Gethsemane*, pp. 189f. Stanley has the right idea when he explains Luke's supposed transformation of Mk. 1:35 as motivated by his desire to show how prayer was essential to "Jesus' earliest efforts at evangelization." However, Lk. 4:14ff is the account of Jesus' earliest efforts, not 5:15ff; this is why the prayer of Mk. 1:35 has already been transposed to Lk. 3:21 (see above).

deliberately in order to pray. In fact, Luke uses two periphrastic imperfects (ἦν ὑποχωρῶν, ἦν προσευχόμενος)[112] emphasising that "retiring to pray" was Jesus' regular habit, not just a unique expedient taken in this particular instance.

The regularity of Jesus' retreats for prayer is couched in a setting which also emphasises the regularity of the crowds coming to hear him teach and be healed. In fact, three thematic elements appear here in much the same way as in 4:14–44: 1) Jesus is anointed with the Spirit to teach and heal; 2) he is popular with the people; and, 3) the effects of his ministry extend throughout the entire countryside. Once again these elements are presented in a parallel fashion, forming an *inclusio* immediately before and after the prayer notice. In this way, Jesus' prayer is intimately associated with each of these activities:

1. Jesus has the power to teach and heal
a) v. 15b ἀκούειν καὶ θεραπεύεσθαι ἀπὸ τῶν ἀσθενειῶν
    αὐτῶν
a') v. 17a καὶ αὐτὸς ἦν διδάσκων...
    17c καὶ δύναμις κυρίου ἦν εἰς τὸ ἰᾶσθαι
    αὐτόν

2. He is popular with the people
b) v. 15a καὶ συνήρχοντο ὄχλοι πολλοὶ
b') v. 17b καὶ ἦσαν καθήμενοι Φαρισαῖοι καὶ
    νομοδιδάσκαλοι

3. The effects of his ministry extend throughout the countryside
c) v. 15a διήρχετο δὲ μᾶλλον ὁ λόγος περὶ αὐτοῦ
c') v. 17b οἳ ἦσαν ἐληλυθότες ἐκ πάσης κώμης τῆς
    Γαλιλαίας καὶ Ἰουδαίας καὶ Ἰερουσαλήμ

It has been suggested that Luke introduces prayer here because of the introduction of those groups who will later comprise Jesus' opposition; thus Jesus prays in preparation for the road of struggle ahead.[113] However, such antagonism is not suggested until 5:21, and is not clearly referred to until 6:11. In addition, the periphrastic pluperfect, which introduces the Pharisees and the Teachers of the Law, sets their gathering on this *particular* occasion apart from the *regular* gatherings of the crowds who come to hear Jesus and be healed. Also, the δέ of v. 16, not to mention the parallel structure outlined above, links Jesus' regular prayer directly with the ongoing assemblies ἀκούειν καὶ θεραπεύεσθαι. When this connection is read in light of the earlier depiction of the praying Jesus as the anointed messianic Deliverer, it becomes less likely that Jesus is again shown praying in order to deal with future conflict, or even to avoid the temptations of populari-

---

[112] Both with iterative meanings; cf. *BDF*, para. 325, 353.
[113] W. Barclay, *The Gospel of Luke*, (Edinburgh, 1954), p. 4.

ty,[114] than it is that his prayer continues to be presented as it was first introduced, in relation to his successfully progressing ministry as messiah.

There is also an important shift of emphasis from vv. 15 to 17 which the intervention of prayer in v. 16 serves to explain. Verse 15 describes the crowds' desires: they come to hear and be healed. After the description of Jesus' prayer habits the reader is told how Jesus was able to meet those desires: he was teaching (ἦν διδάσκων) and the power of the Lord was with him to heal (δύναμις κυρίου ἦν εἰς τὸ ἰᾶσθαι αὐτόν). This movement in the narrative from "expectations" to "prayer" to "performance" seems to be deliberate. It explains how the power and success of Jesus' ministry is to be accounted for. He works through prayer. He retreats not only for his own sake,[115] but for the sake of his ministry to others.

These periods of retreat into the desert provide the explanation of how Jesus' ministry progresses so powerfully. He continues to work through the Spirit, the δύναμις of the Lord (cf. 4:1, 14, 18f, 36,), to teach and heal with power (4:15, 31, 43f; 24:19). As the eschatological Prophet who must suffer, he begins to discover new fronts of future opposition (cf. 4:28–30; 22:2, 66; 23:10). In this capacity, he continues to be widely acclaimed by the people (4:22, 32, 36f, 42; 6:17; 7:16f [!]). And all of this becomes effective, as a part of God's plan, as Jesus prays. In fact, this verse shows that the efficacy of his teaching and healing is actually mediated by these prayers. Consequently, even though Luke does not relate their content, the benefits of these regular prayer retreats are consistently directed outwardly: Jesus is enabled to pursue his popular messianic ministry as he prays.

### 5.2.3 Lk. 6:12–20: The Messiah Assembles His Witnesses and Teaches Them

At this point a new stage is reached in Jesus' ministry. Hostile opposition from the Jewish leaders begins to overtly assert itself (6:11). Luke's phrase "what they might do to Jesus" may appear more circumspect than Mark's (cf. Mk. 3:6), but it is his consistent way of referring to the leaders' plots which eventually issue in Jesus' death (Lk. 19:48; diff. Mk. 11:8; Lk. 23:34). The people are receiving Jesus enthusiastically, but by their hostility the leaders have relinquished their right to rule the people. Consequently, Jesus goes about selecting new leaders, new leaders for the restored people of God being reconstituted through his work (cf. 22:30).[116]

The temporal clause δὲ ἐν ταῖς ἡμέραις ταύταις followed by an infinitive of purpose (προσεύξασθαι) also indicates that Jesus' selection of the Twelve is a

---

[114] Fitzmyer, *The Gospel*, vol. II, p. 576; Marshall, *Commentary*, p. 210; cf. Greeven, *Gebet*, pp. 13, 17; K. Scaria, "Jesus' Prayer and Christian Prayer," p. 181.

[115] Caird, *St. Luke*, p. 92, Jesus withdraws "to recuperate;" Schürmann, *Lukas*, p. 278, Jesus is "at home" (Beheimatung) only with the Father.

[116] See J. Jervell, *Luke and the People of God*, (Minneapolis, 1972), pp. 93f; Lohfink, *Sammlung*, pp. 42, 74–76; Franklin, *Christ the Lord*, p. 170.

response to the leaders' rejection.[117] The choices he eventually makes are demonstrated to have been revealed to him through that prayer.

### 5.2.3.1 The Messiah's Electing Prayers

This is the most emphatic prayer notice yet in Luke.[118] Prayer itself is mentioned twice (προσεύξασθαι, ἐν τῇ προσευχῇ τοῦ θεοῦ; cf. 9:28f), and the duration is stressed as nowhere else in the gospel (ἦν διανυκτερεύων). It is generally agreed that τοῦ θεοῦ stands as a rare use of the objective genitive, which indicates that Jesus' prayer was directed towards God.[119] Why the divine orientation of Jesus' prayer should be made explicit here (as if the reader would assume that Jesus had prayed to anyone else before!) has to do with what follows. Luke wants to make it clear that the choice of the Twelve Apostles was *God's* selection (cf. Acts 1:24), effected through the prayers of his Son.[120] The result is the validation of both the position of the Twelve in God's plan of salvation, and the mediatoral/elective efficacy of Jesus' prayers in the actualisation of that plan.

The opening clause of v. 13 makes this connection plain: καὶ ὅτε... προσεφώνησεν... καὶ ἐκλεξάμενος. The verb ἐκλέγομαι is a Lukan addition (cf. Mk. 3:13f) which most often has God for its subject (Lk. 9:35; Acts 1:24; 13:17; 15:7; cf. Lk. 18:7; 23:35; Acts 13:2; but also cf. Lk. 10:42; 14:7; Acts 15:22, 25). The significance of the verb here is that, through his prayers, Jesus acts for God. God has used this prayer to reveal those whom Jesus should select for apostleship. Jesus discerns the Father's elective will and effects that decision by means of prayer. Jesus, the praying messiah, has been the mediator of divine election,[121] a function

---

[117] Margreth, *Gebetsleben*, p. 199; Feldkämper, *Der betende Jesus*, p. 87; Stanley, *Gethsemane*, p. 190; *pace* Harris, *Prayer*, p. 50.

[118] The language is thoroughly Lukan. Whether it is a unique tradition in Lukan garb or a Lukan creation is a mute point; cf. Schurmann, *Lukas*, p. 319. It is debatable whether it results from Luke's transposition of Mk. 6:46, which was lost in the Great Omission; *pace* Feldkämper, *Der betende Jesus*, p. pp. 84f. Harris is probably correct when he says that such a "compensation" would have appeared later in the gospel; it has already been suggested that the influence of Mk. 6:46 may be seen in Lk. 9:10, 18.

[119] Cf. Rm. 10:2; Jn. 2:17; Mk. 11:22; Gal. 3:22; see Plummer, *St. Luke*, p. 171; Klostermann, *Lukas*, p. 77.

[120] *Not* simply that Jesus is asking for the Father's blessing upon his selection; *pace* Fitzmyer, *The Gospel*, vol. I, p. 616.

[121] This has implications for the translation of Acts 1:2. If this verse were intended to read "the apostles whom he chose through the Holy Spirit" one would expect διὰ πνεύματος ἁγίου to be inserted in between the relative pronoun and the main verb, not before; *pace* Haenchen, *Acts*, p. 139; G. Lohfink, *Die Himmelfahrt Jesu*, (München, 1971), pp. 221, 269; and Feldkämper, *Der betende Jesus*, p. 93. Lohfink (p. 221) admits this grammatical point, but believes the parallel with Lk. 6:12 overrules its significance. He argues that this is Luke's way of emphasising God's hand in the selection of the Twelve (p. 269).However, Luke is consistent in his presentation of prayer and the Spirit: Jesus teaches through the power of the Spirit, received by prayer; but he chooses (on behalf of the Father) through prayer itself. The objective genitive in Lk. 6:12 has already emphasized God's role in the selection, thus Lohfink's argument for "chosen through the Holy Spirit" is nullified. The Spirit is the power behind Jesus' teaching, and prayer is the means of his equipment and choosing.

already seen to be a prerogative of his unique status as Son. Lk. 6:12 makes explicit what was earlier argued to be implicit in Lk. 10:21–24, ie. Jesus exercises the elective will of God through his prayer-life.

This analysis also suggests a second important reason for the absence of any prayer notice in Lk. 4:42. Whereas Mark originally recorded the calling of the first disciples before Jesus' ministry in Capernaum (Mk. 1:16–20), Luke's rearrangement of Mark's order means that Jesus pursues his early ministry as a solitary figure, and the calling of Peter, James and John takes place after Jesus leaves Capernaum to travel throughout Galilee, rather than before. If Luke had retained the prayer notice in Mk. 1:35, the "prayer → election" pattern would have emerged in the juxtaposition of Lk. 4:42–44 and 5:1–11. But Luke apparently wished to avoid this until it could be properly presented as something instigated by the hostility of the Jewish leaders, thus coordinating the election effected through Jesus' prayers with the constitution of a new leadership for Israel.

### 5.2.3.2 More Teaching with Authority (Lk. 6:17–20)

Luke has reversed the order of the material found in Mk. 3:7–10 (par. Lk. 6:17–19; note Mk. 3:11–12 has already been shifted to Lk. 4:41) and Mk. 3:13–19 (par. Lk. 6:12–16) in order to prepare for and offer a better setting for the Sermon on the Plain. Jesus' descent with the newly elected apostles to a level place in v. 17 serves to unify this section with the preceding material (vv. 12–16) in two ways: Jesus is located with respect to the mountain upon which he has recently been praying; and, he is accompanied by the men for whom he has prayed. This connection is important because the relevance of Jesus' prayer on the mountain extends, not only to vv. 12–16, but vv. 17–20 as well.

Aside from the two connections just mentioned, such relevance is conspicuous through the activities referred to in the material itself. Luke once more describes the three-fold pattern of prayer-related messianic activity mentioned earlier in the gospel: 1) Jesus continues his work in the power of the Spirit (ὅτι δύναμις παρ' αὐτοῦ ἐξήρχετο, v. 19); 2) by this power he both teaches and heals (vv. 18, 19, 20 [ἔλεγεν]); and, 3) he ministers to large crowds who come from far and wide (v. 17). The only difference is that the prayer notice is not sandwiched in between two such summary statements. However, as in Lk. 5:16, there is a repetition of the same movement from hope to achievement. The crowds come with definite expectation (ἀκοῦσαι ... ἰαθῆναι), and the praying Jesus fulfills them admirably (ἐθεραπεύοντο ... ἰᾶτο ... ἔλεγεν).

The content, as well as the authority, of Jesus' teaching is determined by his role as eschatological prophet.[122] He has been fulfilling the work of God's messiah,

---

[122] This is true regardless of whether one finds a New Moses motif operating in relation to Jesus' descent from the mountain. The inclusion of the mountain is simply a retention from the tradition (cf. Mk. 3:13), as is also the case with the Transfiguration (9:28; cf. Mk. 9:2). The Mount of Olives in mentioned in Lk. 22:39 under the influence of 21:37. Luke does not consistently portray mountains as *the* locale of spiritual communication, or even as *the* place of prayer (cf. 3:21; 4:1 ff; 5:16; 11:1; *pace* Feldkämper, *Der betende Jesus*, p. 86). Therefore, it is unlikely that there is any

declaring his status and proclaiming the good news of the kingdom ever since Nazareth.[123] He now pronounces the Father's blessings upon "the poor", who have responded to his preaching (v. 20; cf. 4:18; Is. 61:1). He offers hope to the oppressed whom he came to regather (v. 21; cf. 4:18; Is. 55:1 f; 61:2); and he warns them that as the community of God's final prophet they may themselves share in the fate of God's prophets (v. 23).[124] The location of this sermon is important, for it highlights the beginning of Jesus' consolidation of the newly developing community of God. Even more importantly Luke has, once again, made it clear that Jesus is successful in this, as in all other phases of his ministry, in and through his life of prayer.

### 5.2.4 Lk. 11:1: The Disciples Ask to be Taught

It has frequently been suggested that Luke describes Jesus as a man of prayer in order to provide a paradigm of piety for the early church. This is borne out by Lk. 11:1, together with the scene on the Mount of Olives.[125] The language is thoroughly Lukan,[126] and though this cannot settle the question of whether the prayer is Luke's reworking of some tradition or his own creative addition,[127] it does suggest that it functions in a way comparable to Luke's other redactional prayer notices.

The request "teach us to pray" follows a Lukan temporal clause with a present participle, ἐν τῷ εἶναι αὐτὸν... προσευχόμενον, which associates the disciples' request directly with the activity of Jesus' prayer. ὡς ἐπαύσατο does not separate the request from the prayer; it is intended to show that while the disciples' question was framed as Jesus prayed, they did not interrupt, but waited until he was finished praying before asking. A "Model-Learner" relationship between Jesus and the disciples is clearly established.

---

symbolic significance attached to the mountain, Mosaic or otherwise; *pace* Greeven, *Gebet*, p. 18; Harris, *Prayer*, p. 52; Schürmann, *Lukas*, pp. 313, 320; D. Moessner, "Luke 9:1–50: Luke's Preview of the Journey of the Prophet like Moses of Deuteronomy," *JBL.* 102 ('83) 575–605.Cf. Marshall, *Commentary*, pp. 236, 241; Fitzmyer, *The Gospel*, vol. I,pp. 616, 623.

[123] Finkel, "Jesus' Sermon," p. 113 even suggests that the dependence of the Beatitudes upon Is. 61 indicates that at least the first portion of this sermon preserves Jesus' synagogue homily following the reading at Nazareth. But this is unlikely.

[124] Cf. D. Lührmann, "Jesus und seine Propheten Gesprächsbeitrag" in *Prophetic Vocation in the New Testament and Today*, (Leiden, 1977), p. 212.

[125] Ott, *Gebet*, pp. 94–99, especially p. 97; Harris, *Prayer*, pp. 77, 79; F. Lentzen-Deis, "Beten Kraft des Gebetes Jesu," *GL.* 48 ('75) 171; Feldkämper, *Der betende Jesus*, pp. 180, 204; M. Vellanickal, "Prayer-Experience in the Gospel of Luke," *Bibl.* 2 ('76) 37.

[126] Cadbury, *Style*, vol. II, 106; Harris, *Prayer*, pp. 82–83; Feldkämper, *Der betende Jesus*, p. 179; Grundmann, *Das Evangelium*, p. 229; Rengstorf, *Das Evangelium*, p. 143; Marshall, *Commentary*, p. 456.

[127] It is unlikely that the reference to John's disciples is an invention (cf. 5:33). Whether or not v. 1a is traditional, it seems most likely that Luke's arrangement preserves the original setting for the Lord's Prayer; cf. Marshall, *Commentary*, p. 456; W. Manson, *The Gospel*, p. 557; Greeven, *Gebet*, p. 20.

But, as undeniable as this portrayal may be, does it exhaust the significance of the text? Elsewhere Jesus' prayers have regularly been associated with the powerful continuation of his messianic ministry, and the associated benefits accomplished through those prayers on behalf of others. With this in mind, it would not be inappropriate to ask if the coincidental nature of the disciples' request and Jesus' prayer is not also intended to suggest a cause-and-effect relationship between these two, as Luke has done elsewhere. In other words, are the disciples moved to seek Jesus' instruction, not simply as the result of seeing Jesus pray, but as a direct result of the prayer itself? The fact that they ask for teaching, giving Jesus another opportunity to instruct his elect apostles in the nature of their relationship to the Kingdom of God, certainly seems to suggest that this prayer has played an effective role in the scene. Luke has previously gone to great lengths to show that this is exactly the sort of result one would expect from Jesus' prayers. When this evidence is combined with the simultaneous coordination of the disciples' request with Jesus' prayer, this suggestion is transformed from a possibility to a probability, and God's praying messiah once again finds an opportunity to teach his followers in a situation made possible through his prayers.[128]

### 5.2.5 Jesus Enters Jerusalem

Jesus' time in Jerusalem is presented as the climax of the ministry of God's anointed Deliverer. Even though he is proclaimed "king" (19:38) by the disciples, his first response upon seeing Jerusalem is to pronounce the second of his prophetic judgment oracles. The fate of the Jewish leadership is the fate of Israel's principal city (19:41–44). According to Luke, Jesus sees himself as the final Prophet bringing God's final offer of deliverance to the recalcitrant leaders, in an effort to save a city which must otherwise suffer destruction (13:34–35; 21:20–24; 23:28–31). All three of the prayer-related characteristics used by Luke to define Jesus' status elsewhere recur in this section: Jesus teaches; he is followed by large crowds; he works with power.

### 5.2.5.1 Jesus Teaches in Jerusalem

According to Luke, Jesus takes over the Jerusalem temple and makes it the headquarters for his ministry in the city,[129] an action which may well be performed under the auspices of the expectations attached to the coming eschatological

---

[128] Feldkämper, *Der betende Jesu*, p. 290 maintains that this close association implies that the Lord's Prayer "can be nothing less" than what Jesus had just prayed himself. However, the oft repeated difference between Jesus' use of "my Father" and the disciples' "our Father" makes this suggestion less likely than that offered here.

[129] There is no need to follow Conzelmann in positing some geographical ignorance on Luke's part, wherein Jesus does not actually enter the city proper until the night of the Last Supper; cf. *Theology*, p. 75, n. 1. Luke is simply telescoping his story in order to highlight its essential features, and the absence of any mention of the city may simply be the result of his omitting Mark's exit to Bethany and the withering of the fig tree.

Prophet (cf. Mal. 3:1).[130] With the omission of Mark's account of the withering of the fig tree (Mk. 11:12–14, 20–25), Luke also eliminates any hint of judgment against the temple, which might have otherwise been implied in Jesus' "cleansing" (19:45–48).[131] His casting out of the money-changers becomes more a purging of the temple, as Conzelmann has suggested,[132] which serves to prepare its precincts as the focal point for Jesus' teaching in the city. This is an important observation; v. 47a, "and he was teaching daily in the temple," is a Lukan addition which makes this point (diff. Mk. 11:18). It also serves to depict the leaders' antagonism towards Jesus as being the result of his teaching, not of his cleansing the temple as in Mark. Jesus has deliberately usurped the leaders' position; *he* now speaks to the people for God. What was in Mark a sign of the temple's obsolescence becomes for Luke a sign of Jesus' prophetic supremacy. It is not surprising, then, to observe that all of Jesus' work in Jerusalem is surprisingly similar to the ministry of Jeremiah (see especially Jeremiah 6, 26), a connection which Jesus makes himself when he calls the temple a "den of robbers" (Jer. 7:11).[133]

In light of this, Luke's alteration of Mk. 11:17 takes on special significance. His omission of the phrase "for all nations" from Is. 56:7 has most often been explained as Luke's attempt to save Jesus from making a false prophecy, since he knows that the temple never actually achieved such a world-wide, religious status.[134] However, such speculation overlooks the most readily observable effect of Luke's alteration: the temple becomes significant solely as "a house of prayer."[135] This is the crucial factor in Jesus' preparations for his teaching ministry in Jerusalem. He teaches as The Praying final Prophet, and so the temple which he adopts as the seat of his ministry must first be reconstituted as THE house of prayer. Only then will it be serviceable for the task which lies before him.

Jesus' teaching ministry in Jerusalem is reiterated several times throughout chapters 20–21. Lk. 20:1 indicates that it was a ministry of some duration (ἐν μιᾷ

---

[130] Fitzmyer, *The Gospel*, vol. II, pp. 1266; although cf. Marshall, *Commentary*, p. 719 for a more measured evaluation.

[131] Cf. Talbert, *Genre*, p. 21.

[132] Conzelmann, *Theology*, pp. 77f; Tyson, *The Death of Jesus*, pp. 102, 107.

[133] See L. Goppelt, *Typos: The Typological Interpretation of the Old Testament in the New*, (Grand Rapids, 1982), pp. 65f.

[134] Creed, *The Gospel*, p. 242; Prevallet, *Luke 24:26*, p. 135; J. Drury, *Tradition and Design in Luke's Gospel: A Study in Early Christian Historiography*, (London, 1976), p. 106; C. K. Barrett, "The House of Prayer and the Den of Thieves" in *Jesus und Paulus*, (Göttingen, 1978), p. 15; Ernst, *Das Evangelium*, p. 531. In his critique of the use of the OT in this pericope, V. Eppstein says that the allusion to Jer. 7:11 is "inappropriate," but without any real explanation; see "The Historicity of the Gospel Account of the Cleansing of the Temple," *ZNW*. 55 ('64) 43.

[135] Perhaps this emphasis also results from the priority given to the reconstruction of Israel in Luke-Acts. As the eschatological Prophet, Jesus comes to *Israel*; the effects of his prayers concern these people first. The inclusion of "all nations" will eventually be assured, if his ministry of prayer is effective with Israel now; see J. Jervell, "The Divided People of God: The Restoration of Israel and Salvation for the Gentiles" in *Luke and the People of God*, pp. 41–74; N. Dahl, "The Story of Abraham in Luke-Acts" in *Studies in Luke-Acts*, pp. 140, 147, 151.

τῶν ἡμερῶν διδάσκοντος αὐτοῦ),[136] and relates his preaching ministry in Jerusalem (εὐαγγελιζομένου) as a part of his fulfillment of those responsibilities accepted when he was anointed with the Spirit (cf. 4:18).

The Jerusalem material is concluded by a summary statement (21:37) similar to the introduction in 20:1, thus giving yet another example of two summary descriptions forming a thematic *inclusio* around the intervening material. Luke says three times that Jesus taught the people only in the temple (20:1; 21:37, 38); therefore, it is implied that all of the teaching offered in 20:3–21:36 was also given in the courts of Jesus' House of Prayer. But Lk. 21:37 not only complements 20:1, it also foreshadows 22:39; and while this connection would not be apparent to a first-time reader of the gospel, it would become an evocation of 21:37 for anyone who had read the Jerusalem material once before.

Luke has replaced Mark's "Gethsemane" (Mk. 14:32) with the "Mount of Olives" (Lk. 22:39) and added further that when Jesus left the disciples he went out "as was his custom" (κατὰ τὸ ἔθος) *to pray*. That it was Jesus' habit to pray on the Mount is also seen in Luke's use of the article in v. 40: γενόμενος δὲ ἐπὶ τοῦ τόπου. This is "the place" where Jesus prays and now instructs his disciples to pray. Luke's κατὰ τὸ ἔθος thus serves not only to explain how Judas knew where to lead the arresting mob, as many have suggested,[137] but it also re-emphasises that Jesus' teaching in Jerusalem, as all of his teaching elsewhere, was offered by a man who was constantly in prayer.[138] During the day he never left "the house of prayer," and night by night he returned to "the mount of prayer." In fact, Lk. 22:39 brings not only Jesus' teaching, but all of the events in Jerusalem under the rubric of his prayer-life. It also serves to explain why Luke could feel free to describe Jesus as reconstituting the temple but not actually praying there himself.

### 5.2.5.2 Jesus is Followed by Large Crowds

Jesus is accompanied by large crowds of disciples as he approaches Jerusalem (19:37), as he has been all throughout his ministry (6:17; 7:1, 16; 4:42; 5:1, 3, 15, 29; 6:17, 19; 7:9, 11f, 24; 8:4, 19, 40, 42, 45; 9:11f, 37f; 11:14, 29; 12:1, 54; 13:14, 17; 14:25; 18:36). His time in Jerusalem is no exception. All the people hang upon Jesus' teaching, which is primarily directed to them (19:47f; 20:1, 9, 45; 21:38).[139]

---

[136] Grundmann, *Das Evangelium*, p. 370.

[137] Plummer, *St. Luke*, p. 509; Dibelius, "Gethsemane," p. 263; Conzelmann, *Theology*, p. 81; Feldkämper, *Der betende Jesus*, p. 234; Fitzmyer, *The Gospel*, vol. II, p. 1441.

[138] "The counterpart to the teaching by day is Jesus' praying on the Mount of Olives by night..." (Conzelmann, *Theology*, p. 199); also cf. J. Bailey, *The Traditions Common to the Gospels of Luke and John*, (Leiden, 1963), pp. 48f; Harris, *Prayer*, p. 109.

[139] Although the actual examples of teaching (20:3–8, 9–19, 20–25, 27–40, 41–47) are directed to various groups of "leaders," they serve to illustrate the controversy instigated by Jesus. Aside from these instances of Jesus' response to hostility, the general impression is that Jesus spent the majority of his time instructing the sympathetic crowds. Luke's vocabulary for these crowds of people (both λαός and ὄχλος) exhibits definite, albeit not entirely consistent, "trends." Generally, "crowds" are presented as the curious mass from which disciples may be drawn, while "the people" represent the sympathetic nation prepared by baptism to be reconstituted as God's

Jesus is temporarily shielded from the plots to kill him only by his popularity with the people and the leaders' fear of mass retribution (19:47f; 20:6, 19; 22:2, 6). It is not too much to say that Jesus is presented as "taking possession" of the city.[140] This deepens the impressive division between the people and their leaders, which in turn underscores the efficacy of Jesus' work in regathering the people of Israel, and the preparations he has made to supply a new leadership himself.[141] All of these Jerusalem activities have previously been related to Jesus' prayer-life. Now his time in Jerusalem, teaching in the house of prayer, becomes not only the climax of his journey from Galilee, but also a climactic testimony to the power of the Son's prayers. It is as if the praying messiah's destiny has been borne along, guided and now assured through the efficacy of his regular retreats for prayer.

### 5.2.5.3 "By Whose Authority?" (Lk. 20:1–8)

Jesus' reply to the first challenge from the Jerusalem leaders points the reader back to his baptism. While Luke closely follows Mk. 11:27–33, his version acquires a significance not found in Mark's because of the unique features of Luke's baptismal narrative. The leaders inquire about the nature and source of Jesus' ἐξουσία.

---

people; see Lohfink, *Sammlung*, pp. 36–47; N. Dahl, "'A People for His Name' (Acts XV. 14)," *NTS*. 4 ('58) 324; G. Kilpatrick, "ΛΑΟΙ at Luke II. 31 and Acts IV. 24, 27," *JTS*. ns. 16 ('65) 127; J. Baird, *Audience Criticism and the Historical Jesus*, (Philadelphia, 1969), pp. 39–47; P. Minear, "Jesus' Audiences, According to Luke," *NovT*. 16 ('74) 81–109; Kodell, "Luke's Use of LAOS," pp. 327–339; Lentzen-Deis, *Die Taufe*, pp. 35, 91; J. Tyson, "The Jewish Public in Luke-Acts," *NTS*. 30 ('84) 577–582.

[140] Franklin *Christ the Lord*, p. 88.

[141] The well known (possible) exception to this is found in 23:13f. Even many of those who would argue for the identification of ὁ λάος and "the people of God" in Luke-Acts would admit that here the significance of the tradition that Jesus was rejected by *all* the people, not just the leaders, is significant enough for Luke to allow a tension to stand in his presentation; see Neyrey, *The Passion*, p. 110; Lohfink, *Sammlung*, pp. 38, 42–46; Tyson, "The Jewish Public," pp. 578–582. G. Rau, "Das Volk in der lukanischen Passiongeschichte, eine Konjektur zu Lk. 23:13," *ZNW*. 56 ('65) 41–51, follows a suggestion made by P. Winter (*On the Trial of Jesus*, [Berlin, 1961], p. 201 n. 23), and attempts to solve the tension by suggesting a textual corruption which altered an original "leaders of the people" to "leaders and the people" (p. 48). However, this is pure conjecture and has not found much support. Actually, the tension is a confusion born more of Luke's flexibility of language than from any inconsistency in this portrayal. Luke refers to the arresting entourage with Judas as a "crowd" (22:47, 52) even though it is clear from 22:6 that this *cannot* refer to the "crowd" of Jerusalemites who have positively received Jesus' teaching. Therefore, it must refer to the minions of the Jewish leaders. This group (Sanhedrin plus hangers-on) should be understood as the crowd which accompanies "the leaders" all throughout the trial process (23:1, 4). Rau's objection that 23:1 refers to the Sanhedrin alone (cf. 22:66; 23:10), and therefore cannot be identical with 23:13, fails to see the unity of this portrayal beginning with 22:47.It is Luke's habit of stylistic variation which allows him to refer to this same "crowd" as "the people" in 23:13, just as he earlier was free to designate both the sympathetic masses and the arresting body as a "crowd." Furthermore, since the accusation of "the whole assembly" (23:1) is that Jesus has stirred up "the people" (v. 5), it is highly unlikely that "the people" in v. 13, who now call for Jesus' death, refers to that same body. Otherwise, the agitated crowd would be saying, "Kill him, because he has stirred *us* up!"

In Mark this is motivated by Jesus' cleansing of the temple,[142] but in Luke it is due to his teaching. By associating his authority with that of John the Baptist, Jesus connects the source of his ministry with the source of John's ministry, and creates a situation where the leaders can only indict themselves for not submitting to John's baptism (7:30). Above all, he reminds the reader that he first began to wield his ἐξουσία immediately after his baptism, where the Spirit had descended upon him as he prayed. Consequently, even though there is no mention of the Spirit or "power" in this Jerusalem section, the related concept of "authority" (4:36) performs the same function, for it makes clear that Jesus continues to operate in Jerusalem (as perceived by his opposition) as he always has operated elsewhere:[143] he teaches with the divine authority that has consistently characterized his Spirit-filled, prayer-led ministry of messianic deliverance.

## 5.3 Conclusion: The Prayer Experience of the Messianic Deliverer

The wide scope of material covered in this chapter has been bound together by a common thread: Jesus' own personal experience in prayer. The results have indicated that Jesus' prayer-life was both similar and dissimilar to that of the average disciple. As for any other man, Jesus' prayers served as an avenue for the unpredictable, providential communication of God's will for his life. They were a means for his reception of revelation, visions, heavenly encouragement and the confirmation of actions performed in obedience to the Father, just as genuinely and spontaneously as for any later member of the church in Acts. Through prayer he learned what was the Father's will for his life. In this way Jesus prayed as any man would pray.

But Jesus was not just any man, and the life's ministry which unfolded for him as he prayed was not a task which could be fulfilled by any other man. He was the Son of God, the messianic Deliverer, the eschatological Prophet. Therefore, while the general outline of the role played by prayer in his life is certainly paradigmatic for the church, the specific details of his experience are unique. He models for all disciples how the Father may reveal his will through prayer, but he also shows that he was equipped for and then realised his unique function as he exercised a special intimacy with God in prayer. From beginning to end, Luke associates prayer with the initiation and accomplishment of the ingredients distinctive to the fulfillment of Jesus' messianic ministry. He is called the Son and endowed with the Spirit, which fills him with the divine power necessary to effect deliverance, as he prays; he is embraced by the people and enabled to meet their expectations by teaching them with authority, healing their diseases and exorcising their demons after he prays; he exercises God's elective will after discerning the Father's mind through

---

[142] Barrett, The Holy Spirit, p. 81.
[143] Cf. G. S. Shae, "The Question of the Authority of Jesus," NovT. 16 ('74) 1–29.

prayer; and his final days of authoritative teaching in Jerusalem are characterised by long days in the reconstituted House of Prayer, and equally long nights praying upon the Mount. Luke makes it clear that Jesus is not simply the messianic Deliverer, he is *the praying* messianic Deliverer, who is equipped with power, realises the whole of God's plan of salvation, and pursues his course in triumphant obedience by means of prayer.

Finally, Jesus' prayers are unique in that he alone is able to mediate the Father's revelation to others through them. No one else in Luke-Acts superintends the electing arm of God through their intercessions. Only Jesus prays so that others may come to see and hear who he truly is.

Chapter 6

# Jesus, the Heavenly Intercessor on Earth

## Introduction

Jesus' words in Lk. 22:31–32 are unique for a number of reasons. First of all, this is the only occasion in Luke where Jesus relates the subject of his (unrecorded) prayer to the disciples, giving them some insight into what he does when he retreats for prayer. Consequently, it is also the only example in Luke-Acts of a known, specific prayer request receiving an explicit, direct answer from God (at least Jesus assumes its future efficacy in v. 32; and, as will be seen, following events substantiate this confidence). The only other text comparable to this is found in Lk. 23:34, but neither the request nor the consequent "answer" is as specific. What these passages hold in common more directly is the intercessory nature of Jesus' prayers, and for this reason in particular Lk. 22:31 f takes on a great deal of importance for this study, as indeed it must for any study of prayer in Luke's writings.

Jesus functions as the supreme Intercessor in this passage, who not only brings the Father's revelation to his disciples but also brings the disciples' needs before his Father, and is efficacious in both parts of this work. This expansion of Jesus' intercessory task becomes doubly important when it is discovered that Luke presents this prayer not only as part of his story about the earthly Jesus, but also as paradigmatic for the continuing work of the exalted Lord. Or to put it the other way around, the ongoing task of heavenly intercession now conducted by the ascended Lord Jesus actually finds its roots, not in the resurrection/ascension/exaltation, but in Jesus' earthly ministry as the praying messianic Deliverer. A subsequent examination of Stephen's vision in Acts 7 will clarify this point, but it is already implicit in Luke's treatment of Lk. 22:31–46.

## 6.1 Satan's Demand (Lk. 22:31–32)

In explaining this prayer to his disciples, Jesus reveals the cosmic dimensions of impending events. Satan has demanded that he be allowed to sift the disciples like wheat. The similarity in this with the heavenly court scenes of Job 1:8–12; 2:3–7 has been observed many times.[1] The fact that Job and his belongings are given

---

[1] Plummer, *St. Luke*, p. 503; Surkau, *Martyrien*, p. 92; T. Boman, Der Gebetskampf Jesu," *NTS*. 10 ('63–4) 269; Taylor, *Passion Narrative*, p. 66; Beck, "Imitatio," p. 38; Dietrich, *Petrusbild*, p. 123; Foerster, "διάβολος," *TDNT*. vol. II, p. 73; G. Stählin, "αἰτέω," *TDNT*. vol. I, p. 194; Marshall, *Commentary*, p. 820.

over into the Devil's "hands" (Job. 1:12; 2:6) provides a fitting parallel to this demand that Satan be allowed "to sift" the disciples. Interpretive distinctions between Satan as Accuser and as Tempter are not particularly significant here since any accusation would require the evidence which only a temptation could provide.[2] A more comprehensive designation of Satan as Adversary is more appropriate (cf. Zech. 3:1; Rev. 12:10).[3] The enemy of God's people comes before the throne with his demands, but unlike Job's situation (cf. Job 9:33) there is now an Advocate to plead on their behalf.

While it is true that ἐξαιτέομαι could be used of demonic requests for control over individuals (T. Benj. 3:3),[4] it is not necessary to see a technical designation here. Whatever the precise meaning of this verb, or the exact nature of the intended sifting,[5] it is clear that Jesus understands Satan's goal to be the final destruction of the disciples' faith.[6] The juxtaposition of "Satan has demanded…but *I have asked*" (ἐγὼ δὲ ἐδεήθην) indicates that Jesus' prayer has been specifically aimed at effectively countering Satan's interest.[7] And since Jesus understands the result of his prayer to be the insurance that Peter's faith will not be "terminated"

---

[2] Thus Neyrey's (*Passion*, p. 33) objection to the Job parallel is nullified. The Devil's goal in Job is not merely Job's testing, but his ultimate apostasy (Job 1:11; 2:5, 9), just as in Lk. 22:31; also *pace* Ott, *Gebet*, pp. 76 f.

[3] K. de Blois, "How to Deal with Satan?," *BT*. 37 ('86) 301; Foerster, "διάβολος," p. 72. The OT background is that of "Prosecutor" in the heavenly court.

[4] "… even though the spirits of Beliar ask to have you (ἐξαιτήσωνται ὑμᾶς), yet they shall not have dominion over you;" see A. Argyle, "The Influence of the Testaments of the Twelve Patriarchs upon the New Testament," *ExpT*. 63 ('52) 256f.This verb appears nowhere else in either the NT or the LXX; cf. also Stählin, "αἰτέω," pp. 191–195. Boman, citing classical usage, suggests the translation of "demanding someone's surrender for torture" ("Gebetskampf," p. 269); Neyrey (*Passion*, p. 32) suggests a "warlike challenge for total domination;" Stählin prefers simply "to demand the surrender of." Bowman and Neyrey's definitions stretch beyond the evidence; the exact nature of the demand will depend upon the specific details of the request, and not be carried by the verb alone.

[5] See Marshall, *Commentary*, pp. 820 f for a summary of the various options with their adherents and weaknesses. Also, B. Noack, *Satanás und Sotería: Untersuchungen zur Neutestamentlichen Dämonologie*, (København, 1948), pp. 101–102; W. Foerster, "Lk. 22,31 f," *ZNW*. 46 ('55) 130f; G. Klein, "Die Verleugnung des Petrus: Eine traditionsgeschichte Untersuchung," *ZTK*. 58 ('61) 299; reprinted in *Rekonstruktion und Interpretation: Gesammelte Aufsätze zum Neuen Testament*, (München, 1969); Ott, *Gebet*, pp. 75–79; Feldkämper, *Der betende Jesus*, pp. 214–215. Ott correctly concludes that the precise nature of the metaphor is irrelevant, since the point is Satan's destruction of their faith through "violent agitation," whatever image may be intended to convey that agitation (pp. 78 f); so too E. Fuchs, "σινιάζω," *TDNT*. vol. VII, pp. 291–292.

[6] Noack, *Satanas*, p. 102; Dietrich, *Petrusbild*, pp. 124, 130f; Klein, "Verleugnung," p. 304; Ott *Gebet*, pp. 78 f.

[7] The emphatic ἐγώ, parallel as it is with the ἰδοὺ ὁ Σατανᾶς makes this clear; so also Feldkämper, *Der betende Jesus*, pp. 210f; *pace* Klein, "Verleugnung," pp. 299–301, who interprets the δέ as contrasting *Peter* with the other apostles; cf. Dietrich, *Petrusbild*, p. 124.

(μὴ ἐκλίπη ἡ πίστις)[8] it can only be assumed that Satan's intent has been *the destruction* of this faith, not simply its "testing" or "proving."

However, while Jesus' prayer has guaranteed the preservation of Peter's faith, it does not mean that he will not temporarily fail in his commitment. By referring to Peter's responsibilities after "returning" (ποτε ἐπιστρέψας) Jesus indicates in advance that he will succumb, if only temporarily, to the sifting ahead. The promise that his faith will not fail speaks against a transitive meaning for ἐπιστρέφω, ie. "convert your brothers and strengthen them." Unless it is suggested that Jesus' prayer is effective only for Peter and not the other ten –something which is extremely improbable, as will be argued below – then the apostasy of the ten, which would require a renewed "conversion" through Peter, is the very thing which Jesus' prayer has been aimed against. And the use of the aorist tense indicates that Jesus assumes the efficacy of this prayer![9] It also seems more likely that, had this been Luke's intended meaning, he would have written καὶ σύ ποτε στηρίχθεις ἐπιστρέψον τοὺς ἀδελφούς σου. Furthermore, the πότε distinguishes the idea of the participle from that of the principle verb, making a transitive meaning more difficult than an intransitive.[10]

The consensus of scholarly opinion today favours an intransitive meaning for this participle, ie. "when you have turned back."[11] The verb is commonly used by Luke either neutrally or geographically with this sense (Lk. 2:39; 8:55; 17:31; Acts 9:40; 15:36; 16:18), and it is also regularly intransitive when used with a moral/religious significance (Lk. 17:4; Acts 3:19; 9:35; 11:21; 14:15; 15:19; 26:18, 20; 28:27; 8 out of 11 occurrences in Acts). The story of Peter's denial, concluding as it does

---

[8] Cf. Heb. 1:2 of the Lord's years never "ending;" Lk. 16:9 of "death;" 23:45, "eclipse." The verb is regularly used of death; cf. Gen. 49:33; Ps. 17:37 (LXX); Tob. 14:11; Wisd. 5:13; T. Reub. 1:4; Josephus, *Bell.* 4, 68, *Ant.* 2, 184. Whether Jesus conceives of a process of decline or an abrupt end is not particularly germane; cf. Dietrich, *Petrusbild*, pp. 130f.

[9] S. Brown, *Apostasy*, p. 70; E. Linnemann, *Studien zur Passionsgeschichte*, (Göttingen, 1970), p. 75.

[10] Godet, *A Commentary*, vol. II, p. 300.

[11] See E. Sutcliffe, "'Et tu Aliquando Conversus,' St. Luke 22,32," *CBQ.* 15 ('53) 305–310 for a discussion of all the options.There is also the possibility of a Hebraism, "in (one's) turn" (cf. Ps. 85:7, LXX). This is, perhaps, not impossible traditionally, but in the light of Peter's eventual denial (vv. 54–62), predicted as it is so closely to this instruction (v. 34), it is unlikely that an idiosyncrasy of translation alone adequately explains the literary phenomena; *pace* Sutcliffe, "Aliquando," pp. 307–310; cf. Margreth, *Gebetsleben*, p. 231; C. Pickar, "The Prayer of Christ for Saint Peter," *CBQ.* 4 ('42) 137–140; Bailey, *Luke and John*, p. 42 n. 1. Sutcliffe argues for a Hebraism on the basis of a parallel between Jesus' strengthening of Peter and Peter's strengthening of his brothers. But this would seem to require a parallel of means, ie. prayer, as well as of tasks, something neither forseen here nor described later. Also, the verb is never used this way elsewhere in Luke-Acts; cf. Feldkämper, *Der betende Jesus*, pp. 217f. For the arguments in favour of an intransitive meaning see Pickar, "The Prayer," p. 140; P. Thomson, "'Επιστρέφω (Luke xxii. 32)," *ExpT.* 38 ('26–7) 468; Creed, *The Gospel*, p. 269; Harris, *Prayer*, pp. 105–108; G. Schneider, "'stärke deine Brüder!' (Lk. 22,32), die Aufgabe des Petrus nach Lukas," *Cath.* 30 ('76) 202; G. Bertram, "στρέφω," *TDNT.* vol. VII, p. 727; Fitzmyer, *The Gospel*, vol. II, p. 1425; *pace* R. Lee, "Luke xxii. 32," *ExpT.* 38 ('26–7) 233f; Ott, *Gebet*, p. 81.

with his immediate repentance (v. 62),[12] also speaks in favour of a reference to a temporary fall by Peter rather than a complete apostasy by the other ten. Luke's use of στηρίζω elsewhere is in agreement with this conclusion.[13] The only other example of this word being used, as it is here, of interpersonal relationships (Acts 18:23; cf. Lk. 9:51; 16:26) concerns Paul's "strengthening" of the disciples in Galatia and Phrygia; it has nothing to do with conversion. His use of the cognate ἐπιστηπίζω is identical, twice being found in parallel with παρακαλέω (Acts 14:22; 15:32; also cf. 15:41).

The conclusion to be derived from all this is that Satan has demanded of God that he be allowed to try all the disciples in such a way as to demonstrate the precarious nature of their faith in Jesus and so bring about their final apostasy. However, the earthly Jesus has served as the Advocate before the heavenly throne. He, as will soon be argued, has asked that "their faith not fail;" his request was not that they be saved from the trial, but that they be protected through it.[14] By virtue of these prayers, Satan's intentions have been short-circuited. The disciples will not apostasise. Thus *the perseverance of the disciples' faith, the survival of Satanic trials, is shown to be founded upon the intercession of the earthly Jesus.* This is a crucial observation for the proper understanding of Jesus' role as Pray-er in Luke-Acts,[15] especially when it is recalled that Luke has grounded not only this ongoing perseverance, but also the initial perception and confession of Jesus as the Christ, in the power of Jesus' prayers.

Ott devotes some attention to arguing that since Satan is never presented as an Accuser in the gospels, Jesus cannot be seen as an Advocate.[16] But Ott's arguments are misdirected. The description of Jesus is not dependent upon how one describes Satan, but upon the dynamics of the text, ie. Satan demands/Jesus intercedes. And secondly, Satan is at least presented as an Adversary; the OT background to this idea certainly does link the adversarial task with that of heavenly Accuser (cf. Job 31:25). Thus Ott's objections do not stand.

---

[12] *Pace*, those such as Schneider, "stärke deine Brüder!," p. 202 and Bertram, "στρέφω," p. 727, who would date Peter's "return" from Jesus' resurrection appearance to him (24:34).Though this was certainly a step in the process, why overlook a text as striking as 22:62? Cf. Brown, *Apostasy*, p. 71; Neyrey, *The Passion*, p. 35; Linnemann, *Studien*, pp. 72f; "Die Verleugnung des Petrus," *ZTK*. 63 ('66) 3.

[13] See G. Harder, "στηρίζω," *TDNT*. vol. VII, pp. 653–657; Feldkämper, *Der betende Jesus*, pp. 218f.

[14] Dietrich, *Petrusbild*, p. 130. Not giving proper attention to this distinction between being sifted yet not failing is partly responsible for the difficulties which some have in relating this prayer to the tradition of Peter's denial; cf. Klein, "Verleugnung," pp. 301f; *Rekonstruction*, pp. 62f. Thus the period of "sifting" includes the whole of the passion events, which is inclusive of 22:54–62; cf. Noack, *Satanas*, p. 102; P. Minear, "A Note on Luke 22:36," *NovT*. 7 ('64) 130f.

[15] Lentzen-Deis, "Beten Kraft," p. 176 describes this as the church's extrapolating back onto Jesus' earthly life the attitudes about his heavenly mediation which had developed after the ascension. The direction in which this development took place will be discussed more fully later on in this study.

[16] Ott, *Gebet*, pp. 76–78; his argument is largely aimed at Foerster, "Lk. 22,31f'.

## 6.2 For Whom Does Jesus Pray?

One of the curious features of these two verses is the change from the plural ὑμᾶς of v. 31 to the singular σοῦ in v. 32. Satan asks to sift all the disciples, but Jesus prays only for Peter. At least this is the way in which these words are usually interpreted.[17] But how is this to be explained? Do not the other apostles need Jesus' prayers? If not, on what is their perseverance based?

Those who maintain that Jesus prayed only for Peter try to mitigate the difficulties in various ways. Some point out that Peter exercises a representative role as the leader of the other disciples,[18] and the charge to strengthen his brothers shows that Jesus plans to restore the other ten through Peter, in *lieu* of praying for them himself.[19] Or, perhaps, while Satan demanded all the disciples, he was only allowed access to Peter; therefore, only Peter required Jesus' prayer.[20] Still others have suggested that Jesus prays only for Peter because only Peter denies Jesus (cf. 22:28; 23:49; 24:33; omit Mk. 14:27, 50).[21] Or conversely, the verb στήρισον may indicate that only Peter was not handed over to Satan, and so Jesus prays for him to lift his fallen brothers.[22] E. Ellis adopts a variation of the penultimate argument, adding a new twist by suggesting that the plural you envisages not all of the disciples, but only Peter and Judas. Satan asks for these two in particular on the basis of their upcoming faithlessness.[23]

However, all of these solutions face significant difficulties. Regarding Ellis' suggestion, Judas does play a significant role in determining the place of Jesus' prayer in the perseverance of the disciples (see below), but there is no justification for limiting the scope of the ὑμᾶς, as Ellis does, so as not to include all twelve of the apostles. A reference to Judas and Peter alone is anything but clear in v. 31. A solution may be found, not by delimiting the referent of ὑμᾶς, but by extending that of the σοῦ. In addition, it hardly seems reasonable to turn the natural progression of the narrative on its head by asserting that Satan's demand is the consequence of his foreseeing Peter's denial, rather than the more straightforward order of interpreting Peter's denial as a consequence of Satan's sifting. It might also be asked why Jesus' prayer for Judas is ineffective; why does Judas apostasise, while Peter does not?

Those who maintain that Peter was not handed over to Satan have similar problems. On what basis is Peter excluded from the ὑμᾶς? As pointed out above,

---

[17] Plummer, *St. Luke*, p. 504; F. Botha, "'Umâs' in Luke xxii. 31," *ExpT*. 64 ('52–3) 125; W. Tobin, "The Petrine Primacy, Evidence of the Gospels," *LumV*. 23 ('68) 57f; Marshall, *Commentary*, pp. 819f; Fitzmyer, *The Gospel*, vol. II, p. 1424.

[18] Pickar, "Prayer of Christ," p. 134; Plummer, *St. Luke*, p. 504; Major, *The Mission*, p. 174; Ellis, *The Gospel*, p. 256; R. Brown, *Peter in the New Testament*, (Minneapolis, 1973), p. 113.

[19] Minear, "A Note," p. 130; Neyrey, *The Passion*, p. 34; Fitzmyer, *The Gospel*, vol. II, p. 1422.

[20] Suggested in a personal discussion with Prof. I. H. Marshall.

[21] S. Brown, *Apostasy*, p. 73; R. Brown, *Peter*, pp. 120–123.

[22] R. Brown, *Peter*, p. 123.

[23] Ellis, *The Gospel*, p. 256.

the δέ of v. 32 explicitly contrasts Satan and Jesus, not Peter and the others.[24] But this contrast occurs via the relative requests they each make with respect to the disciples. Consequently, the δέ also secondarily associates Peter *with* the larger group being demanded by Satan. It has already been seen that Jesus' prayer is not that Peter not be sifted, but that he not apostasise; the participle ἐπιστρέψας in fact looks forward to just such a temporary denial. Thus the denial scene itself presents a significant obstacle to this interpretation, which is not solved – at least insofar as the literary integrity of Luke is concerned – by a convenient appeal to divergent tradition histories.[25]

On the other hand, to those who maintain that only Peter was sifted by Satan, it may be said that while Luke does not emphasise the apostles' flight from Gethsemane as stridently as Mark – in fact he omits Mk. 14:50 – neither does he present them as pillars of fidelity. If such were the case it would be difficult to explain why only Peter follows Jesus to the house of the high priest (22:54). The remaining disciples' abandonment of Jesus is strongly implied by their conspicuous absence from all of the intervening passion material from 22:52 to 24:9.[26] But this is only what is already implicit in Jesus'·charge that Peter strengthen his brothers anyway. While there may be echoes of Peter's future ministry in Acts here, as some maintain, the primary reference must be to the immediate circumstances involving the other ten apostles.[27] But if only Peter had denied Jesus, the advice in v. 32b is most inappropriate; in that case the charge should have been that the other ten apostles, who had remained steadfast, strengthen Peter not *vice versa*! This suggestion also requires a significant bit of reading between the lines, for according to this approach what Jesus actually meant to say was, "Satan has demanded to sift you all – but his request has been denied for all except Peter – and for you, Peter..." This rewording is much more thoroughgoing than the solution suggested below.

It may be true that Peter acts as the spokesman for the other apostles in the gospel.[28] Luke has introduced Peter in such a capacity at several points in his narrative (Lk. 8:45; diff. Mk. 5:31; Lk. 12:41; diff. Mt. 24:44f; Lk. 22:8; diff. Mk. 14:13), but this does not really solve the problem. Jesus clearly implies that Peter's failure of faith is not permanent only because Jesus has prayed for him, yet Satan has asked that he be allowed to sift all of the apostles; the surrounding context,

---

[24] Dietrich, *Petrusbild*, p. 124; *pace* Klein, "Verleugnung," p. 63 (cf. n. 7).

[25] *Pace* those such as Bultmann, *History*, p. 267; Fuchs, "σινιάζω," p. 292; Klein, "Verleugnung," pp. 298ff, who see in vv. 31–32a a tradition which originally knew nothing of Peter's denial. For a critique of Klein see Linnemann, "Verleugnung," p. 3; *Studien*, p.72. It is worth noting that even Klein (p. 298) admits that *in its present context* Jesus' words must refer to Peter's denial; cf. also Ott, *Gebet*, p. 79 n. 25 who rightly asserts that within the present composition vv. 31f not only know the denial tradition, but presuppose it.

[26] Cf. Dietrich, *Petrusbild*, pp. 125f.

[27] *Pace* R. Brown, *Peter*, pp. 123f; Feldkämper, *Der betende Jesus*, pp. 218f. Brown's argument concerning Acts presupposes that only Peter "fell". However, this assumption has already been overturned.

[28] R. Brown, *Peter*, p. 120.

with its plethora of plural pronouns referring to the apostolic circle, makes this plain (vv. 15, 16, 18, 19, 20, 26, 27, 28, 29, 31, 35, 37). There is not the slightest hint that Jesus denies Satan access to the entire group, quite the contrary.[29] If it were not assumed that they all would be sifted, there would be no need to give Peter the future responsibility of strengthening his brothers. The obvious question then becomes, if Jesus had prayed only for Peter, and it is only by this prayer that Peter perseveres, by what ability does Satan's sifting of the others not result in their permanent apostasy? Any representative role held by Peter would do the others little good in the midst of their own trials. Trying to find a solution in Peter's future role as strengthener does no better.[30] At this point there are two options: First, the other apostles do apostasise completely and it is Jesus' intention that Peter re-evangelise them (v. 32b). Or, secondly, the other apostles do not apostasise, but Peter, for whatever reason, required a special prayer for the maintenance of his faith, a prayer which was unnecessary for the others.

But both of these answers are equally untenable. The first, that the others do apostasise, would require that ἐπιστρέψας be read transitively, but this was already shown to be highly unlikely. Secondly, it is anything but clear that Luke intends his reader to understand all the Twelve as having completely abandoned their faith in Jesus. If this were the case, one would expect rather more explicit mention of it, such as the retention of Mk. 14:50. A later interest in whitewashing the apostolic memory can hardly account for the complete absence of such a tradition from the whole of the gospel material, especially in light of the preservation of the frequent chastisements of the disciples in Mark. If anything, Luke's treatment, while not completely exonerating the inner circle (as previously mentioned; cf. Lk. 9:46–50; 12:28; 22:24–30), treats them more kindly than did the tradition. S. Brown has shown that the uninterrupted continuity of the apostolic faith was an important part of Luke's conception of apostolic witness (cf. Acts 1:21–22).[31] In fact, Luke's presentation of the behaviour of the Twelve is not that different from the portrayal of the other gospels. All the disciples temporarily abandon Jesus in fear, as represented by Peter's denial; however, their continued community together (Lk. 24:10–12, 33–36) testifies to anything but a complete throwing over of the messianic hopes they had attached to Jesus.

But the second answer is no more feasible. Jesus' words in v. 32a make it clear that Peter's faith would have failed were it not for his intercession. But if Jesus has not prayed for the other disciples, and their faith has not failed, then they have been able to withstand Satan's assault through their own abilities. Their personal resources are shown to be equal to the personal intercession of Christ himself. But this surely is not the case. Forthcoming discussions of the significance of both

---

[29] Noack, *Satanas*, p. 102; Dietrich, *Petrusbild*, p. 130.

[30] Feldkämper, *Der betende Jesus*, pp. 217, 222f sees the difficulty, but the solution eludes him. To say, as he does, that Jesus prayed for Peter in a "positive" rather than an "exclusive" sense, due to his unique role in the future, does not solve the present dilemma of the other apostles' perseverance.

[31] *Apostasy*, p. 72.

Satan's attack upon Judas in 22:3 and the disciples sleeping in 22:45 f will make this point quite unequivocally. But even now, in anticipation of those arguments, that Luke could have intended such a possibility seems quite remarkable. In fact, this suggestion destroys the significance of the contrast so deliberately made between Satan and Jesus, wherein Jesus is the powerful Advocate whose intercession successfully opposes the challenges of the Adversary of God's people.[32] Jesus is reduced to simply interceding for one particularly, though inexplicably, weak disciple while the others withstand the Satanic assault quite independently. But is this really the dynamic which Luke intends to offer the reader? "Is it conceivable that Jesus affirmed that all the disciples would be tempted, but that he had prayed only for one of them...?"[33]

However, one further possibility suggests itself which, it is believed, can adequately account for all of the factors involved in this dilemma. Peter is the representative spokesman for the apostles. Therefore, it would not be surprising if Jesus were to address him in particular on a subject which was actually relevant to the whole group. Neither would it be surprising if what Jesus said about Peter, the representative, were actually true of them all. With this in mind, it is worth noting that the first shift from the singular "Simon, Simon" to the plural ὑμᾶς in v. 31 is every bit as odd as the second shift back from ὑμᾶς to the singular σύ in v. 32. This evidence suggests that while Jesus is speaking to Peter, he is actually discussing an issue of significance to the entire group. Furthermore, the narrative development may also have a bearing on this shifting address. In other words, Peter alone is specified, not because Jesus prayed only for him, but because these verses are a part of the literary premonition of Peter's eventual temptation and denial (see vv. 54–62). The spotlight will soon be thrown on Peter's solitary behaviour, demonstrating the appropriateness of the singular Simon/σύ; but Peter's role as representative, together with his future responsibility to restore his fallen brothers, also indicates that neither Satan's testing nor Jesus' prayer were for him alone, thereby also accounting for the plural ὑμᾶς.

Consequently, the fact that Jesus explicitly refers only to having prayed for Peter does not exclude the strong implication that he had actually been praying for all the apostles. If Jesus had prayed for all the disciples he, of course, would have prayed for Peter. Likewise, for Jesus to affirm that he had prayed for Peter is not necessarily to deny that he had prayed for the others. With this in mind, it is suggested that the full intention of Jesus' words be read as: "Satan has demanded all of you that he might sift you as wheat, but I have prayed for you all that your faith will not fail; and furthermore, for you Peter I have prayed with the intention that when you have turned back you will strengthen your brothers." Admittedly, this reads something into the text, but such a "reading between the lines" can be as necessary as it is a common part of communication, especially when it is guided

---

[32] Cf. W. Foerster, "Lukas 22,31 f," pp. 131 f.

[33] Argyle, "Luke xxii.31 f," p. 222; also see Pickar, "The Prayer of Christ," pp. 135 f, who discusses the similarity with Jn. 17.

by discernable indicators. Jesus' intention was not to deny that he had prayed for all the apostles, but to affirm that he had prayed something extra for Peter, their representative head who was about to deny him. If in establishing the latter point the former perspective has become obscured, it must be seen as the kind of confusion which easily accompanies economy of expression.

Finally, while one may still be inclined to debate the exegetical appropriateness of this interpretation, the necessity of including all of the apostles within the matrix of Satan's demand and Jesus' intercession becomes apparent as soon as one tries to step from the tangle of exegetical detail into the full light of theological significance. In the process of trying to abstract principles of theological reality from Luke's account, the importance of integrating all of the disciples within Jesus' prayer becomes self-evident. No explanation which excludes them can prove adequate to answering the residual questions.

## 6.3 The Possession of Judas (Lk. 22:3)

The significance attached by Conzelmann to Lk. 22:3 is well known. According to him it designates the renewal of Satanic temptations alluded to in 4:13, marking the termination of the temptation-free era of salvation present during Jesus' earthly ministry.[34] There can be no doubt that Luke presents the period beginning with 22:3 as something of a turning point. Jesus' own description of the moment of his arrest as the hour of ἡ ἐξουσία τοῦ σκότους (22:53) conjures the image of a final assault by Satan's forces (cf. 4:6). But any "turning point" quality in the passion material is due to the apparent victory of this demonic authority not, as Conzelmann suggests, to the reintroduction of an element absent since 4:13. The connection between the temptation narrative and Lk. 22 occurs, not in 4:13 and 22:3, but through 4:6 and 22:53; it is via this element of ἐξουσία, not the appearance of Satan. A corollary of this is the fact that 4:13 refers to the Devil as Tempter, whereas 22:3 is part of a complex of Lukan material portraying Satan as Adversary. The immediate relevance of Judas' possession by Satan needs to be interpreted with respect to the satanic activity mentioned in 22:31, not the demonic activity of 4:13.[35]

### 6.3.1 Why Does Judas Betray Jesus?

Satan's "entrance" into Judas before the betrayal is a tradition which Luke shares with the gospel of John (Jn. 13:2, 27a; 6:70; cf. also Lk. 22:53 with Jn. 13:30). The development of such an idea, which is noticeably lacking in the other synoptics,

---

[34] Conzelmann, *Theology*, p. 80. For a critique of this aspect of Conzelmann's thesis see Brown, *Apostasy*, pp. 6–10; Marshall, *Historian and Theologian*, pp. 87f, 136f.

[35] *Pace* those such as Fitzmyer, *The Gospel*, vol. II, p. 1374, who follow Conzelmann on this point.

has been accounted for as an attempt to explain an otherwise unbelievable action.[36] However, such explanations seem more concerned with ensuring that Judas is not relieved of any personal responsibility for his betrayal, than with actually coming to grips with the text. Plummer writes that ". . . there is no hint that Judas is now like a demoniac, unable to control his own actions. Judas opened the door to Satan. He did not resist him, and Satan did not flee from him."[37] However, is this really an honest appraisal of the simple phrase, εἰσῆλθεν δὲ Σατανᾶς εἰς Ἰούδαν? It appears to be more a discussion of the epistle of James (1:13–15; 4:7) than of the gospel of Luke.

S. Brown has developed an extensive discussion of Satan's role in Judas' betrayal.[38] He too reiterates that Judas' possession does not mitigate his responsibility. There is no need to discuss the whole of Brown's argument, but it will be helpful to examine a few of those points most pertinent to the present discussion:

1) Judas' unauthorized departure (ἀπελθὼν) from Jesus in v. 4, related as it is to the role which following Jesus plays in Luke's thematic portrayal of discipleship,[39] is symbolic of Judas' apostasy.[40] The consequence is Judas' collusion with Jesus' enemies.

2) Judas' own presence at the Last Supper highlights the importance of individual responsibility in perseverance; participation in the Eucharist is no guarantee of continued discipleship.[41]

3) Satan is merely the "heavenly counterpart" to the "earthly reality" to which Judas becomes captive: money (v. 5).[42]

4) Luke actually highlights Judas' free-will in the matter by emphasising his "bargaining" (v. 4, συνελάλησεν) and ultimate "consent" (v. 6, ἐξωμολόγησεν).[43]

5) The divine necessity of the cross does not relieve Judas of responsibility for

---

[36] K. Hein, "Judas Iscariot: Key to the Last-Supper Narratives?," *NTS.* 17 ('70–71) 229; Fitzmyer, *The Gospel*, vol. II, p. 1374.

[37] Plummer, *St. Luke*, p. 490; similarly Ellis, *The Gospel*, p. 248: "Satan tempts but the responsibility remains on Judas."

[38] S. Brown, *Apostasy*, pp. 82–97.

[39] Cf. Robinson, *Der Weg*, p. 39.

[40] *Apostasy*, p. 82.

[41] *Apostasy*, p. 83.

[42] *Apostasy*, p. 85.

[43] *Apostasy*, pp. 92f. Brown clearly follows Conzelmann's views on election in this part of his analysis; cf. *Theology*, pp. 154–156. According to Conzelmann, how one who was chosen (Lk. 6:13) could apostasise merely demonstrates that Luke does not operate with a personal view of election. However, Brown's dismissal of Acts 13:48 as only "a current expression not to be pressed" (cf. *Theology*, p. 154 n. 2), and 18:10 as "a standard cliché for the suffering Christians" need only be mentioned in order to demonstrate their inadequacy. Conzelmann says even less about these texts in his commentary on Acts. His remark concerning 13:48 (*Apostelgeschichte*, p. 86) is a good example of ignoring the text at hand: "trotz der Ausdrucksweise ist der Erwählungsgedanke bei Lk nicht im Sinne einer Prädestination des Einzelnen ausgebaut." There is no relevant comment at all on 18:7 in either *Apostelgeschichte*, (cf. p. 115) or *Theology* (cf. p. 164 n. 1).

what he has done. The adversative πλήν of 22:22 demonstrates that the betrayal is an act of Judas' own free-will.[44]

Do these points actually prove Brown's argument (and, indeed, the concern of so many commentators) that Judas' treachery was an action taken solely of his own free-will? The first, third and fourth all suffer from the same weakness: they ignore the actual order of events. The sequence is not "Judas leaves Jesus → and joins/bargains with the enemy," or "Judas accepts money → and surrenders himself to Satan." In fact, it is quite the opposite. Satan's entering into Judas precedes all of these other actions. Satan enters Judas *and then* Judas leaves Jesus, bargains with the Jewish leaders and accepts their money. All of this gives the very striking impression that it is the entering in of Satan which serves to explain Judas' subsequent behaviour.

Secondly, Brown's argument (number 2) concerning Judas' presence at the Last Supper appears to be a good example of trying to have one's cake and eating it too. If "being with Jesus" is illustrative of true discipleship in Luke, how is "being with Jesus at the table" an example of the fact that even disciples can apostasise? Judas' presence here has nothing to do with the role of free-will in Jesus' betrayal. Finally, argument 5 overlooks the fact that Luke regularly holds in tension the two aspects of divine sovereignty and individual responsibility without necessarily addressing the question of how this is amenable to the concept of free-will. Thus the πλήν of 22:22 does not introduce an adversative clause giving only the cause of Jesus' betrayal, but a clause which offers *the proper evaluation* of Jesus' betrayal, ie. "do not think that just because the betrayal was predetermined that the betrayer is innocent." The issue in 22:22b is not free-will but guilt.

The goal of this discussion has not been to settle all questions surrounding the relationship of individual free-will to the dual forces of divine and human action. It has simply been to set out that efforts to down-play the significance of Satan's control over Judas, in the interest of vindicating the autonomy of Judas' individual decision in the betrayal of Jesus, do not work. Much of the discussion of Lk. 22:3 has gone astray at this point because it continues, whether consciously or not, to follow Conzelmann's lead in relating Satan's action with Judas solely to his work as Tempter set out in Lk. 4:1–13.[45] And, of course, any discussion of demonic temptation must also consider the role of human consent. However, Satan's action with Judas needs to be interpreted, first, with respect to the more immediate context of Satan as Adversary, which entails the corollary of Jesus as Advocate. Satan does not tempt Judas, *he enters Judas!* As B. Noack has observed, the language of Lk. 22:3 presupposes Satanic possession (cf. especially Lk. 8:30, 32–33//Mt. 12:43–44, 45; Mk. 5:13).[46]

However, even Noack back-tracks from the implications of this observation by

---

[44] Apostasy, p. 92.
[45] Cf. Conzelmann, *Theology*, p. 156.
[46] *Satanas*, p. 91.

referring to Asc. Is. 2:1; 3:11. There he claims that possession language is merely an emphatic way of expressing "yielding to temptation." But Noack's retreat from the plain meaning of possession is unjustified. Apart from the fact that Luke's usage should be allowed to define itself, his examples from the Ascension of Isaiah actually prove the exact opposite of what he claims for them.[47] J. Hull is much more honest when he simply says that Lk. 22:3 presents Judas' real bodily possession by Satan.[48]

But once this is admitted, a number of important questions arise: What is the nature of the relationship between Satan's possession of Judas and his demand to be allowed to sift all of the disciples? What role did Jesus' prayer for the perseverance of the apostles' faith have to play in the life of Judas the Betrayer? Was Jesus' prayer ineffective in his case? The possibility that these two pieces of tradition were originally irrelevant to each other is now overridden by the narrative constraints of Luke's gospel. These questions cannot be avoided.

A synoptic look at the information at hand will lead to the required answer. First, Satan has demanded that he be given the apostles with a view to causing their apostasy. Secondly, Jesus has opposed Satan by interceding before God. Thirdly, Judas is lost to Satan while Jesus promises perseverance to the others as the result of his prayer. From these three propositions there may only be two possible solutions to Judas' possession. Either Jesus had included Judas in his prayers, but God denied this aspect of his request; or Jesus had not included Judas in his intercession, and so without Jesus' protective advocacy Judas was left to experience the full measure of Satan's will.

The first of these possibilities is contradicted by numerous aspects of Luke's gospel. To begin with, Luke has made it clear that one of the distinctive features of Jesus' prayers is that they are always offered in accordance with the Father's will; his choice of revealing and witholding is never outside of the Father's determination (10:21–24; 22:42). Thus, if the Father had already determined that Judas be handed over to Satan, his preservation would not have been a part of Jesus' request.[49] Secondly, Jesus reveals that he already knows about the role which Judas will play in God's plan. Lk. 22:21 shows Jesus' knowledge that his betrayer will be from among the Twelve (cf. Jn. 13:26 f); Luke's omission of "twelve" from 22:30 (cf. Mt. 20:28) emphasises this as well. But the confidence expressed in 22:32 at the

---

[47] Clearer examples of an individual's actions being attributed to the demon who indwells them could not be found; cf. 11:41: "Because of these visions and prophecies Sammael Satan sawed Isaiah the son of Amoz, the prophet, in half by the hand of Manasseh." Also see 1:9; 3:12f; 5:1, 15; 11:43.

[48] Hull, *Magic*, p. 96. He properly relates this to the objective, realistic attitude towards spiritual phenomena found in Luke-Acts.

[49] Marshall, *Kept By the Power of God: A Study of Perseverance and Falling Away*, (Minneapolis, 1969), p. 89 mentions "unfulfilled longings" of Jesus (Mk. 14:36; Lk. 13:34; 19:42) to explain this point. But an unsatisfied desire is different from a request denied.

efficacy of his intercession, combined with the force of the first argument above, makes it difficult to believe that Luke would have the reader think that Jesus was ignorant of which of the disciples would fall outside the saving circle of his intercession. And, finally, if it is in fact Jesus' prayer which preserves the Eleven, as has been argued, then the implication can only be that Judas is lost because Jesus did not pray for him.

It is difficult to avoid the conclusion, the second of the answers above, that Judas is invaded by Satan, in order to fulfil the plan of God, as a result of his exclusion from the prayers of the disciples' earthly Advocate. But this would not be the first time that such a pattern had revealed itself in Luke. Already the prayer notice in 9:18 has been shown to play a similar role with respect to the inquisitive Herod and the disciples; likewise, the prayer at Jesus' baptism, as it stands in relation to the "absent" Baptist and the onlooking crowds.

Jesus' prayer has again served to separate two classes of individuals. In this respect, Judas' fate adds an important element to the understanding of Jesus' work as Advocate, for it effectively links the elective aspect of the revelatory facet of Jesus' prayers with the intercessory aspect of the advocatory facet of Jesus' prayers. Offered as they are, always in agreement with the will of God, Jesus' prayers bring him before the throne of heaven where his intercessory prayers become *the* means of administering, not only the predetermined course of redemptive history as a whole, but also the personal application of individual election.

Furthermore, this insight adds yet another argument in favour of the suggested reconstruction of the "full" prayer intended in 22:32. For, if Judas' fate is that which awaited those who were given unreservedly into Satan's hands, then Jesus' prayer must have been concerned with all of the remaining apostles. If not, only Peter would not have turned to betrayal.[50]

## 6.4 Is Jesus Still Our Advocate?

The question arises whether Luke intends his reader to attach any continuing relevance to Jesus' work as Advocate portrayed in Lk. 22:31f, or whether it is presented as merely a singular course of action taken by Jesus in a unique salvation-historical crisis? The key to answering this important question will be found by way of analysing the relationship between Jesus' prayer for the disciples and the disciples' prayer (or lack thereof) for themselves. The scene on the Mount of Olives forms the pertinent complement to the instruction in 22:31f, and for this reason Lk. 22:39–46 needs to be briefly reexamined from this new perspective.

---

[50] Cf. Franklin, *Christ the Lord*, p. 25.

## 6.4.1 "Pray that you will not enter into temptation" (Lk. 22:39–46)

The distinctive structural elements of Luke's scene on the Mount of Olives have been noticed many times.[51] In Mark Jesus tells the disciples to wait while he prays (14:32); in Luke Jesus exhorts all of the disciples to pray for themselves (v. 40). In Mark Jesus selects Peter, James and John to accompany him (14:33), even though he still withdraws a little further to pray alone (14:35); in Luke all of the disciples follow Jesus to the Mount (v. 39), but none of them accompany him to his place of prayer (v. 41). Consequently, while in Mark only the three who go with him are reprimanded for sleeping (14:37), in Luke all of the disciples are found sleeping when Jesus returns from prayer (v. 45). In Mark Jesus prays three times and returns after each prayer (14:37, 40, 41); in Luke Jesus only returns to the disciples once from his place of prayer (v. 45). The result of this, together with the opening exhortation to pray themselves, is that the charge "to pray in order not to fall into temptation" forms an *inclusio* in Luke around Jesus' own prayer and the disciples' sleep (v. 40, 46; cf. Mk. 14:38). This simplification of Luke's structure does not, however, result in any diminution of the role occupied in the narrative by Jesus' prayer, as one might expect from this description. For within the *inclusio* Luke has three references to Jesus' prayer, two of them unique to Luke (Lk. 22:41//Mk. 14:35; Lk. 22:44, 45), in addition to Jesus' own prayer reported in direct discourse (22:42).[52] Consequently, there is a six-fold repetition of the pressing need for prayer in the situation facing Jesus and the disciples. Jesus' own prayer is framed by the twice repeated exhortation to "pray in order not to fall into temptation." The result is a powerful contrast between Jesus and the sleeping disciples who do not pray. The consensus among interpreters today views Luke as deliberately present-ing Jesus as the paradigmatic pray-er, who survives the moment of *his* greatest temptation through the intense prayer he offers to his Father.

However, not all have been willing to agree with this interpretation. In opposi-tion, some have suggested that Jesus originally had commanded the disciples to pray *for him* that he not enter into temptation, reading a με after the infinitive

---

[51] There is anything but a consensus on the sources of Luke's version, and the question need not be answered here. There are three basic positions: 1) Luke derives his narrative from an indepen-dent, non-Markan source – so Loisy, *Luc*, p. 525; Lagrange, *Luc*, p. 558; Schlatter, *Das Evangelium*, p. 432f; K. Kuhn, "Jesus in Gethsemane" *EvT*. 12 ('52–3) 271f; T. Lescow, "Jesus in Gethsemane bei Lukas und im Hebräerbrief," *ZNW*. 58 ('67) 215–223; Grundmann, *Das Evangelium*, p. 411; Rengstorf, *Das Evangelium*, p. 260; Taylor, *Passion*, pp. 69–72; 2) Luke edits Mark's account – so Klostermann, *Lukas*, p. 215; Creed, *The Gospel*, p. 272; Schmid, *Das Evangelium*, p. 335; Schneider, *Das Evangelium*, p. 457; E. Linnemann, *Studien*, 34–40; Fitzmyer, *The Gospel*, vol. II, p. 1438; or, 3) Luke either combines a redacted Mark with his own material, or adds his own material to a shorter account which lay behind Mark's gospel – so Marshall, *Commentary*, p. 829; Green, "Mount of Olives," p. 37.

[52] Feldkämper, *Der betende Jesus*, pp. 228f proposes an outline for these verses which recognises the *inclusio* of vv. 40, 46, but then attempts to construct a chiasm of the intervening material which is rather artificial.

(εἰσελθεῖν) of v. 40.[53] However, there is no manuscript evidence for such a reading having ever existed.[54] Also, Lagrange has observed that the insertion of a subject (με) for the infinitive which is different from the subject of the main verb (προσεύχεσθε) would be unnatural grammatically.[55] And finally, there are no other instances of Jesus ever asking the disciples to pray for him. Given the consistency with which Luke has portrayed Jesus' prayers as being for the benefit of his disciples elsewhere, and the remarkable confidence expressed in the power of Jesus' prayers against the attacks of Satan so recently expressed (22:31f), it would be quite remarkable for Luke to present Jesus as suddenly, and inexplicably, in need of his disciples' intercession!

It has also been suggested that Jesus is not praying for himself, but for his disciples on the Mount of Olives.[56] However, the two-fold exhortation of vv. 40, 46 indicates that Jesus expected the disciples to be praying for themselves. Jesus' prayer in v. 42 is for himself, and the appearance *to him* of a strengthening angel (v. 43), together with his increased agony (v. 44), all point to the depth of Jesus' struggle as he continues to pray in the vein made explicit in v. 42. Furthermore, the structure of the passage, as already outlined, is most conducive to reading the narrative as contrasting Jesus and the disciples as those who do and do not, respectively, follow the advice to pray for themselves. And finally, the correlation of vv. 39–46 with 31–32 being developed in this section, indicates that Jesus' previous prayers for the disciples are now being contrasted with Jesus' own prayer for himself and the disciples' neglect to do the same.

Luke has made it clear elsewhere that one may persevere in discipleship and overcome temptation only through prayer (21:36). As Satan launches his final attack upon both Jesus and the disciples, Luke presents his reader with a course of events that parallels the fates of Jesus and the disciples as they face their respective trials, in their different ways, with their different outcomes.

Jesus faces temptation on the Mount of Olives.[57] The "sandwiching" of his own prayer for himself in between the two exhortations about temptation make this plain. The irony here is that Jesus' obedience will mean his acceptance of that fate which Satan is now instigating; the very opposite course from what one would

---

[53] So Héring, "Zwei exegetisch Probleme," pp. 64f; Loisy, *Les Evangiles synoptiques*, II, (Ceffonds, 1907–8), p. 562; cf. p. 568 (as cited by Lagrange, *Luc*, p. 559).

[54] Barbour, "Gethsemane," p. 244; Holleran, *Gethsemane*, p. 37.

[55] Langrange, *Luc*, p. 559: "L'insertion de με (Loisy) serait peu naturelle, car le verbe a l'infinitif s'entend naturellement du sujet du verbe défini."

[56] Brown, *Apostasy*, pp. 9f. Though not clearly stated, it may also be suggested by Stanley, *Gethsemane*, p. 220, who believes that Jesus never intended the disciples to remain awake and pray; therefore, they "arise" because Jesus has prayed (for them?). Also cf. Schlatter, *Das Evangelium*, p. 433, and Brun, "Engel," p. 272, who also both imply that Jesus' prayer has been for the disciples by seeking to interpret it as consonant with the previous prayer in 22:32; similarly Boman "Gebetskampf," p. 270, who tentatively suggests that the prayer in 22:32 was overheard by the disciples in Gethsemane.

[57] K. Kuhn, "New Light on Temptation, Sin and Flesh in the New Testament" in *The Scrolls and the New Testament*, (London, 1958), p. 95; Barbour, "Gethsemane," p. 240; Marshall, *Commentary*, p. 828.

normally expect of resisting temptation. However, this only highlights the place of the Passion in God's sovereign plan.

But the disciples are also facing a temptation. The challenge before them is presented paradigmatically in the events of Peter's denial (22:54–62),[58] even as he has regularly served as the spokesman for the apostles elsewhere (cf. 22:33). Will they remain loyal to their Master and willingly follow him, even to death if necessary (cf. 9:23; 14:27; 22:33)? Or will their loyalty be compromised as they deny him?[59]

Jesus follows his own advice and prays in the midst of his temptation. As a result he obeys his Father, withstands the test and pursues his course to the cross. Luke's statement that Jesus "stood up from (his) prayer" (v. 45, ἀναστὰς ἀπὸ τῆς προσευχῆς) may well convey an important symbolic, as well as literal sense, due to the ambiguity of the preposition ἀπό. Jesus literally stood up "from" prayer and returned to the disciples, but he was also now able to stand in the face of his coming trial "because of" (ἀπό) this prayer.[60]

The disciples, on the other hand, have not been praying, but lying down asleep. They have not sought the Father's strengthening, but will instead depend upon their own abilities to withstand the trial ahead. Thus, when the arresting mob appears, they try to resist through human strength (22:49f), while Jesus surrenders himself. But the crucial moment of "resisting" is past; by this display of force the disciples demonstrate that they have not resisted the real Enemy in the proper way. Already, the absence of prayer and their failing the test is revealing itself. Perhaps, this is also why Jesus could know ahead of time that they all would repudiate their loyalty and require future strengthening (22:32). Jesus not only foresaw what was coming, but by understanding their current character also knew that none of the disciples could yet exercise the type of prayer which alone could save them from falling.

The result is that Jesus passes his test and proceeds to the cross, while Peter and

---

[58] Is it possible that Peter's denial is to be compared with Satan's work in Judas, as also constituting a Satanic attack, by way of the popular belief that certain demons were active at night until the moment of cock-crow when their work suddenly ceased? Cf. Davies, *Magic*, p. 112; also Lev. R. 5:1 on 4:3.

[59] Some, such as Pickar, "Christ's Prayer," p. 136; Stanley, *Gethsemane*, p. 75; and Fitzmyer, *The Gospel*, vol. II, p. 1423, dissent from the view that Peter actually denied Jesus by claiming that, according to Luke, Peter only denies "knowing Jesus" (22:57). Stanley further asserts that Peter maintains his discipleship by "following" Jesus even after the arrest (22:54b, 61). But this is certainly overly subtle. It would be difficult to explain Luke's intensification of Peter's anguish, ie. he weeps "bitterly" (πικρῶς; diff. Mk. 14:72), if he had actually intended to lessen the significance of Peter's denial. Furthermore, it is already plain from 22:32 that Peter's discipleship is maintained because of Jesus' prayer, not Peter's own determination to follow Jesus.

[60] The case for this interpretation is especially strengthened by the parallelism with the disciples sleeping "because of grief" (v. 45b, ἀπὸ τῆς λύπης); cf. *BDF*. para. 210; Neyrey, "Emotions," p. 169.

the others fail their test and deny Jesus.[61] Jesus stands by prayer. The disciples fall through the lack of it.

There can be little doubt that this deliberate contrast between Jesus and disciples is offered paradigmatically to the church by Luke.[62] The fact that all of the disciples, and not just the inner circle, are contrasted with Jesus in the drama adds strongly to this impression, which is only what one would expect in the light of what Jesus has taught about temptation elsewhere (21:36). It was as true for Luke's own church, as it was for Jesus and his disciples, as it is for the church today, that one is able to resist temptation only by the divine strength available through prayer.

### 6.4.2 The Disciples' Prayer and Jesus' Prayer: The Continuing Relevance of Both

There is a connection begging to be made between what Jesus foretells about the disciples' temporary fall in 22:32 and the portrait of disciples who succumb to temptation through lack of prayer in 22:39–46.[63] In fact, a hint has already been made in this direction. The disciples' faith is not utterly destroyed because Jesus has prayed for them to be spared, but it undergoes temporary failure because they have not prayed for themselves. The disciples' prayer and Jesus' prayer stand in a complementary relationship one with the other. His is the foundation upon which the disciples permanently stand; theirs is the necessary ingredient of discipleship which ensures continual growth. There is no indication that this relationship exists through any inadequacy on Jesus' part. Quite the contrary. The fact that Jesus has specifically requested "that their faith not fail," as opposed to their being wholly spared from the trial, indicates that the effective boundary of Jesus' prayer is self-

---

[61] Brown, *Apostasy*, pp. 10, 15f, 66f, denies that the Passion events constitute a true temptation for the disciples. He bases his conclusion primarily upon the assertions that Luke does not present Satan as a Tempter (pp. 8, 17) and he only uses the idea of temptation with the negative connotation of "apostasy" (p. 15f). However, without examining all of his arguments in detail (cf. Green, "Mount of Olives," p. 31), Brown admits himself that Jesus' temptation in the desert is an exception, an admission which then opens wide the door for more of them, especially in a scene where Jesus is himself being tempted once again. He claims, further, that the Passion is a "sifting" of the disciples, which may only become a "temptation" if they fail to pray (p. 10). But this is exactly what they do fail to do! Furthermore, the close association of the forecast of Peter's denial (22:34) with Jesus' foretelling of the disciples' "sifting," which will result in their temporary fall, makes it most congenial to interpret all of the following events as the disciples' temptation, the interpretation which Jesus himself places upon the events (22:40, 46).

[62] For Jesus-as-Model see Dibelius, "Gethsemane," p. 260; Aschermann, "Agoniegebet," p. 149; Harris, *Prayer*, p. 112; Barbour, "Gethsemane," p. 240; Feldkämper, *Der betende Jesus*, pp. 230–232; Green, "Mount of Olives," pp. 38f. The evident contrast also speaks strongly against Feldkämper's thesis (p. 226) that Luke intends to underline the disciples' "solidarity" with Jesus in his suffering, and thus their solidarity with him in his prayer (p. 250). It is obvious that there is not solidarity but *disjunction* between Jesus and the others at this point. Ott, *Gebet*, pp. 83–90, also sees the praying Jesus as the paradigm for the church. But his attachment to Conzelmann's views on eschatology and temptation cause him to miss the significance of this material for christology, discipleship, Satan's possession of Judas and the prayer of vv. 31f.

[63] Cf. Harris, *Prayer*, p. 107.

imposed; the implication being that the resulting, complementary interaction between the two sets of prayers is a part of the divine intention.[64] There are several important conclusions which result from this analysis of the relationship between the prayers of Jesus and those of his disciples. Firstly, it has been shown that Luke universalises the paradigmatic significance of the disciples' failure to pray. It is not only Peter who will be tempted, and who will need to pray for himself, but all of the disciples, inclusively. But they all fail only temporarily. The one possible conclusion is that they all have benefitted from Jesus' prayer that their "faith not fail." Here, then, is a final piece of evidence in favour of the reconstructed expansion of the abbreviated report of Jesus' prayer offered in 22:32. Not only the final apostasy of Judas, but the *temporary* failing of the other Eleven indicate that Jesus' prayer was not concerned only with Peter, but had been offered on behalf of all the remaining ten apostles.

Luke's universalising of the lesson in 22:39–46 also has a second important implication. The admonitions to "pray in order to avoid temptation" have a continuing parenetic application to the church; this is a part of Luke's didactic perspective on the role of prayer in the Christian life,[65] and also the fundamental reason for his paradigmatic portrayal of Jesus' prayer on the Mount of Olives. The exhortation in Lk. 21:36 remains applicable until the moment of the parousia. Satan continues in his role as the Adversary of God's people all throughout the era of the church (Acts 5:3; 13:10). Tribulation is a constant factor in all Christian experience (Acts 14:22).[66] In fact, the whole of Paul's missionary enterprise is described as the deliverance of individuals from the "power of Satan" (Acts 26:18).

---

[64] This would be true regardless of whether the ἵνα (22:32) is taken to introduce a final or a content clause. Jeremias (*Sprache*, pp. 58, 291) offers a good analysis in favour of content. Marshall, *Commentary*, p. 821 interprets it as a dual purpose clause; cf. the discussions in C. Cadoux, "The Imperatival Use of ἵνα in the New Testament," *JTS*. 42 ('41) 172 (imperatival); H. Meecham, "The Imperatival Use of ἵνα in the New Testament," *JTS*. 43 ('42) 180 (content); Kuhn, "Gethsemane," p. 285 n. 41 (final); H. Schürmann, *Jesu Abschiedsrede, Lk. 22,21–38,* (Münster, 1957), p. 106 (content); Foerster, "Lukas 22, 31 f," p. 131 (final); Klein, "Verleugnung," p. 300 (content); Holleran, *Gethsemane,* p. 36 (final); Feldkämper, *Der betende Jesus,* pp. 235f (content); both Jeremias and Schürmann provide the evidence attesting to Luke's own aversion to the non-final use of ἵνα. A content clause is most likely here since elsewhere after verbs of asking/speaking Luke's ἵνα clauses deal with content, not purpose or consequence (Lk. 4:3; 7:36; 8:31f//Mk. 5:10; Lk. 9:40//Mk. 9:18; Lk. 10:40; 16:27; 18:39//Mk. 10:48; Lk. 18:41//Mk. 10:51; Lk. 21:36; 22:32; 22:46//Mk. 14:38). Luke prefers to use an infinitive of content; cf. the replacement of Mark's ἵνα in Lk. 8:38//Mk. 5:18; Lk. 8:41//Mk. 5:23; Lk. 8:56//Mk. 5:43; Lk. 9:21//Mk. 8:30. Less often Luke simply uses direct discourse (Lk. 9:3//Mk. 6:8; Lk. 22:42//Mk. 14:35). This evidence indicates that both the infinitive of Lk. 22:40 and the ἵνα of 22:46 introduce content clauses. In the latter instance Luke simply reproduces his source (Mk. 14:38); in the former, which comes from his own hand, Luke reverts to his preferred usage. This evidence also suggests that Lk. 22:32 comes from a pre-Lukan source which Luke does not alter.

[65] Ott, *Gebet,* p. 138f.

[66] Brown's attempt (*Apostasy,* pp. 114–117) to eradicate all hints of trial from the age of the church by means of a "collectivist" interpretation is unsuccessful. It is not readily apparent that all individual concerns vanish once the church becomes labeled a part of salvation-history.

The continuity between this ongoing experience of the church and that of Jesus' disciples is further intimated by the verbal echoes of Lk. 22:32 found in these Acts passages (ἐπιστηρίζοντες, Acts 14:22; ἐπιστρέψαι, Acts 26:18). Paul continues to serve in the work of strengthening the fallen which had earlier been allotted to Peter. Consequently, the importance of prayer in discipleship is as relevant to the post-Pentecostal church as it was in the earthly days of Jesus. But it has already been shown that there are *two facets* to the place of prayer in discipleship: there is the disciple's prayer to avoid temptation, *together with* Jesus' prayer that his faith may not fail! It follows that if the scene on the Mount of Olives is offered by Luke as the paradigm for the ongoing necessity of Christian prayer, then Jesus' intercessory prayer in 22:32 must also be offered as *the paradigm for the continuing reality of Jesus' work as Advocate before the heavenly throne of God.* The currency of this belief elsewhere in the NT (chapter 1), together with its appearance in the book of Acts (see chapter 7) also help to establish its feasibility here in the gospel.

If the apostles had required such intercession for the preservation of their faith, is it possible that later disciples could somehow survive satanic temptation without such prayer? This might be possible if there were some indication that, either Satan had been immobilised after the prayer in 22:32, or that Pentecost had given the disciples new dimensions of authority over Satan not available while Jesus was upon the earth. But there is no such evidence. In fact, all of Jesus' demonstrations of power, as well as his teaching about Satan's ultimate defeat, take place well before the words of 22:31 f, let alone the subsequent events of the apostolic mission (cf. Lk. 4:31–36, 41; 8:28–33; 9:42; 10:18; 11:14–22). And the disciples themselves had exercised spiritual power, of the kind had by Jesus himself, over demons while Jesus was still with them (9:1–6; 10:1, 17). Yet, if this same Satan, who had been so powerfully overrun by the ministry of Jesus and his followers, retained the resources to oppose these very disciples, not only with the intention but also the ability to destroy their confession, then there is no reason to believe that he would not be able to do the same thing in the later era of the church. Whatever else Jesus' exaltation and the dispensation of the Spirit at Pentecost may mean for Luke, they nowhere signify the removal of Satan-the-Adversary from the world now inhabited by the church. If one asks, then, whether Luke presents Jesus' prayer for the disciples as simply a unique event offered in the midst of a singular crisis, the answer must be "No". *Jesus' prayer for his disciples must be an ongoing activity,* as important today as it was during his earthly ministry, as much the foundation of a disciple's perseverance now as it was then. And it must remain so until whatever time Satan is no longer able to demand that he be allowed to sift Christ's disciples like wheat.

### 6.4.3 Further Implications: Jesus' Prayers and the Composition of the Church

The ramifications of the previous conclusion are far-reaching, and much of the next two chapters of this study will be devoted to drawing them out. But several may be briefly mentioned here. To begin with, if the preservation of the eleven apostles by virtue of Jesus' prayer is paradigmatic of the function of Jesus' prayers in the continuation of the post-Pentecostal church, then the apostasy of Judas, resulting as it does from his exclusion from that prayer, must also be paradigmatic for the exclusion of unbelievers from the community of the church.[67]

It appears that the construction of the church is orchestrated by the prayers of its Lord. While this may look as if Luke is articulating a doctrine of double predestination, the decisions of which are executed by the prayers of Jesus, an answer to this question will depend upon exactly what one means by the word "double." Jesus does not pray for Judas' exclusion; he simply does not pray for his inclusion. This distinction agrees with a unique feature in Luke's Son of Man tradition (also see chapter 7). Unlike Matthew (10:32f), Luke does not record that the Son of Man will some day both acknowledge *and* deny men before the Father. He simply says that the Son of Man will acknowledge his own (12:8); he does not deny unbelievers.

Nevertheless, by always praying for the Father's will, the Father's decision both to hide and to reveal (Lk. 10:21) continues to be carried out by the Son. The fact that Judas may have been appointed for loss (Acts 1:16) must be balanced against the fact that the "wise and the learned" are those who exclude themselves from God's purposes. One might want to ask, "To what extent is Judas representative of those outside the church?" To the extent that Satan "entered into him" he must be unique, as the one destined to betray God's messiah. Luke nowhere indicates that all those outside the church are possessed or indwelt by Satan. But, as one who was lost through the oppressive power of Satan, Judas does actually represent all those who never "see" and so never experience the liberating power of God (Acts 26:18). The leaders' rebellion (Acts 4:28) had been predetermined by the Father just as much as Judas' betrayal; thus whether the image is one of wilful rejection or demonic possession the interpretation remains the same: God's will is always being performed in the course of redemptive history as he works to free individuals from the ἐξουσία of Satan (cf. Lk. 4:5–7). Insofar as the Son's prayers administrate the will of God, one may perhaps speak of a doctrine of double predestination executed through the prayers of Jesus in Luke. But this would remain correct only so long as it is remembered that Jesus prays for those whom God has chosen, not against those whom he has not chosen, just as the Son of Man will some day "acknowledge" but not "deny." Luke knows nothing of there being any people who might want to repent and believe but who are excluded from the church simply because they have not been predestined. Here the interpreter runs up against the tension between God's predetermination and the reality of individual responsibility, which Luke nowhere seems interested in explaining. To this end, it is significant that Luke records nothing like the repentance of Judas

---

[67] An observation which further underscores the inadequacy of Conzelmann's treatment of Acts 13:48 and 18:10 (see *Theology*, pp. 154–156; cf. n. 43 above). Conzelmann's oft repeated insistence that Luke knows nothing of anything approaching individual election runs aground on this implication of Lk. 22:32.

found in Mt. 27:1–5.[68] While demon-possessed, Judas was not tricked into doing something against his will, something which would repulse him once the possession had ended.

Finally, there arises the question of Luke's relationship to the thought of the rest of the NT. With respect to Luke and Paul, C. H. Dodd's observations continue to be influential, as is shown by Fitzmyer's reaffirmation of Dodd's three-fold distinction between the Pauline kerygma and that found in the apostolic preaching of Acts:[69] 1) in Acts Jesus is not called the Son of God; 2) Jesus is not said to have died for sins; and, 3) it is not said that "the exalted Christ intercedes for us (cf. Rm. 8:34)." Fitzmyer concludes that "Luke says nothing of Jesus' heavenly intercession for humanity in the Father's presence (contrast Rm. 8:34; Heb. 7:25; 9:24; I Jn. 2:1) ..."

While Dodd's original distinction between Paul and the apostolic kerygma as recorded in Acts may remain sound, Fitzmyer's shift to a distinction between Paul and Luke is not. Lk. 22:32 demonstrates that it is wrong to assert that Luke has nothing to say about either Jesus' or the exalted Christ's heavenly intercession before the Father.

Long ago W. Sanday and J. C. Hawkins exchanged opinions over whether the special material in Luke's passion narrative reflected any elements of Pauline teaching.[70] More recently, Taylor has sided with Sanday in claiming that Luke's special material does "not seem to deal with the special doctrinal teaching of St. Paul."[71] While this study would not want to claim that Luke has necessarily derived his views on this question from the apostle Paul; nor that Lk. 22:31–32 is included in Luke's passion narrative under any peculiarly "Pauline" influence; it is this study's contention that *the question of Christ's intercession for his own can no longer stand among the list of doctrinal issues which distinguish Lukan from Pauline thinking.* Luke is unequivocal on the fact that Jesus interceded for his people, before the heavenly throne of God, during his life on this earth. Furthermore, in his gospel Luke almost inescapably implies, if not explicitly states, that the exalted Jesus continues to offer such intercession in heaven (see chapter 7). Since the concept of Christ-as-Advocate is also found in the epistles to the Hebrews and I John, it is not simply a matter of debating Luke's relationship to Paul, but of establishing his standing within the wider spectrum of early Christian thought. An introduction to this issue was attempted in chapter 1. And evidence is now mounting in support of the suggestion made there, after the examination of Rm. 8:34; Heb. 7:25; and I Jn. 2:1, that Luke is using his story of Jesus' life and ministry to offer a biographical

---

[68] *Pace* Schulz's articulation of fatalism in Luke-Acts, "Vorsehung," pp. 106–112; "Was geschieht, ist vom fatum vorherbestimmt," pp. 111f.

[69] Fitzmyer, *The Gospel*, vol. II, pp. 160f; C. H. Dodd, *The Apostolic Preaching and its Developments*, (London, 1936), pp. 15, 25.

[70] J. C. Hawkins, "Three Limitations to St. Luke's Use of St. Mark's Gospel" in *Studies in the Synoptic Problem*, (Oxford, 1911), pp. 90–94; cf. W. Sanday, "Introductory Essays," *Studies in the Synoptic Problem*, pp. xii-xiv.

[71] Taylor, *The Passion*, p. 6; quoting Sanday, "Introductory Essays," p. xiv.

development of the Christian belief in the ascended Jesus as the church's heavenly Intercessor (see chapters 8 and 9).

## 6.5 Conclusion: Jesus, the Earthly and Heavenly Intercessor

With this study of Lk. 22:31–32, the examination of Luke's prayer materials in his gospel is completed. A variety of purposes have been served by this passage and its juxtaposition with the following scene on the Mount of Olives. Once again, the place of prayer in Christian discipleship, particularly as the chief means of resisting temptation, has been highlighted through the comparison of Jesus with the disciples. Luke provides living examples to illustrate the exhortations made in Lk. 18:1; 21:36; 22:40, 46. Jesus is offered as the paradigm of how to resist temptation through prayer, while the disciples demonstrate how the absence of prayer hastens temptation's victory.

But just as these examples have continuing relevance for Christian behaviour, they also illustrate the continuing necessity of Jesus' intercession. Luke demonstrates that the prayers of Jesus, both in whom he does and does not pray for, are crucial to deciding the question of a disciple's apostasy. This was true not only during Jesus' earthly ministry, but also in the subsequent period of the church. It was suggested in chapter 4 that the Emmaus story hints at an ongoing revelatory significance for Jesus' prayers. Now it is seen that his intercessions not only mediate the Father's revelation, and thus his calling, but they also are fundamental to the disciple's perseverance in that call. Judas illustrates the fate of those who are not included within the intercessory prayers of Christ. The prayers of the ascended Saviour are a wall standing between the Christian professor and the satanic attacker, protecting the believer in the midst of temptation. Without that protection perseverance is impossible. Luke maintains that disciples are still to resist temptation through prayer, but he also teaches that the formation, composition and preservation of the church continues to be a product of the prayers of the ascended Jesus.

Chapter 7

# The Heavenly Intercessor in the Book of Acts

## Introduction

Before beginning a study of Stephen's vision in the book of Acts, it would be helpful to review the results accumulated thus far in this study of Luke's presentation of the role of prayer in the life of Jesus. As one might expect, there are points of similarity and dissimilarity between the prayer-life of Jesus and that of his disciples. On the one hand, Jesus is presented as a model of piety. The course of his ministry is guided through the fellowship which he enjoys with the Father through prayer. He receives the Spirit, wields power for his ministry of teaching and performing miracles, calls the twelve apostles, experiences (sometimes unexpected) revelations/confirmations of the Father's will and obediently pursues his course to Calvary all by means of the resources and direction made available to him through prayer. This paradigmatic significance of Jesus' prayer-life is made particularly explicit in Luke's introduction to the Lord's Prayer (11:1f) and the scene on the Mount of Olives (22:39–46). At both places Luke's juxtaposition of the disciples and the praying Jesus makes his exemplary role clear. According to Luke, Jesus is the man of prayer *par excellence*.

Jesus' model of prayer also provides a source for important correctives to popular understandings of Luke's didactic prayer materials. Luke exhorts his readers to continue in prayer and "not to give up," not primarily (if at all) as a part of his attempt to respond to a delay in the parousia (only Lk. 21:36 is possibly amenable to such an interpretation). Luke urges his readers not to give up on prayer because he understands about the crises of faith which may arise when an individual's prayers are not answered in the way they would like, or do not seem to be answered or even heard at all. It is the theological issue of divine sovereignty, rather than any questions of a parousia delay, which gives rise to Luke's particular didactic emphases. Neither the power of faith nor the weight of pious repetition ensure the granting of requests which do not lie within the scope of God's predetermined will. Yet Jesus both persevered in sincere prayer and pursued a course not of his own making, which was determined by the constraints of divine necessity. Here lies the important point of contact between Jesus' own experience and that of any individual member of the church in Luke's day.

As a result of this interaction between prayer and the will of God, Luke also urges his readers to continue in prayer because it is one of the means by which God reveals his will to his people. Prayer is a prime means of Christian growth in obedience because through it the Father leads the pray-ers in how they may best participate in his plans for salvation-history. The disciple must persevere in prayer because it is the means not only of asking of God but also of hearing from God. This too is illustrated in Jesus' experience.

But Jesus is not only a model for Christian piety; in many ways his prayer experience is more dissimilar than comparable to that of his disciples. He is the eschatological Deliverer. Thus his prayer-life is not merely paradigmatic. It is revealed as integral to the accomplishment of his unique station. Jesus prays as the one who enjoys a unique relationship of Sonship with the Father. His prayers are always offered according to the Father's will. In this way he serves as the mediator of the Father's revelation, both hiding and revealing the things of God as the Father chooses. Through prayer Jesus calls God's elect apostles to himself. Through prayer they come to see his status as messiah, even while it is hidden from others. Through the efficacy of his prayer Jesus ensures the perseverance of the Eleven, the defeat of the satanic Accuser and even his betrayal by Judas. Jesus is not only a pious man, but the unique Intercessor who even while on earth has special access to the throne-room of God. Furthermore, Luke implies that this earthly work of elective/intercessory prayer must continue now in heaven for as long as discipleship is able to be tested here on earth. The success of Jesus' earthly prayer ministry demonstrates the necessity of his filling the role of heavenly Intercessor even after his ascension into heaven.

Thus Luke's portrayal of Jesus at prayer is guided not only by parenetic concerns, but also by definite christological considerations. The question to be addressed at this point is, How does Luke's understanding of Jesus' prayer in the gospel relate to the book of Acts? Is there continuity in Luke's christological presentation? Specifically, is there anything in Acts which makes explicit what Luke seems to imply in the gospel, namely that the exalted Jesus serves as the heavenly Intercessor for his people? If so, is it possible to reach some decision as to the nature of the relationship between Jesus' pre-and post-ascension prayer ministries?[1]

Of course, the problem immediately posing itself for anyone who wants to ask questions about Jesus' prayer-life in Acts is the ascension. How can a person's prayer-life be studied after they are taken up into heaven? However, the implications of this observation are not wholly negative. It serves as a reminder that, even in the best of situations, the material which one could reasonably expect to find having a bearing upon this question in Acts would be minimal.

This is not to embrace the common opinion which sees Christ as totally inactive

---

[1] It would also be interesting to consider the place of Pentecost in Luke's development of Jesus' role as Intercessor, for this would relate Jesus' prayer-life not only to the life of the church but also to the work of the Spirit. The results of the present study suggest that Luke's view of Jesus as a heavenly paraclete is an important factor in understanding the relationship between Lukan christology and pneumatology. It would also be an important consideration in any attempt at explaining the differences between Luke's view of the Spirit and that of the other NT writers, particularly John. However, such a study is beyond the scope of the present work.

in the book of Acts. F. Bovon exemplifies this position when he argues that the most striking difference between Luke and Acts is the activity of Jesus in the gospel and the inactivity of the ascended Christ in Acts.[2] But Bovon also develops this view of christological inactivity in a way particularly relevant to the present discussion. In examining Luke's views on mediation, he claims that Luke focuses his attention upon the need for human mediation/intercession in this world.[3] Therefore, the earthly Jesus could perform this work as a man among men, but after the ascension he had to yield his place to other human mediators, ie. the church. As evidence Bovon cites the promise of the Spirit (Acts 1:2), Ananias' mission to Paul (9:6, 10ff) and Paul's vision in Corinth (18:9f).[4]

However, none of these examples actually prove Bovon's point; quite the opposite. Peter makes it clear that the Spirit is sent from heaven *by* Jesus (2:33); Paul receives Ananias after Jesus has revealed himself from heaven on the road to Damascus; and Paul's vision in Corinth is a vision of Jesus from heaven. Luke actually presents a very active, heavenly Lord, which not only undercuts Bovon's general thesis, but also suggests that there is no reason to believe him to be any less involved in heavenly mediation than Bovon has shown him to have been in earthly mediation (cf. Acts 7:55f; 9:3–19; 22:17–21; 23:11).[5]

The preceding study of Luke's gospel has already suggested that it is not inappropriate to read Acts with the question of Jesus' heavenly activity in mind. But is there any evidence in Acts to confirm the suggestion that Luke believes Jesus continues his work of prayer after the ascension? Short of some explicit piece of instruction to this effect, is the reader given any glimpses of Jesus, whether in visions or revelations, which might substantiate such a view? In fact, there is such a revelation, and it is found in Stephen's vision of the Son of Man.

## 7.1 Acts 7:55–56: Stephen's Vision and Its Various Interpretations

Stephen's vision of Jesus as the Son of Man offers several curious features which have invited many interpretative suggestions. Firstly, it is the only place outside of the gospel tradition where the title Son of Man is applied to Jesus by anyone other than Jesus himself. Secondly, it is the only reference to the Son of Man standing rather than sitting at the right hand of God.[6] Before pursuing the significance of

---

[2] F. Bovon, *L'Oeuvre de Luc: Etudes d'exégèse et de théologie*, (Paris, 1987), pp. 189–192; this chapter was originally printed as L'Importance des Médiations dans le Project Theologique de Luc," *NTS*. 21 ('75) 23–39.

[3] Bovon, *L'Oeuvre de Luc*, p. 189.

[4] Bovon, *L'Oeuvre de Luc*, pp. 190f; Bovon gives no attention to Jesus' prayers.

[5] Cf. Maddox, *Purpose*, p. 108.

[6] The significance of this difference has been questioned by D. Hay, *Glory at the Right Hand: Psalm 110 in Early Christianity*, (Nashville, 1973), who calls it an error to point to Acts 7:56 as the only text where Jesus is not seated, since many passages (referring to Rm. 8:34; Acts 2:33; 5:31; I Pet. 3:22) leave the question of posture open (p. 36 n. 5). Although this is true, Acts 7:56 is the only text where Jesus/the Son of Man is explicitly seen to be standing.

these features for the present study it will prove helpful to summarise and evaluate the many different interpretations which have been offered in the past for this standing Son of Man.[7]

1) Numerous interpretations concern themselves, in one way or another, with the fact that Stephen dies a martyr's death. Beginning with Gregory the Great[8] it has been argued that the Son of Man rises in order to give Stephen the strength he needs to remain faithful in his martyr's struggle.[9]

2) Other possibilities have been suggested which focus upon the imminence of death. Thus Stephen's vision testifies to the early Christian conviction that the faithful martyr is given a vision of heavenly glory before his actual demise.[10] Or such a vision indicates that all martyrs will enter heaven and Christ's glory immediately upon their death.[11] Related to this is Plymale's view that Jesus rises in order to show Stephen that his prayer for the reception of his spirit (v. 59) will be immediately answered.[12]

3) One of the more popular interpretations sees Jesus rising in order to greet his martyr upon his entrance into heaven.[13] W. Grundmann, in his TDNT article on

---

[7] Other useful surveys of the history of the interpretation of Acts 7:55f may be found in W. Grundmann, "στήκω," *TDNT.* vol. VII, pp. 650f; R. Pesch, "Die Vision des Stephanus Apg 7,5f. im Rahmen der Apostelgeschichte," *BL.* 6 ('65) 94–107; *Die Vision des Stephanus: Apg. 7,55–56 im Rahmen der Apostelgeschichte,* (Stuttgart, 1966), pp. 13–37; A. Weiser, *Die Apostelgeschichte,* vol. I, (Gütersloh, 1981), pp. 193f; G. Schneider, *Die Apostelgeschichte,* vol. I, (Freiburg, 1980), pp. 454f; H.-W. Neudorfer, *Der Stephanuskreis in der Forschungsgeschichte seit F. C. Baur,* (Giessen, 1983), pp. 199–207, 284–287, who offers the largest amount of patristic and German evidence; Bock, *Proclamation,* pp. 222–224. Of these, Pesch and Neudorfer are the most exhaustive.

[8] *Homiliarium in Evangelica Lib.* II, 19, 7; as cited by Neudorfer, *Der Stephanuskreis,* pp. 199 n. 134. Also see Pesch, *Vision,* pp. 14f.

[9] Weiser, *Apostelgeschichte,* p. 193 lists this as an alternative view; also see R. F. O'Toole, "Activity of the Risen Jesus in Luke-Acts," *Bib.* 62 ('81) 476. M. Hengel, "Between Jesus and Paul: The 'Hellenists', the 'Seven' and Stephen" in *Between Jesus and Paul: Studies in the Earliest History of Christianity,* (London, 1983), p. 152 n. 141 suggests this view with reference to T. Mos. 10:3, a text which is also important to Pesch for very different reasons (as will been seen); also cf. C. K. Barrett, "Stephen and the Son of Man" in *Apophoreta, Festschrift für Ernst Haenchen,* (Berlin, 1964), p. 36, who (although he is known for a very different view) also suggests this as an important element of the vision's meaning.

[10] K. Holl, "Die Vorstellung vom Märtyrer und die Märtyrerakte in ihrer Geschichtlichen Entwicklung," *NJKA.* 17 ('14) 524; B. Reicke, "Die göttliche Offenbarung und das heilige Land, Apg. 7,1–8,3" in *Glaube und Leben der Urgemeinde, Bemerkungen zu Apg. 1–7,* (Zürich, 1957), p. 163; J. Wilson, *Luke's Role as a Theologian and Historian in Acts 6:1–8:3,* unpublished Ph.D. dissertation, (Emory University, 1962), p. 148; Michaelis, "Ὁράω," pp. 353, 339 n. 119.

[11] Conzelmann, *Apostelgeschichte,* p. 58; G. Schille, *Die Apostelgeschichte des Lukas,* (Berlin, 1983), pp. 188f; Barrett, "Stephen," p. 37 (notice again Barrett's employment of the martyr motif). For further representatives see Neudorfer, *Der Stephanuskreis,* p. 200 n. 139.

[12] Plymale, *The Prayer Texts,* p. 189.

[13] Haenchen, *Acts,* p. 292 n. 4 calls this the most popular interpretation since J. A. Bengel's commentary, (cf. the *Gnomon* on Acts 7:56; reference cited by Neudorfer, *Der Stephanuskreis,* p. 200 n. 138); cf. A. Wikenhauser, *Die Apostelgeschichte,* (Regensburg, 1961), p. 92; Marshall, *Acts,* p. 149 sees this as one aspect of the meaning; Hay, *Glory,* p. 75 refers to this as the "most likely" meaning.

ἵστημι, promotes this view with reference to Jn. 14:2f, where the disciple is promised to be taken home to heaven by the Lord.[14] Haenchen believes there is a parallel with Jesus' words to the thief on the cross (Lk. 23:34).[15] Bauernfeind points to the martyred Eleazar's hopes of being "welcomed by the fathers" in IV Macc. 5:37.[16]

4) Long ago Eb. Nestle asserted that Jesus stands as the High Priest in the heavenly Temple, although he admitted that he was not sure of how to argue for the point convincingly.[17]

5) Several suggestions have tried to explain the vision as an anachronistic remnant of some early christological tradition which has not been fully integrated into the overall presentation of Luke-Acts. H. E. Tödt surmises that originally Jesus was imagined to be standing before God like the angels.[18] Similarly, H. Bietenhard points to various texts in the rabbinic literature where it is said that only God is allowed to sit in heaven.[19] J. Bihler believes that there were originally two distinct circles of Son of Man tradition: one relating the Son of Man with the parousia; and another, perhaps earlier tradition, associating the Son of Man only with exaltation.[20] It is this latter idea which is preserved by Luke in Stephen's vision, in contrast to the gospel material.[21] Again, W. Grundmann has also argued that Acts 7:55f is a piece of early subordinationist christology which dealt with Jesus' exaltation to God's right-hand independently (and probably antecedently) of any apologetic reference to Ps. 110:1.[22]

6) Some have claimed that the Son of Man stands in preparation for the parousia.[23] H. P. Owen has offered a unique argument for this position.[24] He claims that Luke marks the course of Jesus' career from the cross to the second

---

[14] Grundmann, "στήκω," p. 651.

[15] Haenchen, Acts, p. 292 n. 4; Hay, Glory, p. 75 adds Lk. 16:9.

[16] Bauernfeind, Apostelgeschichte, p. 120.

[17] Eb. Nestle, "Acts vii. 55,56," ExpT. 11 (1899–1900) 94; "The Vision of Stephen," ExpT. 22 ('10–11) 423; also see C. P. M. Jones, "The Epistle to the Hebrews and the Lucan Writings" in Studies in the Gospels, (Oxford, 1955), p. 128.

[18] H. E. Tödt, The Son of Man in the Synoptic Tradition, (London, 1965), p. 303. Neudorfer, Der Stephanuskreis, p. 201, also cites E. Preuschen, Die Apostelgeschichte, (Tübingen, 1912), p. 45.

[19] H. Bietenhard, Die himmlische Welt im Urchristentum und Spätjudentum, (Tübingen, 1951), p. 71; cf. F. Neugebauer, "Die Davidssohnfrage und die Menschensohn," NTS. 21 ('74–75) 107 n. 1.

[20] J. Bihler, Die Stephanusgeschichte, im Zusammenhang der Apostelgeschichte, (München, 1963), pp. 131–133. Bihler pursues the exaltation theme against the background of I En. 70–71.

[21] Cf. E. Schweizer, "Der Menschensohn," ZNW. 50 ('59) 204, who also asserts that Acts 7, together with Mk. 14:62 and the gospel of John, are evidence of an exclusive interest only in the exaltation of the Son of Man; also see J. Dupont, Nouvelles Etudes sur les Actes des Apôtres, (Paris, 1984), p. 245 who, apparently abandoning his earlier adherance to the interpretation of R. Pesch (see n. 25), discerns no interest here beyond the glory of the ascended Lord.

[22] W. Grundmann, "Das Problem des hellenistischen Christentums innerhalb der Jerusalemer Urgemeinde," ZNW. 38 ('39) 65; cf. "στήκω," p. 650.

[23] Surkau, Martyrien, p. 117; A. Loisy, Les Actes des Apôtres, (Paris, 1920), pp. 348f.

[24] H. P. Owen, "Stephen's Vision in Acts 7:55–56," NTS. 1 ('54) 224–226. Though his work is often cited, Owen does not seem to have gained any adherents to his interpretation.

coming by means of 6 important words: ἔξοδος (Lk. 9:31); εἰσελθεῖν (Lk. 24:26); ἀναλαμβάνεσθαι (Acts 1:2, 11, 2; 2:34); καθῆσθαι (Lk. 20:42; 22:69; Acts 2:34); ἑστάναι (Acts 7:55–56); ἔρχεσθαι (Lk. 9:26; 12:36f; 18:8; 19:23; 21:27; Acts 1:11). Jesus' standing is the penultimate step in this process. He reveals himself to Stephen because Stephen alone in the early church understood the need for world-mission, which is the necessary presupposition to the parousia.

7) E. Trocmé, seeing a connection between the Stephen material and that which follows concerning Paul, has claimed that the Son of Man stands in order to prepare to meet Paul on the Damascus road.[25]

8) C. K. Barrett has proposed that Stephen's vision offers Luke's rewriting of eschatology in view of the delay of the parousia.[26] That is, Luke interprets each individual Christian's death as a "private and personal parousia of the Son of Man;" the universal appearance of the last day occurs individually when every Christian dies.[27] Only Stephen has such a vision because only Stephen is presented as dying a martyr's death in the book of Acts.

9) Others interpret the Son of Man as rising to execute his work as judge. R. Pesch has argued for this view in some detail.[28] According to Pesch, Stephen's speech marks a turning point in the salvation-historical story-line of Acts. At this point the mission of the church turns away from the Jews and extends itself exclusively to the Gentiles. Pointing to Is. 3:13 and T. Mos. 10:3, where God is said to rise in order to judge his own people, Jesus is likewise seen to stand as a sign of his condemnation of the Jews, and thus also to signify his approval of the Gentile mission.[29]

10) Conversely, there is the dispensational position which argues that Jesus

---

[25] E. Trocme", Le "Livre des Actes" et l'histoire, (Paris, 1957), pp. 187f. While this precise connection is to be rejected, a possible relationship between Paul's conversion and (the content of) Stephen's vision may be suggested along other lines when it is recalled that every other (visionary) appearance of Jesus in Acts is explicitly related to Paul's missionary career (cf. Acts 9:1–19; 16:6–10; 18:9–11; 22:6–15, 17–21; 23:11; 26:12–18).

[26] Barrett, "Stephen," pp. 32–38.

[27] Barrett, "Stephen," p. 35; cf. D. J. Williams, Acts, (San Francisco, 1985), p. 132. The uniqueness of Barrett's position concerns his understanding of the vision as a whole. His interpretation of the "standing" element, as has already been shown, is common to the traditional stream of martyrological interpretation (see nn. 5 and 7 above; and critique below). The general contours of his position are anticipated by Bauernfeind, Apostelgeschichte, p. 120: "...er erlebt heute schon, was andere am Tage des Herrn erleben werden."

[28] Pesch, "Die Vision," pp. 170–183; Vision, pp. 52–58; cf. R. Maddox, "The Function of the Son of Man According to the Synoptic Gospels," NTS. 15 ('68–69) 50 n. 1; The Purpose of Luke-Acts, p. 104; also see Neudorfer, Der Stephanuskreis, p. 206.

[29] See Pesch, Vision, pp. 27f, 30, 32, 38f, 53, 58. Pesch does not seem to have gained many adherents to this position. One of the few commentators to adopt his interpretation is Weiser, Apostelgeschichte, p. 194; also see Dupont, "'Assis à la droite," p.372. In his recent commentary Pesch has modified his former position, combining his "judgment" interpretation with the Advocate position discussed below in connection with C. F. D. Moule; see Die Apostelgeschichte. Apg 1–12, vol. I, (Neukirchener-Vluyn, 1986), pp. 263f.

stands as he postpones taking up his judgment seat, thereby giving the Jews an extended opportunity to repent.[30]

11) Numerous interpreters follow G. Dalman and C. H. Dodd in seeing no particular significance for the Son of Man's "standing;" it is only a particular way of referring to his location.[31] Though neither Dalman nor Dodd elaborated upon their observations, E. Richard[32] and M. Sabbe[33] have both tried to defend this view at length. Richard first of all cites other instances where ἵστημι may simply mean "being, existing," offering such examples as Acts 7:33; 9:7; 24:21.[34] However, the pressing question for anyone who maintains this position is why Luke would change the κάθημαι of Ps. 110:1 (cf. Mk. 14:62; Lk. 22:69) to ἵστημι in the first place? Secondly, then, to answer this question, Richard claims that Stephen's vision is not influenced by Ps. 110:1 (as most interpreters claim) but by Dan. 7:13 (LXX), which has no suggestion of the the Son of Man ever sitting down at all. This Danielic influence does not come by way of Mk. 14:62, where Dan. 7:13 and Ps. 110:1 have been combined, but by way of "an independent formulation of early tradition" which, apparently, was dependent upon Daniel alone.[35]

Sabbe, on the other hand, not only cites instances where the verb "standing" seems to have no real significance, but also attempts to show that Luke has no consistent interest in the "sitting" position either.[36] He surmises that Acts 7:56 is distant enough from Mk. 14:62 that the language of Ps. 110:1 was not even in view when Luke recorded Stephen's vision (cf. the following argument). But the most important point in Sabbe's case is that Luke has deliberately composed the Stephen material so that it will parallel the passion story in the gospel.[37] Therefore, Stephen's vision of the Son of Man is required merely as a corollary to the Son of Man saying in Lk. 22:69,[38] and is simply another opportunity for Luke to ascribe

[30] See W. Kelly, An Exposition of the Acts of the Apostles, (London, 1952, 3rd ed.), pp. 102f, as cited by Bruce, Acts, p.168; and Pesch, Vision, p. 23. Also see Bruce, n. 96 for further bibliography.

[31] Dalman, Words, p. 311 calls it "a verbal change" of expression; C. H. Dodd, According to the Scriptures: The Substructure of New Testament Theology, (London, 1952), p. 35 n. 1 claims that the verb has the simple meaning of "to be situated." Also see G. W. H. Lampe, "The Lucan Portrait of Christ," NTS. 2 ('55–56) 171f; Reicke, "Göttliche Offenbarung," p. 163; B. Lindars, New Testament Apologetic: The Doctrinal Significance of the Old Testament Quotations, (London, 1961), p. 48 n. 2; Jeremias, Theology, p. 273 n. 6. This is also, basically, the position adopted by J. Calvin; see his Commentary upon the Acts of the Apostles, vol. II, (Grand Rapids, 1984), p. 315.

[32] E. Richard, Acts 6:1–8:4, The Author's Method of Composition, (Missoula, 1978).

[33] M. Sabbe, "The Son of Man Saying in Acts 7, 56" in Les Actes des Apôtres: Traditions, rédaction, théologie, (Gembloux, 1979), pp. 242–279.

[34] Richard, Acts 6:1–8:4, pp. 295f; in discussing this position Pesch, Vision, p. 23 n. 63, cites Lk. 5:1f; 8:20; 9:27; 13:25; 17:12; 18:13; Acts 4:14 as examples.

[35] Richard, Acts 6:1–8:4, p. 296. Wilson, Luke's Role, pp. 123, 149f, appears to reach a similar conclusion.

[36] Sabbe, "Acts 7,56," pp. 273–275.

[37] Sabbe, "Acts 7,56," pp. 252–254. This argument has been repeated many times; see Hay, Glory, p. 74; Bruce, Acts, p. 165; Talbert, Genre, p. 76; J. Bihler, "Der Stephanusbericht (Apg 6,8–15 und 7,54–8,2)," BZ. 3/2 ('59) 259.

[38] So also Wilson, Luke's Role, p. 149; Gourgues, A la droite de Dieu, pp. 180, 193f.

an additional christological title to the exalted Jesus. This is made evident through the assimilation of Acts 7:56 to Lk. 22:69, by way of the mutual omission of any reference to "coming on the clouds of heaven" (cf. Mk. 14:62). In this way an allusion to the parousia via Dan. 7:13 is eliminated, and attention is focused upon the theme of exaltation found in the uncomplicated allusion to Ps. 110:1 (cf. the preceding argument).[39]

12) The final body of interpretive opinion is one which is finding increasing acceptance among exegetes. This includes all those who in various ways point to the judicial circumstances surrounding Stephen's vision and interpret the standing Son of Man as (in some sense) a witness on Stephen's behalf. Since the present study will basically align itself with this position, it might be appropriate to discuss the divergent approaches of a few of the more prominent representatives of this view.[40]

C. F. D. Moule has been one of the more long-standing advocates of this witness interpretation.[41] He begins by pointing out that the OT texts (Ps. 110; Dan. 7; Zech. 3) to which Acts 7:55 f has the greatest affinity are all vindication scenes, two of which are described in courtroom language (Zech. 3:1–5; Dan. 7:10, 22, 26).[42] This has a bearing on the standing position of the Son of Man since this was the posture adopted by witnesses in a court of law (cf. Asc. Is. 9:35 f); even the right-hand location is able to have a judical significance. Though this connection of standing with testimony might not be self-evident on its own, the fact that Stephen's vision occurs in the midst of his own trial is determinative. Luke thus presents a double trial scene. The once condemned, but now vindicated Son of Man acts as the Vindicator of his condemned disciple; "as Stephen's witness confessed Christ before men, so Christ is standing to confess him before the angels of God."[43]

---

[39] Sabbe, "Acts 7,56," pp. 256f, 260. Note that these arguments are diametrically opposed to those of Richard.

[40] See T. Preiss, *Life in Christ*, (London, 1954), p. 50; Cullmann, *Christology*, pp. 157f; J. A. T. Robinson, *Jesus and His Coming*, (London, 1957), p. 55; Bruce, *Acts*, p. 168; A. A Trites, *The New Testament Concept of Witness*, (Cambridge, 1977), p. 132; W. R. G. Loader, "Christ at the Right Hand – Ps. CX. 1 in the New Testament," *NTS.* 24 ('78) 204; Schneider, *Apostelgeschichte*, p. 475; Marshall, *Acts*, 149; P. Doble, "The Son of Man Sayings in Stephen's Witnessing: Acts 6,8–8,2," *NTS.* 31 ('85) 75f; and now Pesch, *Apostelgeschichte*, vol. I, pp. 263f.

[41] According to Calvin, it was also espoused by Augustine; see *Acts*, p. 315; cf. Neudorfer, *Der Stephauskreis*, p. 199 n. 132. Augustine maintained that the Son of Man sits as Judge, but stands as Advocate. See C. F. D. Moule, "From Defendant to Judge – And Deliverer: An Inquiry into the Use and Limitations of the Theme of Vindication in the New Testament," originally in the *Bulletin of the Studiorum Novi Testamenti Societas*. No. III('52) 40–53, (reprinted in 1963 by CUP); also reprinted as Appendix I (pp. 82–99) in *The Phenomenon of the New Testament: An Inquiry into the Implications of Certain Features of the New Testament*, (London, 1967). Also see "Neglected Features in the Problem of the Son of Man" in *Neues Testament und Kirche, Festschrift für R. Schnackenburg*, (Freiburg, 1974), reprinted in *Essays in New Testament Interpretation*, (Cambridge, 1982); "The Influence of Circumstances on the Use of Christological Terms," *JTS*. ns. 10 ('59) 247ff, also reprinted in *Essays*; "The Christology of Acts," p. 163.

[42] Moule, *Phenomenon*, pp. 82f.

[43] Moule, *Phenomenon*, pp. 90f; quote from p. 91.

A. J. B. Higgins has also argued for this position.[44] He reaffirms the similarity of Acts 7:55f with Lk. 22:69, as opposed to Mk. 14:62, claiming that this excludes any reference to the parousia and focuses attention upon the present status and activity of the exalted Son of Man. Therefore, Stephen's vision identifies Jesus in terms of the Son of Man referred to in Lk. 12:8f; the Son of Man stands to acknowledge his faithful disciple even as he had promised. In this respect the Son of Man is similar to the angelic intercessors who stand before God (cf. I En. 89:76; 99:3; 104:1), but as the exalted Son of Man he performs his task at God's right hand in accordance with the testimonium of Ps. 110:1.[45] This view also does greater justice to Stephen's prayer in 7:59f; Jesus is seen as the advocate/mediator of his people's requests.

B. Lindars, abandoning his earlier adherence to Dodd's explanation, offers the lengthiest recent defense of this position.[46] He points out that many interpreters have observed, without necessarily pursuing their implications, that Acts 7:55f is closely related to Acts 6:15, and that Stephen's vision serves as confirmation for the contents of the intervening defense speech.[47] However, Lindars further concludes that Stephen's real defense lies not in the speech itself, but in the revelation that heavenly judgment is on his side. Therefore, the close connection between 7:56 and 6:15 "confirms the primarily forensic character" of the vision, showing that the Son of Man stands as Stephen's advocate before God.[48]

Other scholars reach related positions by interpreting Stephen's vision with respect to the messianic expectations contained in the speech. Thus Bihler states that the standing Son of Man is most easily explained in terms of the final eschatological Prophet referred to in Acts 7:37, 52, who has now taken up his office of heavenly Intercessor.[49] M. Scharlemann makes the same observation. Combining it with what he sees as various elements of Samaritan theology in Stephen's speech, he argues that Jesus is presented as the New Moses who now intercedes for the faithful.[50] For these men, the work of heavenly advocacy is not interpreted generally, but in terms of a specific circle of messianic expectation.

---

[44] A. J. B. Higgins, *Jesus and the Son of Man*, (London, 1964), pp. 144–146.

[45] Higgins, *Jesus*, p. 145.

[46] B. Lindars, *Jesus Son of Man: A Fresh Examination of the Son of Man Sayings in the Gospels in the Light of Recent Research*, (London, 1983), pp. 139–142.

[47] Pesch, *Vision*, p. 53, specifies that this confirmation concerns the turning of the gospel to the Gentiles; cf. also Bihler, *Stephanusgeschichte*, p. 17; Weiser, *Apostelgeschichte*, p. 190; Conzelmann, *Apostelgeschichte*, p. 58; Bruce, *Acts*, p. 165; Haenchen, *Acts*, p. 195.

[48] Lindars, *Jesus*, p. 142.

[49] Bihler, *Stephanusgeschichte*, p. 134.

[50] M. Scharlemann, *Stephen: A Singular Saint*, (Rome, 1968), pp. 15f. On p. 173 he suggests that Abraham was a figure comparable to Moses in this respect; cf. C. Colpe, "ὁ υἱὸς τοῦ ἀνθρώπου," *TDNT*. vol. VIII, pp. 462f; *SB*. IV, 425ff. On Moses see J. MacDonald, *The Theology of the Samaritans*, (London, 1964), pp. 147–222; W. A. Meeks, *The Prophet-King*, (Leiden, 1967), p. 216–257. Perhaps Scharlemann's suggestion should be moderated by MacDonald's warnings about the lateness of this tradition; pp. 211–214, 376–379; but cf. Meeks.

# 7.2 An Evaluation of the Positions Concerning Acts 7:55–56

1) Several of the interpretations outlined above are inadequate insofar as they attempt to explain Stephen's vision without giving any attention to the significance of the Son of Man's standing position. The martyrological explanations of Holl and Conzelmann, for example, while ostensibly dealing with the Son of Man's posture, are actually not too dissimilar from the interpretations of Richard or Sabbe in that the "standing" is of little, if any, significance. The same might also be said of the exaltation explanations provided by those such as Schweizer and Dupont.

Plymale attempts to overcome this weakness but is unable to demonstrate any connection between Jesus' standing and a pledge of answered prayer. Indeed, the fact that Stephen offers his prayer *after* he receives his vision makes Plymale's view untenable.

2) Those martyrological interpretations which do attempt to overcome this problem, ie. the Son of Man rises to strengthen his martyr, or to greet his martyr, beg the question insofar as they necessarily presume a particular theology of martyrdom which has yet to be proven. Stephen's vision may have supplied one of the elements eventually used by the early church to construct such a theology, but there is nothing in the vision itself which makes such an interpretation clear. Hay suggests Lk. 16:9 and 23:43 (following Haenchen) as parallels to the idea of the Son of Man rising to greet Stephen, but none of these texts mentions anything about standing.[51] The same could also be said of Bauernfeind's reference to IV Macc. 5:37. Grundmann's discussion of Jn. 14:2f is equally unhelpful since John speaks of Jesus "preparing a place" but says nothing of any "greeting" or "taking home;" nor does John connect this work of preparation with the Son of Man. Finally, as Bihler has pointed out, there is no direct connection between martyrdom and the Son of Man tradition specifically (let alone a standing Son of Man), either in Luke-Acts or the traditions of the early church.[52]

3) The suggestion that Jesus stands as heavenly High Priest also brings numerous theological presuppositions to bear upon the text. It is far from clear that Stephen's speech offers a new/spiritual temple theology, even if it is read (and this too is doubtful) as an uncompromising polemic against the temple in Jerusalem. Nestle's claim that kings sit to rule while priests stand to minister simply reads unproven elements into the text. Hay has convincingly demonstrated that neither

---

[51] Hay, *Glory*, p. 75.

[52] Bihler, *Stephanusgeschichte*, p. 24 The only possible contradiction to this might be Hegesippus' description of the death of James found in Eusebius (*HE.* II, xxiii, 1–18; cf. Josephus, *Ant.* XX, 199–203). But there James simply confesses Jesus to be the Son of Man; there is no vision. It is most likely that the point of connection between Acts and Hegesippus is not the Son of Man, but the fact that here is another pious Jew who is stoned after being condemned by members of the Sanhedrin for confessing Christ. These similarities have caused the tradition of James' martyrdom to be assimilated at key points to the story of Stephen; cf. Scharlemann, *Stephen*, pp. 138–141.

Jewish nor Christian exegesis associated the session at God's right hand "with any single function or activity of that person" whatever their posture.[53] It is also interesting that where priestly activity is associated with God's right hand in the NT (Heb. 1:3; 8:1; 10:12) it is always a sitting High Priest which is portrayed.

4) All those who would see Acts 7:55f as an anachronistic piece of early christology with no further significance must answer Pesch's question as to why Luke not only retains the unusual standing formulation but deliberately doubles it![54] Luke is too good an author to accidentally leave unintegrated pieces of outdated tradition lying about in his story. Whether one believes Dan. 7 or Ps. 110, or neither, or even both texts to be at work in Acts 7:55f, it is already clear from Acts 2:34f that Luke is familiar with the more common tradition which has Christ sitting at God's right hand (cf. Mk. 12:36//Mt. 22:44//Lk. 20:42; Mk. 14:62//Mt. 26:64//Lk. 22:69; Acts 2:34; Eph. 1:20; Col. 3:1; Heb. 1:3, 13; 8:1; 10:12; 12:2; Rev. 5:1,7). This use of Ps. 110:1 was so frequent in the early church that Luke's preservation of this sole witness to Jesus' standing requires a more cogent explanation.[55]

Bock objects to Tödt's angelomorphic explanation on two grounds. First of all, it cannot explain why Stephen would appeal to an angel-like figure for the forgiveness of the leaders' sin in stoning him, since forgiveness was not the work of angels. Secondly, it does not adequately deal with the parallels to the Lukan trial scene, where the Son of Man does not appear "as a mere angel."[56]

However, with some modification Tödt's position is more helpful than many exegetes have recognised. To begin with, it is far from clear that Luke intended Stephen's trial to be read as a strict parallel to that of Jesus. This becomes manifest whenever such parallels are constructed, as seen by the number of times one must appeal to Mark's account of Jesus' trial rather than Luke's.[57] These are hardly good grounds for prejudging the meaning of Acts 7:55f in terms of Lk. 22:69 – something which remains true even if one does accept that the Son of Man in Acts has greater affinity with Lk. 22:69 than Mk. 14:62. An angelic significance to Jesus' standing cannot be ruled out on this basis alone.

Furthermore, to say that Jesus appears angel-like is not to say that he is a "mere angel." If the exalted Son of Man had taken over functions which had previously been associated with the angels, then he might easily appear in what had heretofore been considered an angelic position without this in any sense implying a primitive or subordinationist christology. Rejecting Tödt's view because (whether rightly or wrongly) one cannot accept an angelomorphic christology in Acts 7, does not mean that one should overlook the indicators which led Tödt to this

---

[53] Hay, Glory, pp. 31–33.
[54] Pesch, Vision, p. 32.
[55] Cf. Schneider, Apostelgeschichte, p. 474; Michaelis, "Ὁράω," p. 353.
[56] Bock, Proclamation, p. 222.
[57] Sabbe's discussion ("Acts 7,56," pp. 252f, 256f) is representative: Luke omits the false witnesses (Mk. 14:56; cf. Acts 6:13; Lk. 22:65f); the temple saying (Mk. 14:58; cf. Acts 6:13f); and Jesus is not addresses by the High Priest (Mk. 14:60f; cf. Acts 7:1).

conclusion. Thus, to return to Bock, forgiving sin may not have been the work of angels, but the intercessory work of receiving the prayers of God's people and bringing them before God certainly was (cf. Tob. 12:15).

5) Owen offers an appropriate evaluation of his own work when he describes Luke as having created "a highly imaginative picture" of Jesus' career.[58] The main problem is that there is no objective basis upon which to explain Owen's selection of key words. For example, why should a programmatic schematisation of Jesus' career begin in Lk. 9:31, rather than in Lk. 4 or even earlier in the birth narratives? Why is his "coming into the world" not represented among the career stages? This use of ἔρχεσθαι is also an important part of Luke's understanding of Jesus (cf. Lk. 5:32; 7:19, 34; 19:10, 38).

Owen's six stages are also artificially related. For example, stage 1 might easily be interpreted as inclusive of stages 2–4; that is, the "exodus" referred to at the Transfiguration includes the entire process of death-resurrection-ascension-exaltation. Similarly, there is nothing outside of Owen's scheme to indicate any intrinsic reason for relating the word "standing" to the word "coming." One would expect to see some evidence within the vision itself if its message were eschatological. But this is not the case. Tödt has shown that Owen confuses elements of a vision motif with hints of the parousia.[59] Furthermore, the agreement of Acts 7:56 with Lk. 22:69 in the omission of "the clouds of heaven," thereby distancing the vision from both Mk. 14 and Dan. 7, makes even a preparatory reference to the parousia unlikely.[60]

There might be one way to see an apocalyptic expectation in Stephen's vision, if one were to follow the arguments of D. Carlson.[61] He maintains that I En. 91–104 and T. Mos. 9–10 testify to a belief in God's final judgment being hastened through the intercessory prayers of the heavenly angels, offered on behalf of God's righteous sufferers who cry out for deliverance. The juxtaposition of the praying martyr Stephen and the standing Son of Man is striking when read against Carlson's discussion of the inter-testamental literature. Here "standing" is related to eschatology, however it is not by way of "waiting" but through "intercession."

However, the aforementioned absence of otherwise explicit eschatological factors in Stephen's vision should temper even this approach to finding a parousia reference in Acts 7:55 f. But Carlson's exploration of the role of intercessory angels does coalesce with the preceding evaluation of Tödt's views to further indicate the fruitfulness of pursuing the idea of heavenly intercession for the proper interpretation of Acts 7.

---

[58] Owen, "Stephen's Vision," p. 224.

[59] Tödt, *The Son of Man*, p. 304; cf. "the heavens opening" with Lk. 3:21 pars; Acts 10:11, 16; 11:5.

[60] See the similar discussions in Scharlemann, *Stephen*, p. 121 n. 36; Lindars, *Jesus*, p. 141; M. Casey, *Son of Man: The Interpretation and Influence of Daniel 7*, (London, 1979), p. 200.

[61] D. Carlson, "Vengeance and Angelic Mediation in Testament of Moses 9 and 10," *JBL*. 101 ('82) 85–95; but Carlson does not deal with Acts 7.

6) Trocmé's suggestion regarding the Son of Man and Paul has weaknesses similar to Owen's, in that it is not clear why the standing position should be interpreted as merely preparatory to some other impending action which then bears the real weight of significance. There is no more reason to see the Son of Man as preparing to come to Paul than there is to see him as preparing to come in the parousia. Furthermore, is it justifiable not to see any importance at all in the vision for Stephen himself?

7) Barrett's position also suffers at several of the same points as Owen's. As already mentioned, there is nothing overtly eschatological about the vision to cause one to relate it to the parousia, whether publicly or personally. In any case, the idea of an individualised eschatology is anything but clear in Luke-Acts.[62] Also the idea of "parousia" is generally thought of in terms of the Lord's coming to us, not our going to him. The latter is the language of death, and it is difficult to see how a movement in any other direction could be conceived of between Stephen and Jesus in Acts 7:55 ff. Thus Barrett's interpretation begins to look increasingly like those which see Jesus rising to greet his martyr. But rising is the very idea lacking from the vision.[63] Despite its originality, Barrett's approach cannot deal with Jesus' standing position any more convincingly than the other martyrological interpretations to which it is so similar.

8) The judgment element in Pesch's interpretation is highly questionable with respect both to the theology of Acts and to the background material presented to explain the Son of Man's standing. Firstly, Pesch simply is not true to the story of Acts when he suggests that after chapter 7 the gospel goes out exclusively to the Gentiles (cf. Acts 13:5, 43; 14:1; 17:1–4, 10–12, 17; 18:4, 19; 19:10, 17; 20:21; 21:21; 28:17, 23f). Stephen's death may be a turning point in Acts, but not of the sort claimed by Pesch. Secondly, Pesch fails to show that standing is *necessarily* a feature of judgment, much less the judgment of Israel in particular.[64] God may be presented as standing for any number of reasons: to help the poor (Ps. 12:5); to intervene against his people's enemies (Pss. 3:7; 7:6; 9:19); to judge the earth (Pss. 94:2; 96:13; 98:9; Is. 2:19, 21); or to judge the heathen ( Is. 14:22). In any case, God stands in T. Mos. 10:3 not to judge Israel, but to judge the world in vindication of Israel.[65]

Finally, the logic of Pesch's argument would require him to affirm that the Son of Man sits in Lk. 22:69 in order to judge the Gentiles; yet this is no more evident there than a judgment of Israel is in Acts. In a contrary fashion, Bock maintains that vv. 59 f emphasise the reception of Stephen's spirit by Jesus, and a call for the forgiveness of his Jewish persecutors.[66] Therefore, Stephen cannot view Jesus' role as judicial at all. However, while his observations are valuable, Bock confuses the substance of judicial and judgmental actions. Jesus' role is not *judgmental*, but both

---

[62] See Sabbe, "Acts 7,56," p. 269 for a good development of this objection.

[63] Cf. Bock, *Proclamation*, p. 222.

[64] See Tödt, *Son of Man*, p. 304; Sabbe, "Acts 7,56," pp. 271 f.

[65] See Hengel, "Between Jesus and Paul," p. 152 n. 141.

[66] Bock, *Proclamation*, p. 223.

of Stephen's requests fall very much within the scope of the judicial prerogatives of an heavenly advocate.

Similar arguments pertain to the dispensationalist view. It is not clear in Luke-Acts that the Son of Man's sitting position refers exclusively to the final judgment of the Jews any more than does his standing. Acts 2:34–41, in fact, suggests that the Jews may have opportunity to repent long after Jesus sits down at God's right hand.

9) Those who contend that there is no significance to the standing position have yet to explain this with respect to Ps. 110:1. Regardless of what one considers to be the OT background to Acts 7:55f,[67] the image of a sitting Son of Man (via the use of Ps. 110) is so common in the NT that it is difficult to believe that there is no importance in this single NT exception. The various linguistic discussions of ἵστημι have merely shown that "being" or "location" may be entailed within the meaning of the word; but this is not the same as saying that standing is ever to be positively excluded from that meaning. Obviously the idea of standing will always carry the connotation of "existing" or being located somewhere – as will the ideas of "sitting," "lying down," or "standing on one's head" – but this does not offer a basis for denying the element of standing in the meaning. Neither does the fact that a subject's posture may not have a special significance in every instance prove that the element of posture may be ignored in any particular instance.

10) A frequent argument against the witness interpretation of Moule is the claim that the Son of Man functions as a judge in the gospel tradition, not a witness/advocate.[68] However, Tödt has argued strongly for the latter interpretation of the Son of Man tradition in Luke.[69] Even if one were to conclude that Tödt pushes his case too far, the following discussion concerning the semitic understanding of judges and advocates will show that the hard and fast distinctions made by Moule's critics cannot stand.

Pesch also disagrees with Moule's attaching a judicial significance to the "right hand," claiming that its normal meaning is Lordship (cf. Lk. 22:69). For Pesch the real issue lies in explaining the "standing," not "at the right hand."[70] But it is far from clear that the normal meaning of being located at the right hand is always and only lordship (cf. Rm. 8:34; Heb. 1:3; 8:1; 10:12). Its significance must be interpreted according to the peculiarities of each individual case. Therefore, Pesch's arguments are irrelevant: a judicial significance is possible in Acts 7:55f, as Pesch himself finally admits; and the two elements of "standing" and "at the right hand" cannot be divided from each other. The meaning of this phrase can only be

---

[67] Richard, *Acts 6:1–8:4*, pp. 296 (following Tödt, *Son of Man*, p. 303) seems to argue for the influence of Dan. 7:13 (LXX), as opposed to that of Ps. 110:1, under the erroneous assumption that eliminating Ps. 110 as the background to Acts 7:55f will also eliminate the need to postulate any significance for Jesus' standing position.

[68] Barrett, "Stephen," p. 34; Pesch, *Vision*, p. 55.

[69] Tödt, *Son of Man*, pp. 44f, 56, 98f, 109; also Bihler, *Stephanusgeschichte*, p. 102.

[70] Pesch, *Vision*, pp. 52f.

found through the interrelationship of these two features within their immediate context.

## 7.3 The Judicial Significance of "the Son of Man Standing at the Right Hand"

The proper starting point for any interpretation of this scene must be the context in which Stephen's vision is placed.[71] Moule and his followers set the proper agenda in this respect when they point out that Stephen's vision takes place in the midst of a courtroom battle. Stephen has just concluded his defence against the legal charges brought against him, and the Sanhedrin is on the verge of passing its verdict when the Son of Man appears. This scenario makes the suggestion of a judicial significance to the vision extremely likely. It is noteworthy that the Son of Man saying in Lk. 22:69 serves a similar judicial function: it forecasts heaven's overturning of a lower court's (the Sanhedrin's) decision regarding Jesus. It will be seen that Stephen's vision conveys a similar heavenly overturning of another earthly court's verdict.

A heavenly/judicial significance for the role of the Son of Man is also found in Lk. 12:8f (cf. Mt. 10:32). Here the Son of Man is also not a judge, but an advocate who testifies before the heavenly court on behalf of those who have been faithful in confessing him before their persecutors on the earth.[72] Several significant features are worth highlighting in this passage.

First, it need only briefly to be repeated that in the semitic court witnesses were not interrogated by an attorney, but testified themselves as advocate or prosecutor.[73] Therefore, in "acknowledging" his disciple the Son of Man is not only a witness, but also functions as an heavenly advocate.

---

[71] The possible functions suggested by the Son of Man title alone are not so consistently discernible as to justify setting aside the context of the vision; *pace*, Colpe, "ὁ υἱὸς τοῦ ἀνθρώπου," p. 462.

[72] See Trites, *Witness*, p. 182 for a list of those features which show judicial advocacy to be the issue in Lk. 12:8–12; also see B. Lindars, "Jesus as Advocate: A Contribution to the Christology Debate," *BJRL*. 62 ('80) 476–497.

[73] Trites, *Witness*, p. 21; Z. W. Falk, *Hebrew Law in Biblical Times*, (Jerusalem, 1964), p. 70; also see A. N. Sherwin-White, *Roman Society and Roman Law in the New Testament*, (Oxford, 1963), pp. 18, 22f, 25f, for details of the similar Roman system. Trites also points out that neither were witnesses and judges always differentiated. It is important to observe this flexibility of function because it has sometimes been argued that the parousia doctrine, wherein the Son of Man is seen to come as judge of the world, is a creation of the early church since elsewhere Jesus conceived of his future role not in terms of judgment but advocacy (Mk. 8:38 par; Mt. 7:22f, par; Acts 7:56). The argument assumes that, (1) since Jesus could not have spoken of himself performing both functions simultaneously, and (2) elsewhere judgment is the prerogative of God alone, therefore (3) the idea of Jesus as eschatological judge must have arisen in the post-Easter community; cf. for example Robinson, *Jesus*, pp. 55f. However, given the well attested flexibility of both the language and the functions of the semitic judiciary it is not at all inconceivable that the same individual could have spoken of himself as both advocate and judge; also cf. Moule's discussion of

Secondly, the similar Markan tradition (Mk. 8:38; Lk. 9:26; omit Mt.) does not mention any denial or acknowledgement by the Son of Man, only his being "ashamed" of the faithless at his parousia.

Thirdly, although Lk. 12:8 f is often read as a statement concerning the parousia, there is no obvious reason for doing so. There is nothing overtly eschatological about this teaching, unless one sees the reference to the Son of Man in this light; but then one has to contend with Luke's non-eschatological version of Jesus' words in Lk. 22:69, not to mention such texts as Lk. 5:24; 6:5; 7:34; 9:22, 44, 58. The supposed similarity to Lk. 9:26 evaporates at exactly those points where eschatology comes into view. In fact, its Lukan context, where the Son of Man's testimony is associated with *the present day* challenges of faithful witness in the face of opposition (12:10–12), gives Lk. 12:8 f a decidedly non-eschatological import.

Fourthly, only Luke's version of this "Q" material presents it as a Son of Man saying; in Matthew Jesus speaks in the first person.

Fifthly, in distinction to Mt. 10:33, the Son of Man in Luke has no part in denying those who deny him. He is only shown testifying on their behalf, and in Lk. 9:26 he is merely ashamed of them. Lk. 12:9 employs a passive verb (ἀπαρνηθήσεται) rather than the previous active verb with the Son of Man as subject, implying that it is only God who denies men, while the Son of Man intercedes for the faithful.[74] Each of these features combine uniquely in Luke to offer the picture of a Son of Man who is *presently* acting as the exalted, heavenly advocate for his faithful disciples.

### 7.3.1 Standing at the Right Hand

In the ancient world being "on the right hand" conveyed the idea of power or authority.[75] In Greek thought the right side was the side of luck and good fortune, while the left was weak and unlucky.[76] In the OT the right hand was the hand of blessing (Gen. 48:14, 17f) and the seat of (divine) power (Ex. 15:6, 12; Job 40:14; Pss. 18:35; 20:6; 21:8; Hab. 2:16). Thus to be "on the right hand" was a sign of divine protection and favour (Pss. 16:11; 80:17; 110:1; Jer. 22:24). But the met-

---

the use of metaphor, in *Phenomenon*, pp. 82–85. The rabbis regularly likened God to both an advocate and judge at one and the same time (cf. PsPhilo 22:6; Gen. R. 33:3; 73:3); also see Moore, *Judaism*, vol. I, p. 387.

[74] In *Jesus and the Son of Man* (p. 58) Higgins claimed that the parallelism made it "clear" that the Son of Man was in view in v. 9 as well. However, in his more recent study, *The Son of Man in the Teaching of Jesus*, (Cambridge, 1980), pp. 40, 80–82 he concedes that the passive verb is most likely intended as a circumlocution for God. Lindars, *Son of Man*, p. 49, writes that even though it spoils the symmetry, it may be "that while Luke was content to represent Jesus as advocate in the coming judgement, he wished to avoid representing him as accuser." The error of referring the saying only to the future judgment has already been noted.

[75] See Hay, *Glory*, pp. 52–60 for a good survey of the ancient Near Eastern, Greek, Roman and OT materials; also Gourgues, *A la droite de Dieu*, pp. 38–41, who concentrates on the royal use of the imagery in the ANE; and J. M. Court, "Right and Left: The Implications For Matthew 25:31–46," *NTS.* 31 ('85) 223–233.

[76] W. Grundmann, "δεξιός," *TDNT.* vol. II, p. 38.

aphor was also reversible, for there are those places where God is described as being on the right hand of the one he strengthens (Pss. 16:8; 73:23; 110:5 [!]; Is. 41:13; 45:1; 63:12).

Entailed within this metaphor is the idea of special access to the one on whose right hand a person sits. I Kg. 2:19 offers one of the earliest examples of this thought when Bathsheba is set at Solomon's right hand as she comes to intercede for the life of Adonijah.[77] This particular judicial application of the language undergoes extensive development in Judaism, while retaining every bit of its flexibility.

Standing was the recognised posture for witnesses to adopt, both in the OT and in later Jewish writings (Dt. 19:17; I Kg. 3:16; Acts 4:7; 5:27; 6:13; 22:30; 24:20; 25:10, 18; 26:6; 27:24; b. Sheb. 30b), which meant that it was the attitude for advocates and prosecutors as well. Ps. 109:6 and Zech. 3:1 indicate that in Israelite trials the accuser might stand on the right hand of the defendant. But according to Ps. 109:31, so also does the defending advocate (who in this instance was the Lord himself; in Zech. 3:1 the judge, who is the angel of the Lord, also becomes the advocate).[78] Standing at the right hand was the place from which one, hoping to find favour with the judge, made an appeal.

However, as these legal features developed, distinctions between the right and left hands became more fixed. Normally the advocate came to stand on the judge's right while the accuser stood on the left. Thus in III En. 28:4–9 God sits enthroned as judge while two angels act as advocate and prosecutor. The angel on the right argues his case on the basis of the righteous deeds recorded in the heavenly books, while the angel on the left stands to accuse on the basis of those evil deeds recorded.[79] Similarly, in T. Abr. 12–13 Abraham sees the heavenly court where the angelic advocate, who stands on the right of God's throne, is also the scribe who records the righteous deeds by which he argues his case; the accuser on the left writes down in his own books every individual's sins, and so uses this as evidence against the wicked. In a midrash on the Song of Songs (1:9, par. 1) the entourage of the heavenly court is divided in half; some stand on the right side of the throne, which is the side of acquittal, while others stand on the left, which is the side of condemnation (cf. b. Sanh. 38b; T. Job 33:3).[80] Philo agrees in describ-

---

[77] See H. Gunkel, *Die Psalmen*, (Gottingen, 1968), pp. 191, 481f. Perhaps Ps. 45:9 indicates that the queen or queen-mother regularly stood at the king's right hand in order to have such access; also cf. Jos. Asen. 20:5; 21:5. The LXX of Zech. 6:13 may reflect the same mode of thought when it enthrones Joshua the high priest on the king's right hand.

[78] See R. de Vaux, *Ancient Israel*, (London, 1961), p. 156; Gunkel, *Psalmen*, pp. 479f.

[79] In III En. 30:2, Metatron, the Prince of the World (cf. 10:3), serves as advocate for this world at the daily court of judgment through his reading the books of good and evil deeds.Further visions of the heavenly courtroom reveal that justice stands on the right, mercy on the left, while truth is in front of the throne of judgement (31:3); elsewhere angels of mercy are on the right, angels of peace on the left and angels of destruction are in front (33:1).

[80] Similarly, Midr. Ps. 90 par. 12 describes how prior to creation Eden existed on the right of God's throne, while Gehenna was on the left. Furthermore, according to the rabbis, the good inclination resides in the right side of a man's body, while the evil inclination is found in the left

ing God's right hand as the place of mercy and his left as the place of judgment (Abr. 124; cf. Deus, 73; Gaius 95; Jos. 229; QE. 2.68).

This connection between innocence and the right hand may also be expressed in the location of the defendants in such cases, although this language is less frequent. Thus in the Apoc. Abr. 22:5–7 humanity is divided into two groups; the righteous are placed on the right side of the judgment seat, while the wicked are placed on the left (cf. Mt. 25:31–46). It is important to adequately comprehend the manifold extra-biblical development of this imagery or its importance may be misunderstood. For example, Neudorfer rejects the advocate interpretation of Acts 7:55 f by saying that such figures were only ever presented as standing on the right side of the accused, while the Son of Man stands on the right hand of God.[81] Similarly, Gourgues maintains that since the right hand is the place of giving evidence only the defendant ever adopts that position; "obviously" this can have no christological application.[82] It is clear the latter scholar has not fully appreciated the semitic understanding of giving evidence, while neither of these interpreters fully appreciate the Jewish understanding of "at the right hand."

Although it is true that a judicial significance is not the only possible meaning which might be attached to either "standing" or "at the right hand," when this important judicial background is combined with (a) the legal context of Stephen's vision, (b) the coordination of this particular posture with this location, and (c) the previous presentation of the Son of Man in Luke's gospel *presently* functioning as *a heavenly advocate* for the faithful, the inclination to interpret the standing Son of Man in Acts 7:55–56 in these terms rather than in any others becomes strong indeed. While the false witnesses stand to accuse Stephen (Acts 6:13, ἔστησάν τε μάρτυρας ψευδεῖς), the heavenly witness stands to vindicate him.

### 7.3.2 Acts 7:55–56 and Ps. 110:1?

The preceding arguments indicate that a strong case for the witness interpretation of Acts 7:55–56 may be established independently of the arguments concerning which (if any) specific OT text(s) are alluded to in Stephen's vision. But given the importance of Ps. 110 in the NT, this question needs to be addressed nevertheless.

Acts 7:55–56 has most often been interpreted with reference to Ps. 110 (109):1, the "standing" being either an independent alteration or evidence of the influence

---

(Num. R. 22:9; b. Ber. 61a; here each inclination is located in their respective kidney). Thus to follow on the right side of the Torah is to follow the good inclination and use the law correctly; to pass on the left of Torah is to follow the evil inclination and misuse God's law (b. Shab. 63a, 88b); cf. Court, "Right and Left," p. 224.

[81] Neudorfer, *Der Stephanuskreis*, p. 285. He claims that because of this the idea of advocacy may be found in Acts 7 only if the element of the right hand is ignored, all the emphasis being placed upon the standing. The weakness of this view has already been addressed above with reference to Pesch.

[82] Gourgues, *A la droite de Dieu*, p. 182. He offers this argument in defence of the use of Ps. 110:1 in Acts 7:55 f, although oddly enough he does eventually decide in favour of the advocate interpretation (pp. 183f).

of Dan. 7:13 (LXX). Casey has made out a strong case against any Danielic influence.[83] He argues that the presence of "standing ones" (οἱ παρεστηκότες) in Daniel's vision is not enough grammatically to explain the standing (ἑστῶτα) Son of Man in Acts. However, Casey's arguments do not eliminate the possibility of a conceptual connection, insofar as Dan. 7 presents a heavenly courtroom scene. The LXX translator, understanding the requirements of this scenario, undoubtedly included these "standing ones" as the court-attendants which would be expected in such a situation. This, then, provides a common conceptual framework for both Dan. 7 and Acts 7 (as well as Zech 3; see below); influence from this source remains possible.

But Ps. 110 remains to be dealt with. The important phrase in v. 1 of the psalm is κάθου ἐκ δεξιῶν μου. The relevant portions of Acts 7 read:

v. 55 Ἰησοῦν ἑστῶτα ἐκ δεξιῶν τοῦ θεοῦ
v. 56 τὸν υἱὸν τοῦ ἀνθρώπου ἐκ δεξιῶν ἑστῶτα τοῦ
       θεοῦ

With the change in Acts from sitting to standing the only point of contact remaining in Ps. 110 is ἐκ δεξιῶν μου. Since God is the speaker in Ps. 110 there would be no difficulty in explaining the shift from μου to τοῦ θεοῦ in Acts 7. However, this re-wording could also result from the influence of Lk. 22:69 (diff. Mk. 14:62). While there can be little doubt that the (traditional) influence of Ps. 110:1 is evident in Lk. 22:69, this is made clear by the very element lacking in Acts 7: the Son of Man is sitting. The question which begs to be asked at this point is, Why should anyone see the influence of Ps. 110:1 in Acts 7:55–56?[84] Location at the right hand is not an exclusive characteristic of the sort of enthronement/exaltation motif present in Ps. 110, and can mean a place of honour quite independently of that psalm.[85] Further, as has already been demonstrated, both the right hand *and* the standing position are important elements in judicial proceedings.[86] With such important dissimilarities between the two passages, and a very feasible alternative explanation on hand for the sole point of "contact" (ie. the right hand), there is little compelling reason to see any influence of Ps. 110 upon Acts 7 at all. At best, Ps. 110 may have exerted a mediated influence through Lk. 22:69 and a general awareness of the importance of this OT text for the theology of exaltation in the early church. However, there may be other points of contact in the OT for both the right hand and the standing position which honour the judicial significance of

---

[83] Casey, *Son of Man*, p. 200. The words "Son of Man" are the only possible allusion to Dan. 7:13, and without some other evidence there is no reason to look beyond the gospel tradition itself for the source of this title.

[84] Cf. Gourgues, *A la droite de Dieu*, p. 182.

[85] Grundmann, "Das Problem," p. 65.

[86] At this point, Moule's inclusion of both Ps. 110 and Acts 7 under the general rubric of "vindication scenes," though correct in itself, is seen to be too broad a categorisation to be of help in identifying the specific OT background. Vindication may take various forms.

Stephen's vision. A passage such as Zech. 3:1–10, for instance, appears agreeable at the very points where Ps. 110:1 is unhelpful.

The fourth vision of Zechariah (3:1–10) is also a heavenly court scene. The high priest Joshua has been brought before the Lord and is being accused by Satan as unfit for his ministry. Eventually, the judge intervenes and vindicates Joshua. The important sections of v. 1 read as follows:

Ἰησοῦν ... ἑστῶτα πρὸ προσώπου ἀγγέλου κυρίου
ὁ διάβολος εἱστήκει ἐκ δεξιῶν αὐτοῦ

Of course, there can be no claim to anything as straightforward as the actual quotation of this text in Acts 7; the differences are too great. In Zech. Joshua stands as the defendant, while in Acts Jesus stands as advocate; also in Zech. the accuser stands on the right of the defendant, while in Acts the advocate stands on the right of the judge. However, in spite of these differences there are enough points of resemblance between Zech. 3 and Acts 7 to give cause to suspect that this OT passage may at least provide the conceptual background to the standing Son of Man. What differences there are may be explicable as alterations made necessary by the events of salvation-history which have occurred subsequent to Zechariah's vision, thereby requiring fundamental changes in the way any such scene can now be portrayed.

The visionary revelation of a judicial setting establishes the basic, shared frame of reference for both texts. In both cases the litigant making his appeal stands at the right hand. For anyone who read the LXX as their OT the parallel between Joshua (Ἰησοῦν) standing (ἑστῶτα) and Jesus (Ἰησοῦν) standing (ἑστῶτα) would have been evident. The seeming difference between defendant and advocate disappears when one recalls the semitic expectation that a witness prosecute his own case (and if a defendant had no corroborative testimony, he *was* his own witness/advocate). The difference between Jesus standing at the judge's right as advocate and Satan standing at the defendant's right as accuser makes impossible any neat paralleling of the two visions. But, from Luke's perspective, since the ascension it has become impossible for Zechariah's vision ever to be seen again in its original form. The accuser who once stood in heaven (Zech. 3:1) has been defeated and cast out through the powerful intercessions of Jesus (Lk. 10:18–20; 22:31–32). Jesus is now the ascended Lord, the heavenly Son of Man, who stands as the exalted advocate in heaven's court (Lk. 12:8–9) replacing the accuser. This is why Jesus is not situated before the throne, as was the accuser, but stands at the right hand of God himself.[87]

The reversal of Joshua's fortunes (Zech. 3:3–5) is also reminiscent of the judicial reversal experienced by Jesus. Like Joshua, Jesus had once stood before a judge with his opponents standing by to accuse him (Lk. 23:10, εἱστήκεισαν δὲ οἱ ἀρχιερεῖς ... κατηγοροῦωτες αὐτοῦ; cf. Zech. 3:1; also Lk. 23:2, 14). And just

---

[87] Which is itself not unusual, since elsewhere even defending angels stand at God's right hand. Tödt's observations concerning angelomorphic christology, while misdirected, are seen to be very relevant.

as the Lord had intervened to vindicate Joshua and silence his accuser, so the Father has vindicated Jesus. In each instance, this vindication by God is expressed through a heavenly confirmation of their divine appointment to office (cf. Lk. 22:69).

Zech. 3:1 offers the basic conceptual background for Acts 7:55f, but it has been re-presented after being drawn through the grid of Lukan convictions regarding the present status of the Son of Man and the significance of Jesus' prayer-life. The same essential features are present, but are rearranged according to the constraints of a new theological reality. At the very least, Zech. 3 offers itself as a possible source of influence for the modification of Ps. 110, if one were still to hold to Ps. 110 as the background to Acts 7:55f. But, in either case, it has already been shown that the value of the advocate interpretation of the standing Son of Man stands independently of any particular OT background passage.

It may be concluded from this study that the language of vindication/exaltation can have different origins and be used for different purposes. B. Lindars has made a few relevant observations in this regard in an interesting article entitled "Enoch and Christology."[88] Although there will be more cause to discuss the relationship between the Enoch traditions and NT christology in the next chapter, a few remarks now will be germane to the place of Ps. 110 in the development of the idea of Christ as Intercessor.

Lindars notes that, in spite of the similarites between the Jewish traditions concerning Enoch and those aspects of early christology which drew so freely from Ps. 110:1, this psalm never appears in any of the Enoch literature. This suggests that "the similarities between the primitive christology and the picture of Enoch ... have been reached along separate lines."[89] The present study of Acts 7:55–56 suggests that the exaltation christology of the NT is not a homogeneous derivative of a single-minded reflection upon Ps. 110, which may then be mono-lithically juxtaposed against extra-Biblical traditions. There are independent lines of development, that is strains of thought which are either unrelated to Ps. 110, or are influenced by it only secondarily, within this aspect of NT christology itself.

Thus the description of the standing Son of Man is not simply a different permutation of the exalted, sitting Son of Man; it is a related yet distinct use of imagery, which serves a related but distinct theological purpose. Once this distinc-tion is recognised it may be possible to discern similar differences in other NT texts. For example, in Rom. 8:34 when Paul refers to Christ as "the one who intercedes (ἐντυγχάνει) on our behalf" he does so to affirm that this Christ is not the one who will condemn the elect. This fact, namely that since Christ is our advocate he will not be our judge, suggests a train of thought surprisingly similar to that in evidence behind Luke's unwillingness to credit the Son of Man with the final repudiation of faithless disciples (Lk. 12:8f), and thereby consistently describe him as advocate rather than as judge.

---

[88] ExpT. 92 ('81) 295–299.

[89] The closest passages present the Elect One (I En. 45:3; 61:8) or the Son of Man (I En. 62:5) sitting on his glorious throne of judgment. This is not derived from Ps. 110:1; see "Enoch," p. 298.

Perhaps the common theme of intercession should also cause the interpreter to stop and reflect on Paul's description of Christ ἐν δεξιᾷ τοῦ θεοῦ. In the absence of any reference to posture (standing or sitting), there is no more reason to see an exclusive reference to Ps. 110:1 in Rom. 8:34 than there is in Acts 7:55–56. In fact, the description of Christ as our heavenly advocate would seem to tip the scales in favour of associating this text with the same judicial perspective expressed in Luke, although it must be admitted that in the absence of an explicit reference to a standing position such a connection can only be suggested. Perhaps Rom. 8:34 is evidence of Paul's familiarity with the same circle of christological thought which, without reference to Ps. 110:1, described the exalted Jesus in judicial rather than royal terms as the heavenly advocate at God's right hand.

Heb. 7:25 uses the same vocabulary of intercession as does Paul (ἐντυγχάνειν), also without any reference to posture. Elsewhere the author gives ample evidence that he thinks of Christ as the High Priest who now sits at God's right hand (1:3; 8:1; 10:12). But it is interesting to note that the references to Christ's "sitting" are always used to underscore the *finality* of Christ's work (1:3; 8:1; 10:12; 12:2). However, to refer to Christ as the one who "ever lives in order to intercede" is to describe an ongoing process. Perhaps this is why, when Christ's relationship to God is referred to in Heb. 7:25, he is portrayed as the mediator "who is able to save all those who come to God through him" (τοὺς προσερχομένους δι᾽ αὐτοῦ τῷ θεῷ). The language of Ps. 110:1 is nowhere in sight! Thus, even though the theology of intercession coexisted with the use of Ps. 110:1 in the mind of the author of the epistle to the Hebrews, there was an inherent difficulty in expressing this particular point of theology in the language of that psalm. Sitting could be used to express such ideas as exaltation, rule, judgment and the finality of one's work; but it was inadequate for the present, ongoing task of heavenly intercession, which in any event was (traditionally) expressed through the language of stand-ing, if indeed any posture was referred to at all. In this regard, Hebrews is really not very different from Luke-Acts. For Luke clearly knew of the traditional use of Ps. 110:1 (Acts 2:34), but he too found it inadequate for the expression of his theology of intercession.[90]

## 7.4 The Son of Man as Prophetic Intercessor

A synoptic look at the descriptions of Jesus' heavenly intercession in Hebrews and Luke-Acts raises another obvious point of comparison. While Hebrews integrates the theme of intercession within its broader presentation of Jesus as the heavenly

---

[90] O. Bauernfeind, "τυγχάνω," *TDNT*. vol. VIII, p. 243 surmises that the similar language in Rm. 8:26f, 34 and Heb. 7:25 reflects an underlying tradition which had already received a "fixed form" when employed by these two authors. The present argument sheds further light on the suggestion, showing that the tradition had developed independently of Ps. 110 and was also known to Luke.

High Priest (cf. Ps. 110:4), Luke offers Jesus as the interceding, eschatological Prophet. It is not as Priest but as final Prophet that the Son of Man stands at God's right hand in Acts 7.

That the title Son of Man may entail such prophetic significance is made explicit in Lk. 11:30–32. There the prophet Jonah is compared with the Son of Man as the great preacher of repentance. For the Son of Man (whom Luke plainly identifies as Jesus) to refer to himself, during his earthly ministry, as one greater than Jonah (v. 32) is to confirm the self-identification made by Jesus in the synagogue at Nazareth where he declared himself to be the final Prophet.[91]

Other intimations of there being a prophetic aspect to Jesus' earthly identification as the Son of Man have already arisen from Luke's passion narrative. It will be recalled that Lk. 19:42–44 and 23:28–31 show Jesus speaking prophetic judgment oracles over Jerusalem. The implication is that Jesus goes to the cross as the rejected final Prophet. However, one must also remember that whenever Jesus explicitly speaks of his fate in Jerusalem he always refers to himself as the Son of Man (Lk. 9:22, 44; 17:24–25; 18:31–33; cf. 24:7). The convergence of these two lines of thought in Luke's story-line indicates that it is as the Son of Man that Jesus speaks his words of prophetic judgment against Jerusalem. Also, Luke's particular emphasis upon the fact that it is the special fate of the prophets to suffer (Lk. 4:24; 13:33, 34; Acts 7:42) in Jerusalem – the place of the Son of Man's demise – serves to link the Son of Man title with Jesus' status as final Prophet.

This Lukan portrait of the earthly Son of Man as God's eschatological Prophet leads to the same declaration being made in Acts about the ascended Jesus. Stephen clearly identifies Jesus as the eschatological Prophet (Acts 7:37), not only while he walked upon the earth but also after the ascension. Likewise, Peter's declaration of Jesus as the long awaited Prophet-like-Moses (Acts 3:22–23) must refer to a status enjoyed now by the ascended Jesus. Consequently, the speaking done by this Prophet, which Peter commands the people to obey, must be Jesus' *present* activity; the fulfillment of his promise to the disciples that he would help them with

---

[91] Although one may want to debate the meaning of "the sign of Jonah" more precisely, ie. is it the person of Jesus, his person and message, the resurrection, or the parousia, the concluding phrase of v. 32 (καὶ ἰδοὺ πλεῖον Ἰωνᾶ ὧδε) makes it clear that it is *as* the Greater Prophet that the Son of Man is related to the sign, whatever it may be. For a discussion of alternatives see Marshall, *Commentary*, pp. 484f; Higgins, *The Son of Man in the Teaching of Jesus*, pp. 103–105, 137–139. Higgins attempts to base his parousia interpretation of the sign upon Edwards' arguments concerning his "eschatological correlative." However, it is significant that even Edwards admits that the point of comparison between Jesus and Jonah is their role as vindicated prophets; see R. A. Edwards, *The Sign of Jonah In the Theology of the Evangelists and Q*, (London, 1971), pp. 84, 86, 95. In the end, Fitzmyer's words (*The Gospel*, vol. II, p. 933) express the most probable interpretation: "Just as Jonah was a prophet sent from afar to preach repentance to the Ninevites, so too does Jesus appear to this generation ... He comes from afar in the sense of a heaven-sent prophet like Jonah; but he is something greater than Jonah." Also see T. W. Manson, *Teaching*, p. 219; Lindars, *Son of Man*, pp. 39–42.

their witness in times of trial (Lk. 21:15).[92] Evidently, Luke conceives of the exalted, final Prophet as being presently active in that very capacity as witness (even though in Peter's case, it is a witness spoken through the apostle).

This series of observations, namely (1) that Luke links the title Son of Man with his presentation of Jesus as the final Prophet, (2) that the exalted Jesus is the exalted final Prophet, and (3) that as the final Prophet Jesus is presently active in his church, combine to shed important light on Stephen's vision of the interceding Son of Man, especially when it is recalled that Stephen's vision is given to him immediately after his confession of Jesus as the eschatological Prophet-like-Moses. Pesch has criticised Bihler's identification of the standing Son of Man as the final Mosaic Prophet by claiming that it lacks clarity;[93] and, as presented by Bihler, it does seem to be something of an exegetical leap. But the preceding discussion indicates that Bihler's suggestion should be reappraised. To interpret Stephen's vision as the revelation of the Son of Man, in his capacity as the heavenly Mosaic Prophet, not only fits the christological convictions expressed in Stephen's speech, but is also commensurate with, at least a part of, Luke's definition of the Son of Man, and his description of the post-ascension activity of Jesus. In addition to this literary/exegetical evidence, there also is the evidence of the Jewish background materials which suggest that precisely this expectation could possibly have attached itself to whomever would eventually be revealed as the final Mosaic Prophet (see chapter 8).

Luke has gone to great lengths in his gospel to show that, while pursuing his ministry as final Prophet on the earth, Jesus was a great man of prayer. It should not be surprising, then, to see exactly this prophetic mode of expression surface in Acts 7:55–56; in any event, there are no grounds in either the gospel or Acts for postulating a heavenly High Priest theology. Here is the other important point of contrast between Luke-Acts and the book of Hebrews. According to Luke, Jesus not only prays during his earthly ministry, but also intercedes in his heavenly ministry, as the final Prophet-like-Moses, not as High Priest.

## 7.5 Why Does Stephen see "the Son of Man"?

One of the most enigmatic features of Stephen's vision is the fact that Jesus is seen as the Son of Man. Why does Stephen not identify Jesus as the Son of God? or as Christ? Of course, this sort of question can be asked in any such situation, but its relevance here is made most acute by the well known peculiarities of the Son of Man title itself. Does the preceding discussion offer any possible assistance in answering this question?

---

[92] Cf. O'Toole, "Activity," p. 480; Haenchen, *Acts*, p. 209. This unique, Lukan description of Jesus as the disciples' advocate (diff. Mk. 13:11; Mt. 10:19) is another part of Luke's "paraclete christology," which needs to be kept in mind for any comparative study of NT pneumatology (cf. n. 1).

[93] Pesch, *Vision*, p. 17.

Of course, the first thing some investigators would want to say is that the Son of Man title as used by Stephen is historically accurate. *This* is why it occurs here; and this suggestion cannot be dismissed as quickly as some would like. But it would still be necessary to explain why Stephen interprets his vision of Jesus as a view of the Son of Man in particular, as opposed to applying any other title to Jesus. It also remains to explain the role of this title within the context of Luke-Acts.[94]

One factor which may lead to a possible solution has already been provided. The partial Lukan identification of the Son of Man with the prophetic dimensions of Jesus' ministry would perhaps make this title particularly appropriate for the revelation of Jesus as the heavenly Prophet-Advocate. However, this suggestion alone still does not prove adequate, since for example, the passage which deals paradigmatically with Jesus' role as the prayerful mediator of the things of God (Lk. 10:21–22) refers to him as the Son. The question, then, remains: Why does Stephen not see his heavenly Intercessor as the Son rather than the Son of Man? Perhaps the solution is still to be found in the particular christological interests of Stephen's speech, and the fact that Luke does not associate the title Son with the idea of final Prophet as regularly as he does the title Son of Man.

But there are other suggestions that might be made. Whatever the OT background to the idea, the gospels agree unanimously in saying that it is as the Son of Man that Jesus is located near God's throne. Since an heavenly Intercessor would necessarily be located at God's right hand this makes the Son of Man title a likely candidate for identifying Jesus. This would be especially true for Luke, whose "from now on" (ἀπὸ τοῦ νῦν) in Lk. 22:69 not only helps to purge this Son of Man saying of its eschatological dimensions, but also makes the Son of Man's presence at God's right hand a permanent feature of the era of the church.

Finally, it should also be remembered that Jesus himself describes his role as heavenly advocate precisely as the work of the Son of Man (Lk. 12:8). Thus it simply follows Jesus' own description for Stephen to see Jesus-his-Advocate as the Son of Man. This is an important observation because it raises several questions regarding the use of the title Son of Man in the early church. For instance, Moule has suggested that this title disappeared from current church usage (except for its preservation in the Jesus tradition) because it had no relevance to the church's present situation. The title Son of Man referred either to the sufferings of Jesus, which was an event of the past, or to the return of Jesus, which is an event in the future, but it had no significance for the ongoing experience of the church.[95] The

---

[94] For example, Bauernfeind *Apostelgeschichte*, p. 120 and Trocmé, *Le Livre*, pp. 187f both defend the historicity of the Stephen material. In this case, Acts 7:55f could either provide:a) early evidence of the titular use of the "son of man," thus suggesting that the current preoccupation with Aramaic idioms as the way of accounting for such language is misdirected; or, b) evidence that a Son of Man theology was a very early creation of the church. Theory (a) has the greater probability of being correct since position (b) would have great difficulty accounting for the (near) absence of this title outside the gospels.

title Lord was much more relevant for the church's present predicament and so this became the most common title for Jesus, replacing Jesus' own title of preference. However, according to Luke, the title Son of Man retains a good deal of relevance for the church's present situation. It is as the Son of Man that Jesus serves as every disciple's advocate with the Father. It is as the Son of Man that Jesus intercedes for his elect, prayerfully preserving their discipleship and safeguarding them from the Adversary. According to Luke, the title Son of Man has an important place indeed within the grammar of Christian existence.

Of course, this still leaves unanswered questions. For example, if this is true, why then are there not more appearances of the title Son of Man in this connection, especially since there are other NT references to Jesus' work of intercession? But questions such as this are not easily answered; if answers to them are available at all. Perhaps the scarcity of this title is linked to the paucity of material anywhere in the NT treating Jesus' work of heavenly intercession. Although this might still allow for the possibility of a Son of Man theology finding expression in texts such as Rm. 8:34; Heb. 7:25; I Jn. 2:1, the fact that next to nothing is known about the relationship of Lukan theology to the broader spectrum of theological expression in the early church makes it difficult to know how to offer even intelligent speculation on this matter. It would also presume that such an Intercessor/Son of Man association be agreeable to the other aspects of Son of Man theology already resident in these literary *corpi* and/or their communities of origin (if nothing about the Son of Man were to be found in the writing itself). Given the present state of the question, it seems most likely that just as the language of "at the right hand" may be derived from different sources or realms of thought and therefore serve different purposes, so too might the common concept of Jesus-the-Intercessor have been derived from different contexts and have found expression in different christological formats. Only in the Lukan context did this express itself with reference to the Son of Man title.

## 7.6 Conclusions: The Heavenly and the Earthly Jesus

If the interpretation offered here for Acts 7:55–56 is accepted, then it appears that there is indeed explicit confirmation in Acts for the view implicitly expressed in Luke's gospel, namely that Jesus does continue to pray for his disciples in heaven. The "witness" interpretation of Acts 7:55f integrates Stephen's vision as the climax of a consistently developed christological theme in Luke-Acts.

That Acts actually does confirm the task of heavenly intercession implied within the gospel would suggest that it also confirms the implied reasons for such intercession. In other words, Jesus continues to intercede for his disciples in heaven in order both to testify to their faithfulness in times of trial, and to ensure their perseverance in discipleship at such moments. Both of these reasons appear in the

---

[95] Moule, "The Influence of Circumstances of the Use of Christological Terms," pp. 175f.

gospel (Lk. 12:8f; 22:31–32, 39–46), and both of them admirably fit the context of Stephen's vision. The Son of Man intercedes for Stephen in acknowledgment of his faithful witness, but also to pray, as he did for Peter and the other ten, that his faith might not fail. Both heavenly recognition and earthly perseverance are secured for the church through their ascended advocate.

The apparent change from the prayer oriented language of "intercession" to the legal language of "advocacy" does not hinder this interpretation, since the shift is simply one of changing metaphors. In a legal setting Advocate expresses that status, which in a more overtly religious context, is articulated more appropriately as Intercessor. And it is exactly as the unique Intercessor before God that Jesus is already seen to function in Luke's gospel. In fact, Lk. 22:31–32 has already fused the two metaphors; Jesus' intercessory prayer countermanded the charges of the heavenly Accuser.

This too is an important observation if one is to understand the proper relationship between Jesus' role in the gospel and his status in Acts. Bock, for example, claims that Jesus' status as heavenly advocate in Acts 7 illustrates the "divine prerogatives" assumed by the Son of Man who is now the exalted Lord. No one in the gospel ever prays to Jesus. But now, rather than address his petition for forgiveness to God, as previous Jewish theology·would have demanded, Stephen prays to the Lord Jesus (vv. 59–60). Thus the titles Lord and Son of Man are made synonymous, and the deepening christological insights of the church are reflected as Jesus is now seen to perform the very tasks of God himself.[96]

But this interpretation does not take adequate account of the place of Jesus' prayers in the gospel.[97] While it is true that no one prays to Jesus in Luke's gospel, it is not clear why anyone should have since he was there for anyone to speak with immediately. More to the point, Stephen's vision does not show Jesus doing anything in heaven which he has not already done on earth. The real wonder is not that the heavenly Jesus is now the church's advocate, but that he was able to perform exactly the same task of heavenly advocacy while living here on the earth. If there is any christological development to be seen, it is running in the opposite direction! Thus it is also an error to confuse the significance of the two titles Lord and Son of Man. Stephen's recognition that Jesus is someone who may be prayed to as "Lord" should not obliterate the continuity recognisable between the interceding earthly Jesus and the advocate now in heaven. It is a well known fact that Luke refers to Jesus (in narration) as Lord more than any other evangelist. Just as the earthly Lord Jesus, whom the disciples could speak to face to face, had to pray to his heavenly Father, so after the ascension the disciple must pray to the heavenly Lord Jesus, who is now able to speak and intercede with his heavenly Father face to face. It is this change in the pre-and post-ascension *locations* of Jesus which accounts both for this first prayer being offered to him and for his present

---

[96] Bock, *Proclamation*, pp. 224f.
[97] Not to mention the fact that the earthly Son of Man already forgives men's sins (Lk. 5:24).

status as "heavenly" advocate, *not* some fundamental change in his ability to be such an advocate.[98]

The question which clamours for an answer at this point is one with which this chapter began: What is the nature of the relationship between the pre-and post-ascension prayer ministries of Jesus? An answer to this question may help to explain why Luke includes so much more prayer material in his gospel than the other synoptics. For example, is Luke reading a view of Jesus-as-Intercessor back into his gospel materials? Or does Jesus' earthly prayer ministry somehow serve as a precursor for Luke's convictions that Jesus is now the ascended advocate? Answers to these questions will first require an examination of the place of heavenly intercessors in first century Judaism.

---

[98] Of course, the ascension, as a part of the process of resurrection-exaltation, does affect the status of Jesus; and the title Lord (in Acts 7:59f) may well reflect something of this development. But the point at issue here is that Jesus' work as heavenly Advocate is not the result of any such development or enhancement in his status.

Chapter 8

# Exalted, Human Intercessors in Ancient Judaism

## Introduction

The question which presents itself at this point in the study is: What is the relationship between Luke's description of Jesus' prayer-life during his earthly ministry and the ongoing ministry of intercession taken up by Jesus in heaven? Answering this question will require an investigation into the ideas of heavenly intercession in ancient Judaism.[1] Mediators and/or intercessors such as angels, the merits of the Fathers, the Logos, the Memra, and the Holy Spirit will be referred to occasionally in the course of this study, but they will not comprise this chapter's central concern since the primary objective is to discover how Luke's portrayal of Jesus compares with Jewish beliefs in exalted, human intercessors. Consequently, the main interest will be in other human figures, particularly those whose careers parallel Jesus' in that, having once served as effective intercessors during their earthly lifetimes, they then continue that intercessory role in heaven, after experiencing either death or a miraculous translation. This area of study hardly presents virgin territory, but it is hoped that new perspectives on a well researched subject will emerge through adopting a very particular focus. Firstly, the crucial question is how can this material throw new light on Luke-Acts? Secondly, the most relevant information for answering this question will emerge as the material is sifted with three other specific questions in mind:

1) Which human intercessors are allowed to occupy the place of heavenly intercession?

2) Why are they chosen to fill this role? What suits them in particular for this task?

3) Who do they pray for and what benefits are derived from their prayers?

Specific comparisons with Luke-Acts will be reserved for the end of this study. Although, at times, this may cause the intervening discussion on Judaism to seem a bit like a digression, it will be both easier and more reliable to draw intelligent comparisons after the whole of the material has been examined on its own terms.

---

[1] There is very little possibility of purely Hellenistic influences accounting for *the genesis* of the particular ideas explored in this chapter, which of course is not to deny the influence of Hellenism upon Judaism at large. Johansson has thoroughly discussed the dependence of the Christian belief in Christ's heavenly intercession upon OT/Jewish religion, as opposed to Greek or Gnostic conceptions; see *Parakletoi*, pp. 279–296.

# 8.1 Human Intercessors in the OT

After a comparative study of the concept of mediator/ intercessor in the ANE, J. Scharbert reaches a number of important conclusions, three of which will be particularly pertinent to this study as it unfolds: 1) the standard ANE mediators are the priest and king; the biblical ideas of prophets and special, godly men serving as intercessors are unique to Israel; 2) the idea of the dead continuing to serve presently as intercessors for the living is found only in Egypt; and, 3) ideas of "eschatological mediators," that is figures appearing as intercessors at the final judgment, are unknown in the ANE.[2]

While it is true that Israel was similar to its ancient neighbours in giving both its priests and kings an official role as intercessor for the people, neither of these offices are particularly stressed in this respect in the OT. The priest's task of intercession occurred primarily on the Day of Atonement in association with sacrifice,[3] though there were other official occasions on which priestly intercession was offered (cf. II Chr. 30:27). However, because their responsibilities were largely cultic, priests were not viewed in the first instance as intercessors. While this aspect of their work was to gain increasing importance after the cessation of prophets in post-exilic Israel, the OT, unlike the inter-testamental literature, offers no individual priest as a paradigmatic intercessory figure. The likeliest candidate, Aaron, makes this point quite well, overshadowed as he is by his brother Moses.[4]

Israel also shared with her neighbours a view of their king as the corporate representative of the nation. That the responsibilities of this position entailed prayer is amply attested by the numerous royal psalms in which the king presents himself before God on behalf of the people.[5] However, as with the office of priest, no particular king is ever eulogised as an especially memorable intercessor. In fact, only three kings are specifically mentioned as having ever interceded for the people at all: David (II Sam. 24:17); Solomon (I Kg. 8; II Chr. 6); and Hezekiah (II Kg. 19:4; II Chr. 10:18f; 30:18; Jer. 26:19).[6]

The figures most exalted in Israel as intercessors were those which distinguished Israel from her ancient neighbours: special, chosen men and the prophets. However, even here the development in each case is not commensurate, with the result that the reason for effective prophetic intercession is rather ambiguous, ie. it is not altogether clear whether the prophet intercedes as prophet, or as a man chosen to intercede who is also a prophet. The element of personal piety is not explicitly

[2] J. Scharbert, *Heilsmittler im Alten Testament und im Alten Orient*, (Freiburg, 1964). The religions of Egypt, Babylon, Assyria and Syria-Palestine are compared in pp. 21–63; a summary of conclusions appears on pp. 63–67.

[3] J. Mauchline, "Jesus Christ as Intercessor," *ExpT*. 64 ('52–3) 356.

[4] Scharbert, *Heilsmittler*, pp. 63f notes that in the ANE all but the Hittite priests played a decidedly secondary role as mediators for the people. This means that, for the remainder, the king was the primary figure.

[5] See J. Eaton, *Kingship and the Psalms*, (London, 1976).

[6] See Johansson, *Parakletoi*, pp. 13f; also J. Scharbert, "Die Fürbitte in der Theologie des Alten Testaments," *TG*. 50 ('60) 328.

made a condition for this task, although one would expect a prophet to be a pious man who prayed. However, the relationship between these two elements is clarified with respect to Abraham, who intercedes because he is chosen, not because he has merited the position by his piety (see below).

There are those prophetic figures who appear to make intercession an essential element of their office. Thus Jeremiah maintains that effective intercession is one test of a true prophet (Jer. 27:18);[7] and even though he is speaking ironically he appeals to the people on the basis of a shared assumption. Jeremiah himself is recognised in this capacity by others (Jer. 21:2), as was Isaiah (Is. 37:1–4; II Kg. 19:1–4). Even before the monarchy, Samuel, that important transitional figure in Israel's history, was recognised by the people as their representative intercessor (I Sam. 7:8; 12:19; cf. 8:21), a role which he endorses as an important aspect of the prophetic task (I Sam. 7:5–9; 12:23). In fact, R. Klein writes that I Sam. 12:23 offers "a theological etiology for prophetic intercession."[8]

However, it must be added that the work of intercessory prayer appears much less frequently in the prophets than texts such as these would lead one to expect. Scholars such as N. Johansson,[9] J. Scharbert[10] and H. Greeven[11] agree that the work of intercession is most noticeable in the prophets by its absence. It is never described as characteristic of the cult prophets, is rare in the major writing prophets, and it disappears altogether among the post-exilic prophets. Even in a premier figure such as Isaiah there is precious little one could take as intercession (Is. 22:4; 37:4; 53:12; cf. II Chr. 32:20). And those well known passages in Ezekiel (13:5; 22:30) are unclear as to whether the prophet is able, or even expected, to fill the breach between God and the people.[12]

While Scharbert maintains that the paucity of such materials may as easily be explained by the final literary forms of the prophetic writings,[13] it can also be said that there is still considerable occasion within those writings for at least the mention, if not the recitation, of such prayers. When this observation is combined with the significant intercessory role played by non-prophetic figures in the OT (see below) it would appear likely that while intercession is in some places asserted to be a prophetic characteristic, it may perhaps more accurately be described as a unique task performed by a few select individuals, some of whom were also prophets.

Jeremiah's own predicament should cause one to question a simple prophet-

---

[7] Johannson, *Parakletoi*, p. 20; J. A. Thompson, *The Book of Jeremiah*, (Grand Rapids, 1980), p. 536.

[8] R. W. Klein, *I Samuel*, (Waco, 1983), p. 119. P. K. McCarter, *I Samuel*, (Garden City, 1980), p. 217 explains this verse as demonstrating that kingship does not annul the prophet's role as intercessor; also see H. McKeating, "The Prophet Jesus," *ExpT*. 73 ('61) 7.

[9] Johannson, *Parakletoi*, pp. 16, 20f.

[10] Scharbert, *Heilsmittler*, pp. 162f, 223; "Die Fürbitte," pp. 329f, 332.

[11] H. Greeven, "εὔχομαι," *TDNT*, vol. II, p. 798.

[12] See W. Eichrodt, *Ezekiel: A Commentary*, (London, 1970), pp. 164f, 316; W. Zimmerli, *Ezekiel*, vol. I, (Philadelphia, 1979), pp. 292f, 469.

[13] Scharbert, "Die Fürbitte," pp. 329f.

intercessor equation, for he patently fails to pass his own test of a true prophet! His ministry is scarcely one of effective intercession; God does not forgive Israel, nor does he divert his punishment. Yet this never casts any doubt upon Jeremiah's status. Clearly, his consciousness of being one who has been called to pray for the nation is rooted in something other than this particular criterion of the prophetic office. In this respect it is significant that those passages which highlight Jeremiah's work of intercession are the very places where the Lord exhorts him to stop praying for the people (Jer. 7:16; 11:14; 14:11; cf. 10:23–25; 15:1; 37:3; 42:2f)![14]

Two important conclusions may be derived from Jeremiah's situation. First of all, it is not clear that the importance of Jeremiah's intercession is derived from, or is even dependent upon, his holding the office of prophet. Secondly, intercession cannot annul the proper judgment of God when sinners remain unrepentant. Long before this, Eli had also warned that no man may effectively intercede for one who sins (by implication, unrepentantly) against the Lord (I Sam. 2:25). The importance of this observation will become evident as the study moves on to examine the pseudepigraphal literature.

The final class of people who function as OT intercessors is also the most important. These are the individuals chosen by God to play a special role in his plan of salvation-history. Eventually the element of personal piety will become important in the developing Jewish understanding of such "interceding saints," but in the OT individual righteousness does not occupy as prominent a position as does the element of divine election.[15]

The first such intercessor was Abraham, whose role was to undergo extensive development in Judaism. The classic example was Abraham's intervention on behalf of Sodom and Gomorrah (Gen. 18:16–33). There it is made explicit that the Lord grants such bargaining power to Abraham, not because of any exemplary piety on his part, but because God had chosen him to be his covenant partner (vv. 17–19). Abraham's effective intercession for Abimelech, preceded as it is by the unbelieving subterfuge of passing off Sarah as his sister, demonstrates that it is his status as the chosen patriarch, not his great piety, which gives him the right to intercede with God (Gen. 20:17f).

While other figures also appear in the OT who intercede on another's behalf – Isaac (Gen. 25:21), Job (Job 42:8, 10), an anonymous "man of God" (I Kg. 13:6), Elisha (II Kg. 4:33; 6:17) – the intercessor *par excellence* in OT history was Moses. His role as mediator/intercessor would become archetypical for later Jewish theol-

---

[14] W. McKane, *A Critical and Exegetical Commentary on Jeremiah*, vol. I, (Edinburgh, 1986), p. 245; Thompson, *Jeremiah*, pp. 284, 382, 441. This perspective on "prophetic" intercession has been well established by H. W. Hertzberg, "Sin die Propheten Fürbitter?" in *Tradition und Situation: Studien zur alttestamentlichen Prophetie*, (Göttingen, 1963), pp. 63–74). On p. 74 he correctly concludes: "... von einer 'Amtsfunktion' nicht gesprochen werden.Dass die Fürbitte ihnen, wie anderen Gottesmännern auch Richter, Ältesten und Priestern, zugetraut wird, ist ein davon unabhängige Tatsache... Dass es bei Jeremia anders ist, leigt im wesen dieses Mannes begründet, nicht in einer heir besonders wirksam werdenden Institution."

[15] This is an important observation, often overlooked in the discussions of this subject.

ogy.[16] The greatest example of such intercession was Moses' conversation with God on Mt. Sinai after Israel had constructed the Golden Calf (Ex. 32:11–14, 30–35; Dt. 9:13–29), although it is worth noting that even here Moses' prayers do not completely erase the culpability of those who fell into idolatry (Ex. 32:33–35). While Ex. 32 offers the most important example of intercession, this work actually typifies all of Moses' ministry (Ex. 15:25; 20:19; 33:12f; Num. 9:20, 26; 11:2; 12:13; 21:7; Dt. 5:27). And even though he was called a prophet, as was Abraham (Gen. 20:7, 17), it was not any prophetic "office" which allowed Moses such access to God – indeed, Moses is quite unique even with respect to the later prophets. Rather, Moses was able to speak to God face-to-face, and stand between the Lord and the nation, because God had chosen him to do just this (Ex. 3:1–4:17).

Johansson begins his study of Jewish views on intercession by observing that OT religion never commanded individual intercession as a part of general piety because this was seen to be the role of specially chosen, pious men.[17] As true as this observation may be, it does not answer the prior question of *why* this should be the case. J. Jeremias suggests a solution when he differentiates between "petition" (Fürbitte) and "intercession" (Fürsprache).[18] The former concerns general requests for oneself as well as others, and is the right of everyone; the latter invariably concerns averting the wrath of God and so is reserved for those chosen men of God whom the Lord has appointed to the proper mediatorial position. Scharbert would modify this further by observing that generally such intercession is offered only on behalf of Israel.[19]

In broad terms these observations would appear to be correct. Generally, the intercession of such figures does primarily concern the judgment of God. Even though the prayer of Solomon may be seen to deal with many other contingencies as well, and so might be claimed as an exception, it too is largely concerned with averting future punishment. Likewise, the beneficiary of such prayers is primarily Israel. Again, one might want to argue that Abraham's prayer for Sodom and Gomorrah is an important exception. But, aside from the fact that there is not yet an Israel to pray for in Gen. 18, even here it is very likely that it is Abraham's concern for his own relatives, Lot and his family, which motivates his anxious intercessions with God.[20] In short, there would appear to be a pattern in the OT of God selecting certain individuals to play a mediatorial role between himself and his covenant people. This particularly suited them to intercede on the people's behalf in those situations where God had decided to punish sin. While R. Le Déaut has suggested that this function was orginally limited to official figures

---

[16] See Johansson, *Parakletoi*, pp. 5–11; A. Oepke, "μεσίτης," *TDNT*. vol. IV, pp. 611f; Scharbert, *Heilsmittler*, pp. 82–89.

[17] Johansson, *Parakletoi*, p. 3.

[18] J. Jeremias, *Heiligengräber in Jesu Umwelt (Mt. 23,29; Lk. 11,47): Eine Untersuchung zur Volksreligion der Zeit Jesu*. (Göttingen, 1958), p. 134.

[19] Scharbert, *Heilsmittler*, p. 154.

[20] See Scharbert, "Die Fürbitte," pp. 324f.

such as king, priest or prophet, and then expanded to include certain pious individuals,[21] it would appear more likely to have developed in exactly the opposite direction. The task which was originally unique to certain select individuals, such as the patriarchs, Moses, or certain of the prophets, was eventually expanded to include particular official figures, not because of their office *per se*, but because they too had been chosen by God for this task.[22]

However, the OT did not develop the place of human prayers to include heavenly intercession. The post-exilic literature contains the idea of angelic, heavenly intercession (Zech. 1:12; 3:1–10) as does the book of Job (16:19–22; 19:25; 33:23–28).[23] But the only passages containing possible references to human intercessors are Is. 63:16 and Jer. 15:1. While some have maintained that the former describes the heavenly intercession of Abraham and Jacob,[24] this is not the obvious meaning of the text and would appear unlikely.[25] Targum Jonathan certainly does not understand Is. 63:16 in this way, which is significant given the place occupied by the intercessions of deceased patriarchs elsewhere in the targumic literature (see below).[26]

Jer. 15:1 might be read to mean that Moses and Samuel were interceding for Israel in heaven, but it seems more natural to take this as a reference to the theoretical possibility that even if Israel's two greatest historical intercessors (note the same combination in Ps. 99:6) were alive and praying in Jeremiah's day, they could not avert the punishment which God was sending upon Israel.[27] This is the interpretation placed upon the verse in III En. 48A:5ff. The passage is intended to supplement those texts in which God tells Jeremiah of the futility of his own prayers for Israel. Consequently, while the OT describes men who intercede for Israel on the earth, and angels who pray for men in heaven, there are no examples of exalted men praying for Israel in heaven, which is not surprising given the

---

[21] Le Déaut, "Aspects de l'Intercession," p. 36.

[22] Cf. Hertzberg, "Propheten Fürbitter?," p. 67, who quotes F. Hesse: "... die Fürbitte ist das Amt des machtbegabten Gottesmannes."

[23] For a thorough study of the Job texts, arguing for references to an angelic intercessor, see N. Habel, *The Book of Job*, (London, 1985), pp. 274–276, 305ff, 469f; also Johnstone, *Paraclete*, pp. 96f, 100–102 on the meaning of *melitz*. On angelic intercession see Johansson, *Parakletoi*, pp. 22f, 33–39, 75–95; Le Déaut, "Aspects de l'Intercession," pp. 38f.

[24] G. W. Wade, *Isaiah*, (London, 1911), p. 401; Obeng, *Romans 8:26f*, p. 14.

[25] For more likely alternative interpretations see J. Smart, *History and Theology in Second Isaiah: A Commentary on Isaiah 35, 40–66*, (Philadelphia, 1965), pp. 269f; E. Achtemeier, *The Community and Message of Isaiah 56–66*, (Minneapolis, 1982), p. 116; J. Calvin, *Commentary on Isaiah*, vol. III, (Grand Rapids, 1984), pp. 354f, argues that this verse actually opposes the idea of heavenly intercessors.

[26] The targum reads: "For you are he whose mercies upon us are more than a father's upon son's, for Abraham did not take us up from Egypt and Israel did not do wonders for us in the wilderness..." See B. Chilton, *The Isaiah Targum: Introduction, Translation, Apparatus and Notes*, (Edinburgh, 1987), p. 121; for the Aramaic text see J. F. Stenning, *The Targum of Isaiah*, (Oxford, 1949).

[27] Thompson, *Jeremiah*, p. 387; McKane, *Jeremiah*, p. 334.

absence of any idea in the OT of exalted men residing in heaven for any reason whatsoever.

In conclusion, it is seen that the OT knows of special, chosen men who have been appointed by God to intercede on behalf of the covenant people in times of special need, but particularly at moments of impending judgment. These men have access to God which seems to be denied other men. Not only do they plead uniquely on behalf of others, but they may also be the recipients of special revelations from God, ie. Abraham's receipt of the covenantal promises, Moses' experiences on Mt. Sinai and in the Tent of Meeting, the visions of Isaiah and Jeremiah.

## 8.2 The Apocrypha and Pseudepigrapha[28]

There is considerable development in the ideas concerning human intercession from the OT to the inter-testamental literature.[29] Firstly, the circle of those who are said to offer intercessory prayers is widened. Secondly, these prayers are no longer strictly concerned with judicial situations. Thirdly, the piety of the pray-er now becomes a key to their success.[30] Fourthly, exalted human figures now appear as heavenly intercessors. With respect to the first two points, however, it must be said that the circle of these heavenly figures remains restricted, as would be expected, and the attention of their prayers continues to be focused upon judicial concerns. The relationship between their earthly piety and heavenly status is not always made explicit and will need to be investigated as the study progresses.

### 8.2.1 The Development of Earthly Intercession

A trend which is especially frequent in the inter-testamental literature is the attribution of intercessory prayers to OT figures which are not to be found in the OT itself. In addition to Moses (Jub. 1:19–22), Jacob (T. Reub. 1:7; 4:4; T. Gad 5:9; T. Ben. 3:6; 10:1), Levi (T. Naph. 6:8f), Noah (Jub. 9:3–6; 10:3),[31] Baruch (II

---

[28] The following discussion of extra-biblical literature will include works which are manifestly post-Christian. This is done to give the reader some idea of how Luke-Acts relates to later theological developments as well as earlier. At no point, however, do the arguments of the present study depend upon ideas contained only in this later material.

[29] For a discussion of this development see Johansson, *Parakletoi*, pp. 68–72; Le Déaut, "Aspects de l'Intercession," pp. 40–48.

[30] See the examples of Le Déaut, "Aspects de l'Intercession," p. 50.

[31] Jubilees is generally dated from at least the early 2nd century B.C.; see Charlesworth, *Pseudepigrapha*, vol. II, pp. 43f; E. Schürer, *The History of the Jewish People in the Age of Jesus Christ*, vol. III.1, (Edinburgh, 1986), p. 311. Some, such as M. Stone, *Scriptures, Sects and Visions*, (Philadelphia, 1980), p. 60, would date it to the 3rd century B.C.

Bar. 2:1; 48:1–24; IV Bar. 7:24, 32),[32] Mordecai (Add. Esth. 13:8–17),[33] Esther (Add. Esth. 14:3–19), and even Adam and Eve (LAE [Vita] 20:3; 21:2; 40:2–43:3, including Seth; [Apoc] 31:4)[34] are all discussed in haggadic fashion as having offered intercession at some crucial point in their lives. Furthermore, such intercessory efforts were extended to extra-biblical characters as well, such as Judith (Jud. 8:31; 9:2–14; 11:17; 12:8),[35] and Sedrach (Ap. Sedr. 7:3; 12:2–13:6; 14:2; 16:1–7).[36]

The extent to which successful intercession had also become an element of true leadership is seen in the regularity with which it occurs in the history of the Maccabees (I Macc. 4:30–33; 7:41f; 11:71; II Macc. 11:6ff; 12:36, 43–45; 13:10–12; 15:22–24)[37] and the descriptions of the pre-Hasmonean high priests (II Macc. 3:1, 16f, 31–33; III Macc. 6:1–15; IV Macc. 4:13f).[38] These prayers concern a wide variety of situations, from military conquest to the alleviation of labour pains, and illustrate a two-fold development in inter-testamental thinking which is not without its tensions. For, on the one hand, intercession has become more egalitarian; more people are able to offer such prayers and they are offered for a wider variety of reasons. But, on the other hand, the idea is also strongly maintained that efficacious intercession is the work of special leaders; at least, it is the demonstration that God has selected a person for such a task.

As was mentioned earlier, personal piety also becomes a characteristic of successful intercession in this life. II Bar. 85:1f accounts for the efficacy of the intercessions of the OT saints by their righteousness. The life of Onias the high priest is explained in these terms as well (II Macc. 3:1–33; also cf. I En. 63:1–5; IV Ezra 8:26f; IV Bar. 7:23; III En. 48:5; James 5:16 for further instances).[39] And in an era when the ultimate expression of religious commitment could easily become martyrdom, it should not be surprising to find that martyrs too could now intercede on behalf of the people (II Macc. 7:37f; IV Macc. 6:28f; IV Ezra 8:27). Once again it is the martyred priest Onias (II Macc. 4:33–38) who exemplifies the

---

[32] A. F. J. Klijn dates the final recension of II Baruch from the early 2nd century A.D., although parallels with Pseudo-Philo, IV Ezra and I Enoch indicate the incorporation of much earlier materials; see Charlesworth, *Pseudepigrapha*, vol. I, pp. 616f, 619f.

[33] The Additions to the Book of Esther date from at least the end of the 2nd century B.C.; see B. Metzger, *The Apocrypha of the Old Testament*, (New York, 1965), p. 96.

[34] M. D. Johnson dates the final recension of the Life of Adam and Eve from the end of the 1st century A.D.; see Charlesworth, *Pseudepigrapha*, p. 252.

[35] The book of Judith dates from the middle to the end of the 2nd century B.C.; see Metzger, *Apocrypha*, p. 76; Schürer, *History*, vol. III.1, pp. 218f.

[36] S. Agourides maintains that the Apocalypse of Sedrach, while dating itself from 100–400 A.D., contains Jewish material originating from a much earlier period; see Charlesworth, *Pseudepigrapha*, vol, I, pp. 606, especially n. 4.

[37] I and II Maccabees date from the mid to late 2nd century B.C., and the 1st century B.C., respectively; see Metzger, *Apocrypha*, pp. 221, 263; Schürer, *History*, vol. III.1, p. 181.

[38] III and IV Maccabees were both composed before the destruction of the second temple, and may be as early as the mid 2nd century B.C. and late 1st B.C., respectively; see Charlesworth, *Pseudepigrapha*, pp. 510–512, 533f; Schürer, *History*, vol. III.1, pp. 539, 591.

[39] Le Déaut, "Aspects de l'Intercession," p. 50. Also see A. Büchler, *Types of Jewish-Palestinian Piety from 10 B.C.E. to 70 C.E.: The Ancient Pious Men*, (London, 1922), pp. 260ff.

most extensive development of this concept, when he is seen to be interceding for Jerusalem from heaven (II Macc. 15:12–16).


## 8.2.2 Intercession in This Life and in Heaven

The circle of those who exercise heavenly intercession is not opened as widely as that of earthly intercession. But, of course, given the complete absence of such ideas in the OT any development at all in this area is significant. It would be helpful at this point to see who is able to occupy such a role,[40] and make some attempt at unravelling why they are selected for the task. Specifically, is there any relationship between those prayers offered in life and those offered in heaven?


### 8.2.2.1 Abraham and Other Patriarchs

The patriarchs are all described as interceding before God in heaven. Ap. Zeph. 11:1–6 portrays not only Abraham, Isaac and Jacob, but also a "multitude of the righteous", praying for the souls of those in torment.[41] Similarly, III En. 44:7 describes the souls of Abraham, Isaac and Jacob praying for Israel,[42] and the T. Abr. has the patriarch pray both on the earth and during his translated, visionary state (albeit, before he actually dies) for his own deceased servants as well as other sinners, asking that they be restored to life and saved from judgment, respectively ([A] 14:5–15; 18:9–11; cf. [B] 12:1–12; 14:6).[43]

It is not difficult to see why the patriarchs would be selected for such development. As the fathers of the nation they would be key candidates for any representative or mediatorial positions. But the quality of their lives also plays a part in their elevation to such a status, as the description of "the righteous" in Ap. Zeph. indicates (also, in I En. 39:5 it is the "holy ones" who intercede). Abraham especially becomes the subject of a great deal of early hagiographa. He is extolled for his wisdom and righteousness, but especially for his youthful rejection of

---

[40] For a good introduction to the phenomenon of the exaltation of OT figures in the pseudepigrapha and a discussion of the chief characters involved see, D. S. Russell, *The Old Testament Pseudepigrapha: Patriarchs and Prophets in Early Judaism*, (London, 1987).

[41] The Apocalypse of Zephaniah is dated from between 100 B.C. and 175 A.D. O. S. Wintermute argues that it can be no later than 70 A.D.; see Charlesworth, *Pseudepigrapha*, vol. I, pp. 500f.

[42] P. Alexander and the editors of Schürer argue for a 5th–6th century A.D. date for III Enoch; see Charlesworth, *Pseudepigrapha*, vol. I, pp. 225–229; Schürer, *History*, vol. III.1, p. 274. Odeberg's classic study defends a date from the 2nd half of the 3rd century A.D.; see *III Enoch*, pp. 38–41. In either case, the presence of merkabah-like traits in some of the Qumran literature, together with the similarities to earlier apocalyptic works such as I En. and Ap. Zeph. indicates that much older material is to be found in the work; cf. Stone, *Scripture*, p. 33.

[43] E. P. Sanders dates the Testament of Abraham to approximately 100 A.D.; see Charlesworth, *Pseudepigrapha*, vol. I, pp. 874f.

idolatry (Jub. 11:16–24; 12:1–8, 12–14; Sir. 44:19; PsPhil. 6:1–18).[44] This elevation of Abraham's piety concerns the general quality of his life, and there is no
particular connection made in this literature between his heavenly intercession and
his prayer-life on earth specifically, even though each is discussed in a work such as
the T. Abr. Later works, however, such as the T. Isaac and the T. Jacob, which
contain a significant amount of Christian interpolation, not only portray heavenly
intercession for sinners as a regular part of the patriarchs' task (T. Is. 1:3; T. Jac. 1:3;
7:11), but also directly connect the efficacy of such heavenly work with the
devotion to prayer exhibited by these men during their lives on earth (T. Jac. 1:9;
7:21, 27; 8:3).[45]

### 8.2.2.2 The Prophets

The OT prophets continue to be seen as powerful intercessors, and in some places
intercessory prayer continues to be one of the distinctive activities of their ministry (II Bar. 84:10–85:3, 12; IV Bar. 1:2; 2:3; 7:24, 32; PsPhil. 64:2). However, it is
also important to notice that the same selective emphasis remains in the inter-
testamental literature, with regards to the prophets, as is found in the OT. Only
those figures are exalted as intercessors who are specifically presented as such in the
OT, men such as Samuel, Jeremiah and Isaiah. This is especially noticeable in a
work of hagiographa such as the Lives of the Prophets.[46] In this collection several
prophets are mentioned as having been efficacious intercessors during their lives:
Isaiah (1:2f, 8), Jeremiah (2:3), Ezekiel (3:10), Daniel (4:4, 12), Elijah (21:4f, 7, 9),
and Elisha (22:9, 11, 15). However, even though there are haggadic expansions in
the stories of most of the prophets' lives, there are no accounts of individuals
praying who were not already described as powerful pray-ers in the OT. When
other prophets are mentioned (and there are many) it is without any reference to
prayer whatsoever, and of those who did pray on the earth only two are believed
to have been exalted as heavenly intercessors. Thus, according to LivPro. 1:2f, 8,
the continuity of Jerusalem's water supply is the result of Isaiah's ongoing prayers

---

[44] The book of Sirach dates from the early to mid 2nd century B.C.; see Metzger, Apocrypha, p.
128; Schürer, History, vol. III.1, p. 202. Pseudo-Philo, also known as the Biblical Antiquities
(often referred to by the Latin title Liber Antiquitatum Biblicarum) is dated by D. J. Harrington
to the early 1st century A.D. The editors of Schürer maintain it is pre–70 A.D.; see Charlesworth,
Pseudepigrapha, vol. II, p. 299; Schürer, History, vol. III.1, p. 399.

[45] Both the Testaments of Isaac and Jacob seem to be modelled upon the earlier work the T.
Abr. W. R. Stinespring dates the T. Is. from the 2nd century A.D., and the T. Jac. from the 2nd to
3rd century A.D.; see Charlesworth, Pseudepigrapha, vol. I, pp. 903f, 913. The T. Jac. is the most
christianized of the two, including a reference to the intercessions of the saints and the Virgin
Mary on judgment day (8:8). This illustrates the close connection between Jewish ideas of
heavenly intercessors and the early Christian development of belief in the prayers of the saints.

[46] D. R. A. Hare maintains that the Lives of the Prophets be dated from the first quarter of the
1st century A.D.; see Charlesworth, Pseudepigrapha, vol. II, pp. 380f. Jeremias argues that despite
the Christian form of the final work the book is based upon early Palestinian tradition; Jeremias,
Heiligengraber, pp. 11f.

in heaven, and the efficacy of these prayers are directly related to the power of his prayers for the same thing during his life.

Jeremiah is also referred to as a powerful pray-er (2:3–19), and because of this not only does the soil from his grave-site continue to heal and protect people, but God made him Moses' "partner" so that "they are together to this day" (v. 19). In view of the traditions concerning Moses' heavenly intercession (see below), together with the fact that Moses and Jeremiah were buried quite separately, the idea of Jeremiah becoming Moses' "partner" suggests that Jeremiah now also occupies a role as heavenly intercessor, based upon the power of his prayers on earth. This would agree with the early tradition found in II Macc. 15:12–16, where Judas Maccabeus describes his vision of Jeremiah and Onias praying in heaven for Jerusalem. The connection between Onias' place in this vision and his life of piety has already been pointed out. Even though there is no similar connection made for Jeremiah in II Macc., it would seem likely that the OT tradition of his fervent prayers for Jerusalem, especially when read in conjunction with this tradition found in the LivPro., provides an adequate background to his appearance in Judas' vision.

Jeremias has argued that it is the fact that each of these prophets were believed to have been martyred that they were given such a role in LivPro.[47] However, while this is possible, it is not a connection explicitly made for any of them in that book, nor for Jeremiah in II Macc. In any case, even though the evidence is not abundant, it does appear that there was an early belief in special prophetic figures occupying the place of heavenly intercession for Israel, based upon the efficacy of their earthly prayer-lives, and perhaps also because they had been martyred.

### 8.2.2.3 Moses

Considering the importance given to Moses' earthly prayers for Israel in the OT, there is a surprising paucity of material in the pseudepigraphal literature allowing Moses any present intercessory role in heaven. One must look to the Samaritan and rabbinic literature in order to discover those sectors of ancient Judaism which elevated Moses to anything approaching the status of heavenly mediator/intercessor. Of course, Moses is greatly exalted in the pseudepigrapha, and there is much discussion concerning the place of intercession in Moses' leadership of Israel (Jub. 1:19–22; Sir. 45:1–5; PsPhil. 12:8–10; 19:3, 8f; T. Mos. 1:14; 11:11, 14, 17).[48] But there is very little to suggest that Moses prays now in heaven. T. Mos. 12:6 might

---

[47] Jeremias, *Heiligengräber*, p. 137.

[48] J. Priest dates the Testament of Moses from the end of the 1st century B.C. to the beginning of the 1st century A.D. Nickelsburg, however, followed by those such as Carlson and the editors of Schürer date the body of this document from the period of the Maccabean revolt (mid 2nd century B.C.) with later additions made towards the end of the reign of Herod the Great; see Charlesworth, *Pseudepigrapha*, vol. I, pp. 920f; Carlson, "Angelic Mediation," p. 85, especially nn. 2–3; Schürer, *History*, vol. III.1, pp. 281–283.

contain such teaching,[49] but the text is extremely uncertain and even Priest's suggested reconstruction is ambiguous is this regard.[50] The fact is that much of the material which exalts Moses' earthly status also contains a strain of thought implicitly denying any continuing intercessory role to him, something which is also encountered in both the targumic and rabbinic materials (and will be discussed more extensively below).

The only extant passage which clearly suggests that Moses might offer heavenly intercession is III En. 15B:2–5. Here Moses' ascent up Mt. Sinai for the reception of the Law is interpreted in the typically rabbinic fashion as an heavenly ascent. During his time in heaven Moses not only receives the Torah, but also prays for Israel. He also learns that Israel has 1,800,000 special angelic advocates and that Metatron is given particular responsibility for answering his prayers. That such a tradition should occur in III En. is hardly surprising, given the rabbinic affinities of this work and the recurrence of the idea of Moses' "heavenly ascent" in both rabbinic and merkabah literature (see below).

### 8.2.2.4 Enoch

The single most important exalted intercessor in the inter-testamental literature is Enoch. Why certain circles should have exalted him to a position which is nowhere enjoyed by Moses in comparable literature is an interesting question, and thankfully the progress of this study need not depend upon its answer.[51]

The character of Enoch is greatly extolled at a very early date in Jewish literature. He is the premier righteous man who is translated to heaven as the archetype of repentance for all future generations (Sir. 44:16; 49:14). He is a wise prophet, a visionary, skilled in the arts of literature and astrology; he has been given access to the divine secrets and elected to serve as the eternal scribe for the day of judgment (Jub. 4:17–19, 21–24; 7:38; 19:24–27; 21:10; T. Abr. [B] 11:3f; Pseudo-Eupolemus 8).[52]

---

[49] So W. Meeks, *The Prophet-King: Moses Traditions and the Johannine Christolgy*, (Leiden, 1967), p. 160.

[50] Charlesworth, *Pseudepigrapha*, vol. I, p. 934 n. c.

[51] See P. Davis, "The mythic Enoch: New light on early christology," *SR*. 13 ('84) 340f for a discussion of this issue. He suggests that Jubilees is attempting to harmonize these two circles of tradition, Moses being presented as the restorer of the ancient wisdom revealed to Enoch (cf. 1:14; 4:17; 7:38f; 21:10).The challenge facing any attempted answer is the lack of any Mosaic development in the pseudepigrapha comparable to that undergone by Enoch. The exaltation of Moses takes place in the Samaritan and rabbinic materials, and how these circles interrelate with those which produced the other inter-testamental literature is a question which touches upon the darkest recesses of our ignorance concerning the complex nature of ancient Judaism.

[52] This fragment of Pseudo-Eupolemus is preserved in Eusebius' *Praeparatio Evangelica*, 9.17.8. R. Doran argues that it in fact comes from the authentic Eupolemus whose works are known from the Greek historian Alexander Polyhistor, who wrote during the mid 1st century B.C. Therefore, Pseudo-Eupolemus' account of Enoch as the discoverer of astrology must date from sometime before Alexander Polyhistor; see Charlesworth, *Pseudepigrapha*, vol. II, pp. 861–863, 873–878. The editors of Schürer date it even earlier; *History*, vol. III.1, p. 529f.

Whatever the origins of these Enoch-legends,[53] they appear to be attempts at explaining the OT account which (at least) implies that he was spared from death and translated to heaven because of his exceptional righteousness ("he walked with God"; Gen. 5:21–24). These inter-testamental legends endorse this logic and seek to flesh out the bare statements of the biblical account. But they also go beyond it. For not only must Enoch have been exceptionally righteous in order to enjoy such exceptional treatment by God, he must also have been chosen for an exceptional task in order for God to miraculously elevate him into heaven. And what might this task be? He becomes the heavenly scribe. And his selection for this office not only makes him the great witness at the final judgment – for his books will contain the records of everyone's good and evil deeds, which in turn will constitute the evidence upon which they will be judged – but it also makes him the great heavenly intercessor. For Enoch's records of good works form the only basis upon which any individual might appeal to God; consequently, as scribe Enoch stands between God and all those who would approach him. This is illustrated early on in I En. when the fallen angels ask Enoch to pray for them; he includes his prayers for them in his books (I En. 13:4, 6; 14:4) and is explicitly called their "intercessor" (I En. 15:2; 16:3).[54] Noah also prays to Enoch, asking about the fate of the world, and Enoch comes to him from heaven in order to answer his prayer, having now read all of the heavenly books concerning the future (I En. 65:2–5; 81:1–3; 106:19).

Although most of Enoch's intercession takes place during his temporary translation, this heavenly work and his earthly prayers appear to be extensions of one another. Thus after seeing a vision of the final judgment, he returns temporarily to earth and intercedes for all mankind, a prayer which he then writes down (I En. 83:5f, 10; cf. 89:76; 90:14–17). Enoch intercedes wherever he may be, whether in heaven or on earth. Therefore, the relationship pertaining between the two activities may be more that of habituated expressions of piety, rather than pious qualifications for a heavenly task.

The writings of II and III En. develop these aspects of Enoch's ministry even further. Whereas I En. only implies what Enoch's eternal status will be on the basis of that which is revealed during his translation/visions, II En. explicitly describes him as the eternal scribe and intercessor who is "forever in God's presence" (II En. 7:4f; 18:7; 21:3; 22:6; 24:1; 36:3 [A]; 64:5 [J]; 67:2). He is the eternal mediator (II

---

[53] According to H. Odeberg, Gen. 5:21–24 indicates that such Enoch traditions were already in circulation; see "'Ενώχ" TDNT. vol. II, pp. 556–558. T. Glasson (Greek Influence in Jewish Eschatology, [London, 1961], pp. 8–11) has argued for Greek influence in these legends, while Stone (Scriptures, pp. 39f) maintains that they result from Mesopotamian influences; cf. Bietenhard, Himmlische Welt, pp. 143–160; J. Bowker, The Targums and Rabbinic Literature: An Introduction to Jewish Interpretations of Scripture, (Cambridge, 1969), pp. 143–147.

[54] Based upon the fragments discovered at Qumran, J. T. Milik dates the books of I Enoch, excluding the Similitudes (chapters 37–71), from the early 2nd century B.C. to the last 3rd of the 1st century B.C.; see The Books of Enoch, Aramaic Fragments of Qumran Cave 4, (Oxford, 1976), pp. 5f. F. I. Anderson dates II En. to the late 1st century A.D.; see Charlesworth, Pseudepigrapha, vol. I, pp. 91, 94–97.

En. 33:10 [J]) or intercessor ([A]) who is equated with the archangel Michael; but even more remarkably, he is endowed with the power to thereby take away the sin of the world (II En. 64:5 [J]). The highest point of development is reached in III En. where Enoch is transfigured into Metatron, the prince of all the angels, who is also called the "lesser Yahweh" (see III En. 4:2f, 9; 10:3f; 11:1f; 12:5; 14:2; 48C:7).

The Enoch literature presents a reasonably coherent picture of one who is endowed with exceptional character and sees intercessory prayer as an important part of his life's task. He is then translated to heaven, made privy to the secrets of the ages and installed as the world's heavenly intercessor. Admittedly, the exact nature of the connection between Enoch's life on earth and his office in heaven is not made as explicitly as has been found elsewhere. But it would seem most likely that the legendary developments about his character, including a passage such as I En. 83:10 where Enoch intercedes for the world, are most easily explained as an effort to provide just such a causal explanation for why he, of all people, was chosen to be God's scribal-intercessor.

## 8.2.2.5 Conflicting Opinions

Despite the growth of this belief in exalted heavenly intercessors during the inter-testamental period, it was not an innovation which found universal acceptance. Whether or not the development of this idea sprang from an increasing sense of God's remoteness, as some have claimed,[55] there apparently were others who felt that such human intercessors were a dangerous development. Their hesitations probably arose from the suspicion that such figures, at the very least, would serve to widen any gap felt between an individual and his God; while, at the very worst, they could easily be mistaken for divine figures themselves, competing with God for the attention due only to him. Certainly, a redactor of III En. sensed this danger when he included chapter 16, recounting the dethronement and fiery lashing of Metatron after he is mistaken for a second divine power in heaven.[56]

The earlier literature is not as polemical as this, but often makes it clear nonetheless that there are no human intercessors in heaven by lamenting the passing of effective intercessors from the earth. Thus at the end of the T. Mos., Joshua expresses his fears for Israel's safety once the surrounding nations hear that Moses is dead and his prayers are no longer able to protect them:

... there is now no advocate for them who will bear messages to the Lord on their behalf in the way that Moses was the great messenger. (11:17)

---

[55] For example see N. Johnson, *Prayer in the Apocrypha and Pseudepigrapha: A Study of the Jewish Concept of God,* (Philadelphia, 1948), pp. 51f; O. Betz, *Der Paraklet: Fürsprecher im häretischen Spätjudentum, im Johannes-Evangelium und im neu gefundenen gnostischen Schriften,* (Leiden, 1963), p. 82.

[56] Cf. Charlesworth, *Pseudepigrapha,* vol. I, p. 268, nn. a, e, g. Also see the discussion of b. Hag. 15b and the controversy over the "two powers" heresy in the rabbinic literature below. For more discussion on the ambivalence towards human intercessors see D. R. de Lacey, " Jesus as Mediator," *JSNT.* 29 ('87) 109; Le Déaut, "Aspects de l'Intercession," p. 51

Such fears make it clear that there is no belief in Moses' continuing prayers for Israel from heaven.

The same line of thought recurs elsewhere. In PsPhil. 19:3 the entire nation repeats these fears about Moses' death; in PsPhil. 19:8f Moses expresses them himself. The Philistines say the same thing after the death of Samuel in PsPhil. 64:2; and, as will be seen, some of the rabbis were also known to use this line of argument in their own discussions about Moses. It is not surprising then that III En. 48A:5–8, in an explicit exposition of Jer. 15:1, laments that the era of great intercessors such as Moses and Samuel lies in the past so that Israel is without anyone to pray for them effectively. II Bar. 85:1–3 also makes it clear that the time of powerful intercessors is a bygone era; they once intervened with God, but "now the righteous have been assembled and the prophets are sleeping," and they evidently do not continue their work in heaven.

Thus there was an important tension in the theological development of inter-testamental Judaism, a tension which was never fully reconciled even within the later rabbis (see below). Some, undoubtedly for various reasons, continued to maintain the OT position denying the possibility of exalted, human intercessors in heaven. But alongside this conservatism existed, sometimes simultaneously in the same works, the new, developing hope of human intercessors, who had not only been elevated to this status through their piety, but were also able to empathise with the individual because of their shared humanity.

### 8.2.2.6 Is Heavenly Intercession Always Effective?

Having presented the evidence of conflicting opinions concerning heavenly inter-cession in the pseudepigrapha, it is now time to add a proviso to the effect that this opposition to human, heavenly intercession is not as extensive as is often main-tained. It is common, for example, to read that such passages as II En. 53:1f; PsPhil. 33:5; IV Ezra 7:102ff; II Bar. 85:12 all explicitly combat the idea of human intercession in heaven.[57] However, this is to misunderstand an entire category of passages which are not combating human intercession *per se*, but are attempting to maintain the OT conviction that another's prayers cannot eradicate the judgment which must fall upon unrepentant sinners.[58]

The most frequently quoted text in this regard is II En. 53:1–2:

So now, my children, do not say, "Our father is with God, and he will stand in front of God for us, and he will pray for us concerning our sins." For there is no helper there – not even for any one person who has sinned.

The scene envisaged in this passage is the last judgment where Enoch's records of

---

[57] Andersen, in Charlesworth, *Pseudepigrapha*, vol. I, p. 96; Le Déaut, "Aspects de l'Interces-sion," pp. 44f; W. O. E. Oesterley, *The Jews and Judaism During the Greek Period: The Background of Christianity*, (London, 1941), p. 173; H. Wicks, *The Doctrine of God in the Jewish Apocryphal and Apocalyptic Literature*, (London, 1915), p. 329; Longenecker, *Christology*, p. 29.

[58] According to J. W. Bowker, this tension continues to be reflected in the Koran; see "Interces-sion in the Qur'an and the Jewish Tradition," *JSS.* 11 ('66) 69–82.

the sins committed by the unrighteous will serve to condemn them to hell. The point of Enoch's warning is that no prayer offered by another may amend an evil life, nor negate God's just punishment. That may only be done through an individual's own repentance and reformation before the moment of judgment arrives. Once the final judgment begins it is too late for appeasement.

Similarly, in PsPhil. 33:4–5, while contemplating their uncertain future after the death of Deborah, Israel asks her to pray for them "and after your departure your soul will be mindful of us forever." However, Deborah replies that a person may only pray for himself or others while still alive, "after his end he cannot pray or be mindful of anyone. Therefore, do not hope in your fathers. For they will not profit you at all unless you be found like them."

Admittedly, the exact line of thought in this passage is not easy to sort out. If it is intended to disclaim any ideas of human intercession, it may be due to the author's view of the after-life rather than any prejudice against heavenly intercession itself. The story of Saul and the witch of Endor (PsPhil. 64) indicates that the dead were thought to remain in an intermediate state of "soul sleep" until the final judgment, so that an ongoing ministry of intercession would have been impossible. In any event, there is the strong appeal not to let the hope of another's intercession distract one from the obligations of personal righteousness. One's only hope is "to be found" like the righteous fathers. That this is the burden of the passage is also suggested by an earlier text where Israel has rebelled against God by refusing to enter into Canaan (PsPhil. 15:5). God extracts his judgment by commanding Israel's guardian angels to cease their intercessions. There is a belief in angelic intercession, but as in II En., no one's prayers may undo the need to punish the sins of the unrepentant.

Consequently, it is faithfulness to the words of Eli (I Sam. 2:25) which give rise to this line of thought in the apocrypha and pseudepigrapha. Wisdom 12:12 asks, "Who will come before thee to plead as an advocate for unrighteous men?"[59] So, when in Jub. 1:19–22 Moses himself asks God to save Israel from their sin, avoiding the need for future punishment, God replies that Israel must be punished until they repent (vv. 22ff; similarly, II Bar. 48:26–41; 85:12; III En. 44:9f; LAE [Vita] 40:2–43:3).

But the most thorough, self-conscious development of this theme is found in IV Ezra.[60] Ezra states the issues involved quite explicitly and assumes his self-appointed task of interceding for the sinners of the world precisely because of the finality of God's judgment. Thus Ezra inquires about the fate of those sinners for

---

[59] The Wisdom of Solomon is dated from 200 B.C. to the mid 1st century A.D.; see Metzger, *Apocrypha*, p. 102; Schürer, *History*, vol. III.1, pp. 572f.

[60] It is generally accepted that IV Ezra dates from the end of the 1st century A.D., perhaps near the close of Domitian's reign (A.D. 81–96); see Charlesworth, *Pseudepigrapha*, vol. I, pp. 520–522; Schürer, *History*, vol. III.1, p. 300. However, it seems dubious to maintain that the author's wrestling over issues of theodicy arose *ex nihilo* out of the disaster in A.D. 70. This was not the first time in Israel's history that the Jews had to come to terms with the destruction of Jerusalem.

whom he prays and asks whether the righteous may intercede for the ungodly on the judgment day (7:46, 102f). God replies that "no one shall ever pray for another on that day, neither shall anyone lay a burden on another, for then everyone shall bear his own righteousness or unrighteousness" (7:105). When Ezra then asks how the OT saints could have prayed for the living the answer is that they operated prior to the final judgment (7:112–115; cf. IV Bar. 2:3); consequently, Ezra takes up his task to intercede for the world while there is still some hope of repentance (8:17, 19–36, 37–40; 12:48; 13:14). However, even then God reminds him that his prayers will not benefit those who finally refuse to turn from their sins (8:41). As a result of his commitment to pray for sinners, God promises to take Ezra into heaven to be with his son; although, significantly, there is no suggestion that he will continue his intercession from there (also cf. the later Ezra literature: Grk Ap. Ezra 1:6, 10ff; 2:2–7, 31; 7:13; Vis. Ezra 18; Quest. Ezra 7).

Perhaps this line of thought also explains why the book of Jubilees omits any mention of Abraham's intercession for Sodom and Gomorrah (Jub. 16:5f). The fate of those two cities was used from an early date as a picture of God's final judgment upon the unrepentant (Jub. 16:6; Mt. 10:15 par; II Peter 2:6; Jude 7). Thus, within this frame of reference, Abraham's prayers would have been inappropriate.

Consequently, it appears that there was a conservative element in the pseudepigraphal literature which resisted the idea of human intercession, but it was not as thoroughgoing as is often maintained. Rather, it was a complementary concern for another point of OT theology, that is the immutable justice of God which gave rise, not to scepticism about intercession itself, but to the affirmation of individual responsibility to the demands of righteousness.

However, as always seems to be the case with the inter-testamental literature, there appears to be a conflicting line of thought on this point as well! It is rather later, and much less developed, but there is also the idea that the intercessions of a righteous man *can* save a sinner from punishment. Thus in T. Abr. (A) 14:10–15 Abraham prays that God would save a group of "sinners" from judgment, and on the basis of Abraham's prayer alone they are received into heaven. However, it is possible that this is a special case since Abraham is simply rectifying the results of the impetuous condemnations which he had brought upon these people earlier until God, in his greater mercy, intervened to stop him (T. Abr. [A] 10:4–15).

A more relevant text may be T. Abr. (A) 14:5–9. Here Abraham prays for those whose sins and righteousness are evenly balanced at the judgment, and on the basis of this intercession God accepts them, although it is noteworthy that they do possess a measure of righteousness of their own. They are not abject sinners saved by Abraham's prayers. Once again it is the T. Jac. which institutionalises this role of the patriarchs. There the patriarchs (together with the virgin Mary and all the saints) do intercede for sinners to save them from hell (7:11, 21; 8:8).

These conflicting lines of thought form a complex picture of theological development in inter-testamental Judaism. Since there is no systematic attempt to harmonise them it is difficult to know how any one individual would have conceived of the idea of exalted heavenly intercessors. The different attitudes undoubtedly express the conflicting opinions of different circles within Judaism, although this does not explain how the opposing views can coexist (as they sometimes do) within the same pieces of literature. However, it is clear that there was a growing, if not universally accepted, belief in the existence of archetypical, pious men from the past, known for the efficacy of their prayer-lives, who had been elevated to the status of heavenly intercessors. Sometimes they prayed permanently in heaven; at other times it was only a temporary station adopted during their translation to heaven. Sometimes they interceded only for Israel; more often they prayed for sinners and Gentiles as well. This latter perspective is especially true in those works where the possibility of that moral complacency which may result from a misplaced confidence in covenantal privileges is combated by an emphasis upon the universality of human sin. Occasionally this intercession had a role to play in the final judgment, but usually it could only hope to effect repentance before the Judge had made his final decisions.

# 8.3 The Targums

The dating of the targumic materials and the nature of the relationships existing between their various circles of tradition are difficult issues which have yet to be settled by a universal consensus of opinion. Without going into a detailed study of these questions, it will be enough for the present purposes to notice that all of the midrashic elements in the targums pertaining to human intercession are paralleled in the apocryphal and pseudepigraphal literature which can be given a pre-Christian date with greater or lesser degrees of confidence.[61]

The proliferation of extra-biblical prayer notices in the targumic midrash continue, as was seen in the pseudepigrapha. Such additions may be found, to list just a few examples, concerning Abraham (Onkelos on Gen. 18:22),[62] Isaac (ps-

---

[61] For arguments that the Palestinian targums especially, and pseudo-Jonathan in particular, derive from pre-Christian tradition see A. Marmorstein, "Einige vorläufige Bemerkungen zu den neuentdeckten Fragmenten des jerusalemischen (palästinensischen) Targums," *ZAW.* 8 ('31) 234 f, 241 f; R. Le Déaut, *La Nuit Pascale: Essai sur la signification de la Pâque juive à partir du Targum d'Exode XII 42*, (Rome, 1963), pp. 41–65; Bowker, *Targums*, pp. 22–28; M. McNamara, *Targum and Testament: Aramaic Paraphrases of the Hebrew Bible, a Light on the New Testament*, (Shannon, 1972), pp. 81 f, 86–89, 175–186; *The New Testament and the Palestinian Targum to the Pentateuch*, (Rome, 1978), pp. 60–65. M. Klein, *The Fragment-Targums of the Pentateuch According to their Extant Sources*, vol. I, (Rome, 1980), pp. 23–26, is more hesitant about any date prior to the 2nd century, but admits that he can only comment on the present, extant form of the collections. Mc-Namara, *The New Testament*, p. 65, concludes by saying: "Since the western rabbis, by and large, appear to have interfered little with the (text of the Palestinian targum), it would follow that the present text of this targum has been faithfully transmitted from early, even pre-Christian, times."

[62] M. Aberbach, *Targum Onkelos to Genesis: A Critical Analysis Together with an English Translation of the Text*, (Denver, 1982), p. 110.

Jon. on Gen. 26:27–31),[63] but especially Moses (Onkelos, ps-Jon. and the targum fragments on Ex. 17;[64] Onkelos, ps-Jon. and Neofiti on Dt. 9:19 and 10:10).[65] While such additions may have served to strengthen the image of these leaders as great men of prayer, I. Drazin accounts for them as simply the elimination of anthropomorphisms which might suggest that God was man's peer.[66] But even if this had been the orginal motivation behind some of these additions, it can hardly serve to explain them all (the account of Ex. 17 for example), and does not necessarily negate what would have been their lasting effect in the minds of the people.

One of the most interesting instances of such prayer "additions" is found in targum Jon. on Is. 53, where in addition to the original mention of intercession in v. 12, the targum adds three other such notices in vv. 4, 7, 11 and gives the passage an explicitly messianic significance (v. 10).[67]

There is also an important strain in the targums which develops Moses' place as special mediator between God and the nation. According to Onkelos on Dt. 5:5 the people were so overwhelmed by the Lord's awesomeness that they were afraid to have dealings with him except through Moses.[68] This naturally meant that Moses filled an important role as intercessor, although it is interesting that the key OT passages illustrating this task (Ex. 32; Dt. 9) are not elaborated upon as fully as one might have expected, given the importance of Moses' position.[69] However, ps-Jon. on Dt. 34:5 does relate the tradition about Moses' heavenly ascent from

---

[63] J. W. Etheridge, *The Targums of Onkelos and Jonathan ben Uzziel on the Pentateuch with the Fragments of the Jerusalem Targum*, (New York, 1968), p. 245.

[64] Etheridge, *The Targums*, pp. 385, 502f; Klein, *The Fragment Targums*, vol. II, pp. 49, 131.

[65] I. Drazin, *Targum Onkelos to Deuteronomy: An English Translation of the Text with Analysis and Commentary*, (New York, 1982), p. 128; for both ps-Jon. and Neofiti see R. Le Déaut, *Targum du Pentateuque: Traduction des deux recensions palestiniennes complètes avec introduction, parallèles, notes et index*, vol. IV, (Paris, 1980), pp. 96f, 102f.

[66] Drazin, *Targum Onkelos*, pp. 129 n. 21, 133 n. 5.

[67] For a discussion of this passage see R. A. Aytoun, "The Servant of the Lord in the Targum," *JTS*. 23 ('22) 175f; P. Seidelin, "Der 'Ebed Jahwe' und die Messiasgestalt im Jesajatargum" *ZNW*. 35 ('36) 212, 215f; Mowinkel, *Cometh*, p. 332f; Le Déaut, "Aspects de l'Intercession," pp. 56f; S. Levey, *The Messiah: An Aramaic Interpretation, The Messianic Exegesis of the Targum*, (Cincinnati, 1974), pp. 63–67; Chilton, *The Aramaic Bible*, pp. 103–105. These alterations suggest the perspective found in b. Sot. 14a, where Is. 53:12 is interpreted with reference to Ex. 32:32. Later rabbinic interpretation of Is. 53 was to explicitly ascribe this work to Moses, as well as R. Akiba and the men of the Great Synagogue (cf. j. Shekalim 48c); see Moore, *Judaism*, vol. I, p. 229 n. 3; Le Déaut, "Aspects de l'Intercession," p. 57 (see n. 104 below).

[68] Etheridge, *The Targums*, p. 486; Drazin, *Targum Onkelos*, p. 98. This conviction that the greatness of God was the justification for Moses' status is something which also finds particular development in Philo (see below).

[69] The Mishnah (Meg. 4:10) lists a number of OT passages which were prohibited from being rendered into Aramaic in the targums, one of these being the second story of the Golden Calf (Ex. 32:21ff); see McNamara, *The New Testament*, pp. 46–49. Perhaps this lacunae in the targums is evidence for the early date of the mishnaic ruling; or, it may be the result of later rabbinic editing of the extant targum collections.

Mt. Sinai to receive the law, so that (by implication) the prayers recorded in Ex. 32 were made before God in heaven.[70]

An even more illuminating passage, preserved only by ps-Jon. (on Gen. 9:19), combines the importance of Moses' earthly intercession with the heavenly intercession of the patriarchs.[71] There the Lord tells Moses to stop his praying so that he might destroy the nation, at which point God unleashes five destroying angels against Israel. But when Moses heard this he continued his prayers and immediately "Abraham, Isaac and Jacob arose from their tomb, and stood in prayer before the Lord." Their intercessions restrained three of the angels so that by his continued prayers Moses could stop the remaining two.

This passage poses a number a interesting questions, not the least of which is how concretely such a story would have actually been envisaged. The idea of holy tombs is similar to that found in the LivPro. However, unlike the development there the patriarchs seem not to permanently reside as intercessors in heaven, but "arise" from the dead at times of special need. Their prayers are required to supplement Moses', but theirs are not as powerful as Moses', for they are able to stop only one angel each while Moses stops two!

Very similar ideas are found in a more ambiguous passage which will also serve to introduce a contrary line of thought opposed to the portrayal of Moses as Israel's special intercessor. Again, in a haggadic passage preserved only in ps-Jon. (on Dt. 28:15), after Moses has warned Israel of the penalty they must pay for breaking the covenant, cosmic tremors commence and the patriarchs cry out "from their sepulchres":[72]

"Woe to our children should they sin, and bring these maledictions upon them: for how will they bear them, lest destruction be executed on them and no merit of ours protect, and there be no man to stand and intercede on their behalf!" Then fell the Bath-Qol from the high heavens, and said, "Fear not, you fathers of the world; if the merit of all generations should fail, yours shall not . . ."

Once again, the patriarchs intercede from their graves in a moment of crisis. And, oddly enough, they repeat the argument which has already been seen in the pseudepigraphal literature, assuming the non-existence of heavenly intercessors. The answer which comes from heaven concerns the ongoing efficacy of the patriarch's merits, and so tacitly accepts their assumption that there is no human intercessor for Israel in heaven. How this aligns with the patriarchs' own appearance from the dead is probably found in the brevity of their showing; they do not pray like this regularly; nor is there any need to, for their past righteousness continues to prevail on behalf of the nation, even in this situation.

In league with a passage such as this is a tradition which serves to minimise even Moses' earthly role as intercessor for Israel. The entire Palestinian tradition (ps-Jon., the targum fragments, and Neofiti, all on Ex. 14:15) agrees that God

---

[70] Meeks, *Prophet-King*, pp. 191 f; Etheridge, *The Targums*, p. 683.

[71] Etheridge, *The Targums*, p. 589; Le Déaut, *Targum du Pentateuque*, vol. IV, p. 97.

[72] Etheridge, *The Targums*, p. 642; Le Déaut, *Targum du Pentateuque*, vol. IV, p. 223.

censured Moses as he prayed for Israel before the parting of the Red Sea.[73] In ps-Jon. the Lord answers Moses' prayer by saying, "Why do you stand praying before me? Behold, the prayers of my people have come before your own." These arguments seem to reflect an aversion towards giving any one individual a special status as pray-er which could not be enjoyed by anyone else in the nation. Such hesitations towards entrenching Moses as "the" intercessor continue to appear in the rabbinic literature (see below; cf. the Mekilta on 14:15 and 17:11),[74] and may also be found in the pseudepigrapha. For example, while Sir. 45:1–5 goes to great lengths to exalt Moses' leadership, it says nothing about his being Israel's intercessor. The book of Judith, in particular, reflects this attitude. At several points in the recitation of Israel's history ample opportunity is afforded, and passed over, to mention important leaders. It is made quite explicit that God delivers his people from Egypt in response to *the nation's* prayers (Jud. 5:12ff; 6:18f, 21; 4:11–13). Moses does not figure in any of these events at all!

As with the pseudepigrapha, the targums reflect conflicting beliefs about the importance of special, human intercessors. The patriarchs are presented as powerful men of prayer, and in some places they intercede for Israel after death. But this latter point is not universally accepted. In some contexts Moses is exalted as Israel's special intercessor, an opinion which may include the belief that he was translated into heaven during his time on Mt. Sinai. But at other times all of these ideas are decidedly denigrated.

## 8.4 Qumran

The attitudes at Qumran towards human intercessors would appear to be similar to those in other quarters of ancient Judaism. The presence of the books of I En. (excluding chapters 37–71) and Jub. in the Qumran library indicates their acceptance of the intercessory traditions developed in those bodies of literature (see above). This is substantiated by similar material in the pertinent sectarian documents. For example, 4QEnGiants[b] 2:14, 22 and 4QEnGiants[a] 8:4 contain exalted descriptions of Enoch which are in complete agreement with the traditions of the other Enoch literature.[75] Also 4QEnGiants[a] 9 and 10 both contain fragments of prayers offered by Enoch which, once again, indicate his place as intercessor.

The importance of the prayers of other key biblical figures is also developed, as

---

[73] Etheridge, *The Targums*, p. 487; Klein, *The Fragment Targums*, vol. II, pp. 42, 128; Le Déaut, *Targum du Pentateuque*, vol. II, p. 114, 115; "Aspects de l'Intercession," pp. 53f.

[74] Le Déaut, "Aspects de l'Intercession," p. 53.

[75] See Milik, *Enoch*, pp. 306f. It has been suggested that the Qumran Book of Giants occupied the position given to the Similitudes in the Ethiopic version of Enoch.

has been seen elsewhere. A midrash on Gen. 12:10–20, found in 1QapGen. 20:12–16, describes the healing power of Abraham's intercession for the king of Egypt. And at the beginning of column II in 4QDibHam., Moses' intercession for the Israelites in Ex. 32 is referred to as an act of atonement.[76]

The Qumranians would also appear to have sided with those who rejected the possibility of intercession being able to reverse God's decision against unrepentant sinners on the judgment day. A passage such as 1QS 2:4–9, describing the last judgment, makes it clear that God's punishment of the wicked is inevitable and irreversible; no intercessions by another, nor even petitions for oneself will be heard, for on that day he will not give heed to any who "call upon him" (cf. especially vv. 8f).[77]

There is also additional evidence in the specifically sectarian literature from Qumran (1QH 6:13f) to indicate a shared belief in angelic intercession.[78] But what is missing from this body of material is any suggestion of a belief in human intercessors in heaven. Of course, the presence of I En. indicates that such ideas would have circulated here as elsewhere. But the particular interest which attaches itself to the texts peculiar to Qumran is, of course, their attitude towards the Teacher of Righteousness.

Numerous suggestions have been made about the Teacher which could, conceivably, have a bearing on this point. For example, O. Betz has given a great deal of attention to the Qumran angelology and has said that the Teacher of Righteousness corresponds to the archangel Michael, whom he claims is the "spirit of truth."[79] Meeks has argued that the Teacher shows all the traits of being a "prophet like Moses," whether or not he was actually viewed as "the" eschatological prophet.[80] Either of these convictions, if correct, could have conceivably provided ample reason for styling the Teacher of Righteousness as the community's intercessor. But this does not seem to have been the case. Aside from the fact that Betz's comparison with Michael has serious weaknesses, there is no indication that Michael, in particular, interceded for the community. And even if the Hodayoth had been composed by the Teacher *qua* prophet, as corporate prayers offered on behalf of the community, there is no evidence to suggest that he was conceived of as fulfilling this task continually in heaven.

---

[76] T. H. Gaster, *The Dead Sea Scriptures*, (Garden City, 1964), pp. 261, 357.

[77] G. Vermes, *The Dead Sea Scrolls in English*, (London, 1987, 3rd ed.), p. 63; cf. Betz, *Paraklet*, p. 81; Johnstone, *The Spirit-Paraclete*, p. 82 n. 3.

[78] M. Mansoor, *The Thanksgiving Hymns: Translated and Annotated with an Introduction*, (Leiden, 1961), p. 143, nn. 2 and 3; Johnstone, *Paraclete*, p. 101.

[79] Betz, *Paraklet*, pp. 100–106, especially p. 104. For a thorough critique of Betz's overall thesis see Johnstone, *Paraclete*, pp. 102–118.

[80] Meeks, *Prophet-King*, pp. 169f.

## 8.5 Philo

Philo discusses the historical intercession of a few biblical characters in his writings:[81] Abraham's prayer for Sodom and Gomorrah (*De Migr. Abr.* 122, [LCL, IV, 201 f]), and the office of the High Priest as mediator/intercessor (*De Spec. Leg.* III, 131, [LCL, VII, 559]; *De Vit. Mos.* II, 133 f, [LCL, VI, 513 f]). But it is Moses who occupies the premier position of intercessor in Philo's works (*De Migr. Abr.* 122, [LCL, IV, 201 f]; *De Vit. Mos.* II, 166, [LCL, VI, 531]).[82] Moses is installed as Israel's intercessor because God is too awesome for the people to approach themselves, even in the best of circumstances (*De Somn.* I, 142 f, [LCL, V, 373]; *De Post. Cain.* 143, [LCL, II, 413]). He is superbly fitted for this task since he had merely been "loaned to the earthly sphere" by God for work such as this (*De Sacr. Abel. Cain.* 9, [LCL, II, 101]). In fact, at one point, Moses is even equated with the heavenly Logos who "stands on the border" between creature and Creator, and so being able to "offer a surety to both sides," is perfectly suited to the task of intercession (*Quis Rer. Div. Her.* 205, [LCL, IV, 385]).

In the midst of views such as this it would not, perhaps, be surprising to find Moses also presented as offering ongoing heavenly intercession. But there are no straightforward examples to this effect. While Philo knows about angelic intercession (*De Somn.* I, 141, [LCL, V, 373]), as well as the tradition about Enoch's translation being a symbol of repentance (*De Abr.* 17–26, [LCL, VI, 13–17]), there is no explicit evidence of any human, heavenly intercession in his writings. The closest one gets to this idea is found in the mystical descriptions of Moses' ascent upon Mt. Sinai. As in the rabbinic and merkabah literature, Moses' sojourn on Mt. Sinai is consistently interpreted as a mystical ascent to heaven, and so his prayers for Israel are interpreted as having been offered in heaven.[83] In addition, the death of Moses in Dt. 34:5 is explicitly interpreted by Philo as a translation into heaven much like Enoch's, and the language which is used there clearly parallels the descriptions of Moses' heavenly ascent on Sinai (*De Vit. Mos.* II, 288–292, [LCL, VI, 593–595]; *De Sacr. Abel. Cain.* 8, [LCL, II, 99]). The words of Dt. 5:31, where the Lord tells Moses (on Sinai) "to stand here with me," are applied to his eternal condition in heaven, so that he now stands by the Lord forever. Does this also suggest that Moses will be able to eternally intercede for Israel? It would appear to make such a position possible for Moses; but *eternal* heavenly intercession, offered by anyone other than the angels, is nowhere made explicit in Philo. Even if this were a valid implication of Philo's description of Moses it would be more the result of his unique nature, as the embodiment of the Logos, than of any straightforward "earthly piety → heavenly intercession" equation.

---

[81] All references are to the Loeb Classical Library edition (abbreviated LCL); see F. H. Colson and G. H. Whitaker, *Philo*, 10 vols., and 2 supplementary vols. edited by R. Marcus, (London, 1929–1962).

[82] For a very thorough discussion of Moses' place in Philo see, Meeks, *Prophet-King*, pp. 100–131.

[83] See the detailed discussion in Meeks, *Prophet-King*, pp. 122–125.

# 8.6 The Rabbinic Literature

The volume of the rabbinic materials is too extensive to be thoroughly discussed here, but an abbreviated treatment of the thoughts of the rabbis on heavenly intercession may be justified by the fact that there is very little to be found in their works which has not already been seen in the earlier Jewish literature. These parallels also indicate the presence of very early traditions in the post-christian writings of the rabbinical schools.

## 8.6.1 The Patriarchs and Other Powerful Pray-ers

The rabbinic literature continues to perpetuate the nostalgic portraits of ancient, holy men who could gain special access to God through their prayers. The prophets, as a class of men, do not occupy even as marginally an exalted position in this respect as has been found elsewhere. However, there are exceptions; for example, Daniel is said to offer heavenly prayer for Israel in Ex. R. 43:1 on 32:11.[84] This passage explains Ex. 32:11 by way of a midrash on Ps. 106:23:

Moses was one of the two advocates that arose to defend Israel and set themselves, as it were, against the Holy One, blessed be He. These were Moses and Daniel. That Moses was one we deduce from: "Had not Moses His chosen, etc.," [Ps. 106:23] and that Daniel was the other we infer from: "And I set may face unto the Lord God, to seek by prayer, etc." [Dan. 9:3].

This text is particularly interesting for several reasons. Firstly, in a fashion not unusual for rabbinic exegesis, it ignores the apparent chronological difficulties involved in making the prayers of Daniel assist those of Moses on Mt. Sinai. Secondly, in spite of this problem, it implies that Daniel is also praying in the heavenly court with Moses (see below). Thirdly, it links Daniel's intercession to that of Moses in a manner also regularly done with the patriarchs. Fourthly, and most importantly, it explicitly relates Daniel's ability to offer this intercession in terms of the effectiveness of his intercessory prayer recorded in Dan. 9:3ff.

This scheme of earthly prayer leading to heavenly intercession is also developed with respect to Abraham. According to Gen. R. 49:1–4 on 18:17–19, God decided to consult with Abraham about Sodom and Gomorrah because of his great righteousness; the remainder of this section then likens Abraham's intercession for those cities to Moses' own prayers for Israel at Sinai (also see Num. R. 19:23 on 21:7; Lev. R. 10:1 on 8:1), giving Abraham's efforts the same sort of paradigmatic significance commonly ascribed to Moses. Of course, this link between Abraham's piety and heavenly intercession is at the heart of all those passages which refer to the eternal value of the merits of the fathers. On numerous occasions even Moses' prayers find their efficacy only through his appeal to the

---

[84] All references to the Babylonian Talmud and the Midrash Rabbah are to the Soncino editions. References to the Midrash on Psalms and Pesikta Rabbati are to the editions found in the Yale Judaica Series.

patriarch's merits (b. Ber. 32a; Sotah 14a; Shab. 3a; Lev. R. 10:1; 29:8; Dt. R. 3:15; Cant. R. I, 2,3).[85] In Dt. R. 3:15f on 10:1 Moses makes a proleptic appeal asking that, in the light of the coming resurrection, God "count it as if the patriarchs were now beseeching you . . ." This not only presumes the efficacy of patriarchal prayer, but also implies that at the resurrection they will once again pray for Israel.

But Abraham was also known to pray himself from heaven. Ex. R. 25:26 on 12:2 maintains that the patriarchs have been interceding for Israel from the moment of their death until the destruction of the first temple. Similarly, in b. Men. 53b God discovers Abraham in the temple at the time of the Babylonian exile, pleading on behalf of the nation; the two then engage in a dialogue about Jerusalem which is modelled upon the discourse of Gen. 18, indicating once again both the paradigmatic and preparatory significance of Abraham's earthly intercessions for Sodom and Gomorrah. Finally, in a passage reminiscent of the belief in holy graves found in LivPro. and ps-Jon. (on Dt. 9:19 and 28:15), the Mekilta on Ex. 16:14 accounts for God's giving the manna in the wilderness as his answer to the prayers of Abraham "who lay in the (grave)-dust."[86]

### 8.6.2 Enoch

The rabbinic treatment of Enoch differs significantly from that seen in the pseudepigraphal literature. There is no exaltation of this figure at all; in fact, Gen. R. 25:1 on 5:24 explicitly denounces Enoch as a wicked hypocrite, whom God deliberately caused to die while in a temporary state of righteousness. Thus Enoch was not translated to heaven, and there is no indication anywhere in the rabbinic literature that he was thought to intercede. M. Aberbach believes that this attitude was intended to counteract sectarian interests (Jewish or otherwise) in the exaltation of Enoch,[87] which could well be true. But the rabbinic perspective at this point is not a totally new innovation. At best it is the highlighting of a tradition which had long run parallel to that which had exalted Enoch, for the belief that Gen. 5:24 recounts Enoch's death, and not his translation, is also found in Wisd. 4:10–14, 16 and targum Onkelos on Gen. 5:24.[88]

Beliefs similar to those in III En., where Enoch is transfigured into Metatron, may be found in the Babylonian Talmud (also see ps-Jon. on Gen. 5:25 and Dt. 34:6), but they concern only Metatron and give no indication of this angelic figure

---

[85] This association of Moses and the patriarchs is reminiscent of those passages in ps-Jon. which linked their intercessions at Sinai and the recitation of the covenantal curses. As always, there is also a contradictory tradition which may be found in b. Ber. 10b. There God rejects Moses' appeal to the patriarchs' merits and listens to him solely on the basis of his own merit.

[86] See Jeremias, *Heiligengraber*, p. 135. It is unclear exactly how Abraham is conceived of praying from the grave. Perhaps he rises to pray for Israel in situations of extreme duress, as in ps-Jon.; or perhaps the thought is similar to that found in Pes. R. 40:6, where Abraham asks that his prayer offered in Gen. 22:14 will have an eternal value against all of Israel's accusers.

[87] Aberbach, *Targum Onkelos*, pp. 48f n. 5.

[88] See L. Ginzberg, *The Legends of the Jews*, (Philadelphia, 1909–1938), vol. V, p. 156; Bowker, *Targums*, pp. 143–150 for discussion.

being viewed as a trasmuted Enoch (see b. San. 38b; Ab. Zar. 3b; Hag. 15a). Neither is there any suggestion that Metatron functions as an heavenly intercessor; he is said to write down the merits of Israel, but this is merely a cursory notice in the midst of a retelling of the story about Metatron's "lashings" found in III En. 16 (b. Hag. 15a). In fact, two of the three talmudic passages are clearly polemical, minimising the status of Metatron, and associating him with the dangers of the "two powers" heresy (also see b. San. 38b).[89]

Thus both Enoch and Metatron are given little place in rabbinic literature. Whether this was due to suspicion of anything resembling merkabah mysticism, or the more general fear that such figures posed a threat to monotheism, is unclear. There were certainly many other traits of merkabah which were not censored by the rabbis,[90] and why the extolling of Enoch should have been any more suspicious than that of Moses or the patriarchs is uncertain, unless it was thought that his comparatively minor role in the OT story ill suited him for such development, or that he presented the thin edge of a wedge which might lead to the introduction of more dangerously esoteric beliefs from among those circles which did elevate Enoch.

### 8.6.3 Moses

No human figure is exalted as highly as Moses in the rabbinic literature. His righteousness and the effectiveness of his prayers are expostulated upon at great length (Ex. R. 21:3 on 14:15; 18:3 on 12:29; all of Ex. R. 43; Lev. R. 1:3 on 1:1; Num. R. 12:1 on 7:1; 19:23 on 21:7; Dt. R. 3:15 on 10:1; 3:17 on 10:1; Pes. Rab. 17:5; b. Ber. 32a, to list just a few pertinent passages). In fact, so powerful are Moses' prayers that in several places the words of Ex. 32:32 are related to Is. 53:12, so that by his intercessions on Sinai Moses made atonement for the sins of Israel (b. Sot. 14a; Mek. on Ex. 12:1).[91]

However, it was debated whether Moses continued to offer such prayers for Israel from heaven. The rabbis certainly knew, and developed, the tradition of Moses' mystical ascent on Mt. Sinai (Ex. R. 40:2 on 31:2; 43:4 on 32:11; Dt. R. 11:10; Pes. Rab. 20:4; Midr. Ps. 7:6).[92] Consequently, the discussions of Ex. 32 invariably assume that Moses spoke with God face to face in the heavenly courts. Some rabbis also believed that Moses continues to pray in heaven. For example, in

---

[89] See Odeberg, *III Enoch*, pp. 36–41, 91–95; for a discussion of these talmudic references and rabbinic polemic against the two powers heresy, see A. Segal, *Two Powers in Heaven: Early Rabbinic Reports about Christianity and Gnosticism*, (Leiden, 1977), pp. 60–69.

[90] See I. Chernus, *Mysticism in Rabbinic Judaism: Studies in the History of Midrash*, (Berlin, 1982). The merkabah-like story of the ascent of the four rabbis, which has numerous points of contact with III En. and the Metatron traditions (cf. especially b. Hag. 15a), may be found in b. Hag. 14a; see Segal, *Two Powers*, p. 62.

[91] Moore, *Judaism*, vol. I, p. 550; J. Jeremias, "Μωυσῆς," *TDNT*. vol. IV, p. 853 n. 80. The same thing is said about the merits of Abraham in Lev. R. 29:8 on 23:24.

[92] It is interesting to observe that Midr. Ps. 7:6 contains a modified version of the midrash concerning the five destroying angels found in ps-Jon. on Dt. 9:19.

b. Sot. 13b, in the midst of a section discussing Moses' death, it is admitted that "others declare that Moses never died," pointing out that Ex. 34:28 indicates that he is forever "standing and ministering" with the Lord.[93] Such statements assume a belief in Moses' final, bodily translation to heaven. While other passages strongly deny this teaching (for example, Mek. on Ex. 19:20), Meeks[94] has pointed out, probably correctly, that the very strength of this denial may indicate the general popularity of the belief being attacked. It is not surprising then that both Origen (*In Josuam*, homily 2:1) and Clement of Alexandria (*Stromata* vi. 15) refer to a tradition recounting that there were two Moses visible at the moment of his death/translation.[95] This must be the remnant of an attempt to harmonise the conflicting Jewish beliefs over Moses' final estate. In any event, it is apparent that some did believe in Moses' ongoing prayers from heaven.

### 8.6.4 Conflicting Opinions

However, there were other areas of conflict as well, dealing not only with the nature of Moses' eternal condition, but also the question of intercession in general. Thus Dt. R. 11:10 and b. Sot. 13b, 14a relate a midrash based upon Ps. 94:16 where God laments Moses' death because Israel will no longer have an intercessor,[96] which is the same implicit argument against heavenly intercession that has already been seen many times in the inter-testamental literature. Similarly, Dt. R. 2:3 on 3:23 and Dt. R. 11:10 both relate God's rejection of Moses' request that he be allowed to enter Canaan. When Moses asks why his previous prayers for Israel had always been effective but now his prayers for himself are not, God's answer is two-fold: Moses' prayers cannot controvert God's prior decree; and, Moses' era as intercessor has come to an end. This passage shares both the conviction that Moses does not intercede after his death, and the belief represented so strongly elsewhere, that intercession can never undo the judgments of God.

Finally, the midrash discovered in the Palestinian targums on Ex. 14:15 also finds its way into Ex. R. 21:1, 4, 5 on 14:15. There again God rebukes Moses for

---

[93] Meeks, *Prophet-King*, p. 210. For a thorough discussion of Moses' temporary ascent and (possible) final translation to heaven see Ginzberg, *Legends*, vol. II, pp. 305–315; vol. V, pp. 416–418; Meeks, *Prophet-King*, pp. 191–210; "Moses as God and King" in *Religions in Antiquity: Essays in Memory of Erwin Ramsdel Goodenough*, (Leiden, 1968), pp. 354–371. Teeple, *Mosaic Prophet*, pp. 38–43, especially p. 42, provides additional references (Sifre on Dt. 34:7 and Midr. Tannaim 224).

[94] Meeks, *Prophet-King*, p. 205.

[95] Teeple, *Mosaic Prophet*, p. 43 nn. 64, 65. See W. Baehrens, *Origenes Werke*, vol. 7, (Leipzig, 1921), p. 297; A. Roberts and J. Donaldson, *The Writings of Clement of Alexandria*, vol. 2, (Edinburgh, 1869), p. 382. Clement talks about two "seeings," one from above and the other from below, in a fashion similar to b. Sot. 13b. However, in the talmud the object is to elucidate the phrase "no one knows where he is buried," while Clement is discussing the higher, spiritual meaning of Scripture.

[96] For additional references see, Odeberg, *III Enoch*, p. 93; Meeks, *Prophet-King*, p. 202.

praying on Israel's behalf when he has already heard the nation's own prayers; this proves that Moses' prayers were no greater than those of "any poor man in Israel."

The motivation for arguments such as these would appear to be a rejection of the idea that anyone, whether in heaven or on earth, need come between an Israelite and his God. Of course, the idea of directly addressing one's prayers to anyone but God is rejected outright (j. Ber. 13a),[97] but praying to an intermediary and believing that an intermediary may pray on one's behalf are two different ideas. However, they must have been similar enough in the minds of some that rejecting the latter was believed to be an important part of protecting against the former. Thus in a highly polemical passage found in b. Shab. 89b, which is also reminiscent of targum Jon. on Is. 63:16, God forgives all of Israel's sins when they complain of the inadequacies of the patriarchs' intercessions and so turn directly to God, rejecting all intermediaries.

## 8.7 Conclusions for Luke-Acts

Before relating the findings of this brief look at ancient Judaism with the portrait of Jesus as Intercessor found in Luke-Acts, it would be helpful to return to the three questions which began the study and summarise the answers that have appeared.

First, who serve as heavenly intercessors? The patriarchs, certain of the prophets, and specially chosen, godly men are allowed to pray in heaven. They are distinguished in life through God's selecting them for a special relationship with himself. Associated with this election (as it develops in the inter-testamental period) is a great degree of personal piety and a powerful prayer-life.

Second, what makes them suitable for the station of heavenly intercessor? Most fundamentally, the answer is found in their sovereign election by God. The pseudepigrapha attempts to explain God's election of Abraham and Moses through their antecedent piety and personal stature, but this is certainly not the OT position. However, all the evidence is consistent in describing these men as great men of prayer, so that what they do in heaven is simply a continuation of what they have performed with such efficacy in their earthly life. Powerful (elect), earthly pray-ers may become powerful heavenly pray-ers.

Third, who do they pray for and what are the benefits? They pray primarily for the covenant people, although occasionally the entire world is included. Their prayers concern moments of special, extenuating need, particularly judgment and the punishment of wrongdoing. The requests, thus, concern the protection and forgiveness of God.

However, this study has also demonstrated the diversity of beliefs in ancient

---

[97] Heinemann, *Prayer in the Talmud*, p. 249, observes that no prayers of the talmudic period are addressed to intermediaries. An English text of j. Ber. 13a may be found in R. Herford, *Pharisaism, Its Aim and Its Method*, (London, 1912), pp. 262f; also cf. Moore, *Judaism*, vol. I, pp. 438f; Longenecker, *Christology*, p. 29 n. 13.

Judaism. Since there was no single, harmonious picture of human intercession in Jewish thought, Luke's perspective has as many dissimilarities as it does similarities with the attitudes found in the OT and the extra-biblical literature. And while it is impossible to be absolutely certain about authorial intent in the absence of an explicit, intentional statement by the author, it is possible to draw reasonable inferences on the basis of parallels which could only result from the author's deliberate composition.[98]

To begin with, the distinctive element of OT religion is maintained, in that Jesus' prayers are related not so much to the categories of king or priest, but to those of prophet, and especially the divinely chosen man of God. Repeatedly it has been seen that Luke highlights Jesus' status as the final, eschatological Prophet, and while not all of the prayer notices in his gospel relate immediately to this theme, Jesus' place as the uniquely Chosen One of the Father, the messianic Deliverer, who always prays according to the will of his Father, and who fulfills his mission through the agency of such prayer, is a cardinal aspect of the prayer theme in Luke. It is also worth repeating in this context that Luke nowhere presents Jesus' intercessory prayers as a priestly activity.

Luke's portrayal also shows greater affinity to the OT than to the extra-biblical developments with respect to the beneficiaries of his intercessory prayers. Jesus' intercessions are solely for the benefit of his disciples. The inter-testamental idea of prayers being offered for the unrepentant wicked is not found in Luke-Acts. Jesus' prayers are the instrument of the election of the apostles; they are the means by which God's revelation is given to the elect and withheld from the wicked; they protect the disciples from temptation and apostasy, and ensure the heavenly vindication of his martyrs.

However, the importance of Jesus' prayers for all aspects of the lives of his disciples also reveals a point at which Luke partially embraces the inter-testmental development of intercessory prayer.

First of all, in contrast to the OT, Jesus' intercessory prayers are not limited to judicial situations. He does not simply pray in order to avert God's wrath. His intercession encompasses the whole of the initiation and maintanence of the disciples' confession. When his prayer does appear in a judicial context it is not to turn away God's wrath, but to testify on behalf of his persecuted follower and, by implication, to endorse God's judgment upon his rebellious people. This is a significant development within the canon which illustrates the importance of the inter-testamental literature for drawing proper lines of conceptual connection between the thought of the two testaments.

Secondly, the selective principle which has determined how Luke will weave together, or re-interpret, the various opinions available to him is the conviction that Jesus is the final Prophet come as God's Messiah. It is an individual's response

---

[98] Cf. Wellek and Warren, *Theory*, p. 148: "... for most works of art we have no evidence to reconstruct the intentions of the author except the finished work itself." In the absence of such explicit statements of intent, this is also true for works such as Luke-Acts, insofar as they partake of the qualities of literature as well as historical narrative.

to him which determines whether he become a beneficiary of Jesus' prayers (remembering that Luke is not concerned with how this logically coheres with the belief that it is also Jesus' prayers which make it possible for one to recognise his messiahship). Therefore, Jesus now divides the people in a fashion reminiscent of the final judgment in IV Ezra and the messianic work in targumic interpretation.[99] He does not stand between God and the entire nation, no matter how rebellious they may be, as Moses had done. Rather, as the final Prophet-like-Moses he stands between the faithful and the faithless, not only among the people of Israel but also the entire world, mediating the salvation of God to the former by his intercessions. Perhaps one may see here a development of the idea that the assembly of Christ's disciples (both Jew and Gentile) will replace the nation of Israel as God's covenant people, so that, insofar as Jesus continues to pray for his own, he does in fact mirror the work of Moses who interceded for all the people of Israel.

While there was no uniform development of the relationship between earthly prayer and heavenly intercession in ancient Judaism there was an important belief, which makes its appearance in numerous places throughout the literature, that heavenly intercessors simply continued to do in heaven what they had done so successfully on earth. Thus a powerful prayer-life before death is an important presupposition for ascension to the role of heavenly intercessor. Without prejudging the issue of the sources from which Luke derived his fuller picture of Jesus' prayer-life, it may be seen that his picture of Jesus' pre-and post-ascension prayer-life fits into this Jewish scheme quite well. The important role played by prayer in general, and intercession in particular, in Jesus' life, combined perhaps with the fact that Jesus dies a martyr's death, lays the groundwork for Luke's vision of the exalted Son of Man standing at the right hand of God.

What Luke has done is to develop the earlier traditions about the heavenly intercessions of the exalted Lord that are reflected in such passages as Rom. 8:34, Heb. 7:25 and I John 2:1. In the earliest stages of development, Jesus was seen to intercede at the right hand of God as a result of his ascension and exaltation. It was a function of that universal lordship acquired when he ascended on high. Consequently, it was expressed in language reminiscent of Ps. 110:1. Even though the actual roots of this expression were to be found elsewhere in the judicial context of heavenly court-room proceedings, the actual terms of this intercessory tradition were similar enough to those of heavenly Lordship that the functions of the first were subsumed among those already connected with the second.

However, when these beliefs were juxtaposed with contemporary Jewish traditions, Luke perceived even further reasons for Jesus' exaltation to this position. If Jesus was now the heavenly intercessor, it implied that he had exercised a particularly powerful prayer-life during his earthly ministry; that he had been chosen by God for a special role of Revealer/Intercessor; and that even the ascension/exaltation was predicated (at least in part) upon the efficacy of Jesus' having fulfilled this role. This "biographical" perspective on Jesus' heavenly intercession was not

---

[99] Levey, *The Messiah*, p. 143.

entirely unique to Luke; the raw materials for just such a development were already lying dormant in the earlier tradition, as may be seen in Heb. 5:7–10 (cf. Heb. 7:25–28; also see I Joh. 2:1, and the discussion in chapter 1). However, it was left to Luke to make these relationships explicit. When viewed in this light the traditions of Jesus' earthly prayer habits took on an entirely new significance. Consequently, in composing his gospel Luke was motivated to highlight this particular aspect of Jesus' career by definite christological concerns.[100] Jesus' earthly prayers present their own apologetic for both who he is and what he is able to do now in heaven.

If one were to ask how it is that Jesus' earthly prayers enjoy such singular success – in other words, what is the antecedent to *their* efficacy – the answer must be Jesus' status as the Elect One, the Son of God (Lk. 9:35; 10:22). Jesus' election is again reminiscent of the OT solution to the question of why particular men were successful as powerful intercessors. But his unique status as Son, who has been given all knowledge and authority by the Father, and who has been delegated the right to dispose of God's revelation by means of prayer, is also suggestive of the mystical/apocalyptic revelations of divine knowledge given to such figures as Enoch, Moses and Abraham in the OT, pseudepigraphal and rabbinic literature. As the Elect, Jesus is privy to special revelation from the Father; as the Elect, he also lives in perfect righteousness and obedience, exercising his prayer-life in accordance with the will of God. Thus his prayers are uniquely effective.

Without digressing too severely, since it is not the purpose of this study to address the historical-critical questions surrounding Luke-Acts, it should perhaps be mentioned here that maintaining that Luke's composition of the gospel was influenced by his convictions concerning the status of the exalted Lord – as indicated by this study – is quite a different thing from saying that those particular aspects of Luke's gospel story have no roots in the tradition. There is no *a priori* reason to assume that Luke could not maintain his abilities as an historian, even while being influenced by this Jewish perspective on what typifies the career of a worthy Intercessor. Certainly, since Luke alone penned a sequel to his gospel story, only Luke among the evangelists would have had the literary opportunity either to evaluate Jesus' earthly prayer-life in the light of his ongoing work as the ascended Christ, or to provide the temporal antecedents which justify Jesus' exalted status. The gospel story requires a sequel if this "career pattern" is to be displayed. Thus it is not surprising that it is the author of Acts who shows an unparalleled interest in the effects of Jesus' earthly prayers.

The approach being adopted here, of elucidating christology through the examination of existing figures and the course of their careers, provides an impor-

---

[100] The existence of a passage such as Heb. 5:7–10 indicates the circulation of early (oral) traditions about the fervency of Jesus' prayer-life. This suggests a reservoir of tradition from which Luke may have derived his prayer notices; cf. Lescow, "Jesus in Gethsemane bei Lukas und im Hebräerbrief," pp. 215–239; Jones, "Hebrews and the Lucan Writings," p. 121; Boman, "Der Gebetskampf Jesu," pp. 261–273. It is not self-evident that Heb. 5 is referring only to Gethsemane; in fact, quite the opposite.

tant supplement to the more common method of studying isolated christological titles. For it was probably through the interaction of both these processes that early christology actually developed. For example, the functions of Christ have as much if not more resemblance to the tasks of Enoch than to the recoverable meaning of any single christological title or term.[101] That the early church made just such wholistic comparisons is seen not only through this study of the prayer motif in Luke-Acts, but also by a passage such as the Acts of Pilate 16:6f, where the translation of Enoch (and possibly Moses) is used to illustrate the ascension of Christ.[102] This sort of comparison of events is not far removed from the comparison of functions associated with those events, whereby the tasks of the exalted Enoch would be used to illustrate those functions now performed by the exalted Christ. The parallels found between the Jewish attitudes towards exalted intercessors and Luke's treatment of Jesus' prayer-life suggests that just such career comparisons were in operation early on in the church.

Perhaps Luke's most innovative contribution to NT christology is his presentation of a praying Messiah. It is difficult to find an appropriate antecedent for this perspective in ancient Judaism. Enoch's transmutation into the Son of Man in the Similitudes is a suggestive development, but apart from the problem of dating this section of I Enoch, neither Enoch nor the Son of Man ever intercede in any of those chapters. It is also the general consensus in (at least) English speaking scholarship today that the Son of Man does not represent an established cosmic/messianic figure in ancient Judaism.[103]

An expectation of an interceding Messiah could possibly have been foreseen as a part of the ministry of the final Mosaic Prophet, given that this work played such a vital part in the ministry of the first Moses. But this can only be assumed, and there is little if any evidence that such implications were ever drawn out by those circles which looked forward to a prophetic messiah. The only place where the messiah is plainly said to come as a powerful intercessor is in targum Jon. on Is. 53[104] and while this is significant (and, admittedly, could be influenced by an expection of the final Mosaic Prophet), it should be remembered that Isaiah

---

[101] See C. H. Talbert, "Shifting Sands: The Recent Study of the Gospel of Luke," *Int.* 30 ('76) 387; Davis, "Mythic Enoch," p. 343f for a fuller discussion of this approach to christological investigation.

[102] Bowker, *Targums*, p. 146 n. a. For an English text see E. Hennecke and W. Schneemelcher, *New Testament Apocrypha*, vol. I, (London, 1963), pp. 468f; or M. James, *The Apocryphal New Testament*, (Oxford, 1924), pp. 112f. The discussion concerning Moses' body, and the ambivalence as to whether he actually died, is reminiscent of that in b. Sot. 13b.

[103] For a good, recent survey of this debate see "The Myth of the Son of Man" in Lindars, *Son of Man*, pp. 1–16; also cf. M. Stone, "The Concept of the Messiah in IV Ezra" in *Religions in Antiquity*, pp. 307f.

[104] Cf. Levey, *The Messiah*, p. 67: "A new messianic note is sounded in the intercessory power of the Messiah, who pleads for pardon for Israel's sins, which are forgiven for his sake. While this is intercession, it is not vicarious atonement; for the Messiah . . . does not suffer." However, it is very possible that Luke-Acts antedates this targumic development, so that it is Luke, not targum Jon., who sounds this "new messianic note"; see S. Levey, "The Date of Targum Jonathan to the Prophets," *VT.* 21 ('71) 186–196.

describes only a this-worldly ministry and knows nothing of intercession in heaven. However, this should not be too surprising since it appears that while Judaism knew of human messiahs raised up by God on the earth, and cosmic messiahs revealed by God from heaven, there was no exact parallel to the NT description of the experience of Jesus, which would have required the combination of both these sets of expectations. In any event, this study has shown that Luke, surprisingly, does not make use of the relevant portions of Is. 53.

Consequently, Luke's portrait of Jesus is unique in the NT, not only for what it says about him, but also for how he says it. For Luke's presentation of a messianic career distinguished by powerful prayer and effective intercession in its earthly phase, and ascension to the place of exalted intercessor in its heavenly phase, offers a distinctive combination of messianic expectation with beliefs in non-messianic heavenly intercessors.

Chapter 9

# Luke's Understanding of Prayer and Christology

When Luke picked up his pen to write a two-volume work on the life of Jesus and the early years of the Christian church he did so as one who was himself part of an ongoing process of thought and reflection on these very issues. His dependence upon a pre-existent tradition is seen in his indebtedness to anonymous writers of earlier gospels (Lk. 1:1–4). But being part of a developing tradition not only meant dependence upon one's predecessors, it also meant that Luke could combine his own insights and new discoveries with those established traditions already available to him from the well of inherited theological convictions, both Jewish and Christian.

As Luke reflected upon the role of prayer in the life of Jesus there were at least two relevant traditions already in place. First of all, it was widely believed within the church that the ascended Lord now served as the heavenly Advocate and Intercessor for the people of God; and he fulfilled this role as the One who had been exalted to the right hand of the Father. Secondly, the rich seed-bed of contemporary Judaism, out of which Christianity had sprung, allowed for the existence of numerous heavenly intercessors, many of them exalted men who had been chosen for this office by God and were distinguished by the miraculous efficacy of those prayers offered during their lives on earth. Doubtless it was under the very influence of these Jewish beliefs that the early church had developed its own convictions concerning the ascended Christ. Exactly how this development may have transpired is shrouded in the pre-literary mists of early Christian thought, but there are a few indicators within the NT that hint at the different avenues which may have been pursued.

One line of thought interpreted Christ's ascension in terms of the Lordship spoken of in Ps. 110:1. Thus the language of "sitting at the right hand" would connote "dominion." The establishment of Christ's heavenly rule would also imply the prior completion of all work preparatory to that rule. Therefore, "sitting" signified finality as well as authority.

But Christ's location at the right hand could have been deduced from texts other than Ps. 110, and these other passages would lend a wholly different significance to that position. This second line of development would have understood the outcome of Christ's ascension in terms of various vindication scenes and judicial passages found in both the OT and the extra-biblical, Jewish literature; Christ's ascension would be interpreted as his establishment at the right hand of God in order to serve as the new Advocate/Intercessor in the heavenly court. Current Jewish theology would have lent legitimacy to this line of thought, and

Christian belief in the supremacy of Christ could easily have allowed for his assuming heavenly tasks which had previously been allotted to less grand characters.

But this line of development is less clearly defined than the first. For some the language of standing was preferable to sitting since this was the attitude adopted by court witnesses. It might also have been assumed that the element of finality implied by sitting was incompatible with the belief in an ongoing ministry of heavenly intercession. Perhaps an eventual attempt at merging these two traditions into a single, unified depiction of Christ's heavenly status produced a compromise formulation wherein any reference to Christ's posture was omitted; Christ is simply "at the right hand," either to rule or to intercede. In other circles the solution was found in avoiding altogether anything even remotely reminiscent of Ps. 110:1. For them the idea of Christ's heavenly intercession was established firmly enough on other grounds that reference could be made to this activity independently of any allusion to either posture or location; Christ simply "intercedes with God for us." In some circles this activity was related to Christ's role as Paraclete.

As Luke gathered the materials for his literary undertaking he would have been able to reflect upon the traditions concerning Jesus' own prayer-life in the light of both Christian convictions concerning the work now performed by Jesus in heaven, whatever the details of their development, and Jewish beliefs in exalted, human intercessors. These Jewish beliefs entailed several other important elements. Firstly, there was the assumption that such figures had lived an antecedent life on earth that was characterised by powerful, effective prayer. Secondly, it was believed that such intercessors were elected to this mediatorial office by the sovereign choice of God. And thirdly, there was an important strain of thought which attributed such an exalted, intercessory position to Moses.

Writing with these convictions in mind, the gospel traditions about Jesus' earthly prayer-life would have taken on important new dimensions for Luke. He could have seen his gospel as an opportunity to provide the biographical antecedents which, within a Jewish frame of reference, would have been presumed of anyone now believed to occupy the position of heavenly Intercessor. To say this is not to attempt a sweeping explanation for the whole of Luke's purposes in writing Luke-Acts. It is simply an attempt to offer a partial explanation for Luke's special interest in Jesus' prayer-life. The fuller concluding summary of Luke's theology of prayer offered below will posit other complementary motivations for Luke's interest in the gospel prayer materials/traditions, but it is important to notice at this point that Luke's presentation of Jesus as the paradigmatic pray-er is not simply due to didactic or pastoral concerns, though these are a factor; it is the result of definite christological considerations. Luke offers the biographical details which explain how Jesus can be conceived of as the church's heavenly Intercessor, that is, he was the Chosen of God, the eschatological Deliverer, who exercised a powerful ministry of prayer and intercession during his life on this earth.

Luke's particular interest in those Jewish expectations which conceived of the messianic Deliverer as an eschatological, Mosaic Prophet would also have served to encourage Luke in his depiction of Jesus as the praying Messiah. Moses had been the paradigmatic earthly intercessor; in certain strains of Judaism he continued to occupy this position as an exalted, heavenly intercessor; furthermore, certain other of the prophets were also seen to occupy a special place as heavenly pray-ers. As soon as Luke incorporated Jewish prophetic messianism within the framework of his own christology he provided a context in which an interest in Jesus' prayer-life could grow. For, while there was no explicit Jewish expectation of the final Mosaic Prophet reproducing this particular aspect of the first Moses' ministry (as some thought he would recapitulate the exodus), thereby returning as an inter-ceding prophet-like-Moses, the connection was there to be made by any Christian who embraced this particular brand of messianic expectation and accepted the belief in Jesus as their exalted, heavenly Intercessor. Luke stepped into this gap, brought these disparate yet interrelated pieces of Jewish and Christian belief together, and offered the story of the praying, eschatological Prophet to the world. In doing this he not only took a new step in the continuing development of early christology, he created a narrative explanation and/or justification for what had previously been only a confessional statement. He also firmly fixed the significance of Jesus' heavenly intercession within a prophetic, as opposed to a priestly, frame of reference. It should also be noticed that by explicating these lines of connection between Luke's christology and his depiction of prayer in the life of Jesus the present study has supplemented the christological work of Feldkämper, providing the explanations of causal relationships which were absent from Feldkämper's own treatment of Jesus' prayer-life. It can now be seen why and how Jesus enjoys intimacy with his Father and mediates salvation through his prayers.

Of course, the complete picture of Luke's theology of prayer is more complex than this. Jesus' experience is both similar and dissimilar to that of his disciples (chapter 5). As one born of a human mother, who prays as a man like other men, Jesus is the church's model of true piety. The paradigmatic emphases of Monlou-bou, and to a lesser extent of Ott, have been reaffirmed. But in addition, Jesus' prayer-model demonstrates, as is also seen in the church's experience throughout Acts, that prayer is a prime means by which God reveals his will to his children. Through prayer the individual participates in a dialogue with heaven and is allowed to discover how he or she may be involved in God's sovereign plans for the church and the world. At times this will mean the revelation of unexpected things at unexpected moments. But the challenge of genuine prayer lies in the disciple's willingness to yield himself to whatever guidance or instruction God's answer may bring, however suprising it may be. In this obedience Jesus' life is exemplary: he only prays according to the will of the Father; and he always obeys the Father's revealed will. In this way, the present work has offered a significant modification of Harris' thesis concerning prayer and salvation-history. Prayer is not so much the means by which God guides salvation-history as it is a means for the individual to become attuned to God's plan.

It is this dynamic interaction between personal prayer and divine sovereignty which accounts for Luke's exhortations to perseverance in prayer, not any fears resulting from a delayed parousia. Thus the alteration in Harris' views concerning prayer and *Heilsgeschichte* is related to a similar readjustment in Ott's opinions on prayer and eschatology. Luke's teaching on persistent prayer is the result of his doctrine of God, and how that God relates to history, not any particular views on the last things, as Ott maintained. Luke presents his material in such a way as to eliminate any idea that prayer petitions will inevitably be granted exactly as requested, if only they are offered with enough faith and/or persistence. Luke realises that disappointment can lead to discouragement, and discouragement can result in one's giving up on prayer altogether. Therefore, he exhorts his reader never to abandon regular prayer simply because one does not always receive what one desires. God gives what he knows is best for his children, even if it is not always anticipated. By persisting in faithful prayer, even when discouraged, disciples keep open their main lines of communication with God; they are able to receive the good things which God wants to bestow upon their lives; and they follow in the footsteps of Jesus who pursued his own difficult course to the end through prayer (chapters 5 and 6).

But Jesus is also dissimilar to his disciples insofar as his task and status were unique. In fact, the paradigmatic dimensions of Luke's depiction of Jesus are partially derived from this very element of "uniqueness;" this is why Luke's description of Jesus' prayer-life is able to serve in this double capacity. Jesus is the praying messianic Deliverer. As the uniquely chosen Son he possesses a unique relationship with God which is the presupposition to his unique ministry on earth (chapter 3). And prayer, the chief means by which the Son maintains his intimate fellowship with the Father, also becomes a chief means of pursuing his ministry as final Prophet (chapters 4 and 5). Thus it is as Pray-er that Jesus executes the will of God (chapters 2 through 4); successfully pursues the course of his own Spirit-endowed ministry of preaching and healing (chapter 5); superintends the revelation of his own messianic identity to his followers (chapters 2 through 4); extends repentance and salvation to the lost (chapter 4); effects God's election through calling those who are chosen into God's Kingdom (chapters 3 and 5); confirms God's intention to withhold his revelation from those who have not been chosen (chapters 2 and 3); and ensures the final perseverance of all true disciples (chapter 6). Jesus is the heavenly Intercessor who prayed on earth as he now prays in heaven (chapters 6 and 7).

Consequently, the exact role played by prayer in Jesus' own life is multi-faceted. From one angle, Jesus prayed as any other man would pray. Prayer functioned in his life as it would in the life of any Christian; in this he is the church's paradigm. Prayer was integral to the accomplishment of Jesus' mission, but this was not unique to him. His model demonstrates that every Christian can only expect to discern the mind of God and discover the resources necessary for the fulfillment of their special task in life through their own prayers.

But from a second angle, Jesus is unique even in this, for the peculiar efficacy of his prayers are the result of his peculiar status. Jesus is the only Intercessor who can hope to mediate the will of God for the world through his prayers; no disciple ever shares this role with him. As the Son, only Jesus perfectly knows the mind of God and so perfectly prays according to the Father's will. Only the Son's prayers may serve to illuminate the hearts and minds of God's people.

From yet a third perspective, Jesus' prayer-life serves as the presupposition to his exalted status as heavenly Intercessor. But he is not simply one among many heavenly figures; he is the sole Intercessor in heaven. His heavenly status is as unique as was his earthly status; just as no one else had ever prayed with his power, authority or effectiveness in this life, so no one else can now pray at the right hand of God but him.

Luke's portrait of the praying Jesus offers a complex picture which resists simplistic, unidimensional categorisations. This remains true regardless of what one concludes about the previous hypothesis concerning the formation of extra-Lukan, intercessory traditions in the early church. Luke demonstrates that an exclusive concern with exaltation christology in Luke-Acts is inappropriate. The earthly Jesus already exercised extraordinary functions which were also to be his after his ascension and exaltation. But simple functional explanations are to be rejected as well. The earthly Jesus is not an "Intercessor designate" who takes up a new position in heaven strictly on the basis of his successfully completing a prerequisite prayer ministry on the earth. He is already the Heavenly Intercessor praying on the earth; this status is not rooted in what he does, but in who he is, the only Son of the Father.

The complexity of Luke's portrayal is unified by the simplicity of its central concern. Luke is especially interested in Jesus' prayer-life because he believes that the Saviour is especially interested in praying for his own. Luke conveys important didactic and paradigmatic dimensions of the gospel material concerning prayer, which are of immense importance to the proper pursuit of Christian discipleship. But beyond this, he also demonstrates why and how the prayers of Christ can have a continuing relevance for the church today. In achieving this end Luke clarifies the most important factor of all in Christian discipleship, for Jesus says, "I have prayed for you that your faith may not fail."

# Bibliography

## 1. Reference Works

Aberbach, Moses and Grossfeld, Bernard. *Targum Onkelos to Genesis: A Critical Analysis Together with an English Translation of the Text.* Denver: KTAV Publishing House, 1982.

Baehrens, W. A. *Origenes Werke.* vol. VII. Leipzig: J. C. Hinrichs, 1921.

Bardenhewer, Otto. (translated by Thomas J. Shahan). *Patrology: The Lives and Works of the Fathers of the Church.* Freiburg: B. Herder, 1908.

Baron, Solo Wittmayer. *A Social and Religious History of the Jews.* 19 vols. New York: Columbia University Press, 1952–1983 (2nd ed.).

Bauer, Walter. (translated and adapted by William F. Arndt and F. Wilbur Gingrich). *A Greek-English Lexicon of the New Testament and Other Early Christian Literature.* Chicago: University Press, 1957.

Blass, F. and Debrunner, A. (translated and revised by Robert W. Funk). *A Greek Grammar of the New Testament and other Early Christian Literature.* Chicago: University Press, 1961.

Box, G. H. *The Apocalypse of Ezra.* London: SPCK, 1917.

–, *The Apocalypse of Abraham.* London: SPCK, 1918.

Braude, William G. *The Midrash on Psalms.* 2 vols. New Haven: Yale University Press, 1959.

–, *Pesikta Rabbati: Discourses for Feasts, Fasts, and Special Sabbaths.* 2 vols. New Haven: Yale University Press, 1968.

Charles, R. H. *The Apocrypha and Pseudepigrapha of the Old Testament in English.* 2 vols. Oxford: Clarendon Press, 1913.

Charlesworth, James H. (ed.). *The Old Testament Pseudepigraph.* 2 vols. London: Darton, Longman & Todd, 1983, 1985.

Chilton, Bruce D. *The Isaiah Targum: Introduction, Translation, Apparatus and Notes.* Edinburgh: T. & T. Clark, 1987.

Colson, F. H. and Whitaker, G. H. *Philo.* 10 vols and 2 supplementary vols. edited by R. Marcus. Loeb Classical Library. London: William Heinemann Ltd., 1929–1962.

Danby, Herbert. *The Mishnah.* Oxford: Clarendon Press, 1933.

de Jonge, M. (with H. W. Hollander, H. F. de Jonge and Th. Korteweg). *The Testaments of the Twelve Partriarchs: A Critical Edition of the Greek Text.* Leiden: E. J. Brill, 1978.

Drazin, Israel. *Targum Onkelos to Deuteronomy: An English Translation of the Text with Analysis and Commentary.* New York: KTAV Publishing House, 1982.

Epstein, I. (ed.). *The Babylonian Talmud.* 35 vols. London: Soncino Press, 1935–1952.

Etheridge, J. W. *The Targums of Onkelos and Jonathan ben Uzziel on the Pentateuch with the Fragments of the Jerusalem Targum.* New York: KTAV Publishing House, 1968.

Freedman, H. and Simon, Maurice. *The Midrash Rabbah.* 5 vols. London: Soncino Press, 1977.

Ginzberg, Louis. (translated by Henrietta Szold). *The Legends of the Jews.* 7 vols. Philadelphia: The Jewish Publication Society of America, 1909–1938.

Goldschmidt, Lazarus. *Der Babylonische Talmud.* 8 vols. Berlin: S. Calvary & Co., 1897–1909.

Hatch, Edwin and Redpath, Henry A. *A Concordance to the Septuagint.* 2 vols. Oxford: Clarendon Press, 1897.

Hawkins, John C. *Horae synopticae: Contributions to the Study of the Synoptic Problem.* Oxford: Clarendon, 1899.

Hennecke, E. and Schneemelcher, W. (translated by R. McL. Wilson). *New Testament Apocrypha.* 2 vols. London: Lutterworth Press, 1963, 1965.

Herford, R. Travers. *Pirke Aboth.* New York: Jewish Institute Press, 1925.

Jackson, F. J. Foakes, and Lake, Kirsopp and Ropes, J. H. *The Beginnings of Christianity.* 5 vols. London: Macmillan & Co., 1920–1933.

James, Montaque Rhodes. *The Apocryphal New Testament.* Oxford: Clarendon Press, 1924.

Kenyon, Frederic G. *The Chester Beatty Biblical Papyri: Descriptions and Texts of Twelve Manuscripts on Papyrus of the Greek Bible.* fasciculus I–II.2. London: Emery Walker Ltd., 1933–1934.

Klein, Michael L. *The Fragment-Targums of the Pentateuch According to their Extant Sources.* 2 vols. Rome: Biblical Institute Press, 1980.

Kleist, James A. *Ancient Christian Writers.* vol. VI. London: Longmans, Green and Co., 1948.

Lake, Helen and Kirsopp. *Codex Sinaiticus Petropolitanus et Friderico-Augustanus Lipsiensis.* 2 vols. Oxford: Clarendon Press, 1911, 1922.

Lampe, G. W. H. *A Patristic Greek Lexicon.* Oxford: Clarendon Press, 1961.

Le Déaut, Roger. *Targum du Pentateuque: traduction des deux recensions palestiniennes complètes avec introduction, parallèles, notes et index.* 4 vols. Paris: Les Editions du Cerf, 1978–1980.

Lightfoot, J. B. *The Apostolic Fathers.* London: Macmillan and Co., 1898.

Lindell, Henry George and Scott, Robert (eds.). *A Greek-English Lexicon.* Oxford: Clarendon Press, 1940 (9th ed.).

Mansoor, Menahem. *The Thanksgiving Hymns: Translated and Annotated with an Introduction.* Leiden: E. J. Brill, 1961.

Martin, Victor. *Papyrus Bodmer II: Evangile de Jean chap. 1–14.* Geneva: Bibliotheca Bodmeriana, 1956.

–, and Kasser, Rodophe. (eds.). *Papyrus Bodmer XIV–XV, Evangiles de Luc et Jean.* 2 vols. Geneva: Bibliotheca Bodmeriana, 1961.

Mattill, A. J. and Mattill, Mary Bedford. *A Classified Bibliography of Literature on the Act of the Apostles.* Leiden: E. J. Brill, 1966.

McCown, Chester Charlton. *The Testament of Solomon: Edited from Manuscripts at Mount Athos, Bologna, Holkam Hall, Jerusalem, London, Milan, Paris and Vienna, with Introduction.* Leipzig: J. C. Hinrichs'sche Buchhandlung, 1922.

Metzger, Bruce M. (ed.). *Annotated Bibliography of the Textual Criticism of the New Testament, 1914–1939.* Copenhagen: Ejnar Munksgaard, 1955.

–, (ed.). *The Oxford Annotated Apocrypha.* Oxford: University Press, 1965.

–, *Index to Periodical Literature on Christ and the Gospels.* New Testament Tools and Studies, VI. Leiden: E. J. Brill, 1966.

–, *A Textual Commentary on the Greek New Testament.* London/ New York: United Bible Societies, 1971.

Milik, J. T. *The Books of Enoch, Aramaic Fragments of Qumrân Cave 4.* Oxford: Clarendon Press, 1976.

Moore, George Foot. *Judaism in the First Centuries of the Christian Era: The Age of the Tannaim.* 3 vols. Cambridge: Harvard University Press, 1954 (7th ed.).

Moulton, James Hope and Milligan, George (eds.). *The Vocabulary of the Greek Testament, Illustrated from the Papyri and Other Non-Literary Sources.* London: Hodder and Stoughton, 1930.

Moulton, W. F. and Geden, A. S. *A Concordance to the Greek Testament.* Edinburgh: T. and T. Clark, 1978 (5th ed.).

Odeberg, Hugo. *3 Enoch. The Hebrew Book of Enoch.* KTAV Publishing House, 1973 (reprint, 1928).

Prior, Tomus. *Codes Bezae Cantabrigiensis.* 2 vols. C. J. Clay & Sons, 1899.

Rahlfs, Alfred (ed.). *Septuaginta.* Stuttgart: Deutsche Bibelgesellschaft, 1979 (2nd ed.).

Rengstorf, Karl Heinrich (ed). *A Complete Concordance to Flavius Josephus.* 4 vols. Leiden: E. J. Brill, 1973.

Roberts, Alexander and Donaldson, James (eds.). *The Writings of Clement of Alexandria.* vol. II. Edinburgh: T. & T. Clark, 1869.

Robertson, A. T. *A Grammar of the Greek New Testament in the Light of Historical Research.* London: Hodder and Stoughton, 1914.

Schürer, Emil. (revised and edited by Geza Vermes, Fergus Millar and Matthew Black). *The History of the Jewish People in the Age of Jesus Christ.* 3 vols. Edinburgh: T. & T. Clark, 1973–1986.

Scrivener, Frederick H. *Bezae Codex Cantabrigiensis.* Cambridge: Deighton, Bell & Co., 1864.

Staniforth, Maxwell (translator). *Early Christian Writings: The Apostolic Fathers.* Middlesex: Penguin Books, 1968.

Stenning, J. F. *The Targum of Isaiah.* Oxford: Clarendon Press, 1949.

Strack, Hermann L. and Billerbeck, Paul. *Kommentar zum Neuen Testament aus Talmud und Midrasch.* 4 vols. München: C. H. Becksche, 1922–1928.

Thackeray, Henry St. John. *A Lexicon to Josephus.* part. I. Paris: Librairie Orientaliste Paul Geuthuer, 1930.

Turner, Nigel. *A Grammar of New Testament Greek.* vol. III. Edinburgh: T. & T. Clark, 1963.

Vermes, Geza. *The Dead Sea Scrolls in English.* London: Penguin Books, 1987 (3rd ed.).

Wagner, Günter (ed.). *An Exegetical Bibliography of the New Testament, Luke and Acts.* Macon, Georgia: Mercer University Press, 1985.

Westcott, B. F. and Hort, F. J. A. *The New Testament in the Original Greek.* 2 vols. Cambridge: Macmillan and Co., 1881.

# 2. Commentaries

Achtemeier, Elizabeth. *The Community and Message of Isaiah 56–66.* Minneapolis: Augsburg Publishing House, 1982.

Balz, Horst. *Die Katholischen" Briefe.* Göttingen: Vandenhoeck & Ruprecht, 1973.

Barrett, C. K. *The Epistle to the Romans.* London: Adam & Charles Black, 1962.

Bauernfeind, Ott. *Die Apostelgeschichte.* Leipzig: A. Deichertsche Verlagsbuchhandlung, 1939.

Baur, Ferdinand Christian. *Kritische Untersuchungen über die kanonischen Evangelien.* Tübingen: Verlag und Druckt von Ludw. Fr. Fues., 1847.

Beare, Francis W. *The Gospel According to Matthew.* Oxford: Basil Blackwell, 1981.

Braun, Herbert. *An die Hebräer.* Tübingen: J. C. B. Mohr(Paul Siebeck), 1984.

Brown, Raymond E. *The Birth of the Messiah: A Commentary on the Infancy Narratives in Matthew and Luke.* London: Geoffrey Chapman, 1977.

Bruce, F. F. *The Acts of the Apostles.* Grand Rapids: Eerdmans Publishing Co., 1951.

–, *Commentary on the Epistle to the Hebrews.* London: Marshall, Morgan & Scott, 1964.

Bultmann, Rudolf. *Die drei Johannesbriefe.* Göttingen: Vandenhoeck & Ruprecht, 1969.

Caird, G. B. *The Gospel of Saint Luke.* Middlesex: Penguin Books Ltd., 1963.

Calvin, John. *Commentary on the Book of the Prophet Isaiah.* vol. III. Grand Rapids: Baker Book House, 1984.

–, *Commentary upon the Acts of the Apostles.* vol. I. Grand Rapids: Baker Book House, 1984.

Conzelmann, Hans. *Die Apostelgeschichte.* Tübingen: J. C. B. Mohr (Paul Siebeck), 1972.

Creed, John Martin. *The Gospel According to St. Luke.* London: Macmillan and Co., Ltd., 1953 (4th ed.).

Danker, Frederick W. *Jesus and the New Age, According to St. Luke: A Commentary on the Third Gospel.* St. Louis: Clayton Publishing House, 1974.

Dodd, C. H. *The Johannine Epistles.* London: Hodder & Stoughton, 1946.

Dupont, Jacques. *Les Actes des Apôtres.* Paris: Cerf, 1953.

Eichrodt, Walter. (translated by Cosslett Quin). *Ezekiel: A Commentary.* London: SCM Press, 1970.

Ellis, E. Earle. *The Gospel of Luke.* Grand Rapids: Eerdmans, 1981 (3rd ed.).

Ernst, Josef. *Das Evangelium nach Lukas.* Paderborn: Friedrich Pustet Regensburg, 1977.

Fitzmyer, Joseph A. *The Gospel According to Luke.* 2 vols. New York: Doubleday and Co., 1981, 1985.

Godet, F. (translated by E. W. Shalders). *A Commentary on the Gospel of St. Luke.* 2 vols., Edinburgh: T.& T. Clark, 1976 (5th ed.).

Grundmann, Walter. *Das Evangelium nach Lukas.* Berlin: Evangelische Verlagsanstalt, 1969.

Gundry, Robert H. *Matthew, A Commentary of His Literary and Theological Art.* Grand Rapids: Eerdmanns, 1982.

Gunkel, Hermann. *Die Psalmen.* Gottingen: Vandenhoeck & Ruprecht, 1968 (5th ed.).

Habel, Norman C. *The Book of Job.* London: SCM Press, 1985.

Hauck, Friedrich. *Das Evangelium des Lukas.* Leipzig: A. Deichertsche Verlagsbuchhandlung, 1934.

Haenchen, Ernst. (translated by Bernard Noble and Gerald Shinn). *The Acts of the Apostles.* Oxford: Basil Blackwell, 1971.

Hill, David. *The Gospel of Matthew.* London: Marshall, Morgan and Scott, 1972.

Houlden, J. L. *A Commentary on the Johannine Epistles.* London: Adam & Charles Black, 1973.

Hughes, Philip Edgcumbe. *A Commentary on the Epistle to the Hebrews.* Grand Rapids: Eerdmanns, 1977.

Jeremias, Joachim. *Die Sprache des Lukasevangeliums: Redaktion und Tradition in Nicht-Markusstoff des dritten Evangeliums.* Göttingen: Vandenhoeck & Ruprecht, 1980.

Käsemann, Ernst. (translated by Geoffrey W. Bromiley). *Commentary on Romans.* Grand Rapids: Eerdmans Publishing Co., 1980.

Klein, Ralph W. *I Samuel.* Waco: Word Books, 1983.

Klostermann, Erich. *Das Lukasevangelium*. Tübingen: J. C. B. Mohr, 1975.

Lagrange, M. -J. *Evangile selon Saint Luc*. Paris: J. Gabalda, 1921.

Leenhardt, Franz J. (translated by Harold Knight). *The Epistle to the Romans*. London: Lutterworth Press, 1961.

Loisy, ALfred. *Les Actes des Apôtres*. Paris: Emile Nourry, 1920.

–, *L'Evangile selon Luc*. Paris: Minerva G.M.B.H., 1924.

Manson, William. *The Gospel of Luke*. London: Hodder and Stoughton, 1930.

Marshall, I. Howard. *The Epistles of John*. Grand Rapids: Eerdmans, 1978.

–, *The Gospel of Luke: A Commentary on the Greek Text*. Grand Rapids: Eerdmans, 1978.

–, *The Acts of the Apostles*. Leicester: Inter-Varsity Press, 1980.

McCarter, P. Kyle. *I Samuel*. Garden City: Doubleday & Co., 1980.

McKane, William. *A Critical and Exegetical Commentary on Jeremiah*. vol. I. Edinburgh: T. & T. Clark, 1986.

Michel, Otto. *Der Brief an die Römer*. Göttingen: Vandenhoeck & Ruprecht, 1955.

–, *Der Brief an die Hebräer*. Göttingen: Vandenhoeck & Ruprecht, 1984.

Michl, Johann. *Die katholischen Briefe*. Regensburg: Friedrich Pustet, 1968.

Munck, Johannes. *The Acts of the Apostles*. Garden City: Doubleday & Co., 1967.

Murray, John. *The Epistle to the Romans*. London: Marshall, Morgan & Scott, 1967.

Pesch, Rudolf. *Die Apostelgeschichte*. 2 vols. Neukirchener-Vluyn: Neukirchener Verlag, 1986.

Plummer, Alfred. *The Gospel According to Luke*. Edinburgh: T. & T. Clark, 1981 (5th ed.).

Robinson, Theodore H. *The Epistle to the Hebrews*. London: Hodder & Stoughton, 1933.

Sanday, William and Headlam, Authur. *A Critical and Exegetical Commentary on the Epistle to the Romans*. Edinburgh: T. & T. Clark, 1930 (5th ed.).

Schille, Gottfried. *Die Apostelgeschichte des Lukas*. Berlin: Evangelische Verlagsanstalt, 1983.

Schlatter, Adolf. *Der Evangelist Matthäus*. Stuttgart: Calwer Verlag, 1948.

–, *Das Evangelium des Lukas*. Stuttgart: Calwer Verlag, 1960, (2nd ed.).

Schmid, Josef. *Das Evangelium nach Lukas*. Regensburger: Friedrich Pustet, 1960 (4th ed.).

Schnackenburg, Rudolf. *Die Johannesbriefe*. Freiburg: Herder, 1963.

Schneider, Gerhard. *Das Evangelium nach Lukas*. 2 vols. Gütersloh: Gütersloher Verlagshaus Mohn, 1977.

–, *Die Apostelgeschichte*. 2 vols. Freiburg: Herder, 1980, 1982.

Schunack, Gerd. *Die Briefe des Johannes*. Zürich: Theologischer Verlag, 1982.

Schürmann, Heinz. *Das Lukasevangelium*. Freiburg: Herder, 1969.

Schweizer, Eduard. (translated by David E. Green). *The Good News According to Luke*. London: SPCK, 1984.

Smalley, Stephen S. *1, 2, 3 John*. Waco: Word Books, 1984.

Smart, James D. *History and Theology in Second Isaiah: A Commentary on Isaiah 35, 40–66*. Philadelphia: Westminster Press, 1965.

Spicq, C. *L'Epitre aux Hébreux*. 2 vols. Paris: J. Gabalda et Cie, 1953.

Thompson, J. A. *The Book of Jeremiah*. Grand Rapids: Eerdmans Publishing Co., 1980.

Wade, G. W. *Isaiah*. London: Methuen & Co., 1911.

Weiser, Alfons. *Die Apostelgeschichte*. 2 vols. Gütersloh: Güterslohar Verlagshaus Mohn, 1981.

Wikenhauser, Alfred. *Die Apostelgeschichte*. Regensburg: Friedrich Pustet, 1961.

Wilckens, Ulrich. *Der Brief an die Römer (Röm 6–11)*. vol. II. Zürich: Benziger/Neukirchener, 1980.

Williams, David John. *Acts.* San Francisco: Harper & Row, 1985.
Zimmerli, Walter. (translated by Ronald E. Clements). *Ezekiel.* 2 vols. Philadelphia: Fortress Press, 1979, 1983.

# 3. Secondary Literature

Abba, R. "Jesus – Man or Mediator?" *ExpT.* 55 ('43–44) 61–65.
Achtemeier, Paul J. "The Lucan Perspective on the Miracles of Jesus: A Preliminary Sketch" *JBL.* 94 ('75) 547–562.
Adler, Nikolaus. *Taufe und Handauflegung, Eine Exegetisch-Theologische Untersuchung von Apg 8,14–17.* Münster: Aschendorffsche, 1951.
Aland, Kurt. "Neue Neutestamentliche Papyri II" *NTS.* 12 ('65–66) 193–210.
–, and Aland, Barbara. (translated by Erroll F. Rhoads). *The Text of the New Testament: An Introduction to the Critical Editions and to the Theory and Practice of Modern Textual Criticism.* Grand Rapids: Eerdmans, 1987.
Alsup, John E. *The Post-Resurrection Appearance Stories of the Gospel Tradition.* London: SPCK, 1975.
Allen, Leslie C. "The Old Testament Background of (PRO)HORIZEIN in the New Testament" *NTS.* 17 ('70–71) 104–108.
Allen, P. M. S. "Luke xvii. 21" *ExpT.* 49 ('37–38) 476–477; 50 ('38–39) 233–235.
Alter, Robert. *The Art of Biblical Narrative.* New York: Basic Books, Inc. 1981.
–, "A Response to Critics" *JSOT.* 27 ('83) 113–117.
Anderson, Hugh. "The Easter Witness of the Evangelists" in *The New Testament in Historical and Contemporary Perspective: Essays in Memory of G. H. C. Macgregor.* edited by Hugh Anderson. Oxford: Basil Blackwell, 1965.
Argyle, A. W. "Luke xxii. 31f" *ExpT.* 64 ('52–53) 222.
–, "The Influence of the Testaments of the Twelve Patriarchs upon the New Testament" *ExpT.* 63 ('52–53) 256–258.
Armbruster, Carl J. "The Messianic Significance of the Agony in the Garden" *Scr.* 16 ('64) 111–119.
Arvedson, Tomas. *Das Mysterium Christi: Eine Studie zu Mt. 11:25–30.* Leipzig: Alfred Lorentz, 1937.
Aschermann, Hartmut. "Zum Agoniegebet Jesu, Luk. 22, 43–44" *TV.* 5 ('53–54) 143–149.
Audet, J. P. "Literary Forms and Contents of a Normal Εὐχαριστία in the First Century" *SE.* in *TU.* 73 ('59) 643–662.
Aune, D. E. "A Note on Jesus' Messainic Consciousness and 11Q Melchizedek" *EvQ.* 45 ('73) 161–165.
–, "Magic in Early Christianity" in *ANRW.* II.23.2. ('80) 1507–1557.
–, "The Problem of the Genre of the Gospels: A Critique of C. H. Talbert's 'What is a Gospel?'" in *Gospel Perspectives: Studies of History and Tradition in the Four Gospels.* vol. II. edited by R. T. France and David Wenham. Sheffield: JSOT Press, 1981.
–, "The Use of ΠΡΟΦΗΤΗΣ in Josephus" *JBL.* 101 ('82) 419–421.
Aytoun, Robert A. "The Servant of the Lord in the Targum" *JTS.* 23 ('22) 172–180.
Bachmann, Michael. "Johannes der Täufer bei Lukas: Nachzügler oder Vorläufer?" in *Wort in der Zeit: Neutestamentliche Studien Festgabe für Karl Heinrich Rengstorf.* Leiden: E. J. Brill, 1980.

Bacon, Benjamin W. "Stephen's Speech: Its Argument and Doctrinal Relationship" in *Biblical and Semitic Studies*. New York: Charles Scribner's Sons, 1901.

Baigent, John W. "Jesus As Priest: An Examination of the Claim that the Concept of Jesus as Priest May be Found in the New Testament Outside the Epistle to the Hebrews" *VE*. 12 ('81) 34–44.

Bailey, John Amedee. *The Traditions Common to the Gospels of Luke and John*. Leiden: E. J. Brill, 1963.

Bailey, Kenneth Ewing. *Poet and Peasant: A Literary Cultural Approach to the Parables in Luke*. Grand Rapids: Eerdmans, 1976.

Baird, J. Arthur. *Audience Criticism and the Historical Jesus*. Philadelphia: Westminster Press, 1969.

Baltzer, Klaus. "Considerations Regarding the Office and Calling of the Prophet" *HTR*. 61 ('68) 567–581.

Bammel, Ernst. "Is Luke 16:16–18 of the Baptist's Provenience?" *HTR*. 51 ('58) 101–106.

Banks, J. S. "Professor Deissmann on Jesus at Prayer" *ExpT*. 11 ('1899) 270–273.

Barbour, R. S. "Gethsemane in the Tradition of the Passion" *NTS*. 16 ('69–70) 231–251.

Barker, Margaret, "Some Reflections upon the Enoch Myth" *JSOT*. 15 ('80) 7–29.

Barnard, L. W. "Saint Stephen and Early Alexandrian Christianity" *NTS*. 7 ('60) 31–45.

Barrett, C. K. *The Holy Spririt and the Gospel Tradition*. London: SPCK, 1947.

–, "Luke 22:15: To Eat the Passover" *JTS*. ns. 9 ('58) 305–307.

–, *Luke the Historian in Recent Study*. London: Epworth Press, 1961.

–, "Stephen and the Son of Man" in *Apophoreta, Festschrift für Ernst Haenchen*. edited by W. Eltester and F. H. Kettler. Berlin: Alfred Töpelmann, 1964.

–, "The House of Prayer and the Den of Thieves" in *Jesus und Paulus*. edited by E. Earle Ellis and Erich Grässer. Göttingen: Vandenhoeck & Ruprecht, 1978.

–, "Light on the Holy Spirit from Simon Magus (Acts 8,4–25)" in *Les Actes des Apôtres: Traditions, rédaction, théologie*. edited by J. Kremer. Gembloux: J. Duculot, 1979.

Bate, H. N. "Luke xxii 40" *JTS*. 36 ('35) 76–77.

Bauernfeind, Otto. "τυγχάνω" *TDNT*. vol. VIII, pp. 238–245.

Beasley-Murray, G. R., "The Two Messiahs in the Testaments of the Twelve Patriarchs" *JTS*. 48 ('47) 1–12.

–, "Jesus and the Spirit" in *Mélanges bibliques en hommage an R. P. Béda Rigaux*. edited by A. Descamps and A. de Halleux. Gembloux: Duculot, 1970.

Beck, Brian E. "'Imitatio Christi' and the Lucan Passion Narrative" In *Suffering and Martyrdom in the New Testament: Studies Presented to G. M. Styler by the Cambridge New Testament Seminar*. edited by William Horbury and Brian McNeil. Cambridge: University Press, 1981.

Behm, Johannes. "δεῖπνον, δειπνέω" *TDNT*. vol. II, pp. 34–35.

–, "ἐσθίω" *TDNT*. vol. II, pp. 689–695.

–, "κλάω" *TDNT*. vol. III, pp. 726–743.

–, "παράκλητος" *TDNT*. vol. V, pp. 800–814.

Benoit, Pierre. (translated by Benet Weatherhead). *The Passion and Resurrection of Jesus Christ*. New York: Herder & Herder, 1969.

Bentzen, Aage. *King and Messiah*. Oxford: Basil Blackwell, 1970.

Bergmann, J. "Gebet und Zauberspruch" *MGWJ*. 74 ('30) 457–463.

Bernadicou, Paul J. "The Spirituality of Luke's Travel Narrative" *RevRel*. 36 (3,'77) 455–466.

–, "Luke-Acts and Contemporary Spirituality" *ST*. 31 ('79) 137–148.

Bertram, Georg. "νήπιος" *TDNT.* vol. IV, pp. 912–923.

–, "στρέφω" *TDNT.* vol. VII, pp. 714–729.

Betz, Hans Dieter. "The Logion of the Easy Yoke and of Rest (Matt. 11:28–30)" *JBL.* 86 ('67) 10–24.

–, "The Origin and Nature of Christian Faith According to the Emmaus Legend" *Int.* 23 (1,'69) 32–46.

Betz, Otto. *Der Paraklet: Fürsprecher im härestischen Spätjudentum, im Johannes-Evangelium und in neugefundenen gnostischen Schriften.* Leiden: E. J. Brill, 1963.

Bieneck, Joachim. *Sohn Gottes als Christusbezeichnung der Synoptiker.* edited by W. Eichrodt and O. Cullmann. Zurich: Zwingli-Verlag, 1951.

Bietenhard, Hans. *Die himmlische Welt im Urchristentum und Spätjudentum.* Tübingen: J. C. B. Mohr (Paul Siebeck), 1951.

Bihler, Johannes. "Der Stephanusbericht (Apg 6,8–15 und 7,54–8,2)" *BZ.* 3/2 ('59) 252–270.

–, *Die Stephanusgeschichte, im Zusammenhang der Apostelgeschichte.* München: Maax Hueber Verlag, 1963.

Black, Matthew. "The 'Fulfillment' in the Kingdom of God" *ExpT.* 57 ('45–6) 25–26.

–, "The Arrest and Trial of Jesus and the Date of the Last Supper" in *New Testament Essays: Studies in Memory of Thomas Walter Manson.* edited by A. J. B. Higgins. Manchester: Universty Press, 1959.

–, "The Holy Spirit in the Western Text of Acts" in *New Testament Textual Criticism, Its Significance for Exegesis.* edited by Eldon Jay Epp and Gordon D. Fee. Oxford: Clarendon Press, 1981.

Blakiston, Herbert E. D. "The Lucan Account of the Institution of the Lord's Supper" *JTS.* 4 ('02–03) 548–555.

Bligh, John. "Christ's Death Cry" *HeyJ.* 1 ( 60) 142–146.

Blinzler, Josef. *Die Neutestamentliche Berichte über die Verklärung Jesu.* Münster: Aschendorffschen Verlagsbuchhandlung, 1937.

Bloch, Renée. "Quelques Aspects de la Figure de Moïse dans la Tradition Rabbinique in *Moïse L'Homme de L'Alliance.* Tournai: Desclée & Co., 1955.

Blomberg, Craig L. "Miracles as Parables" in *Gospel Perspectives: The Miracles of Jesus, vol. 6.* edited by D. Wenham and C. Blomberg. Sheffield: JSOT Press, 1986.

Bock, Darrell L. *Proclamation from Prophecy and Pattern: Lucan Old Testament Christology.* Sheffield: JSOT Press, 1987.

Boismard, M. -E. "The Texts of Acts: A Problem of Literary Criticism?" in *New Testament Textual Criticism, Its Significance for Exegesis.* edited by Eldon Jay Epp and Gordon D. Fee. Oxford: Clarendon Press, 1981.

Boman, Thorleif. "Der Gebetskampf Jesu" *NTS.* 10 ('63–4) 261–273.

Boozer, Jack. "A Biblical Understanding of Religious Experience" *JBR.* 26 ('58) 291–297.

Boring, M. Eugene. *Sayings of the Risen Jesus: Christian Prophecy in the Synoptic Tradition.* Cambridge: University Press, 1982.

Bornkamm, Gunther. (translated by Irene and Fraser McLuskey, with James M. Robinson). *Jesus of Nazareth.* London: Hodder & Stoughton, 1960.

Borremans, John. "The Holy Spirit in Luke's Evangelical Catechesis" *LV.* 25 ('70) 279–298.

Botha, F. J. "'Umâs' in Luke xxii. 31" *ExpT.* 64 ('52–53) 125.

Bousset, Wilhelm. (translated by John E. Steely). *Kyrios Christos: A History of the Belief in Christ from the Beginnings of Christianity to Irenaeus.* Nashville: Abindon Press, 1970.

Bovon, Francois (translated by Alfred M. Johnson). "French Structuralism and Biblical Exegesis" in *Structural Analysis and Biblical Exegesis*. edited by Dikran Y. Hadidian. Pittsburgh: Pickwick Press, 1974.

–, "L'Importance des Médiations dans le Project Theologique de Luc" *NTS*. 21 ('75) 23–39.

–, *L'Oeuvre de Luc: Etudes d'exégèse et de théologie*. Paris: Cerf, 1987.

Bowen, Clayton Raymond. "The Emmaus Disciples and the Purposes of Luke" *BW*. 35 ('10) 234–245.

Bowker, John. "Intercession in the Qur'an and the Jewish Tradition" *JSS*. 11 ('66) 69–82.

–, *The Targums and Rabbinic Literature: An Introduction to Jewish Interpretations of Scripture*. Cambridge: University Press, 1969.

Box, G. H. "The Jewish Antecedents of the Eucharist" *JTS*. 3 ('02) 357–369.

–, "St. Luke xxii 15,16" *JTS*. 10 ('08–09) 106–107.

Bratcher, Robert G. " A Note on υἱὸς Θεοῦ (Mark xv. 39)" *ExpT*. 68 ('56) 27–28.

Braumann, Georg. "Das Mittel der Zeit: Erwägungen zur Theologie des Lukasevangeliums" *ZNW* 54 ('63) 117–145.

Braun, Herbert. "Entscheidende Motive in den Berichten über die Taufe Jesu von Markus bis Justin" *ZTK*. 50 ('53) 39–43.

Bretscher, Paul G. "Exodus 4:22–23 and the Voice from Heaven" *JBL*. 87 ('68) 301–311.

Bretscher, Paul M. "Luke 17:20–21 in Recent Investigations" *CTM*. 22 ('51) 895–907.

Brockington, L. H. *Ideas of Mediation between God and Man in the Apocrypha*. University of London: The Athlone Press, 1962.

Brower, Kent. "Mark 9:1, Seeing the Kingdom in Power" *JSNT*. 6 ('80) 17–41.

Brown, Colin. *Miracles and the Critical Mind*. Grand Rapids: Eerdmans, 1984.

Brown, Peter. "Sorcery, Demons and the Rise of Christianity, from Late Antiquity into the Middle Ages" in *Religion and Society in the Age of Saint Augustine*. edited by P. Brown. London Faber and Faber, 1972.

Brown, Raymond E., Donfried, Karl P., and Reumann, John (eds.). *Peter in the New Testament*. Minneapolis: Augsburg Publishing House, 1973.

Brown, Schuyler. *Apostasy and Perseverance in the Theology of Luke*. Rome: Pontifical Biblical Institute, 1969.

–, "'Water-Baptism' and 'Spirit-Baptism' in Luke-Acts" *ATR*. 59 (2,'77) 135–151.

Brownlee, W. H. "Messianic Motifs of Qumran and the New Testament" *NTS*. 3 ('56–57) 12–30.

Bruce, F. F. "Herod Antipas, Tetrarch of Galilee and Peraea" *ALUOS*. 5 ('63–65) 6–23.

–, "The Holy Spirit in the Acts of the Apostles" *Int*. 27 ('73) 166–183.

Brun, Lyder. "Engel und Blutschweiss, Lc 22, 43–44" *ZNW*. 32 ('33) 265–276.

Büchele, Anton. *Der Tod Jesu im Lukasevangelium: Eine redaktionsgeschichtliche Untersuchung zu Lk. 23*. Frankfurt am Main: Josef Knecht, 1978.

Büchler, Adolph. *Types of Jewish-Palestinian Peity from 70 B.C.E. to 70 C.E., The Ancient Pious Men*. London: Jews' College, 1922.

Büchsel, Friedrich. "δίδωμι" *TDNT*. vol. II, pp. 166–173.

Buck, Erwin. "The Function of the Pericope 'Jesus before Herod' in the Passion Narrative of Luke" in *Wort in der Zeit: Festgabe für Karl Heinrich Rengstorf*. Leiden: E. J. Brill, 1980.

Bultmann, Rudolf. (translated by Kendrick Grobel). *Theology of the New Testament*. 2 vols. London: SCM Press, 1952, 1955.

– "History and Eschatology in the New Testament" *NTS*. 1 ('54) 5–16.

–, (translated by Louise Pettibone Smith and Erminie Huntress Lantero). *Jesus and the Word*. New York: Charles Scribner's Sons, 1958 .

–, (translated by John Marsh). *The History of the Synoptic Tradition*. Oxford: Basil Blackwell, 1968.

–, "ἀγαλλιάομαι, ἀγαλλιάσις" *TDNT*. vol. I, pp. 19–21.

–, "γινώσκω" *TDNT*. vol. I, pp. 689–719.

Burnham, Sylvester. "Jesus as Prophet" *BW*. 10 (1897) 327–332.

Burkill, T. A. "Mysterious Revelation" in *The Messianic Secret*. edited by Christopher Tuckett. London: S.P.C.K., 1983.

Burkitt, F. C. and Brooke, A. E. "St. Luke xxii 15, 16: What is the General Meaning?" *JTS*. 9 ('07–08) 569–572.

–, "W and Θ: Studies in the Western Text of St. Mark" *JTS*. 17 ('16) 1–21.

–, "The Baptism of Jesus" *ExpT*. 38 ('26–27) 198–202.

Burney, C. F. *The Poetry of Our Lord: An Examination of the Formal Elements of Hebrew Poetry in the Discourses of Jesus Christ*. Oxford: Clarendon Press, 1925.

Buse, S. I. "St. John and the Passion Narratives of St. Matthew and St. Luke" *NTS*. 7 ('60–61) 65–76.

Butler, E. M. *Ritual Magic*. Cambridge: University Press, 1949.

Cadbury, Henry J., "The Internal Evidence of Acts" in *The Beginnings of Christianity*. vol. II. edited by F. J. Jackson Foakes and Kirsopp Lake. London: Macmillian and Co., 1922.

–, "Jesus and the Prophets" *JR*. 5 ('25) 607–622.

–, *The Style and Literary Method of Luke*. 2 vols. Cambridge: Harvard University Press, 1920.

–, *The Making of Luke-Acts*. London: Macmillian and Co., 1927.

–, "Acts and Eschatology" in *The Background of the New Testament and its Eschatology*. edited by W. D. Davies and D. Daube. Cambridge: University Press, 1956.

–, "Four Features of Lucan Style" in *Studies in Luke-Acts*. edited by Leander E. Keck and J. Louis Martyn. Philadelphia: Fortress Press, 1966.

Cadoux, C. J. "The Imperatival Use of ἵνα in the New Testament" *JTS*. 42 ('41) 165–173.

Caird, G. B. *The Language and Imagery of the Bible*. London: Duckworth, 1980.

Calloud, Jean (translated by Daniel Patte). *Structural Analysis of Narrative*. Philadelphia: Fortress Press, 1976.

Carlson, David C. "Vengeance and Angelic Mediation in Testament of Moses 9 and 10" *JBL*. 101 ('82) 85–95.

Carmignac, Jean. *Recherches sur le "Notre Père"*. Paris: Letouzey & Ané, 1969.

Case, Shirley J. "The Circumstances of Jesus' Baptism: An Exposition of Luke 3:21" *BW*. 31 ('08) 300–302.

Casey, Maurice. *Son of Man: The Interpretation and Influence of Daniel 7*. London: SPCK, 1979.

Casey, R. P. "Gnosis, Gnosticism and the New Testament" in *The Background of the New Testament and its Eschatology*. edited by W. D. Davies and D. Daube. Cambridge: University Press, 1956.

Catchpole, David R. "Q and 'The Friend at Midnight' (Luke xi. 5–8/9)" *JTS*. 34 ('83) 407–424.

Cave, C. H. "Lazaraus and the Lukan Deuteronomy" *NTS*. 15 ('68–69) 319–325.

Chamblin, K. "John the Baptist and the Kingdom of God" *TB*. 15 ('64) 10–16.

Chapman, John. "Dr. Harnack on Luke 10:22: No Man Knoweth the Son" *JTS*. 10 ('08–09) 552–566.

Chilton, Bruce David. *God in Strength: Jesus' Announcement of the Kingdom of God.* Freistadt: F. Plöchl, 1979.

–, "'Not to Taste Death': a Jewish, Christian and Gnostic Usage" in *Studia Biblica 1978, II. Papers on the Gospels.* edited by E. A. Livingstone. Sheffield: JSOT Press, 1980.

–, "Announcemnet in Nazara: An Analysis of Luke 4:16–21" in *Gospel Perspectives: Studies of History and Tradition in the Four Gospels.* vol. II. edited by R. T. France and David Wenham. Sheffield: JSOT Press, 1981.

–, "The Transfiguration: Dominical Assurance and Apostolic Vision" *NTS*. 27 ('81) 115–124.

Clark, Kenneth Willis. "The Text of the Gospel of John in Third-Century Egypt" *NovT*. 5 ('62) 17–24.

–, "The Theological Relevance of Textual Variation in Current Criticism of the Greek New Testament" *JBL*. 85 ('66) 1–16.

Collins, Raymond F. "Luke 3:21–22, Baptism or Anointing?" *BT*. 84 ('76) 821–831.

Collison, J. G. F. "Linguistic Usages in the Gospel of Luke" in *New Synoptic Studies: The Cambridge Gospel Conference and Beyond.* edited by William R. Farmer. Macon, Georgia: Mercer University Press, 1983.

–, "Eschatology in the Gospel of Luke" in *New Synoptic Studies: The Cambridge Gospel Conference and Beyond.* edited by William R. Farmer. Macon, Georgia: Mercer Univeristy Press, 1983.

Colpe, E. "ὁ υἱὸς τοῦ ἀνθρωπου," *TDNT*. vol. VIII, pp. 400–477.

Congar, Y. M. J. "The Prayer of Christ" *RevRel*. 24 (2,'65) 221–238.

Conolly, R. H. "Syriacisms in St. Luke" *JTS*. 37 ('36) 374–385.

Conybeare, F. C. "The Stoning of St. Stephen" *Exp*. 6/8 ('13) 466–470.

Conzelmann, Hans. "Gegenwart und Zukunft in der synoptischen Tradition" *ZTK*. 54 ('57) 277–296.

–, (translated by Geoffrey Buswell). *The Theology of St. Luke.* Philadelphia: Fortress Press, 1961.

–, "σύνεσις, συνέτος" *TDNT*. vol. VIII, pp. 888–896.

–, "Luke's Place in the Development of Early Christianity" in *Studies in Luke-Acts.* edited by Leander E. Keck and J. Louis Martyn. Philadelphia: Fortress Press, 1966.

Corbin, M. "Jésus devant Hérode. Lecture de Luc 23, 6–12" *Chr*. 25 ('75) 190–197.

Court, J. M. "Right and Left: The Implications For Matthew 25:31–46" *NTS*. 31 ('85) 223–233.

Cranfield, C. E. B. "The Baptism of Our Lord – A Study of St. Mark 1:9–11" *SJT*. 8 ('55) 53–63.

Crockett, Larrimore C. "Luke 4:25–27 and Jewish-Gentile Relations in Luke-Acts" *JBL*. 88 ('69) 177–183.

Crowe, Jerome. "The Laos at the Cross: Luke's Crucifixion Scene" in *The Language of the Cross.* edited by Aelred Lacomara. Chicago: Franciscan Herald Press, 1977.

Culley, Robert C. "Strutural Analysis: Is it Done with Mirrors?" *Int*. 28 ('74) 165–181.

Cullmann, Oscar. (translated by J. G. Davies). "The Meaning of the Lord's Supper in Primitive Christianity" in *Essays on the Lord's Supper.* edited by O. Cullmann and F. J. Leenhardt. London: Lutterworth Press, 1958.

–, (translated by Shirlie C. Guthrie & Charles A. M. Hall). *The Christology of the New Testament.* London: SCM Press, 1959.

–, (translated by S. G. Sowers). *Salvation in History.* London: SCM Press, 1967.

–, (translated by Floyd V. Filson). *Peter: Disciple-Apostle – Martyr, A Historical and Theological Study.* Philadelphia: Westminster Press, 1962 (2nd ed.).

Dahl, Nils Alstrup. "'A People for His Name' (Acts XV. 14)" *NTS.* 4 ('58) 319–327.

–, "Form-Critical Observations on Early Christian Preaching" in *Jesus in the Memory of the Early Church: Essays by Nils Alstrup Dahl.* Minneapolis: Augsburg Publishing House, 1976.

–, "The Story of Abraham in Luke-Acts" in *Jesus in the Memory of the Early Church.* Minneapolis: Augsburg Publishing House, 1976.

–, "The Purpose of Luke-Acts" in *Jesus in the Memory of the Early Church.* Minneapolis: Augsburg Publishing House, 1976.

Dalman, Gustaf (translated by D. M. Kay). *The Words of Jesus.* Edinburgh: T. and T. Clark, 1902.

–, (translated by Paul P. Levertoff). *Jesus – Jeshua: Studies in the Gospels.* London: SPCK, 1929.

Dammers, A. H. "Studies in Texts, Luke xxiii, 34a" *Th.* 52 ('49) 138–139.

Danker, Frederick W. "Luke 16:16 – An Opposition Logion" *JBL.* 77 ('58) 231–243.

D'Arc, Jeanne. "Catechesis on the Road to Emmaus" *LV.* 32 ('77) 143–156.

Daube, David. "ἐξουσία in Mark 1:22 and 27" *JTS.* 39 ('38) 45–59.

–, *The New Testament and Rabbinic Judaism.* London: Athlone Press, 1956.

–, "A Prayer Pattern in Judaism" *SE.* in *TU.* 73 ('59) 539–545.

–, "'For they know not what they do:' Luke 23:34" *SP.* IV in *TU.* 79 ('61).

Davies, J. H. "The Lucan Prologue (1–3): An Attempt at Objective Redaction Criticism" *SE.* VI in *TU.* 112 ('73) 78–85.

Davies, J. G. "The Prefigurement of the Ascension in the Third Gospel" *JTS.* ns. 6 ('55) 229–233.

Davies, Paul E. "Jesus and the Role of the Prophet" *JBL.* 64 ('45) 241–254.

Davies, T. Witton. *Magic, Divination and Demonology among the Hebrews and their Neighbours.* London: James Clarke & Co., 1898.

Davies, W. D. "'Knowledge' in the Dead Sea Scrolls and Matthew 11:25–30" *HTR.* 46 ('53) 113–139.

–, *The Setting of the Sermon on the Mount.* Cambridge: University Press, 1964.

Davis, Philip G. "The mythic Enoch: New light on early christology" *SR.* 13 ('84) 335–343.

de Blois, K. F. "How to Deal with Satan?" *BT.* 37 (3,'86) 301–309.

Dechent, H. "Der Gerechte – eine Bezeichnung für den Messias" *TSK.* 100 ('27–28) 438–443.

Deissmann, Adolf. "Der Beter Jesus" *CW.* 13 (1899) 701–707.

–, (translated by William E. Wilson). *The Religion of Jesus and the Faith of Paul.* London: Hodder and Stoughton, 1923.

Deitrich, Wolfgang. *Das Petrusbild der lukanischen Schriften.* Stuttgart: W. Kohlhammer, 1972.

de Jonge, Henk J. "Sonship, Wisdom, Infancy: Luke II. 41–51a" *NTS.* 24 ('78) 317–354.

de Jonge, M. "The Use of the Word 'Anointed' in the Time of Jesus" *NovT.* 8 ('66) 132–148.

–, and A. S. van der Woude. "11Q Melchizedek and the New Testament" *NTS.* 12 ('66) 301–326.

de Lacey, D. R. "Jesus as Mediator" *JSNT.* 29 ('87) 101–121.

Delzant, A. "Les disciples d'Emmaus (Luc 24, 13–35)" *RSR.* 73 ('85) 177–186.

Derrett, J. Duncan M. "The Friend at Midnight – Asian Ideas in the Gospel of St. Luke" in *Donum Gentilicium: New Testament Studies in Honour of David Daube.* edited by E. Bammel, C. K. Barrett and W. D. Davies. Oxford: Clarendon Press, 1978.

Descamps, Albert. *Les Justes et la Justice dans les évangiles et le christianisme primitif hormis la docrine proprement paulinienne.* Louvain: Universitaires de Louvain, 1950.

de Vaux, Roland. (translated by John McHugh). *Ancient Israel.* London: Darton, Longman & Todd, 1961.

Dibelius, Martin. "Herodes und Pilates" *ZNW.* 16 ('15) 113–126.

–, "Gethsemane" *CQ.* 12 ('35) 254–265.

–, (translated by Mary Ling). *Studies in the Acts of the Apostles.* London: SCM Press, 1956.

–, (translated by Bertram Woolf). *From Tradition to Gospel.* London: Redwood Press, 1971.

Dietrich, Wolfgang. *Das Petrusbild der lukanischen Schriften.* Stuttgart: Kohlhammer, 1972.

Dillon, Richard J. *From Eye-Witnesses to Ministers of the Word: Tradition and Composition in Luke 24.* Rome: Biblical Institute Press, 1978.

Dinkler, Erich. (translated by C. E. Carlston and R. P. Scharlemann). "Peter's Confession and the 'Satan' Saying: The Problem of Jesus' Messiahship" in *The Future of Our Religious Past: Essays in Honour of Rudolf Bultmann.* edited by James M. Robinson. London: SCM Press, 1971.

Doble, P. "The Son of Man Saying in Stephen's Witnessing: Acts 6.8–8.2" *NTS.* 31 ('85) 68–84.

Dodd, C. H. "Jesus as Teacher and Prophet" in *Mysterium Christi: Christological Studies by British and German Theologians.* edited by G. K. A. Bell and D. Adolf Deissmann. London: Longmans, Green and Co., 1930.

–, "The Kindom of God has Come" *ExpT.* 48 ('36–7) 138–142.

–, *The Parables of the Kingdom.* London: Nisbet & Co., 1948 (3rd ed.).

–, *According to the Scriptures: The Substructure of New Testament Theology.* London: Nisbet & Co., 1952.

–, "The Appearances of the Risen Christ: An Essay in Form-Criticism of the Gospels" in *Studies in the Gospels: Essays in Memory of R. H. Lightfoot.* edited by D. E. Nineham. Oxford: Basil Blackwell, 1957.

–, "Une parabole cachée dans le quatriéme Evangile" *Revue d'Histoire et de Philosophie religieuses.* 42 ('62) 107–115.

Dodds, E. R. *Pagan and Christian in an Age of Anxiety: Some Aspects of Religious Experience from Marcus Aurelius to Constantine.* Cambridge: University Press, 1965.

Dowd, William A. "Breaking Bread, Acts 2:46" *CBQ.* 1 ('39) 358–362.

Driver, G. R. "Two Problems in the New Testament" *JTS.* ns. 16 ('65) 327–337.

Drumright, Huber L. "The Holy Spirit in the Book of Acts" *SwJT.* 17 ('74) 3–17.

Drury John. *Tradition and Design in Luke's Gospel: A Study in Early Christian Historiography.* London: Darton, Longman and Todd, 1976.

Dungan, David Laird. "Mark – The Abridgement of Matthew and Luke" in *Jesus and Man's Hope.* edited by David G. Buttrick. Pittsburgh: Pittsburgh Theological Seminary, 1970.

Dunn, James D. G. *Jesus and the Spirit: A Study of the Religious and Charismatic Experience of Jesus and the First Christians as Reflected in the New Testament.* London: SCM Press, 1975.

–, "Spirit and Kingdom" *ExpT.* 82 ('70–71) 36–40.

–, *Christology in the Making: An Inquiry into the Origins of the Doctrine of the Incarnation.* London: SCM Press, 1980.

–, "The Messianic Secret in Mark" in *The Messianic Secret.* edited by Christopher Tuckett. London: SPCK, 1983.

Duplacy, J. "La préhistoire du texte en Luc 22:43–44" in *New Testament Textual Criticism, its Significance for Exegesis.* edited by E. J. Epp and G. D. Fee. Oxford: Clarendon Press, 1981.

Dupont, Jacques. "Le Repas D'Emmaüs" *LumV.* 31 ('57) 77–92.

–, (translated by E. M. Stewart). "The Meal at Emmaus" in *The Eucharist in the New Testament.* London: Geoffrey Chapman, 1964.

–, "Les 'simples' (petâyim) dans la Bible et à Qumrân: A propos des νήπιοι de Mt. 11,25; Lc. 10,21" in *Studi sull' Oriente e la Bibbia.* Genoa: S. G. Emilian, 1967.

–, "Jésus et la Prière Liturgique" *Maison-Dieu.* 95 ('68) 16–49.

–, "'Assis à la droite de Dieu' l'interpretation du Ps 110,1 dans le Nouveau Testament" in *Resurrexit: Acts du Symposium International sur la Résurrection de Jésus (Rome 1970).* edited by Edouard Dhanis. Rome: Citta del Vaticano, 1974.

–, "La Prière et Son Efficacité dans L'Evangile de Luc" in *La Parole de Grâce: Etudes lucaniennes à la mémoire d'Augustin George.* edited by J. Delorma and J. Duplacy. Paris: Recherches de Science Religieuse, 1981.

–, *Nouvelles Etudes sur les Actes des Apôtres.* Paris: Cerf, 1984.

Easton, Burton Scott. "Luke 17:20–21. An Exegetical Study" *AJT.* 16 ('12) 275–283.

Eaton, J. H. *Kingship and the Psalms.* London: SCM Press, 1976.

Edmonds, Peter. "The Lucan Our Father: A Summary of Luke's Teaching on Prayer?" *ExpT.* 91 ('79–80) 140–143.

Edwards, Richard A. "The Redaction of Luke" *JR.* 49 ('69) 392–405.

–, *The Sign of Jonah In the Theology of the Evangelists and Q.* London: SCM Press, 1971.

Ehrhardt, Arnold, "The Disciples of Emmaus" *NTS.* 10 ('63–64) 182–201.

Ehrman, Bart D. and Plunkett, Mark A. "The Angel and the Agony: The Textual Problem of Luke 22:43–44" *CBQ.* 45 ('83) 401–416.

Ellis. E. Earle. "Present and Future Eschatology in Luke" *NTS.* 12 ('65–66) 27–41.

–, "The Composition of Luke 9 and the Sources of Its Christology" in *Current Issues in Biblical and Patristic Interpretation: Studies in Honor of Merrill C. Tenney.* edited by Gerald F. Hawthorne. Grand Rapids: Eerdmans, 1975.

Epp, Eldon Jay. "The 'Ignorance Motif' in Acts and Anti-Judaic Tendencies in Codex Bezae" *HTR.* 55 ('62) 51–62.

–, *The Theological Tendency of Codex Bezae Cantabrigiensis in Acts.* Cambridge: University Press, 1966.

–, "The Ascension in the Textual Tradition of Luke-Acts" in *New Testament Textual Criticism, Its Significance for Exegesis.* edited by Eldon Jay Epp and Gordon D. Fee. Oxford: Clarendon Press, 1981.

Eppstein, Victor. "The Historicity of the Gospel Account of the Cleansing of the Temple" *ZNW.* 55 ('64) 42–58.

Evans, Christopher. "Christ at Prayer in St. John's Gospel" *LV.* 24 ('69) 579–596.

Falk, Z. W. *Hebrew Law in Biblical Times.* Jerusalem: Wahrmann Books, 1964.

Fee, Gordon D. "P66, P75 and Origen: The Myth of Early Textual Recension" in *New Dimensions in New Testament Study.* edited by Richard N. Longenecker and Merrill C. Tenney. Grand Rapids: Zondervan, 1974.

–, "'One Thing is Needful'?, Luke 10:42" in *New Testament Textual Criticism, Its Significance for Exegesis.* edited by Eldon Jay Epp and Gordon D. Fee. Oxford: Clarendon Press, 1981.

Feldkämper, Ludger. *Der betende Jesus als Heilsmittler nach Lukas.* Bonn: Steyler Verlag, 1978.

Feuillet, A. "Le Symbolisme de la colombe dans les récits Evangéliques du baptême" *RSR.* 46 ('58) 524–544.

Filson, Floyd v. "The Journey Motif in Luke-Acts" in *Apostolic History and the Gospels: Biblical and Historical Essays Presented to F. F. Bruce.* edited by W. Ward Gasque and Ralph P. Martin. Exeter: Paternoster Press, 1970.

Finkel, Asher. "Jesus' Sermon at Nazareth (Luk. 4, 16–30)" in *Abraham unser Vater: Juden und Christen im Gespräch über die Bibel.* edited by Otto Betz, Martin Hengel and Peter Schmidt. Leiden: E. J. Brill, 1963.

Fisher, Fred L. *Prayer in the New Testament.* Philadelphia: Westminster Press, 1964.

Fitzmyer, Joseph A. "Papyrus Bodmer XIV: Some Features of Our Oldest Text of Luke" *CBQ.* 24 ('62) 170–179.

–, "Jewish Christianity in Acts in Light of the Qumran Scrolls" in *Studies in Luke-Acts.* edited by Leander E. Keck and J. Louis Martyn. Philadelphia: Fortress Press, 1966.

–, "Further Light on Melchizedek from Qumran Cave 11" *JBL.* 86 ('67) 25–41.

–, "The Priority of Mark and the 'Q' Source in Luke" in *Jesus and Man's Hope.* edited by David G. Buttrick. Pittsburgh: Pittsburgh Theological Seminary, 1970.

–, "The Composition of Luke, Chapter 9" in *Perspectives on Luke-Acts.* edited by Charles H. Talbert. Danville, VA.: Associaion of Baptist Professors of Religion, 1978.

–, "Crucifixion in Ancient Palestine, Qumran Literature, and the New Testament" *CBQ.* 40 ('78) 493–513.

–, "The Ascension of Christ and Pentecost" *TS.* 45 ('84) 409–440.

Flender, Helmut. (translated by Reginald H. and Ilse Fuller). *St. Luke: Theologian of Redemptive History.* London: S.P.C.K., 1967.

Flusser, David. "The Crucified One and the Jews" *Immanuel.* 7 ('77) 25–37.

Foakes-Jackson, F. J. "Stephen's Speech in Acts" *JBL.* 49 ('30) 283–286.

Foerster, Werner. "Lukas 22:31 f" *ZNW.* 46 ('55) 129–133.

–, "διάβολος" *TDNT.* vol II, pp. 71–81.

–, "σατανᾶς *TDNT.* vol. VII, pp. 151–163.

Francis, Fred O. "Eschatology and History in Luke-Acts" *JAAR.* 37 ('69) 49–63.

Franklin, Eric. "The Ascension and the Eschatology of Luke-Acts" *SJT.* 23 ('70) 191–200.

–, *Christ the Lord: A Study in the Purpose and Theology of Luke-Acts.* London: S.P.C.K., 1975.

Frei, Hans W. *The Eclipse of Biblical Narrative: A Study in Eighteenth and Nineteenth Century Hermeneutics.* New Haven/London: Yale University Press, 1974.

Friedrich, G. "προφήτης." *TDNT.* vol. VI, pp. 781–861.

Frye, Northrop. *Anatomy of Criticism.* Princeton: Princeton University Press, 1957.

–, *The Great Code: The Bible and Literature.* London: Routledge and Kegan Paul, 1982.

Frye, Roland Mushat. "A Literary Perspective for the Criticism of the Gospels" in *Jesus and Man's Hope, II.* edited by Donald G. Miller and Dikran Y. Hadidian. Pittsburg: Pittsburg Theological Seminary, 1971.

–, "The Jesus of the Gospels: Approaches Through Narrative Structures" in *From Faith to Faith: Essays in Honour of Donald G. Miller on HIs Seventieth Birthday.* edited by Dikran Y. Hadidian. Pittsburgh: Pickwick Press, 1979.

Fuchs, Ernst. "σινιάζω" *TDNT.* vol. VII, pp. 291–292.

Fuhrman, Charles Michael. *A Redactional Study of Prayer in the Gospel of Luke.* unpublished Ph.D. dissertation. Southern Baptist Theological Seminary, 1981.

Fuller, R. H. "The Clue to Jesus' Self-Understanding" *SE*. III. in *TU*. 88 ('64) 58–66.

Galizzi, Mario. *Gesu nel Getsemani (Mc 14,32–42; Mt 26,36–46; Lc 22,39–46)*. Zürich: Pas Verlag, 1972.

Gasque, W. Ward. "The Speeches in Acts: Dibelius Reconsidered" in *New Dimensions in New Testament Study*. edited by Richard N. Longenecker and Merrill C. Tenney. Grand Rapids: Zondervan, 1974.

Geddert, Timothy J. *Mark 13 in its Markan Interpretive Context*. unpublished Ph.D. disssertation. University of Aberdeen, 1986.

George, A. Raymond. *Communion with God in the New Testament*. London: Epworth Press, 1953.

George, Augustin. "Jésus Fils de Dieu dans l'évangile selon saint Luc" *RB*. 72 ('65) 185–209.

–, "Le sens de la mort de Jésus pour Luc" *RB*. 80 ('73) 186–217.

–, *Etudes sur L'Oeuvre de Luc*. Paris: Gabalda et Cie, 1978.

Gibbs, James M. "Luke 24:13–33 and Acts 8:26–39: The Emmaus Incident and the Eunuch's Baptism as Parallel Stories" *BTF*. 7 ('75) 17–30.

Giblin, Charles Homer. *The Destruction of Jerusalem According to Luke's Gospel: A Historical-Typological Moral*. Rome: Biblical Institute Press, 1985.

Ginzberg, Louis, "Some Observations on the Attitude of the Synagogue Towards the Apocalyptic-Eschatological Writings" *JBL*. 41 ('22) 115–136.

Glasson, T. Francis. *Greek Influence in Jewish Eschatology*. London: SPCK, 1961.

Glöckner, Richard. *Die Verkündigung des Heils beim Evangelisten Lukas*. Mainz: Matthias-Grünewald, 1975.

Goppelt, Leonard. (translated by Donald G. Madvig). *Typos: The Typological Interpretation of the Old Testament in the New*. Grand Rapids: Eerdmans, 1982.

Gourgues, M. *A la droite de Dieu: Résurrection de Jésus et actualisation du Psaume 110:1 dans le Nouveau Testament*. Paris: J. Gabalda, 1978.

Grant, Robert M. *Miracle and Natural Law in Graeco-Roman and Early Christian Thought*. Amsterdam: North-Holland Publishing Co., 1952.

Grassi, Joseph A. "Emmaus Revisited (Luke 24:13–35 and Acts 8:26–40)" *CBQ*. 26 ('64) 463–467.

Green, Joel B. "Jesus on the Mount of Olives (Luke 22. 39–46): Tradition and Theology" *JSNT*. 26 ('86) 29–48.

Greenwood, D. S. "Poststructuralism in Biblical Studies" in *Gospel Perspectives: Studies in Midrash and Historiography, vol. III*. edited by R. T. France and D. Wenham. Sheffield: JSOT Press, 1983.

Greeven, Heinrich. *Gebet und Eschatologie im Neuen Testament*. Gütersloh: C. Bertelsmann, 1931.

–, and Hermann, Johannes. "εὔχομαι" *TDNT*. vol. II, pp. 775–808.

Grelot, Pierre. "Etude critique de Luc 10,19" in *La Parole de Grâce: Etudes lucaniennes à la mémoire d'Augustin George*. edited by J. Delorme and J. Duplacy. Paris: Recherches de Science Religieuse, 1981.

Griffiths, J. Gwyn. "ἐντὸς ὑμῶν (Luke xvii. 21)" *ExpT*. 63 ('51–52) 30–31.

Grimm, Werner A. "Selige Augenzeugen, Luk. 10,23f. Alttestamentlicher Hintergrund und ursprünglicher Sinn" *TZ*. 26 ('70) 172–183.

–, "Der Dank für empfangene Offenbarung bei Jesus und Josephus. Parallelen zu Mt. 11:25–27" *BZ*. 17 ('73) 249–256.

Grundmann, Walter. "δεξιός," *TDNT*. vol. II, pp. 37–40.

–, "στήκω," *TDNT*. vol. VII, pp. 636–653.

–, "Das Problem des hellenistischen christentums innerhalb der Jerusalemer Urgemeinde," *ZNW*. 38 ('39) 45–73.

–, "Die νήπιοι in die Urchristlichen Paränese" *NTS*. 5 ('59) 188–205.

–, "Mt. 11:27 und die johanneischen 'Der Vater – Der Sohn' Stellen" *NTS*. 12 (1,'65) 42–49.

Gundry, Robert H. "The Narrative Framework of Matthew xvi 17–19" *NovT*. 7 ('64–65) 1–9.

–, "Recent Investigations Into the Literary Genre 'Gospel'" in *New Dimensions in New Testament Study*. edited by Richard N. Longenecker and Merrill C. Tenney. Grand Rapids: Zondervan, 1974.

Gunkel, Hermann. (translated by Roy A. Harrisville and Philip A. Quanbeck). *The Influence of the Holy Spirit: The Popular View of the Apostolic Age and the Teaching of the Apostle Paul*. Philadelphia: Fortress Press, 1979.

Guy, Harold A. "Matthew 11:25–27; Luke 10:21–22" *ExpT*. 49 ('37–38) 236–237.

Habel, Norman C. "The Form and Significance of the Call Narratives" *ZAW*. 77 ('65) 297–323.

–, "The Narrative Art of Job: Applying the Principles of Robert Alter" *JSOT*. 27 ('83) 101–111.

Haenchen, Ernst. "Judentum und Christentum in der Apostelgeschichte" *ZNW*. 54 ('63) 155–187.

Hahn, Ferdinand. (translated by Harold Knight and George Ogg). *The Titles of Jesus in Christology*. London: Lutterworth Press, 1969.

–, (translated by David E. Green). *The Worship of the Early Church*. Philadelphia: Fortress Press, 1973.

Hamm, Dennis. "Sight to the Blind: Vision as Metaphor in Luke" *Bib*. 67 ('86) 457–477.

Hamman, Adalbert. "The Prayer of Jesus" *Way*. 3 (3,'63) 174–183.

–, (translated by Paul J. Oligny). *Prayer: The New Testament*. Chicago: Franciscan Herald Press, 1971.

–, "La prière chrétienne et la prière païenne, formes et différences, *ANRW*. II.23.2, pp. 1190–1247.

Hanson, Anthony Tyrrell. *The Image of the Invisible God*. London: SCM Press, 1982.

Hanson, R. P. C. "Does δίκαιος in Luke XXIII. 47 Explode the Proto-Luke Hypothesis?" *Hermathena*. 60 ('42) 74–78.

Harder, Günther. *Paulus und das Gebet*. Gütersloh: C. Bertelsmann, 1936.

–, "στηρίζω" *TDNT*. vol. VII, pp. 653–657.

Harnack, Adolf. "Probleme im Texte der Leidensgeschichte Jesu" *SPAW*. 11 ('01) 251–266.

–, (translated by J. R. Wilkinson). *The Sayings of Jesus: The Second Source of St. Matthew and St. Luke*. London: Williams and Norgate, 1908.

Harris, J. Rendel. "New Points of View in Textual Criticism" *Exp*. 8, 7 ('14) 316–334.

Harris, Lindell O. "Prayer in the Gospel of Luke" *SwJTh*. 10 ('67) 59–69.

Harris, Oscar G. *Prayer in Luke-Acts: A Study in the Theology of Luke*. unpublished Ph.D. dissertation. Vanderbilt University, 1967.

Harris, Rendel. "The Origin of a Famous Lucan Gloss" *ExpT*. 35 ('23–24) 7–10.

Hastings, Adrian. *Prophet and Witness in Jerusalem: A Study of the Teaching of Saint Luke*. London: Longmans, Green and Co., 1958.

Hay, David M. *Glory at the Right Hand: Psalm 110 in Early Christianity*. Nashville: Abington Press, 1973.

Hebbelthwaite, Peter. "Theological Themes in the Lucan Post-Resurrection Narratives" *ClRev.* 50 ('65) 360–369.

Hedinger, Ulrich. "Jesus und die Volksmenge: Kritik der Qualifizierung der óchloi in der Evangelienauslegung" *TZ.* 32 ('76) 201–206.

Heiler, Friedrich. (translated by Samuel McComb). *Prayer: A Study in the History and Psychology of Religion.* London: Oxford University Press, 1932.

Hein, Kenneth. "Judas Iscariot: Key to the Last-Supper Narratives?" *NTS.* 17 ('70–71) 227–232.

Heinemann, Joseph. *Prayer in the Talmud: Forms and Patterns.* Berlin: Walter de Gruyter, 1977.

Hengel, Martin. *Nachfolge und Charisma: Eine exegetisch-religionsgeschichtliche Studie zu Mt 8:21f und Jesu Ruf in die Nachfolge.* Berlin: Alfred Töpelmann, 1968.

–, (translated by John Bowden). "Between Jesus and Paul: The 'Hellenists', the 'Seven' and Stephen" in *Between Jesus and Paul: Studies in the Earliest History of Christianity.* London: SCM Press, 1983.

Henry, Donald M. "'Father, forgive them; for they know not what they do' (Luke xxiii. 34)" *ExpT.* 30 ('18–19) 87.

Herford, R. Travers. *Pharisaism, Its Aim and Its Method.* London: Williams and Norgate, 1912.

Héring, J. "Zwei exegetische Probleme in der Perikope von Jesus in Gethsemane (Markus xiv 32–42; Matthäus xxvi 36–46; Lukas xxii 40–46)" in *Neotestamentica et Patristica.* Leiden: E. J. Brill, 1962.

Hertzberg, H. W. "Sin dei Propheten Fürbitter?" in *Tradition und Situation: Studien zur alttestamentlichen Prophetie.* edited by E. Würthwein and W. Kaiser. Göttingen: Vandenhoeck & Ruprecht, 1963.

Hicks, R. Lansing. "Messiah, Second Moses, Son of Man" *ATR.* 33 ('51) 24–29.

Hiers, Richard H. "Why Will They Not Say, 'Lo, here!' Or 'There!'?" *JAAR.* 35 ('67) 379–384.

Higgins, A. J. B. "Jesus as Prophet" *ExpT.* 57 ('45–46) 292–294.

–, *The Lord's Supper in the New Testament.* Studies in Biblical Theology. London: SCM Press, 1952.

–, "Priest and Messiah" *VT.* 3 ('53) 321–336.

–, "The Old Testament and Some Aspects of New Testament Christology" *CJT.* 6 ('60) 200–210.

–, *Jesus and the Son of Man.* London: Lutterworth Press, 1964.

–, *The Son of Man in the Teaching of Jesus.* Cambridge: University Press, 1980.

Hill, David. "The Rejection of Jesus at Nazareth (Luke iv 16–30)" *NovT.* 13 ('71) 161–180.

–, "The Spirit and the Church's Witness: Observations on Acts 1:6–8" *IBS.* 6 ('84) 16–26.

Hill, E. "Messianic Fulfillment in St. Luke" *SE.* in *TU.* 73 ('59) 190–198.

Hoehner, Harold W. *Herod Antipas.* Cambridge: University Press, 1972.

–, "Why did Pilate hand Jesus over to Antipas?" in *The Trial of Jesus: Cambridge Studies in honour of C. F. D. Moule.* Studies in Biblical Theology, second series, 13. London: SCM Press, 1970.

Hoffmann, P. "Die Offenbarung des Sohnes: Die apokalyptischen Voraussetzungen und ihre Verarbeitung im Q–Logion Mt. 11:27 par. Lk. 10:22" *Kairos.* 12 ('70) 270–288.

–, *Studien zur Theologie der Logienquelle.* Münster: Verlag Aschendorff, 1972.

Holl, Karl. "Die Vorstellund vom Märtyrer und die Märtyrerakte in ihrer Geschichtlichen Entwicklung" *NJKA*. 17 ('14) 521–556.

Holleran, J. Warren. *The Synoptic Gethsemane: A Critical Study*. Analecta Gregoriana, 191. Rome: Universita Gregoriana Editrice, 1973.

Hoskier, H. C. *Codex B and Its Allies*. London: Bernard Quaritch, 1914.

Howard, J. K. "The Baptism of Jesus and its Present Significance" *EvQ*. 39 ('67) 131–138.

Hubbard, Benjamin J. "Commissioning Stories in Luke-Acts: A Study of their Antecedents, Form and Content" *Sem*. 8 ('77) 103–126.

–, "The Role of Commissioning Accounts in Acts" in *Perspectives on Luke-Acts*. edited by Charles H. Talbert. Danville: Association of Baptist Professors of Religion, 1978.

Huffard, E. W. "The Parable of the Friend at Midnight: God's Honor or Man's Persistence?" *RQ*. 21 (3,'78) 154–160.

Huffman, Norman. "Emmaus among the Resurrection Narratives" 64 ('45) 205–226.

Hull, J. H. E. *The Holy Spirit in the Acts of the Apostles*. London: Lutterworth Press, 1967.

Hull, John M. *Hellenistic Magic and the Synoptic Tradition*. London: SCM Press, 1974.

Hultgren, Arland J. "Interpreting the Gospel of Luke" *Int*. 30 (4,'76) 353–365.

Hunter, A. M. "Crux Criticorum – Matt. 11:25–30 – A Re-Appraisal" *NTS*. 8 ('62) 241–249.

Hunter, W. Bingham. *The Prayers of Jesus in the Gospel of John*. unpublished Ph.D dissertation. University of Aberdeen, 1979.

Jacobson, Richard. "The Structuralists and the Bible" *Int*. 28 ('74) 146–164.

Jeremias, Joachim. "Das Gebetsleben Jesu" *ZNW*. 25 ('26) 123–140.

–, *Heiligengräber in Jesu Umwelt (Mt. 23, 29; Lk. 11, 47): Eine Untersuchung zur Volksreligion der Zeit Jesu*. Göttingen: Vandenhoeck & Ruprecht, 1958.

–, (translated by Norman Perrin). *The Eucharistic Words of Jesus*. London: SCM Press, 1966.

–, (translated by John Bowden). *The Prayers of Jesus*. London: SCM Press, 1967.

–, (translated by John Bowden). *New Testament Theology*. London: SCM Press, 1971.

–, (translated by S. H. Hooke). *The Parables of Jesus*. New York: Charles Scribner's Sons, 1972 (2nd ed.).

–, "Ἠλ (ε)ίας," *TDNT*. vol. II, pp. 928–941.

–, "Μωυσῆς," *TDNT*. vol. IV, pp. 848–873.

–, "παῖς θεοῦ," *TDNT*. vol. V, pp. 654–717.

–, "πάσχα" *TDNT*. vol. V, pp. 896–904.

Jervell, Jacob. *Luke and the People of God*. Minneapolis: Augsburg Publishing House, 1972.

Jobling, David. "Robert Alter's 'The Art of Biblical Narrative'" *JSOT*. 27 ('83) 87–99.

Johansson, Nils. *Parakletoi, Vorstellungen von Fürsprechern für die Menschen vor Gott in der Alttestamentlichen Religion, im Spätjudentum und Urchristentum*. Lund: Gleerup, 1940.

Johnson, A. F. "Assurance for Man: The Fallacy of Translating ANAIDEIA by 'Persistence' in Luke 11:5–8" *JETS*. 22 ('79) 123–131.

Johnson, Luke T. *The Literary Function of Possessions in Luke-Acts*. Missoula: Scholars Press, 1977.

Johnson, M. D. *The Purpose of the Biblical Genealogies with Special Reference to the Setting of the Genealogies of Jesus*. Cambridge: University Press, 1969.

Johnson, Norman B. *Prayer in the Apocrypha and Pseudepigrapha: A Study of the Jewish Concept of God*. Philadelphia: Society of Biblical Literature and Exegesis, 1948.

Johnston, George. *The Spirit-Paraclete in the Gospel of John*. Cambridge: University Press, 1970.

Johnston, William H. *A Historical and Theological Study of Daily Prayer Times in the Ante-Nicene Church.* unpublished Ph.D. dissertation. University of Notre Dame, 1980.

Jones, C. P. M. "The Epistle to the Hebrews and the Lucan Writings" in *Studies in the Gospels.* edited by D. E. Nineham. Oxford: Basil Blackwell, 1955.

Jones, Maurice. "The Significance of St. Stephen in the History of the Primitive Christian Church" *Exp.* 8/13 ('17) 161–178.

Karris, Robert J. "Windows and Mirrors: Literary Criticism and Luke's Sitz im Leben" in *Society of Biblical Literature 1979 Seminar Papers vol. I.* edited by Paul J. Achtemeier. Missoula: Scholars Press, 1979.

–, *Luke, Artist and Theologian: Luke's Passion Account as Literature.* New York: Paulist Press, 1985.

Käsemann, Ernst. (translated by W. J. Montague). "The Problem of the Historical Jesus" in *Essays on New Testament Themes.* London: SCM Press, 1964.

–, (translated by Wilfred F. Bunge). "Paul and Early Catholicism" in *New Testament Questions of Today.* London: SCM Press, 1969.

Keck, Leander E. "Jesus' Entrance Upon His Mission" *RevExp.* 64 ('67) 465–483.

–, "The Spirit and the Dove" *NTS.* 17,('70–71) 41–67.

–, "Toward the Renewal of New Testament Christology" *NTS.* 32 ('86) 362–377.

Kee, Howard C. "Aretalogy and Gospel" *JBL.* 92 ('73) 402–422.

–, *Medicine, Miracle and Magic in New Testament Times.* Cambridge: University Press, 1986.

Kelber, Warner H. "Mark 14:32–42: Gethsemane, Passion Christology and Discipleship Failure" *ZNW.* 63 ('72) 166–187.

Kennett, R. H. "Jesus the Prophet" *HibJ.* 5 ('06–7) 136–155.

Kenny, Anthony. "Transfiguration and the Agony in the Garden" *CBQ.* 19 ('57) 444–452.

Kenyon, F. G. *The Text of the Greek Bible.* London: Duckworth & Co., 1975 (3rd ed.).

Kiddle, M. "The Passion Narrative in St. Luke's Gospel" *JTS.* 36 ('35) 267–280.

Kilpatrick, G. D. "A Theme of the Lucan Passion Story and Luke xxiii. 47" *JTS.* 43 ('42) 34–36.

–, "ΛAOI at Luke II. 31 and Acts IV. 25, 27" *JTS.* ns. 16 ('65) 127.

Kittel, Gerhard. "ἀκούω" *TDNT.* vol. I, pp. 216–225.

Klein, Günter. *Die zwölf Apostel: Ursprung und Gehalt einer Idee.* Göttingen: Vandenhoeck & Ruprecht, 1961.

–, "Die Verleugnung des Petrus: Eine traditionsgeschichte Untersuchung" *ZTK.* 58 ('61) 285–328.

–, *Rekonstruktion und Interpretation: Gesammelte Aufsäfze zum Neuen Testament.* München: Chr. Kaiser Verlag, 1969.

Klijn, A. F. J. "Papyrus Bodmer II (John I–XIV) and the Text of Egypt" *NTS.* 3 ('56–57) 327–334.

–, "Stephen's Speech – Acts VII. 2–53" *NTS.* 4 ('57) 25–31.

–, "In Search of the Original Text of Acts" in *Studies in Luke-Acts.* edited by Leander E. Keck and J. Louis Martyn. Philadelphia: Fortress Press, 1966.

–, "Matthew 11:25//Luke 10:21" in *New Testament Textual Criticism, Its Significance for Exegesis.* edited by Eldon Jay Epp and Gordon D. Fee. Oxford: Clarendon Press, 1981.

Kloppenborg, John S. "Wisdom Christology in Q" *LTP.* 34 ('78) 129–147.

Kodell, Jerome. "Luke's Use of LAOS, 'People', Especially in the Jerusalem Narrative (Lk. 19,28 – 24,53)" *CBQ.* 31 ('69) 327–343.

Koet, B. -J. "Some Traces of a Semantic Field of Interpretation in Luke 24, 13–35" *Bij.* 46 ('85) 59–73.

Kremer, Jacob. *Die Osterbotschaft der vier Evangelien.* Stuttgart: Katholisches Bibelwerk, 1968.

Kruse, H. "Die 'Dialektische Negation' als Semitisches Idiom" *VT.* 4 ('54) 385–400.

Kuhn, Karl Georg. "Jesus in Gethsemane" *EvT.* 12 ('52–53) 260–285.

–, "The Lord's Supper and the Communal Meal at Qumran" in *The Scrolls and the New Testament.* edited by Krister Stendahl. London: SCM Press, 1958.

–, "New Light on Temptation, Sin and Flesh in the New Testament" in *The Scrolls and the New Testament.* edited by Krister Stendahl. London: SCM Press, 1958.

Kümmel, W. G. (translated by Dorothea M. Barton). *Promise and Fulfillment: The Eschatological Message of Jesus.* London: SCM Press, 1969 (3rd ed.).

–, (translated by C. E. Carlston and R. P. Scharlemann). "Eschatological Expectation in the Proclamation of Jesus" in *The Future of Our Religious Past.* edited by James M. Robinson. London: SCM Press, 1971.

Kunjummen, Raju D. "The Single Intent of Scripture – Critical Examination of a Theological Construct" *GTJ.* 7 ('86) 81–110.

Künzi, Martin. *Das Naherwartungslogion Markus 9,1 par: Geschichte seiner Auslegung.* Tübingen: J. C. B. Mohr, 1977.

Lammers, Klaus. *Hören, Sehen und Glauben im Neuen Testament.* Stuttgart: Katholisches Bibelwork, 1966.

Lampe, G. W. H. "The Lucan Portrait of Christ" *NTS.* 2 ('55–6) 160–175.

–, "The Holy Spirit in the Writings of St. Luke" in *Studies in the Gospels.* edited by D. E. Nineham. Oxford: Basil Blackwell, 1955.

–, "Miracles in the Acts of the Apostles" in *Miracles: Cambridge Studies in their Philosophy and History.* edited by C. F. D. Moule. London: A. R. Mowbray & Co., 1965.

Langton, Edward. *The Ministries of the Angelic Powers, According to the Old Testament and Later Jewish Literature.* London: James Clarke & Co., Ltd., 1936.

Larkin, William J. "The Old Testament Background of Luke XXII. 43–44" *NTS.* 25 (2,'79) 250–254.

Laurentin, René. *Structure et Théologie de Luc I–II.* Paris: J. Gabalda, 1964.

Leaney, Robert. "Jesus and Peter: the Call and Post-resurrection Appearance (Lk. v. 1–11 and xxiv. 34)" *ExpT.* 65 ('53–4) 381–382.

–, "Jesus and the Symbol of the Child (Luke 9:46–48)" *ExpT.* 66 ('54) 91–92.

–, "The Resurrection Narratives in Luke (24:12–53)" *NTS.* 2 ('55–6) 110–114.

–, "The Lucan Text of the Lord's Prayer (Lk. 11:2–4)" *NovT.* 1 ('56) 103–111.

Le Déaut, Roger. *La Nuit Pascale: Essai sur la signification de la Pâque juive à partir du Targum d'Exode XII 42.* Rome: Pontifical Biblical Institute, 1963.

–, "Aspects de l'Intercession dans Le Judaïsme Ancien *JSJ.* 1 ('70) 35–57.

Ledogar, Robert J. Verbs of Praise in the LXX Translation of the Hebrew Canon," *Bib.* 48 ('67) 29–56.

Légasse, S. "La Révélation aux NEPIOI" *RevBibl.* 67 (3,'60) 321–348.

–, *Jésus et l'enfant: "enfants," "petits" et "simples" dans la tradition synoptique.* Paris: J. Gabalda, 1969.

Legrand, L. "Christ the Fellow Traveler: The Emmaus Story in Lk. 24:13–35" *IndTS.* 19 (1,'82) 33–44.

Lentzen-Deis, Fritzleo. *Die Taufe Jesu nach den Synoptikern: Literarkritische und gattungsgeschichtliche Untersuchungen.* Frankfurt am Main: Josef Knecht, 1970.

–, "Beten Kraft des Gebetes Jesu" *GL.* 48 ('75) 164–178.

Léon-Dufour, Xavier. (translated by Geoffrey Chapman). *Resurrection and the Message of Easter*. London: Geoffrey Chapman, 1974.

Lescow, Theodor. "Jesus in Gethsemane" *ET*. 26 ('66) 141–159.

Levey, Samson H. "The Date of Targum Jonathan to the Prophets" *VT*. 21 ('71) 186–196.

–, *The Messiah: An Aramaic Interpretation, The Messianic Exegesis of the Targum*. Cincinnati: Hebrew Union College Press, 1971.

Levison, N. "Importunity?" *Exp*. 9th ser. 3 ('25) 456–460.

Lewis, F. Warburton. "'I beheld Satan fall as lightning from heaven' (Luke x. 18)" *ExpT*. 259'13–14) 232–233.

Liefeld, Walter L. "Exegetical Notes, Luke 24:13–35" *TJ*. ns. 2 ('81) 223–229.

Lietzmann, Hans. (translated by Dorothea H. G. Reeve). *Mass and Lord's Supper: A Study in the History of the Liturgy*. Leiden: E. J. Brill, 1979.

Lindars, Barnabas. *New Testament Apologetic: The Doctrinal Significance of the Old Testament Quotations*. London: SCM Press, 1961.

–, "Jesus as Advocate: A Contribution to the Christology Debate" *BJRL*. 62 ('80) 476–497.

–, "Enoch and Christology" *ExpT*. 92 ('81) 295–299.

–, *Jesus Son of Man: A Fresh Examination of the Son of Man Sayings in the Gospels in the Light of Recent Research*. London: SPCK, 1983.

Lindijer, C. H. "Two Creative Encounters in the Work of Luke (Lk. xxiv 13–35 and Acts viii 26–40)" in *Miscellanea Neotestamentica*. Leiden: E. J. Brill, 1978.

Linnemann, Eta. "Die Verleugnung des Petrus" *ZTK*. 63 ('66) 1–32.

–, *Studien zur Passionsgeschichte*. Göttingen: Vandenhoeck & Ruprecht, 1970.

Loader, W. R. G. "Christ at the Right Hand – Ps. CX. 1 in the New Testament" *NTS*. 24 ('78) 199–217.

Lohfink, Gerhard. *Die Himmelfahrt Jesu: Untersuchungen zu den Himmelfahrts-und Erhöhungstexten bei Lukas*. München: Kösel Verlag, 1971.

–, *Die Sammlung Israels: Eine Untersuchung zur lukanischen Ekklesiologie*. München: Kösel-Verlag, 1975.

–, (translated by Bruce J. Malina). *The Conversion of St. Paul: Narrative and History in Acts*. Chicago: Franciscan Herald Press, 1976.

Lohmeyer, Ernst. (translated by John Bowden). *The Lord's Prayer*. London: Collins, 1965.

Lohse, Eduard. "Lukas als Theologe der Heilsgeschichte" in *Die Einheit des Neuen Testaments: Exegetische Studien zur Theologie des Neuen Testaments*. Göttingen: Vandenhoeck & Ruprecht, 1973.

Loisy, Alfred (translated by L. P. Jacks). *The Origins of the New Testament*. London: George Allen and Unwin Ltd., 1950.

Long, Burke O. "Reports of Visions Among the Prophets" *JBL*. 95 ('76) 353–365.

Longenecker, Richard N. *The Christology of Early Jewish Christianity*. London: SCM Press, 1970

Lowther-Clarke, W. K. "Studies in Texts, St. Luke x. 18" *Th*. 7 ('23) 103–104.

–, "A Prophet Like Unto Me" *Th*. 12 ('26) 163–168.

Lührmann, Dieter. "Jesus und seine Propheten. Gesprächsbeitrag" in *Prophetic Vocation in the New Testament and Today*. Leiden: E. J. Brill, 1977.

Luz, Ulrich. "The Secrecy Motif and the Marcan Christology" in *The Messianic Secret*. edited by Christopher Tuckett. London: SPCK, 1983.

MacDonald, John. *The Theology of the Samaritans*. London: SCM Press, 1964.

Macgregor, W. M. "The Words from the Cross. II. The Penitent Thief (Lk. xxiii. 39–43)" *ExpT*. 41 ('29–30) 151–154.

Mackinnon, D. M. "Sacrament and Common Meal" in *Studies in the Gospels: Essays in Memory of R. H. Lightfoot*. edited by D. E. Nineham. Oxford: Basil Blackwell, 1957.

Maddox, Robert. "The Function of the Son of Man According to the Synoptic Gospels" *NTS*. 15 ('68–69) 45–74.

–, *The Purpose of Luke-Acts*. Edinburgh: T. & T. Clark, 1982.

Major, H. D. A., Manson, T. W., and Wright, C. J. (eds). *The Mission and Message of Jesus*. London: Ivor Nicholson and Watson, 1937.

Mánek, Jindrich. "On the Mount – On the Plain (Mt. v 1 – Lk. vi 17)" *NovT*. 9 ('67) 124–131.

Manson, T. W. "Entry into Membership of the Early Church" *JTS*. 48 ('47) 25–33.

–, *The Sayings of Jesus*. London: SCM Press, 1949 (2nd ed.).

–, *The Teaching of Jesus*. Cambridge: University Press, 1951.

Margreth, Jakob. *Gebetsleben Jesu Christi, des Sohnes Gottes*. Münster: Aschendorffschen Buchhandlung, 1902.

Marmorstein, A. "Einege vorläufige Bemerkungen zu den neuentdeckten Fragmenten des jerusalemischen (palästinensischen) Targums" *ZAW*. 8 ('31) 231–242.

Marshall, I. H. "The Synoptic Son of Man Sayings in Recent Discussion" *NTS*. 12 ('65–66) 327–351.

–, "The Development of Christology in the Early Church" *TB*. 18 ('67) 77–93.

–, "Son of God or Servant of Yahweh? A Reconsideration of Mark 1:11" *NTS*. 15 ('68–69) 326–336.

–, "Tradition and Theology in Luke (Luke 8:5–15)" *TB*. 20 ('69) 56–75.

–, *Kept by the Power of God: A Study of Perseverance and Falling Away*. Minneapolis: Bethany Fellowship, 1969.

–, "The Resurrection in the Acts of the Apostles" in *Apostolic History and the Gospels: Biblical and Historical Essays Presented to F. F. Bruce*. edited by W. Ward Gasque and Ralph P. Martin. Exeter: Paternoster Press, 1970.

–, *Luke: Historian and Theologian*. Grand Rapids: Zondervan, 1970.

–, "Palestinian and Hellenistic Christianity: Some Critical Comments" *NTS*. 19 ('72–73) 271–287.

–, "The Resurrection of Jesus in Luke" *TB*. 24 ('73) 55–98.

–, "'Early Catholicism' in the New Testament" in *New Dimensions in New Testament Study*. edited by Richard N. Longenecker and Merrill C. Tenney. Grand Rapids: Zondervan, 1974.

–, *The Origins of New Testament Christology*. Leicester: Inter-Varsity Press, 1976.

–, *Last Supper and Lord's Supper*. Exeter: Paternoster Press, 1980.

–, "Luke and his 'Gospel'" in *Das Evangelium und die Evangelien: Vorträge vom Tübinger Symposium 1982*. edited by Peter Stuhlmacher. Tübingen: J. C. B. Mohr (Paul Siebeck), 1983.

–, "Apg 12 – ein Schlüssel zum Verständnis der Apostelgeschichte" in *Das Petrusbild in der neueren Forschung*, edited by C. P. Thiede. Wuppertal, 1987.

Martin, A. D. "The Parable Concerning Hospitality" *ExpT*. 37 ('25–6) 411–414.

Martin, Ralph P. "Salvation and Discipleship in Luke's Gospel" *Int*. 30 (4,'76) 366–380.

Matera, Frank J. "The Death of Jesus according to Luke: A Question of Sources" *CBQ*. 47 ('85) 469–485.

Mattill, A. J. "The Purpose of Acts: Schneckenburger Reconsidered" in *Apostolic History and the Gospels: Biblical and Historical Essays Presented to F. F. Bruce.* edited by W. Ward Gasque and Ralph P. Martin. Exeter: Paternoster Press, 1970.

–, *Luke and the Last Things: A Perspective for the Understanding of Lukan Thought.* Dillsboro, NC: Western North Carolina Press, 1979.

Mauchline, John. "Jesus Christ as Intercessor" *ExpT.* 64 ('52–53) 355–360.

May, Eric. "'... For power went forth from him ...' (Luke 6:19)" *CBQ.* 14 ('52) 93–103.

McArthur, H. K. "The Eusebian Sections and Canon" *CBQ.* 27 ('65) 250–256.

McCaughey, J. D. "Literary Criticism and the Gospels" *ABR.* 29 ('81) 16–25.

McKeating, H. "The Prophet Jesus" *ExpT.* 73 ('61) 4–7.

McNamara, Martin. *Targum and Testament, Aramaic Paraphrases of the Hebrew Bible: A Light on the New Testament.* Shannon: Irish University Press, 1972.

–, *The New Testament and the Palestinian Targum to the Pentateuch.* Rome: Biblical Institute Press, 1978.

McNicol, Allen James. *The Relationship of the Image of Highest Angel to the High Priest Concept in Hebrews.* unpublished Ph.H. dissertation. Vanderbilt University, 1974.

McPolin, James. "Holy Spirit in Luke and John" *ITQ.* 45 ('78) 117–131.

Meecham, H. G. "The Imperatival Use of ἵνα in the New Testament" *JTS.* 43 ('42) 179–180.

Meeks, Wayne A. *The Prophet-King: Moses Traditions and the Johannine Christology.* Leiden: E. J. Brill, 1967.

–, "Moses as God and King" in *Religions in Antiquity: Essays in Memory of Erwin Ramsdel Goodenough.* edited by Jacob Neusner. Leiden: E. J. Brill, 1968.

Metzger, Bruce M. "Seventy or Seventy-Two Disciples?" *NTS.* 5 ('58–59) 299–306.

–, "The Bodmer Papyrus of Luke and John" *ExpT.* 73 ('62) 201–203.

–, *Chapters in the History of New Testament Textual Criticism.* Leiden: E. J. Brill, 1963.

–, *The Text of the New Testament, Its Transmission, Corruption, and Restoration.* Oxford: Clarendon Press, 1964.

–, *The Early Versions of the New Testament: Their Origin, Transmission, and Limitations.* Oxford: Clarendon Press, 1977.

–, *Manuscripts of the Greek Bible: An Introduction to Palaeography.* Oxford: University Press, 1981.

Ménard, Jacques E. "'Pais Theou' as Messianic Title in the Book of Acts" *CBQ.* 19 ('57) 83–92.

Michael, J. Hugh. "The Text of Luke xxiv. 34" *ExpT.* 60 ('48–49) 292.

Michaels, J. Ramsey. "The Centurion's Confession and the Spear Thrust" *CBQ.* 29 ('67) 102–109.

Michaelis, W. "ὁράω" *TDNT.* vol V, pp. 315–367.

Michalczyk, John J. "The Experience of Prayer in Luke-Acts" *RevRel.* 34 (5,'75) 789–801.

Michel, O. "ὁμολογέω" *TDNT.* vol. V, pp. 199–220.

Millar, Merrill P. "The Function of Isa. 61:1–2 in 11Q Melchizedek" *JBL.* 88 ('69) 467–469.

Milne, H. J. M. and Skeat, T. C. *Scribes and Correctors of the Codex Sinaiticus.* London: British Museum, 1938.

Minear, Paul. "A Note on Luke 22:36" *NovT.* 7 ('64) 128–134.

–, "Audience Criticism and Markan Ecclesiology" in *Neues Testament und Geschichte.* edited by Heinrich Baltensweiler and Bo Reicke. Tübingen: J. C. B. Mohr(Paul Siebeck), 1972.

–, "Jesus' Audiences, According to Luke" *NovT.* 16 ('74) 81–109.

–, *To Heal and To Reveal: The Prophetic Vocation According to Luke*. New York: Seabury Press, 1976.

–, "Luke's Use of the Birth Stories" in *Studies in Luke-Acts*. edited by Leander E. Keck and J. Louis Martyn. Philadelphia: Fortress Press, 1980 (2nd ed.).

Miyoshi, Michi. *Der Anfang des Reiseberichts Lk. 9:51–10:24; Eine redaktiongeschitliche Untersuchung*. Rome: Biblical Institute Press, 1974.

Moehring, Horst R. "The Verb akouein in Acts 9:7 and 22:9" *NovT*. 3 ('59) 80–99.

Moessner, David P. "Jesus and the 'Wilderness Generation': The Death of the Prophet Like Moses According to Luke" in *Society of Biblical Literature 1982 Seminar Papers*. edited by K. H. Richards. Chico: Scholars Press, 1982.

–, "Luke 9:1–50: Luke's Preview of the Journey of the Prophet like Moses of Deuteronomy" *JBL*. 102 ('83) 575–605.

Mobley, Richard A. *Structure and Theological Significance in the Lukan Concept of Prayer*. unpublished Ph.D. dissertation. Southwestern Baptist Theological Seminary, Fort Worth, Texas, 1983.

Moffatt, James. "Exegetica: Lk. xxii 44" *Exp*. 8/7 ('14) 90–92.

–, "Exegetica: Lk. xxiii 34" *Exp*. 8/7 ('14) 92–93.

Monloubou, Louis. *La Prière selon Saint Luc: Recherche d'une structure*. Paris: Cerf, 1976.

Montefiore, C. G. and Loewe, H. *A Rabbinic Anthology*. New York: Schocken, 1974.

Mosley, A. W. "Jesus' Audiences in the Gospels of St. Mark and St. Luke" *NTS*. 10 ('63–64) 139–149.

Moule, C. F. D. "The Post-Resurrection Appearances in the Light of Festival Pilgrimages" *NTS*. 4 ('57) 58–61.

–, *The Phenomenon of the New Testament: An Inquiry into the Implications of Certain Features of the New Testament*. London: SCM Press, 1967.

–, "The Christology of Acts" in *Studies in Luke-Acts*. edited by Leander E. Keck and J. Louis Martyn. Philadelphia: Fortress Press, 1980 (2nd ed.).

–, "Neglected Features in the Problem of the Son of Man" in *Essays in New Testament Interpretation*. Cambridge: University Press, 1982.

–, "The Influence of Circumstances on the Use of Christological Terms" in *Essays in New Testament Interpretation*. Cambridge: University Press, 1982.

Mouson, J. "Présence du Ressuscité: Les récits évangéliques d'apparitions" *CMCSE*. 54 ('69) 178–220.

Mowinckel, Sigmund. "Die Vorstellungen des Spätjudentums von heiligen Geist als Fürsprecher und der johanneischen Paraklet" *ZNW*. 32 ('33) 97–130.

–, "'The Spirit' and the 'Word' in the Pre-Exilic Reforming Prophets" *JBL*. 53 ('34) 199–227.

–, (translated by G. W. Anderson). *He That Cometh*. Oxford: Basil Blackwell, 1959.

Müller, Ulrich. "Vision und Botschaft" *ZTK*. 74 ('77) 416–448.

Mullins, Terence. "New Testament Commission Forms, Especially in Luke-Acts" *JBL*. 95 ('76) 603–614.

Münsser, F. "'Wann kommt das Reich Gottes?' Die Antwort Jesu nach Lk. 17, 20b, 21" *BZ*. 6 ('62) 107–111.

Nardoni, Enrique. "A Redactional Interpretation of Mark 9:1" *CBQ*. 43 ('81) 365–384.

Navone, John. "Prayer" *Scr*. 20 (52,'68) 115–125.

–, *Themes of St. Luke*. Rome: Gregorian University Press, 1970.

Neirynck, F. "Minor Agreements Matthew-Luke in the Transfiguration Story" in *Orientierung an Jesus: Zur theologie der Synoptiker für Josef Schmid*. edited by P. Hoffmann, N. Brox, W. Pesch. Freiburg: Herder, 1973.

Nestle, Eb. "Acts vii. 55, 56" *ExpT.* 11 ('1899–1900) 94.

–, "The Vision of Stephen" *ExpT.* 22 ('10–11) 423.

Neudorfer, Heinz-Werner. *Der Stephanuskries in der Forschungsgeschichte seit F. C. Baur.* Giessen: Brunnen, 1983.

Neugebauer, Fritz. "Die Davidssohnfrage (Mark xii. 35–7 parr.) und der Menschensohn" *NTS.* 21 ('74–75) 81–108.

Neyrey, Jerome H. "The Absence of Jesus' Emotions – The Lucan Redaction of Lk. 22, 39–46" *Bib.* 61 ('80) 153–171.

–, "Jesus' Address to the Women of Jerusalem (Lk. 23. 27–31) – A Prophetic Judgement Oracle" *NTS.* 29 ('83) 74–86.

–, *The Passion According to Luke: A Redaction Study of Luke's Soteriology.* New York: Paulist Press, 1985.

Noack, Bent. *Satanás und Sotería: Untersuchungen zur Neutestamentlichen Dämnologie.* København: G. E. C. Gads Forlag, 1948.

Norden, Eduard. *Agnostos Theos: Untersuchungen zur Formengeschichte Religiöser Rede.* Leipzig: B. G. Teubner, 1923.

Nuttall, Geoffrey F. *The Moment of Recognition: Luke as Story-Teller.* London: Athlone Press, 1978.

Nützel, Johannes M. *Die Verklärungserzählung im Markusevangelium: Eine redaktionsgeschichtliche Untersuchung.* Würzburg: Echter Verlag, 1973.

–, *Jesus als Offenbarer Gottes nach den lukanischen Schriften.* Würzburg: Echter Verlag, 1980.

Obeng, Emmanuel Adow. *A Study of Romans 8:26f.* unpublished Ph.D. dissertation, University of Aberdeen, 1980.

–, "The Origins of the Spirit Intercession Motif in Romans 8:26" *NTS.* 32 ('86) 621–632. O'Brien, P. T. "Prayer in Luke-Acts" *TB.* 24 ('73) 111–127.

Odeberg, Hugo. "Ἐνώχ," *TDNT.* vol. II, pp. 556–560.

Oepke, Albrecht. "γρηγορέω" *TDNT.* vol. II, pp. 333–339.

–, "καλύπτω, ἀποκαλύπτω" *TDNT.* vol. III, pp. 556–592.

–, "κρύπτω" *TDNT.* vol. III, pp. 957–978.

–, "μεσίτης," *TDNT.* vol. IV, pp. 598–624.

Oesterley, W. O. E. *The Jewish Doctrine of Mediation.* London: Skeffington and Son, 1910.

–, *The Jews and Judaism During the Greek Period: The Background of Christianity.* London: SPCK, 1941.

Oliver, Harold H. "The Epistle of Eusebius to Carpianus: Textual Tradition and Translation" *NovT.* 3 ('59) 138–145.

–, "The Lucan Birth Stories and the Purpose of Luke-Acts" *NTS.* 10 ('63–64) 202–226.

O'Neill, J. C. "The Use of KYRIOS in the Book of Acts" *SJT.* 8 ('55) 155–174.

–, *The Theology of Acts in its Historical Setting.* London: SPCK, 1961.

–, "The Silence of Jesus" *NTS.* 15 ('68–69) 153–167.

Orlett, Raymond. "Influence of the Early Liturgy upon the Emmaus Account" *CBQ.* 21 ('59) 212–219.

–, "The Breaking of Bread in Acts" *BibT.* 1 ('62) 108–113.

O'Toole, R. F. "Activity of the Risen Jesus in Luke-Acts" *Bib.* 62 ('81) 471–498.

–, "Parallels between Jesus and His Disciples in Luke-Acts: A Further Study" *BZ.* 27 (2,'83) 195–212.

Ott, Wilhelm. *Gebet und Heil: Die Bedeutung der Gebetsparänese in der lukanischen Theologie.* München: Kösel-Verlag, 1965.

Owen, H. P. "Stephen's Vision in Acts 7:55–56" *NTS.* 1 ('54) 224–226.

Parsons, Mikeal C. "A Christological Tendency in P75" *JBL*. 105 ('86) 463–479.

Paton, W. R. "'Αγωνία (Agony)" *ClassRev*. 27 ('13) 194.

Patsch, Hermann. "Abendmahlsterminologie ausserhalb der Einsetzungsberichte" *ZNW*. 62 ('71) 210–231.

Patte, Daniel. *What is Structural Exegesis?*. Philadelphia: Fortress Press, 1976.

–, and Patte, Aline. *Structural Exegesis: From Theory to Practice*. Philadelphia: Fortress Press, 1978.

Paul, Shalom M. "Heavenly Tablets and the Book of Life" *JANESCU*. 5 ('73) 345–353.

Pegg, Herbert. "'A Scorpion for an Egg' (Luke xi. 12)" *ExpT*. 38 ('26–27) 468–469.

Percy, Ernst. *Die Botschaft Jesu: eine Traditionskritische und Exegetische Untersuchung*. Lund: C. W. K. Gleerup, 1953.

Perrin, Norman. "The Composition of Mark ix I" *NovT*. 11 ('69) 67–70.

–, "The Evangelist as Author: Reflections on Method in the Study and Interpretation of the Synoptic Gospel and Acts" *BR*. 17 ('72) 5–18.

–, *Rediscovering the Teaching of Jesus*. New York: Harper & Row, 1976.

–, *Jesus and the Language of the Kingdom: Symbol and Metaphor in New Testament Interpretation*. London: SCM Press, 1976.

Pesch, Rudolf. "Die Vision des Stephanus Apg 7,55f. im Rahmen der Apostelgeschichte" *BL*. 6 ('65) 92–107, 170–183.

–, *Die Vision des Stephanus: Apg. 7,55–56 im Rahmen der Apostelgeschichte*. Stuttgart: Katholisches Bibelwerk, 1966.

–, *Jesu ureigene Taten? Ein Beitrag zur Wunderfrage*. Freiburg: Herder, 1970.

Petersen, Norman R. *Literary Criticism for New Testament Critics*. Philadelphia: Fortress Press, 1978.

Petuchowski, Jakob B. and Brocke, Michael (eds.). *The Lord's Prayer and Jewish Liturgy*. London: Burns and Oates, 1978.

Pickar, Charles H. "The Prayer of Christ for Saint Peter" *CBQ*. 4 ('42) 133–140.

Pjetzner, Victor C. "'Pneumatic' Apostleship? Apostle and Spirit in the Acts of the Apostles" in *Wort in der Zeit: Festgabe für Karl Heinrich Rengstorf*. edited by Wilfred Haubeck and Michael Bachmann. Leiden: E. J. Brill, 1980.

Plevnik, Joseph. "The Origin of Easter Faith according to Luke" *Bib*. 61 ('80) 492–508.

Plymale, Steven Frederick. *The Prayer Texts of Luke-Acts*. unpublished Ph. D. dissertation, Northwest University, 1986.

Pobee, John. "The Cry of the Centurion – A Cry of Defeat" in *The Trial of Jesus: Cambridge Studies in honour of C. F. D. Moule*. edited by Ernst Bammel. London: SCM Press, 1970.

Pollard, Edward B. "The Prophetic Activity of Jesus" *BW*. 24 ('04) 94–99.

Porter, Calvin L. "Papyrus Bodmer (P75) and the Text of Codex Vaticanus" *JBL*. 81 ('62) 363–376.

Preiss, Théo. *Life in Christ*. London: SCM Press, 1954.

Prevallet, Elaine M. *Luke 24:26: A Passover Christology*. unpublished Ph.D. dissertation. Marquette University, 1968.

Prokulski, Walenty. "The Conversion of St. Paul" *CBQ*. 19 ('57) 453–473.

Radermakers, Jean. "The Prayer of Jesus in the Synoptic Gospels" *LV*. 24 (4,'69) 561–578.

Rau, Pjarrer Gottfried. "Das Volk in der lukanischen Passionsgeschichte, eine Konjecktur zu Lk. 23:13" *ZNW*. 56 ('65) 41–51.

Reicke, Bo. "Die göttliche Offenbarung und das heilige Land, Apg. 7,1–8,3" in *Glaube und Leben der Urgemeinde, Bemerkungen zu Apg. 1–7.* edited by W. Eichrodt and O. Cullmann. Zürich: Zwingli-Verlag, 1957.

–, "Instruction and Discussion in the Travel Narrative" in *The Gospels Reconsidered.* Berlin: Akademie-Verlag, 1958.

–, "The Risen Lord and His Church: The Theology of Acts" *Int.* 13 (2,'59) 157–169.

–, "Jesus in Nazareth" in *Das Wort und die Wörter: Festschrift Gerhard Friedrich zum 65. Geburtstag.* edited by Horst Balz and Siegfried Schulz. Stuttgart: W. Kohlhammer, 1973.

–, "πᾶς" *TDNT.* vol. V, pp. 886–896.

Reid, James. "The Words from the Cross. I. 'Father, forgive them' (Lk. xxiii. 34)" *ExpT.* 41 ('29–30) 103–107.

Rengstorf, Karl Heinrich. *Die Auferstehung Jesu: Form, Art und Sinn Der Urchristlichen Osterbotschaft.* Witten: Luther Verlag, 1960.

Rese, Martin. *Altestamentliche Motive in der Christologie des Lukas.* Gütersloh: Gerd Mohn, 1969.

Rhoads, David. "Narrative Criticism and the Gospel of Mark" *JAAR.* 50 ('82) 411–434.

Rice, George E. "The Anti-Judaic Bias of the Western Text in the Gospel of Luke" *AUSS.* 18 ('80) 51–57.

–, "Some Further Examples of Anti-Judaic Bias in the Western Text of the Gospel of Luke" *AUSS.* 18 ('80) 149–156.

–, "The Role of the Populace in the Passion Narrative of Luke in Codex Bezae" *AUSS.* 19 ('81) 147–153.

Richard, Earl. *Acts 6:1–8:4 The Author's Method of Composition.* Missoula: Scholars Press, 1978.

–, "Luke – Writer, Theologian, Historian: Research and Orientation of the 1970's" *BTB.* 13 ('83) 3–15.

Rickards, Raymond R. "The Translation of Luke 11.5–13" *BT.* 28 ('77) 239–243.

Riddle, Donald W. "The Martyr Motif in the Gospel According to Mark" *JR.* 4 ('24) 397–410.

Riesenfeld, H. "τηρέω" *TDNT.* vol. VIII, pp. 140–151.

–, "'Εμβολεύειν – 'Εντός" *NSNU.* 2 ('49) 12.

Roberts, Colin H. "The Kingdom of Heaven (Lk. XVII. 21)" *HTR.* 41 ('48) 1–8.

Robertson, David. *The Old Testament and the Literary Critic.* Philadelphia: Fortress Press, 1977.

Robinson, B. P. "The Place of the Emmaus Story in Luke-Acts" *NTS.* 30 ('84) 481–497.

Robinson, James M. "Die Hodajot-Formel in Gebet und Hymnus des Frühchristentums" in *Apophoreta: Festschrift für Ernst Haenchen,* edited by W. Eltester and F. H. Kettler. Berlin: Alfred Töpelmann, 1964.

–, "On the 'Gattung' of Mark (and John)" in *Jesus and Man's Hope.* edited by David G. Buttrick. Pittsburgh: Pittsburgh Theological Seminary, 1970.

Robinson, John A. T. *Jesus and His Coming: The Emergence of a Doctrine.* London: SCM Press, 1957.

–, "Elijah, John and Jesus: An Essay in Detection" in *Twelve New Testament Studies.* edited by J. A. T. Robinson. London: SCM Press, 1962.

–, "The Most Primitive Christology of All?" in *Twelve New Testament Studies.* edited by J. A. T. Robinson. London: SCM Press, 1962.

Robinson, William C. *The Way of the Lord: A Study of History and Eschatology in the Gospel of Luke.* unpublished Ph.D. dissertation. University of Basel, 1962.

–, Der Weg des Herrn: Studien zur Geschichte und Eschatology im Lukasevangelium, ein Gesprach mit Hans Conzelmann. Hamburg: H. Reich, 1964.

–, "On Preaching the Word of God (Luke 8:4–21)" in Studies in Luke-Acts. edited by Leander E. Keck and J. Louis Martyn. Philadelphia: Fortress Press, 1966.

Rohr, Ignaz. Das Gebet im Neuen Testament. Münster: Aschendorffsche Verlagsbuchhandlung, 1924.

Roloff, Jürgen. Das Kerygma und der irdische Jesus: Historische Motive in den Jesus-Erzählungen der Evangelien. Göttingen: Vandenhoeck and Ruprecht, 1970.

Rose, A. "L'Influence des Psaumes sur les Annonces et les Récits de la Passion et de la Résurrection dans les Evangiles" in Le Psautier: Ses origines, Ses problemes littéraires, Son influence. Louvain: Publications Universitaires, 1962.

Ruppert, Lothar. Jesus als der leidende Gerechte? Der Weg Jesu im Lichte eines alt- und zwischentestamentlichen Motivs. Stuttgart: Katholisches Bibelwerk, 1972.

Russell, D. S. The Old Testament Pseudepigrapha: Patriarchs and Prophets in Early Judaism. London: SCM Press, 1987.

Rüstow, A. "Entos hymon estin. Zur Deutung von Lukas 17:20–21" ZNW. 51 ('60) 197–224.

Ryken Leland. "Literary Criticism of the Bible: Some Fallacies" in Literary Interpretations of Biblical Narratives. edited by Kenneth R. R. Gros Louis, James L. Ackerman and Thayer S. Warshaw. Nashville/New York: Abingdon Press, 1974.

Sabbe, M. "The Son of Man Saying in Acts 7,56" in Les Actes des Apôtres: Traditions, rédaction, théologie. edited by J. Kremer. Gembloux: J. Duculot, 1979.

–, "Can Mt 11,25–27 and Lc 10,22 Be Called a Johannine Logion?" in Logia: Les Paroles de Jésus – The Sayings of Jesus. edited by J. Delobel. Leuven: University Press, 1982.

Sanday, William (ed.). Oxford Studies in the Synoptic Problem. Oxford: Clarendon Press, 1911.

Sanders, James A. "From Isaiah 61 to Luke 4" in Christianity, Judaism and Other Greco-Roman Cults. part I. edited by Jacob Neusner. Leiden: E. G. Brill, 1975.

Sanders, J. N. "Peter and Paul in the Acts" NTS. 2 ('55–6) 133–143.

Sawyer, John F. A. "Why is a Solar Eclipse Mentioned in the Passion Narrative (Luke XXIII. 44–5)?" JTS. ns. 23 ('72) 124–128.

Scaria, K. J. "Jesus' Prayer and Christian Prayer (Lk. 10:21–22)" Bib. 7 ('81) 160–185.

–, "Christian Prayer" Bib. 7 ('81) 201–224.

Scharbert, Josef. "Die Fürbitte in der Theologie des Alten Testaments" TG. 50 ('60) 321–338.

–, Heilsmittler im Alten Testament und im Alten Orient. Freiburg: Herder, 1964.

Scharlemann, Martin H. Stephen: A Singular Saint. Rome: Pontifical Biblical Institute, 1968.

Schermann, Theodor. "Das 'Brotbrechen' im Urchristentum" BZ. 8 ('10) 33–52, 162–183.

Schlier, Heinrich. "ἀμήν" TDNT. vol. I, pp. 335–338.

–, "Die Verkündigung der Taufe Jesu nach den Evangelien" GL. 28 ('55) 414–419.

Schmidt, Daryl. "Luke's 'Innocent' Jesus: A Scriptural Apologetic" in Political Issues in Luke-Acts. edited by Richard J. Cassidy and Philip J. Scharper. New York: Orbis Books, 1983.

Schmidt, Hermann. Wie betet der heutige Mensch? Dokumente und Analysen. Freiburg: Herder, 1972.

Schneider, Gerhard. "'stärke deine Brüder!' (Lk. 22,32), die Aufgabe des Petrus nach Lukas" Cath. 30 ('76) 200–206.

–, "Engel und Blutschweiss (Lk. 22,43–44) 'Redaktionsgeschichte' im Dienste der Textkritik" *BZ.* 20 ('76) 112–116.

Schnider, F. and Stenger, W. "Beobachtungen zur Struktur der Emmausperikope" *BZ.* 16 ('72) 94–114.

Schnider, Franz. *Jesus der Prophet.* Göttingen: Vandenhoeck and Ruprecht, 1973.

Schniewind, Julius. *Die Parallelperikopen bei Lukas und Johannes.* Darmstadt: George Olms, 1958 (reprint 1914).

Schrenk, G. "βιάζομαι" *TDNT.* vol. I, pp. 609–614.

–, "δίκη, δίκαιος," *TDNT.* vol. II, pp. 174–225.

Schubert, Paul. "The Structure and Significance of Luke 24" in *Neutestamentliche Studien für Rudolf Bultmann.* Berlin: Alfred Töpelmann, 1954.

Schulz, Siegfried. "Gottes Vorsehung bei Lukas" *ZNW.* 54 ('63) 104–116.

–, *Q Der Spruchquelle der Evangelisten.* Zürich: Theologischer Verlag, 1972.

Schumacher, Heinrich. *Die Selbstoffenbarung Jesu bei Mat. 11,27 (Luc 10,22): Eine kritisch-exegetische Untersuchung.* Freiburg: Herdersche Verlagshandlung, 1912.

Schürmann, Heinz. *Jesu Abschiedsrede, Lk. 22,21–38.* Münster: Aschendorffsche, 1957.

Schütz, Frieder. *Der leidende Christus: Die angefochtene Gemeinde und das Christuskerygma der lukanischen Schriften.* Stuttgart: W. Kohlhammer, 1969.

Schweizer, Eduard. "Der Menschensohn" *ZNW.* 50 ('59) 185–209.

–, "πνεῦμα." *TDNT.* vol. VI, pp. 332–455.

Scrivener, Frederick Henry Ambrose. (4th ed., edited by Edward Miller). *A Plain Introduction to the Criticism of the New Testament.* 2 vols. London: George Bell& Sons, 1894.

Seidelin, Paul. "Der 'Ebed Jahwe' und die Messiasgestalt im Jesajatargum" *ZNW.* 35 ('36) 194–231.

Segal, Alan F. *Two Powers in Heaven: Early Rabbinic Reports about Christianity and Gnosticism.* Leiden: E. J. Brill, 1977.

–, "Heavenly Ascent in Hellenistic Judaism, Early Christianity and their Environment," *ANRW.* II.23.2, pp. 1333–1394.

Shae, G. S. "The Question of the Authority of Jesus" *NovT.* 16 ('74) 1–29

Simon, Marcel. "Saint Stephen and the Jerusalem Temple" *JEH.* 2 ('51) 127–142.

–, *St. Stephen and the Hellenists in the Primitive Church.* London: Longmans, Green and Co., 1958.

Sledd, Andrew. "The Interpretation of Luke xvii. 21" *ExpT.* 50 ('38–39) 235–237.

Sloan, Robert Bryan. *The Favorable Year of the Lord: A Study of Jubilary Theology in the Gospel of Luke.* Austin, Texas: Schola Press, 1977.

Smalley, Stephen S. "The Christology of Acts" *ExpT.* 73 ('61–2) 358–362.

–, "The Christology of Acts Again" in *Christ and Spirit in the New Testament: Festschrift for C. F. D. Moule.* edited by Barnabas Lindars and Stephen Smalley. Cambridge: University Press, 1973.

–, "The Spirit, Kingdom and Prayer in Luke-Acts" *NovT.* 15 ('73) 59–71.

Smith, Harold. "Acts xx. 8 and Luke xxii. 43" *ExpT.* 16 ('04–05) 478.

Smith, Morton. *Jesus the Magician.* London: Victor Gollancz Ltd., 1978.

Snodgrass, Klyne. "Western Non-Interpolations" *JBL.* 91 ('72) 369–379.

Soards, M. L. "Tradition, Composition, and Theolgy in Luke's Account of Jesus Before Herod Antipas" *Bib.* 66 ('84) 344–363.

Soltau, W. "Die Herkunft der Reden in der Apostelgeschichte" *ZNW.* 4 ('03) 128–154.

Sparks, H. F. D. "The Semitisms of St. Luke's Gospel" *JTS.* 44 ('43) 129–138.

–, "The Semitisms of the Acts" *JTS.* ns 1 ('50) 16–28.

Spitta, Friedrich. "Der Satan als Blitz" *ZNW*. 9 ('08) 160–163.

Spivey, Robert A. "Structuralism and Biblical Studies" *Int*. 28 ('74) 133–145.

Stählin, G. "αἰτέω" *TDNT*. vol. I, pp. 191–195.

Stanley, David M. "Liturgical Influences on the Formation of the Four Gospels" *CBQ*. 21 ('59) 24–38.

–, *Jesus in Gethsemane: The Early Church Reflections on the Suffering of Jesus*. New York: Paulist Press, 1980.

Stanton, Graham. "Stephen in Lucan Perspective" in *Studia Biblica 1978, III. Papers on Paul and Other New Testament Authors*. edited by E. A. Livingstone. Sheffield: JSOT Press, 1980.

Stauffer, Ethelbert. "ἀγών" *TDNT*. vol. I, pp. 134–140.

Stone, Michael Edward. "The Concept of the Messiah in IV Ezra" in *Religions in Antiquity: Essays in Memory of Erwin Ramsdell Goodenough*. edited by Jacob Neusner. Leiden: E. J. Brill, 1968.

–, *Scriptures, Sects and Visions*. Philadelphia: Fortress Press, 1980.

Stonehouse, N. B. *The Witness of Luke to Christ*. London: Tyndale Press, 1951.

Strathmann, H. and Meyer, R. "λάος" *TDNT*. vol. IV, pp. 29–57.

Strauss, David Friedrich. *The Life of Jesus Critically Examined*. London: SCM Press, 1973.

Stravinskas, P. M. "The Emmaus Pericope: Its Sources, Theology and Meaning for Today" *Bibl*. 3 ('77) 97–115.

Streeter, B. H. "On the Trial of Our Lord Before Herod: A Suggestion" in *Studies in the Synoptic Problem*. edited by W. Sanday. Oxford: Clarendon Press, 1911.

–, *The Four Gospels: A Study of Origins*. London: Macmillan and Co., 1964 (11th ed.).

Stronstad, Roger. *The Charismatic Theology of St. Luke*. Peabody, Massachusetts: Hendrickson Publications, Inc., 1984.

Styler, G. M. "Stages in Christology in the Synoptic Gospels" *NTS*. 10 ('63–64) 398–409.

Suggs, M. J. "The Use of Patristic Evidence in the Search for a Primitive New Testament Text" *NTS*. 4 ('58) 139–147.

Surkau, Hans Werner. *Martyrien in jüdischer und frühchristlicher Zeit*. Göttingen: Vandenhoeck & Ruprecht, 1938.

Sutcliffe, Edmund F. "'Et tu Aliquando Conversus,' St. Luke 22,32" *CBQ*. 15 ('53) 305–314.

Sylva, Dennis D. "The Temple Curtain and Jesus' Death in the Gospel of Luke" *JBL*. 105 ('86) 239–250.

Talbert, Charles H. *Luke and the Gnostics: An Examination of the Lucan Purpose*. Nashville: Abingdon Press, 1966.

–, "The Lukan Presentation of Jesus' Ministry in Galilee: Luke 4:31–9:50" *RevExp*. 64 ('67) 482–497.

–, "The Redaction Critical Quest for Luke the Theologian" in *Jesus and Man's Hope*. edited by David G. Buttrick. Pittsburgh: Pittsburgh Theological Seminary, 1970.

–, *Literary Patterns, Theological Themes and the Genre of Luke-Acts*. Missoula: Scholars Press, 1974.

–, "The Concept of Immortals in Mediterranean Antiquity" *JBL*. 94 ('75) 419–436.

–, "Shifting Sands: The Recent Study of the Gospel of Luke" *Int*. 30 ('76) 381–395.

–, "Prophecies of Future Greatness: The Contribution of Greco-Roman Biographies to an Understanding of Luke 1:5–4:15" in *The Divine Helmsman: Studies on God's Control of Human Events*. edited by James L. Crenshaw and Samuel Sandmel. New York: KTAV Publishing House, 1980.

–, "The Way of the Lukan Jesus: Dimensions of Lukan Spirituality" *PRS.* 9 ('82) 237–249.

Tarelli, C. C. "The Chester Beatty Papyrus and the Caesarean Text" *JTS.* 40 ('39) 46–55.

–, "The Chester Beatty Papyrus and the Western and Byzantine Texts" *JTS.* 41 ('40) 253–260.

Tasker, R. V. G. "The Chester Beatty Papyrus and the Caesarean Text of Luke" *HTR.* 29 ('36) 345–352.

Tatum, W. Barnes. "The Epoch of Israel: Luke I–II and the Theological Plan of Luke-Acts" *NTS.* 13 ('66–67) 184–195.

Taylor, Vincent. "The Narrative of the Crucifixion" *NTS.* 8 ('61–62) 333–334.

–, *The Text of the New Testament.* London: Macmillan & Co., 1963 (2nd ed.).

–, *The Passion Narrative of St. Luke: A Critical and Historical Investigation.* Cambridge: University Press, 1972.

Teeple, Howard M. *The Mosaic Eschatological Prophet.* Philadelphia: Society of Biblical Literature, 1957.

Thompson, G. H. P. "Called – Proved – Obedient: A Study in the Baptism and Temptation Narratives of Matthew and Luke" *JTS.* 11 ('60) 1–12.

Thomson, P. "Ἐπιστρέφω (Luke xxii. 32)" *ExpT.* 38 ('26–27) 468.

Tobin, William J. "The Petrine Primacy Evidence of the Gospels" *LV.* 23 ('68) 27–70.

Tödt, H. E. (translated by Dorothea M. Barton). *The Son of Man in the Synoptic Tradition.* London: SCM Press, 1965.

Townsend, John T. "The Speeches in Acts" *ATR.* 42 ('60) 150–159.

Trites, Allison A. *The New Testament Concept of Witness.* Cambridge: University Press, 1977.

–, "The Prayer Motif in Luke-Acts" in *Perspectives on Luke-Acts.* edited by Charles H. Talbert. Danville: Association of Baptist Professors of Religion, 1978.

Trocmé, Etienne. *Le "Livre des Actes" et l'historie.* Paris: Presses Universitaires de France, 1957.

Turner, M. M. B. "Spirit Endowment in Luke/Acts: Some Linguistic Considerations" *VE.* 12 ('81) 45–63.

–, "The Significance of Receiving the Spirit in Luke-Acts: A Survey of Modern Scholarship" *TJ.* ns. 2 ('81) 131–158.

–, "Jesus and the Spirit in Lucan Perspective" *TB.* 32 ('81) 3–42.

Tyson, Joseph B. "The Lukan Version of the Trial of Jesus" *NovT.* 3 ('59) 249–258.

–, "Jesus and Herod Antipas" *JBL.* 79 ('60) 239–246.

–, "The Problem of Food in Acts: A Study of Literary Patterns with Particular Reference to Acts 6:1–7" in *Society of Biblical Literature 1979 Seminar Papers vol. I.* edited Paul J. Achtemeier. Missoula: Scholars Press, 1979.

–, "The Blindness of the Disciples in Mark" in *The Messianic Secret.* edited by Christopher Tuckett. London: S.P.C.K., 1983.

–, "Conflict as a Literary Theme in the Gospel of Luke" in *New Synoptic Studies: The Cambridge Gospel Conference and Beyond.* edited by William R. Farmer. Macon, Georgia: Mercer University Press, 1983.

–, "The Jewish Public in Luke-Acts" *NTS.* 30 ('84) 574–583.

–, *The Death of Jesus in Luke-Acts.* Columbia: University of South Carolina Press, 1986.

van Cangh, J. M. "'Par l'esprit de Dieu – par le doigt de Dieu' Mt 12,28 par. Lc 11,20" in *Logia: Les Paroles de Jésus – The Sayings of Jesus.* edited by J. Delobel. Leuven: University Press, 1982.

van de Woude, A. S. "Melchisedek als himmlische Erlösergestalt in der neugefundenen eschatologischen Midraschim aus Qumran Höhle XI" *OS.* 14 ('65) 354–375.

van Iersel, B. M. F. *"Der Sohn" in den Synoptischen Jesusworten.* Leiden: E. J. Brill, 1964.

van Iersel, Bas. "Terug van Emmaüs" *TT.* 18 ('78) 294–323.

van Stempvoort, P. A. "The Interpretation of the Ascension in Luke and Acts" *NTS.* 5 ('58–59) 30–42.

van Unnik, W. C. "Eléments artistiques dans l'évangile de Luc" in *L'Evangile de Luc: Problemes littéraires et théologiques.* edited by F. Neirynck. Gembloux: J. Duculot, 1973.

Vellanickal, M. "Prayer-Experience in the Gospel of Luke" *Bibl.* 2 (1,'76) 23–43.

Varrall, A. W. "Christ before Herod" *JTS.* 10 ('08–09) 321–353.

Vielhauer, Philipp. "On the 'Paulinism' of Acts" in *Studies in Luke-Acts.* edited by Leander E. Keck and J. Louis Martyn. Philadelphia: Fortress Press, 1966.

von Baer, Heinrich. *Der heilige Geist in den Lukasschriften.* Stuttgart: Kohlhammer, 1926.

Vööbus, Arthur. "The Shorter and Longer Text in Luke" *NTS.* 15 ('68–69) 457–463.

Waetjen, H. C. "Is the Imitation of Christ Biblical?" *Dialog.* 2 (2,'63) 118–125.

Walaskay, Paul W. "The Trial and Death of Jesus in the Gospel of Luke" *JBL.* 94 ('75) 81–93.

Walker, William O. "Postcrucifixion Appearances and Christian Origins" *JBL.* 88 ('69) 157–165.

Walther, O. Kenneth. " A Solemn One Way Trip Becomes a Joyous Roundtrip! A Study of the Structure of Luk3 24:13–35" *AshTJ.* 14 ('81) 60–67.

Wanke, Joachim. *Die Emmauserzählung: eine redaktions-geschichtliche Untersuchung zu Lk. 24:13–35.* Leipzig: St. Benno Verlag, 1973.

–, *Beobachtunen zum Eucharistieverständnis des Lukas.* Leipzig: St. Benno Verlag, 1973.

–, "'. . . wie sie ihn beim Brotbrechen erkannten' sur Auslegung der Emmauserzählung Lk. 24, 13–35" *BZ.* 18 ('74) 180–192.

Watson, Francis. "The Social Function of Mark's Secrecy Theme" *JSNT.* 24 ('85) 49–69.

Webster, Charles A. "St. Luke x. 18" *ExpT.* 57 ('45–6) 52–53.

Weinert, Francis D. "Luke, the Temple and Jesus' Saying about Jerusalem's Abandoned House" *CBQ.* 44 ('82) 68–76.

–, "The Multiple Meanings of Luke 2:49 and their Significance" *BTB.* 13 ('83) 19–22.

Weiss, Johannes. "Das Logion Mt. 11:25–30" in *Neutestamentliche Studien für Georg Heinrici.* edited by Hans Windisch and Adolf Deissmann. Leipzig: J. C. Hinrichs Buchhandlung, 1914.

Wellek, René and Warren, Austin. *The Theory of Literature.* Middlesex: Penguin Books, 1973 (3rd ed.).

Wendland, Paul. *Die Hellenistisch-Römische Kultur in ihren Beziehungen zu Judentum und Christentum: Die Urchristlichen Literaturformen.* Tübingen: J. C. B. Mohr (Paul Siebeck), 1912.

Wensley, J. Ivor. "The Heavenly Intercession of Christ" *ExpT.* 40 ('28–29) 559–563.

Whybray, R. N. "On Robert Alter's 'The Art of Biblical Narrative'" *JSOT.* 27 ('83) 75–86.

Wicks, Henry J. *The Doctrine of God in the Jewish Apocryphal and Apocalyptic Literature.* London: Hunter & Longhurst, 1915.

Wilckens, Ulrich. "Kerygma und Evangelium bei Lukas (Beobachtungen zu Acta 10, 34–43)" *ZNW.* 49 ('58) 223–237.

–, *Die Missionsreden der Apostelgeschichte: Form- und traditionsgeschichtliche Untersuchungen.* Neukirchen-Vluyn: Neukirchener Verlag, 1974 (3rd ed.).

Wilcox, Max. *The Semitisms of Acts.* Oxford: Clarendon Press, 1965.

Wilder, Amos N. "Variant Traditions of the Resurrection in Acts" *JBL*. 62 ('43) 307–318.

–, *Early Christian Rhetoric: The Language of the Gospel*. Cambridge: Harvard University Press, 1971.

Wiles, Gordon P. *Paul's Intercessory Prayers: The Significance of the Intercessory Prayer Passages in the Letters of St. Paul*. Cambridge: University Press, 1974.

Wilkens, W. "Die Auslassung von Mark 6:45–8:26 bei Lukas im Licht der Komposition Luk. 9:1–50" *TZ*. 32 ('76) 193–200.

Wilkinson, John. "The Seven Words from the Cross" *SJT*. 17 ('64) 69–82.

Williams, C. S. C. *Alterations to the Text of the Synoptic Gospels and Acts*. Oxford: Basil Blackwell, 1951.

Williams, G. O. "The Baptism in Luke's Gospel" *JTS*. 45 ('44) 31–38.

Williams, N. P. "Great Texts Reconsidered: Mt. 11:25–27 = Lk. 10:21–24" *ExpT*. 51 (4,'40) 182–186; 51 (5,'40) 215–220.

Wilson, Jack Howard. *Luke's Role as a Theologian and Historian in Acts 6:1–8:3*. unpublished Ph.D. dissertation. Emory University, 1962.

Wilson, S. G. "Lukan Eschatology" *NTS*. 16 ('70) 330–347.

Wink, Walter. *John the Baptist in the Gospel Tradition*. Cambridge: University Press, 1968.

Winter, Paul. "Matthew 11:27 and Luke 10:22 from the First to the Fifth Century: Reflections on the Development of the Text" *NovT*. 1 ('56) 112–148.

–, *On the Trial of Jesus*. Berlin: Walter de Gruyter, 1974 (2nd ed.).

Wood, H. G. "The Conversion of St. Paul: Its Nature, Antecedents and Consequences" *NTS*. 1 ('54) 276–282.

Woods, G. F. "The Evidential Value of the Biblical Miracles" in *Miracles: Cambridge Studies in their Philosophy and History*. edited by C. F. D. Moule. London: A. R. Mowbray & Co., 1965.

Wrede, William. (translated by J. C. G. Greig). *The Messianic Secret*. Cambridge and London: James Clarke & Co. Ltd., 1971.

Wulf, Friedrich. "'Jesus, gedenke meiner, wenn du in dein Königtum kommst'" *GL*. 37 ('64) 1–3.

–, "Sie erkannten ihn beim Brechen des Brotes (Lk. 24,35)" *GL*. 37 ('64) 81–83.

Wurzinger, Anton. "'Es komme Dein Königreich': zum Gebetsanliegen nach Lukas" *BLit*. 38 ('64–65) 89–94.

Yamauchi, Edwin. "Magic or Miracle? Diseases, Demons and Exorcisms" in *Gospel Perspectives: The Miracles of Jesus*. vol. 6. edited by David Wenham and Craig Blomberg. Sheffield: JSOT Press, 1986.

Yates, Thomas. "The words from the Cross. VII. 'And when Jesus had cried with a loud voice, he said, Father into thy hands I commend my spirit' (Luke xxiii. 46)" *ExpT*. 41 ('29–30) 427–429.

Young, Franklin W. "Jesus the Prophet: A Re-Examination" *JBL*. 68 ('49) 285–299.

# Index of Biblical References

## Old Testament

# New Testament

# Index of Extra-Biblical References

# Index of Modern Authors

# Subject Index